Cavanagh, John R   1904-
    Counseling the homosexual / John R. Cavanagh, in theological collaboration with John F. Harvey. — Huntington, Ind. : Our Sunday Visitor, c1977.

    352 p. ; 24 cm.

    Bibliography: p. 316-341.
    Includes index.
    ISBN 0-87973-761-1 : $14.95

    1. Homosexuality. 2. Counseling.   I. Harvey, John Francis, 1918-
    joint author. II. Title.

RC558.C33   301.41'57   77-81951
                                                        MARC

    Library of Congress   78

COUNSELING
THE
HOMOSEXUAL

COUNSELING THE HOMOSEXUAL

John R. Cavanagh, M.D., F.A.P.A., F.A.C.P., K.S.G.

In Theological Collaboration With
Rev. John F. Harvey, O.S.F.S.

Our Sunday Visitor, Inc.
Huntington, Indiana 46750

Nihil Obstat:
Rev. Lawrence A. Gollner
Censor Librorum

Imprimatur:
✠William E. McManus, D.D.
Bishop of Fort Wayne-South Bend
April 28, 1977

ISBN: 0-87973-761-1
Library of Congress Catalog Card Number: 77-81951

Cover Design by James E. McIlrath

Published, printed and bound in the U.S.A. by
Our Sunday Visitor, Inc.
Noll Plaza
Huntington, Indiana 46750

761

Some persons find themselves through no fault of their own to have a homosexual orientation. Homosexuals, like everyone else, should not suffer from prejudice against their basic human rights. They have a right to respect, friendship and justice. They should have an active role in the Christian community. Homosexual activity, however, as distinguished from homosexual orientation is morally wrong. Like heterosexual persons, homosexuals are called to give witness to chastity, avoiding with God's grace, behavior which is wrong for them just as nonmarital sexual relations are for heterosexuals. Nonetheless, because heterosexuals can usually look forward to marriage, and homosexuals, while their orientation continues, might not, the Christian community should provide them with a special grace of pastoral understanding and care.

National Conference of Catholic Bishops
November 11, 1976

Contents

Foreword

The fact that a new edition of this work is to be published in 1977 is testimony to the usefulness of the work and the continued interest in the subject. A look at the foreword of the first edition, written in 1966, indicates that events which have transpired since that time have made that foreword completely outdated. The problem remains, mind you, and is even more demanding of attention and understanding; but the manner in which it is now regarded has changed markedly. The subject is now "out in the open" and is looked upon with a great deal more understanding and a modicum of charity.

Dr. Cavanagh offers a fair and comprehensive survey of the situation as it exists today in a book directed toward clergy and counselors, the two groups most often consulted by patients, relatives, and friends. The community is still broadly divided, and understanding comes hard to many citizens; some are mildly understanding, whereas many are unreasonable in their views. The origins of the situation are still under debate — some of the debate is scientific and some of the reasoning prejudicial and unjust.

One thing is certain, namely, that more and more individuals are coming "out of the closet." They have organized and are becoming more assertive and not at all hesitant about demanding what they believe are their rights. One group became overactive at a convention of the American Psychiatric Association (APA); at another time a quieter group, yet one no less determined, waited while the APA trustees voted that homosexuality be eliminated from the illness category in its nomenclature.

This action, eventually approved by a majority of those who voted in a membership referendum, left mixed feelings in the Association; the wisdom of establishing or removing illness

9

categories from the nomenclature by means of a vote was called into question.

One positive advance is that the clergy in general and the physiciàns, though still puzzled about the handling of homosexuality, are now much more intelligent in dealing with it. Physicians are less hostile and clergymen have given up a belief once prevalent years ago that marriage would solve the situation.

One other problem has come starkly to the fore since the first edition of this book was published, and that something must be sharply differentiated from homosexuality — namely the phenomenon of transsexuality. With the relaxed attitude of the laws in the past decade, along with the advances in surgery, transsexual operations have become much more common. The individuals are usually not overt homosexuals but rather they believe themselves to be women in men's physical habiliments, or vice versa.

As yet the reports are not all in on this surgical sex reassignment, and the follow-up reports about it are mixed. Some individuals claim to be quite content postoperatively, while a number of others are not quite so sure.

Female homosexuality has never created as much a stir as has its male counterpart, and that situation has changed little in the past decade, although some Lesbians have joined their brothers out in the open and even have publicly marched and demonstrated with them. Usually female homosexuality can be easily concealed and detection of it, unless a scandal erupts, is often only a matter of conjecture. When it is detected it still does not call forth the serious reactions caused by the discovery of male homosexuality. In fact, some women prominent in the visual arts write in their memoirs about their participation. Furthermore, the law holds that sexual acts with willing adult participants are legal, and unless there is a public outcry or a tragedy, nothing is done about them.

Father John Harvey, O.S.F.S., discusses in this edition both "The APA Change in Nomenclature" and "Homosexuality and Theology," and both of his chapters are welcome additions. Dr. Cavanagh considers "Marriage and the Homosexual," "Homosexuality in the Religious Life," and "Pastoral Counseling of Homosexuals," along with other topics listed in the table of contents.

The work is important; the outlook on the subject is not a run-of-the-mill type. As in the earlier edition, the information this book contains will be helpful to pastors, physicians, and all individuals who deal with people in difficulty. The knowledge gained in the reading of the work might in some instances prove to be a deterrent to tragedy.

Francis J. Braceland, M.D.

Author's Preface

Homosexuality is a continuing problem. So you may ask why we need a new edition of this book not too many years after its original publication. Many questions have arisen in the past decade which are not really new, but nonetheless provide new perspectives for viewing an old problem. Recently many new theological problems have been raised. The answers to some of these may not be readily available to the Catholic counselor. Other questions of terminology need discussion and should be known to the counselor.

Homosexuality is a little understood subject. There has been very little serious effort to illuminate this area of deviant sexuality. Clergymen who wield so much influence over the lives of others have not always been well informed. Problems concerning the marriage of homosexuals and their entry into seminaries in particular need attention.

This book attempts to provide the information which is needed to answer some of the questions in this area. It makes no attempt to tell all that is known about homosexuality. It does make an effort to supply those who need to know with enough background information to do their jobs well. It may help the homosexual himself to have some information about the development of his disorder, and not only what is necessary to eliminate it but also the knowledge that it can be treated if the individual so desires.

For the counselor, suggestions are made in the text as to methods of handling problems as they arise and also techniques of long-term treatment. For the clinical psychologist and the psychiatrist, in addition to the suggestions for counseling, there is a discussion of methods of physical and psychotherapeutic treatment.

An attempt to provide a treatment of the subject of interest to such diverse groups may seem presumptuous. It would have been so a few years ago. Today, however, clergymen, social workers, probation officers, clinical psychologists and others are well versed in psychology and psychopathology. Almost daily they are confronted with psychological problems. In this book an effort is made to give them in one source the information for which they would otherwise have to delve through the bookshelves.

Basically I believe that homosexuality is a psychiatric problem and is best studied as such. I have no illusions, however, that any high percentage of homosexuals will ever seek psychiatric help. It is the duty of the medical profession to supply those who will serve the homosexual with whatever information will be helpful in his management. This I shall attempt to do in these chapters. No effort has been made to exhaust the subject, but I hope that a fair cross section has been presented.

I wish to thank all those authors and publishers who have given permission to quote from their works. I am grateful to Rev. John F. Harvey, O.S.F.S., who has contributed largely of his theological expertise. My thanks also go to my secretary, Mrs. Denyse Kline, to Mrs. Mary Cavanagh White, Mrs. Martha Young and others for their help.

John R. Cavanagh, M.D.

CHAPTER ONE

The Community
and the Homosexual

Man's sexual role has presented a problem on various levels throughout history. From age to age, from one social situation to another, man has expressed and fulfilled his sexual nature in different ways.

The problem of homosexuality has plagued man from earliest times. The Old Testament mentions it, and even a superficial knowledge of history demonstrates the presence of homosexuality in ancient kingdoms, to the extent that some historians list homosexuality as a sign of impending disaster for a state. The presence of homosexuality in American society today tends to send some people into a state of puritanical shock.

Americans on the whole have been intolerant of the homosexual and his orientation. The average man-on-the-street has made him the butt of his most lewd barroom or clubhouse jokes. When a situation of an individual instance of homosexuality confronts most Americans, they will either condemn the person or persons involved, or they will pretend it did not happen.

Also most discouraging is the attitude among many of the clergy concerning the homosexual. Thanks to many pioneers in the fields of pastoral psychology and counseling, attitudes of disdain, which some attribute to real fear on the part of the priests, is disappearing. The Catholic homosexual will most likely approach his pastor or confessor with his problem as a moral issue and truly be seeking help on all levels affected. One wonders how many people have been more solidly confirmed in their way of homosexuality by the instant and often brutal rebuff by a representative of the loving Christ.

The field of psychology has many approaches to the homosexual problem. There are some psychologists, although they are in the minority, who feel that homosexuality is biologically caused (see Chs. 5 and 6). Other counselors feel that there is no physical basis for homosexuality and treat it exclusively by means of psychotherapy. A variety of opinions arises when a group of professionals discusses this area.

One of the most striking phenomena in studying the clinical aspects of treating homosexuality is the discovery that the number of homosexuals who desire to become heterosexual is small. The number who seek professional help is less than three percent. Few homosexuals approach a psychiatrist to be "cured"; most come only to become better adjusted to their state. There are many doctors who believe that even the relatively few who desire to live normal lives cannot be cured but can only be assisted to adjust better to their homosexual tendencies.

The homosexual is basically a most unhappy individual since he has accepted as his lot constant frustration and the endless pursuit of the impossible. He believes he has a great potential for human love, which he may indeed have. He has a constant, strong craving for friendship that is more singular than plural. Most often he feels quite inferior and is constantly striving for acceptance by a society which abhors his sexual expression. He has lived in fear that his "abnormal" tendencies will be found out and made public, for most homosexuals have led double lives. But despite all this frustration and anxiety there are, relatively speaking, only a handful who seek to be changed.

In this book, even when dealing with the role of the priest in counseling the homosexual, I shall not attempt any discussion of the morality of homosexuality *per se* nor its relation to the natural law. I will leave this to the moralists and to Father John F. Harvey, O.S.F.S. In later chapters I do, however, hope to point out the importance of a knowledge and understanding of homosexuality for anyone doing counseling work and for priests in particular.

Finally, the difficulty of adequate information for research must be pointed out. Much of what has been written on this topic is of little value or is merely opinion. Few truly authoritative works have been done in this field, although more are beginning to appear as the discussion of sex and sexuality becomes more open. One of the more valuable contributions is *Homosexuality: An Annotated Bibliography* by Martin S. Weinberg and Alan P. Bell of The Institute for Sex Research founded by Alfred C. Kinsey.[1] However, much that has been written has been of a sensational nature and even some of the articles in the professional journals may be classified as such.

It is my opinion that my own studies of the subject of homosexuality have increased my understanding of a problem that we have all too often ignored in the past. Today we must come to grips with it so that we can adequately assist the homosexual who opens himself to us. Recently I was impressed by the human reaction of a friend of mine when confronted with a transvestite who was living in the same hotel as he. I would have expected shock and disdain, but was most pleased at a reaction of sympathy and concern. The true Christian cannot turn his back "in shock" to the plight of any of his fellow human beings. We must see these individuals as troubled persons who, above all, need our understanding.

Human Sexuality

The homosexual's view of human sexuality is incomplete and shallow. By "homosexual" here, I refer to those individuals and groups who hold homosexuality to be perfectly natural for them and believe in the validity of homosexual expression. At the base of their beliefs is a lack of understanding concerning the depths of the human person to which sexuality reaches. They view sex as just one means in a whole range of possibilities that is open for man to express himself. Human sexuality is just one instinct among many that man possesses. However, in fact, it is radically different from all the other instincts.

> It has first a kind of depth that neither thirst, nor hunger, nor the need to sleep, nor any desire for other bodily pleasure possesses. . . . Above all, sexual ecstacy goes to the very depth of bodily existence: it has in its overwhelming power something extraordinary, to which terrible body pains are alone a counterpart.[2]

Thus we can see that sex is a biological phenomenon. It is something that reaches to the very core of an individual, and for this reason it must hold a special place among his bodily faculties. However, it can honestly be said that society has distorted

17

and exploited the role of sex in the human personality. Sex by itself is not to be considered the primary factor one uses in determining the value of a relationship. But these facts are in no way solid reasons for downgrading sex to a place of equality with the other bodily functions.

Sex is very intimate and personal. It is wrapped up in the total structure of the human person and, therefore, it is like telling a secret, the release of something of value, of great significance. "Indeed, sex in its true setting goes far beyond mere bodily functions of sex because it is in the texture of the person."[3] This is not to say that man is only a sex-being. Sexual drives must be mastered. An individual's conduct in every way is influenced by his sex drives and how they are controlled. At the same time, this sex control depends on the person's attitude and structure.

> The realm of the sexual presents a challenge to man who is made in the image of God. He must take up the sublime task of subordinating the passions to the spirit without hostility to the body or bodily things. For man, who accepts this challenge, sex is indeed a service to life through the call to marriage, ultimately a service to the building up of the Mystical Body of Christ.[4]

Sex, Procreation, and Love

Because sex is so much a part of the complete person, it necessarily involves a giving of self. In sex man gives himself to another. Man is called to give himself to the female of the species, and vice versa. This is surely indicated by their biology, and their biology is an integral part of their personality. The structure of their bodies attests to the fact that they are made to complement one another. Psychologically and socially the complementarity of man and woman can also be affirmed. These varied aspects of sex must be kept in mind in studying its function. The homosexual, however, stresses the purely physical aspect of sexual relations and sees little beyond this level.

> When acting sexually, human persons are involved as whole persons. A purely biological interpretation of human sexuality is contrary to the nature of man. Human sexuality has a psycholog-

ical component too, and cannot be understood in the absence of this element.[5]

What is the relationship between sex and procreation? The connection in a normal heterosexual relationship is somewhat obvious. But the homosexual does not view this connection as one of primary importance in his life. Since he views sex only as a means of expression for man, although a much deeper expression than any other, its procreative function is not stressed. This view of sex as only a morally neutral need is a failure to understand its nature.

Sex, procreation, and love are joined together in marriage in perfect fulfillment. This, of course, is the ideal. Sexual relations between man and wife must have both functions — procreation and love — because they are essential aspects of human sexuality. "The goals of human sexuality and personality demand that the sexual faculty have its proper function within the family framework. The procreation and education of children remains a very important goal of marriage for those who believe that the purpose of mutual expression of love is as important as the rearing of children."[6]

The relationship of love to sex is one of ultimate goal. "Since God is love and thinks of man only to love him, man in his entirety, including sex, is the object of divine love. As seen in this light, sex has no other end, no other meaning than love."[7] There is a profound link between love and procreation. God's love is the creative principle in the universe, so it can be seen that love is creative. The creativity of human sexual love is seen in procreation. In heterosexual union, a new human being proceeds from the act of love of a man and a woman. All possibility of this is absent from the homosexual's love relationship.

Homosexuality in the Bible

The earliest mention of homosexuality in the Bible is the Sodom and Gomorrah account (Genesis 19:4-11). From this the sin of sodomy derives its name. This account is now controverted, although in past ages it was assumed to be the *locus classicus* of the divine condemnation of homosexual acts as the most heinous sin.[8] Unfortunately, the "traditional" interpretation of

19

this story has given the impression that homosexuals are moral monsters for whom God has selected special punishments. St. Paul, however, mentions other kinds of sins which deprive one of the kingdom of God (cf. 1 Corinthians 6:10, Romans 1:28-32 and Galatians 5:19-21). The Genesis account is as follows:

They [the two angels] had not yet retired when the townsmen, the men of Sodom, all the people from every quarter, both young and old, surrounded the house, and called Lot, and said to him, "Where are the men who came to your house tonight? Bring them out that we may abuse them." Lot went out to the men, and shut the door behind him, and said, "I entreat you, brethren, do not act wickedly. I have two daughters that have not known man. Let me bring them out to you; do as you please with them. Only do nothing to these men, for they have come under the shelter of my roof."

Other references in the Old Testament are more specific. For example, in the Book of Leviticus it is stated:

You shall not lie with a male as with a woman; such a thing is an abomination (Leviticus 18:22).
If a man lies with a male as with a woman, both of them shall be put to death for their abominable deed; they have forfeited their lives (Leviticus 20:13).

In the New Testament St. Paul makes frequent references to homosexuality. His clearest and most unmistakable statement is in his Epistle to the Romans:

For this cause has given them up to shameful lusts; for their women have exchanged the natural use for that which is against nature, and in like manner the men also, having abandoned the natural use of the woman, have burned in their lusts one towards another, men with men doing shameless things and receiving in themselves the fitting recompense of their perversity (Romans 1:26-27).

The Jerome Biblical Commentary interprets these scriptural references as follows. "The men of Sodom desire the

20

two visitors for unnatural purposes (whence the term, 'sodomy')." Chapter 18 of Leviticus is chiefly concerned with sexual matters and is formed around a series of apodictic laws which prohibit relations within determined degrees of consanguinity and affinity and *outlaw certain other forms of abnormal behavior.* "Personal sanction in verse 29 takes the form of the offender's severance from the community without the specific delineations given elsewhere, e.g., death for sodomy (20:13)."

The contrast between "females" and "males" in Romans 1:27 makes it clear that the sexual perversion of which Paul speaks is homosexuality. "The depravity of the perversion is the merited consequence of pagan impiety; having exchanged the true God for a false one (1:25), pagans inevitably exchanged their true natural functions for perverted ones."[9]

From these biblical references we can see that the attitude toward homosexual acts is not a supportive one. The passages must be read in context. But no matter how they are read, the Bible in no way lends credence to the possibility of valid homosexual expression. It is always considered an offense against the laws of God, and is not looked upon favorably in any instance. The Bible takes a definite stand against homosexual expression.

A further discussion on homosexuality in the Bible appears in Chapter 16 of this book.

Genuine Love Is Not Selfish

We now come to the point of this entire discussion. Is there a possibility for valid homosexual expression of human sexual love? The answer that some give is in the affirmative: The conclusion of this chapter must be in the negative. This is based on an understanding of the close and inseparable relationship between sex, procreation, and love. It has already been stated that the procreative meaning of human sexuality is an essential aspect of the sex act and can never be totally separated from it. By their very nature homosexual acts exclude any possibility of procreation of life.

The homosexual act by its essence excludes all possibility of transmission of life; such an act cannot fulfill the procreative purpose of the sexual faculty and is, therefore, an inordinate use

21

of that faculty. Since it runs contrary to a very important goal of human nature, it is a grave transgression of the divine will. It is also a deviation from the normal attraction of man for woman, which leads to the foundation of the basic stable unit of society, the family.[10]

The purposes of sexual love are procreation, mutual expression of love between husband and wife, self-fulfillment, and the ultimate giving of self to another, although not necessarily in that order. Homosexual acts stress self-fulfillment and miss the social aspect of sexuality. Their purpose is too selfish and individualistic. It is an incomplete view of human sexuality. "The two-in-one flesh in marriage is the most comprehensive embodiment of the 'we,' of personal community, particularly in the extension to familial society with children."[11] For these reasons homosexual acts constitute a transgression of the goals of human sexuality, of human personality, and of the divine will.

The homosexual strives for a fulfilling human relationship. However, within the homosexual act there are both subjective and objective elements that must be considered. Fulfillment for the homosexual does not necessarily have to involve sexual expression. He can sublimate his sexual desires. There is no denying that the lot of the homosexual is a difficult one. That human fulfillment which he will find will never be as complete and deep as that of the heterosexual in conjugal love. The Church and society have a grave obligation to give the homosexual a chance. Through the acceptance of others, the homosexual might come to an understanding of himself and how he must grow in God's love.

The validity of homosexual acts cannot be condoned, but each individual case must be judged separately. While life in accordance with fundamental principles of natural moral law may be difficult for the homosexual, it is not impossible.

Contemporary Views

"There is nothing new under the sun." Although we have all heard this expression and can attest to its validity, we definitely have been witnessing new ideas on homosexuality during recent years. It is "new" for several Catholic priests to speak favorably

22

of the morality of homosexual acts, arguing that such acts can be truly good and wholesome. To repeat what I will say again and again, there is no problem in the morality of being a homosexual; the moral question arises when homosexuals express their feelings in a sexual manner.

It is "new under the sun" when a Catholic priest, Charles Curran, a professor of moral theology at the Catholic University of America, defends the morality of homosexual acts under "The Theory of Compromise."[12] By this he means that if one is an "irreversible homosexual," he may engage in homosexual acts with another "irreversible homosexual" as long as it is within the context of a permanent commitment. Psychiatrically, I am not sure of the psychodynamics of this. Theologically, I will leave the discussion to Father John Harvey in a later chapter.

While holding that homosexual acts performed by "irreversible homosexuals" within the context of a permanent commitment are justifiable by way of a compromise, Father Curran nonetheless maintains that there is something amiss with them and that they surely cannot be regarded as being the ideal of human sexual behavior. Another theologian, Father John McNeill, S.J., goes further than this and argues that such homosexual acts are positively good in every way. I am afraid that Father McNeill is in error. I will leave the judgment of his theological position to Father Harvey, but as a psychiatrist I can say that I find Father McNeill's book[13] to be replete with rationalizations and wishful thinking.

Other moral theories could be mentioned here, but we need only to bear in mind that priests and theologians are fallible. Too many times they are accepted by lay people as infallible. Perhaps good will come out of this present situation in that the laity will recognize that at times the priest and even the theologian is not always right.

Fairness for Homosexuals

Fairness for homosexuals is not "new." An editorial in *The Washington Post* in 1971 reported:

When the private lives of men or women embrace associations or activities of which they are ashamed — or the exposure of which would be profoundly embarrassing to them — they become

23

vulnerable to blackmailers who may discover their secret. It makes sense, therefore, to exclude such persons from public employment involving access to classified information. This has commonly been cited as a justification for barring homosexuals from jobs which are sensitive from a security point of view. Often, however, this justification has been a mere pretext for denying employment to homosexuals.

The American Civil Liberties Union has served the cause of decency as well as fairness by going to court in behalf of a man denied industrial security clearance solely because he is a homosexual. The man cannot conceivably be considered more subject to blackmail than any other men for the simple reason that he has made no attempt to conceal his homosexuality. For more than 10 years he has been an avowed homosexual, a member of the Washington Mattachine Society; he acknowledged all this quite candidly in filling out a security questionnaire, balking only at what he deemed prurient, intrusive questions about his private sexual habits bearing no relation whatever to his trustworthiness in handling classified material.

Persecution of homosexuals is as senseless as it is unjust. They may have valuable gifts and insights to bring to public service. If they are qualified for a job in terms of intelligence, experience and skill, if they conduct themselves, like other employees, with reasonable circumspection and decorum, their private sexual behavior is their own business; it is none of the government's business as long as it does not affect their independence and reliability. Like anyone else, they have a right to privacy, a right to opportunity and a right to serve their country.[14]

This is all very true and hardly anyone doubts it. But when a Catholic bishop speaks on the rights for homosexuals (*Time,* March 8, 1976) it is made to sound like a new pronouncement. It is clear that Bishop Francis J. Mugavero of Brooklyn, New York, referred only to civil, legal rights, not acceptance of the homosexual way of life.

In his work entitled *The Law of Christ,* German Redemptorist Father Bernard Häring, while admitting that some homosexuals were limited in their moral freedom by psychic defects, said, "They are responsible to the measure or degree of freedom which they still possess."

He continued: "For this reason we must energetically op-

24

pose the campaign emanating from the circle of homosexuals in favor of general impunity, particularly since they attempt to base their position on the claim that the vice is something natural. In many instances of sexual offenses there is no evidence at all of a predisposition to depravity justifying the claim that responsibility is essentially diminished."[15]

Another "new under the sun" is the fact that a neighboring university, the University of Maryland, is now offering a one-semester course in the Department of Philosophy on the "Ethics of Homosexuality." Their textbook is *The Homosexual Matrix* by C. A. Tripp, Ph.D.[16] In my opinion this is not the best study of the topic.

CHAPTER TWO

The Incidence
of Homosexuality

Traditional Attitudes Toward Homosexuality

An unworthy prejudice against the homosexual has existed from the days when homosexuality was "that horrible sin, not to be mentioned among Christians."[1] This attitude is imperfectly understood by many counselors and helps to perpetuate the concept that the homosexual is a being set apart as evil and unclean.

Such prejudice probably arose from a variety of causes. The Catholic Church has traditionally condemned homosexual acts as contrary to nature and, therefore, as "unnatural." Sodomy as related to the sin of the inhabitants of Sodom constituted what was considered ample biblical proof for this belief. Since one of the human (not merely biological) purposes of the sex act is procreation, it is clear that homosexual acts bring about a frustration of this generative function. Bailey states this quite well:

> Starting from the universally accepted premise that the primary purpose of the sexual organs is procreation — from which it followed that they may only be used legitimately for such acts as do not exclude the possibility (though they may not express the intention) of generation — he [St. Thomas Aquinas] found no difficulty in showing that all homosexual practices are *ex hypothesi* unnatural, lustful, and sinful. Thus he established the principal argument upon which moral theologians were to rely in the future when treating of venereal acts between members of the same sex.[2]

From this traditional background many counselors look upon the homosexual with mixed feelings. They have been known

26

to be fearful, mistrusting, resentful, and sometimes overcome by feelings of inadequacy. Many have frightened the deviate away with their rudeness and hostility. They may associate all homosexuals with willful depravity, seduction of the young, effeminacy, and moral perversion.

The tragic reception which many a homosexual has received from a well-meaning but uninformed priest, or ineffectual or sometimes even hostile priest at least partially explains how so many of these unfortunates leave the Church in frustrated rebellion or deep despair . . . it is easy for him to conclude that the Church has abandoned him too.[3]

Because of these attitudes many homosexuals do not seek advice, which may lead some counselors to believe that homosexuality is a rare thing. I have been told by priests of over twenty years' experience that they have never seen a homosexual.

The Incidence of Homosexuality

Because of these traditional attitudes in society toward the homosexual, the frequency of homosexuality in the population as a whole is very difficult to determine. There are many who do not admit their homosexuality because of fear, confusion, or shame. There seems, however, to be no lack of sexual companions for homosexuals. The exact incidence of homosexuality is not known.

In primitive societies Ford and Beach found that forty-nine percent of seventy-six societies which they studied considered that homosexual behavior was normal and socially acceptable. The usual custom was to allow the male to dress like a woman and vice versa. Males dressed as women were also permitted to perform sodomy in many societies. In other societies the male homosexual was considered to have magical powers. In still others the majority or, in some instances, all the male population practiced homosexuality. In others, sodomy was part of the puberty rites. It was, as a matter of fact, considered necessary in some societies for the health of the growing boy.

In twenty-eight of the seventy-six societies studied, homosexual behavior was condemned and disapproved. In these societies children who showed any such tendency were punished, while penalties for adults ranged from ridicule and social condemnation to death.[4]

Magnus Hirschfeld stated that if homosexuality were defined as an abiding sexual interest only in members of the self-sex, the number of homosexuals was probably 1.5 percent of the population of Germany. Hirschfeld also maintained that if inclusion were made of persons whose interest was predominantly in members of their own sex, the percentage would approximate 2.3.[5]

The Kinsey Report on the male, although greatly criticized for statistical and other errors, cannot be completely put aside. Kinsey's study of 5,300 American males revealed some interesting figures. Using as his criterion "physical contact to the point of orgasm," his study revealed that, if projected to the whole population thirty-seven percent of American males have had "some homosexual experience" between adolescence and old age. This estimate is misleading and likely to be an overestimate. Further, his figures showed that: (1) 50 percent of males who were single to the age of 35 had had homosexual experience (many of which were undoubtedly experimental); (2) 25 percent had experience, or reaction, for at least 3 years between the ages of 16 and 35 years; (3) 10 percent of males were more or less exclusively homosexual between the ages of 16 and 55 years; (4) 8 percent of males were exclusively homosexual for at least 3 years between age 16 to 55 years; (5) 4 percent of males were exclusively homosexual throughout their active sex life.[6]

More recent figures concerning the incidence of homosexuality were given by the Wolfenden Committee. This committee estimated that a very large segment of the British population was homosexual and in its report gave the impression that the controversial Kinsey estimates for the United States might be quite applicable to Great Britain.[7]

Mead in 1961 pointed out that statements on the absence of homosexual behavior in cross-cultural studies must be viewed with caution because of such factors as language barriers, unbreakable cultural taboos, need for personal privacy, distrust of Caucasian investigators, retrospective falsification, and, in some nonliterate societies, conventions of courtesy that demand telling a questioner what he presumably wants to hear.[8]

Another complication stems from the fact that different investigators often use widely varying definitions of homosexuality — from the exploratory same-sex play of adolescents to highly institutionalized, often religious, gender role changes to genuine adult homoerotic practices. Thus it is probable that actual incidence figures are higher than studies have reported.

The Hite Report in studying 3,000 women all over the country since 1972 found that 145 or 8 percent of the number questioned said that they prefer sex with women. Another 73 identified themselves as "bisexual," and 84 more women (another 9 percent) had had experiences with both men and women but did not answer to preference.[9]

Oliven summarizes the incidence in these words:

> Best available estimates indicate that approximately 4 to 5 percent of adult men in the civilized Western world have predominantly or exclusively homosexual inclinations of one clinical type or another. Types of "facultative" homosexuality are more frequent, and in some regions of the world (Levant, Eurasian Middle East and elsewhere) it seems to be traditionally "endemic."[10]

It can be seen from the above figures that there is no accurate estimate of the number of homosexuals. Most figures average out to estimate that 10 percent of the male population in the United States (22 million) and 8 percent of the female population (18 million) are homosexual in their sexual orientation.

Gay activists claim that there are 20 million male and female homosexuals in the United States.[11] The National Task Force on Homosexuality estimated in 1969: "There are currently at least three to four million adults in the United States who are predominantly homosexual and many more individuals in whose lives homosexual tendencies or behavior play a significant role."

Whatever the number may be, it is generally assumed that there are more male than female homosexuals and that most of them — male and female — continue to hide their homosexuality. Moreover, homosexuals who have worked hard to be accepted by heterosexual ("straight") society resent attempts by militants to set homosexuals apart as a distinct group. But there is virtually unanimous support among homosexuals for their attempts to secure full civil rights.

CHAPTER THREE

Changes in Nomenclature and Their Probable Effect

(John F. Harvey, O.S.F.S.)

On December 16, 1973, the *Washington Sunday Star* carried the headline, "Victory for Homosexuals," because the previous day the trustees of the American Psychiatric Association (APA) by unanimous vote, with two abstentions and four absentees, ruled that "homosexuality" shall no longer be listed as a "mental disorder" in its official nomenclature of mental disorders, the *Diagnostic and Statistical Manual of Mental Disorders* (DSM II). As this book goes to press, *Psychiatric News*, the official newspaper of the APA (March 18, 1977), published a provisional draft of the third revision of the manual (DSM III), in which various disorders are classified into more specific categories and related to coexisting psychological phenomena. On the question of homosexuality, however, it is not significantly different from DSM II (pp. 1, 26-27, 33). In the DSM II manual the category of homosexuality is replaced by "sexual orientation disturbance," which is described in this fashion: "This is for individuals whose sexual interests are directed primarily toward people of the same sex and who are either bothered by, in conflict with, or wish to change their sexual orientation. This diagnostic category is distinguished from homosexuality, which by itself does not constitute a psychiatric disorder. Homosexuality *per se* is a form of sexual behavior and, with other forms of sexual behavior which are not by themselves psychiatric disorders, is not listed in this nomenclature."[1]

When this statement was formulated in June, 1973, its author, Dr. Robert L. Spitzer, foretold that the gay community would draw the conclusion that psychiatry had at long last recognized that homosexuality is as normal as heterosexuality. To date that is the way the community has responded.

In Dr. Spitzer's statement, however, he observed that in

30

removing homosexuality *per se* from the nomenclature, the APA was only recognizing that by itself homosexuality does not meet the criteria for being considered a psychiatric disorder. "We will in no way be aligning ourselves with any particular viewpoint regarding the etiology or desirability of homosexual behavior."[2]

Reasons for the New Category

Several reasons were given for creating the new category, *sexual orientation disturbance.* The first is that the label would apply only to those homosexuals who are in some way bothered by their sexual orientation, and who may come to the psychiatrist for help. If a homosexual accepts his orientation and shows no generalized impairment in social effectiveness, he will not be labeled as sick. Thus the APA has replied to the charge that by labeling people they act as agents of social control — a thesis of Thomas Szasz (*Myth of Mental Illness*).

A second reason for the change of nomenclature is to remove any justification for the denial of civil rights to individuals whose only crime is that their sexual orientation is to members of the same sex. In the past, homosexuals have been denied civil rights in many areas of life on the score that they suffer from a mental illness, and that it is necessary for them to demonstrate their competence and reliability in spite of their homosexuality. This does not mean that the APA approves the irrational denial of civil rights to individuals who do suffer from true psychiatric illness.

This revision in the nomenclature provides the opportunity of finding a homosexual free of psychiatric disorder, and allows the psychiatrist to focus on a mental disorder whose central feature is conflict about homosexual behavior. Dedicated doctors who have devoted themselves to helping homosexuals unhappy with their lot are encouraged to continue doing so.

The resolutions of the board of trustees in December, 1973, led to a referendum of the members of the APA, in which the majority supported the trustees' statement, but a minority of roughly forty percent did not support it (5,854 members approved; 3,810 opposed; 367 abstained; *The Washington Post,* April 9, 1974, confirmed by the APA Public Relations Department, November 11, 1976). One of the principal opponents, Dr.

31

Irving Bieber, pointed out that while he does not regard homosexuality as a mental illness, he sees it as a developmental abnormality, and feels that it should be so listed in the nomenclature. (Bieber's position, it can be noted, is quite similar to that taken by Dr. Cavanagh in this book.) It might be called "heterosexual dysfunction" or "heterosexual inadequacy."

The new terminology assumes that only homosexuals who are bothered about their orientation and seek treatment have a psychiatric problem. Likewise Dr. Bieber is concerned about the effect of this resolution on prevention. A prehomosexual child is easy to identify; and if the child and parents are treated early, there is a good chance that such a child will develop normal heterosexual responses. "The decision distorts the relation between homosexuals and therapy. Now it appears that those homosexuals whose potential for the restoration of heterosexual functioning is minimal will not be designated as having a *sexual orientation disturbance*. This does disservice to potential patients, especially children and their parents, who will be led to believe that homosexuality is simply another alternative life style."[3]

Before discussing the effects of these resolutions it should be stressed that no one has challenged the second resolution which deplored all public and private discrimination against homosexuals in such areas as employment, housing, public accommodation, and licensing.

The second resolution would seem to be far more beneficial than the first in terms of long-term advancement of the rights of homosexuals. One does not have to agree with various analyses of the etiology and nature of homosexuality in order to work for the full recognition of his person. No matter what view one takes on the morality of homosexual acts, one can respect the homosexual person, and insist that his human rights be respected. The National Task Force on Homosexuality in October, 1969, reporting to the National Institute of Mental Health, recommended that there be "a reassessment of current employment practices and policy relating to the employment of homosexual individuals with a view toward making needed changes. . . . Discrimination in employment can lead to economic disenfranchisement, thus engendering anxiety and frustrating legitimate achievement motivation."[4]

The Task Force admitted that some homosexuals might not be suited for certain jobs, but this is not the same as a policy of general disqualification of homosexuals. In 1969 the Task Force was concerned whether sensitive positions would be denied homosexuals because of the threat of blackmail (see p. 189); during the intervening seven years the growth of the Gay Liberation Movement and several U.S. District Court decisions in San Francisco and Washington, in which the Civil Service Commission's dismissals of persons known to be homosexual were overthrown, have lessened the power of blackmail.[5] In the past blackmail had been used on many prominent persons,[6] but with the shift of public attitude following upon the above events and the APA change of nomenclature, it is likely that blackmail will become a less frequent phenomenon.

Effect on Legislation

As a result of the change in nomenclature, various civil rights bills pending in urban and state legislative assemblies will have a better chance of becoming law. At the risk of oversimplification, these bills include the right of the homosexual not to suffer discrimination in applications for employment, housing, and public accommodations. Since homosexuality is no longer classified as a mental illness, it cannot be adduced as a reason for refusing employment to a homosexual. If one argues in a particular case that the condition of homosexuality impedes the person from quality performance, he must show the nexus beyond reasonable doubt. On the other hand, change in nomenclature and even changes in civil laws will not dissipate overnight the plethora of prejudices against homosexuals.

When the nomenclature was changed it was not known whether homosexuals would seek the same legal protections for their "holy unions" as heterosexuals possess. "In Baker *vs.* Nelson, the Minnesota Supreme Court held that the state statute concerning marriage did not authorize issuance of a license to two persons of the same sex and that the statute so construed did not violate the U.S. Constitution. An appeal to the U.S. Supreme Court was dismissed."[7]

Since then there have been literally hundreds, perhaps thousands, of homosexual marriages, usually called "holy unions" celebrated in at least half of the states of our country. In the overwhelming majority of the states the statutes do not explicitly exclude same-sex marriages, but in view of the rash of applications and homosexual-union ceremonies with consequent publicity, a number of states have considered or have enacted anti-homosexual marriage laws.

Homosexuals have fought for the marriage right in the Churches, Assemblies, Legislatures, Television, Newspapers, highest State Courts, the U.S. Supreme Court, Internal Revenue Service, Veterans Administration, Immigration and Naturalization Service, Governors' Offices, Adoption Agencies, Insurance Companies and anywhere else they might set a legal precedent. Gay activism, becoming obviously more political day-by-day, will undoubtedly increase pressure by attempting to influence Churchmen, lawmakers and society-at-large of the homosexuals' asserted right to a same-sex marriage with all its attendant legal benefits [see p. 221].[8]

From perusal of letters to the editor in the APA's *Psychiatric News*, it is safe to say that there is much dissatisfaction with the change in nomenclature and no disapproval of the resolution concerning discrimination against homosexuals. Like Bieber, several psychiatrists (among them William Green of Dallas, Texas, and Doris Milman of Brooklyn, New York) fear that this ruling will encourage the "sexually untried adolescent boy" to enter the gay life without real knowledge of his options.[9] "At a critical juncture in his psychosexual evolution he is subjected to ambiguity where he needs direction, to uncertainty where he needs definition, to abdication of responsibility where he needs a fixed point of reference. My concern is less for the adult homosexual than for the adolescent whose options are still open."[10]

This judgment is supported on the basis of personal counseling experience.[11] The conscientious homosexual will avoid inducing an adolescent into his own way of life, but gay literature does not distinguish between adolescents and adults, and its impact, together with the need of the adolescent to identify with a group, may cause him to give himself over to a gay way of life.

Effect of Change on Moral Responsibility

No matter how psychiatric manuals describe homosexuality, the moralist must see the same kind of behavior in a different perspective. It is necessary to review the difference between the analysis of actions in themselves and the evaluation of the motivation and freedom of the person acting. The former is regarded as objective morality, and the latter is called subjective, or the analysis of subjective responsibility. Surely, into this latter analysis psychological considerations enter. From the objective morality viewpoint it is difficult to see how the controversy concerning nomenclature affects the widely held conclusions of Catholic moralists. As long as the basic principles of Christian sexual morality are derived from the Church's teaching on marriage, there is no way of justifying homosexual actions. The only way to justify such actions is to reject the principles of sexual morality more recently reaffirmed in Vatican II's statement on marriage[12] and in the encyclical *Humanae Vitae.*

If, on the other hand, we view the homosexual's condition in terms of moral knowledge, personal history, and degree of freedom, then the current controversy does impinge upon the evaluation of subjective factors. Many will be inclined to believe that the removal of homosexuality from the category of mental illness means that homosexual behavior is as normal as heterosexual behavior and therefore is regarded as morally good. It is just a different form of natural behavior. One should be allowed to fulfill his sexual needs, hetero-, homo- or bisexual. Legalization of adult, consensual private acts of homosexuality will tend to confirm this view. Such legislation will have the bad effect of giving the impression that something is morally good because it is legally permitted. There is still another element of confusion. The fact that one has deeply ingrained inclinations to some form of sexual action does not make the act good. Impulses to masturbation, fornication, and adultery are distortions of the natural inclination to sexual union.

Nonetheless, it is noted that many homosexuals who belong to gay groups *seem* convinced that they have a right to lead a gay life. This apparent conviction is doubted because "they protest too much." When their point of view is opposed it is met with strong hostility, not only verbally, but also in the gay media.[13] A former gay journalist, now advocating a chaste way of life for homosexuals, said that whenever he organized panels in the past he made sure they were stacked in one direction. Many gay persons do not want to hear the other side of the question. It appears that such individuals do not incur grave personal guilt for homosexual behavior. They have rationalized themselves into the seeming conviction that they have a right to a different form of sexual expression, but they are not really at ease within themselves.

The Moralist's Responsibility

This possible form of good faith, however, does not excuse the moralist from responsibility to teach the immorality of homosexual acts. At the same time he will note that homosexual actions are frequently of diminished responsibility. There are many degrees of compulsion found in homosexual acts, just as there are in heterosexual acts. Any counselor who has listened to the counselee's account of "cruising" with its consequent promiscuous pattern of behavior realizes that one is dealing here with obsessive-compulsive behavior. *Sometimes*, however, such persons do have moments of freedom when they can stop the buildup of fantasy which leads to cruising and action. Call this moment, if you will, the moment of truth.

If they accept the insight that they can turn back to some other activity and self-control, they will be able to lead a chaste life, perhaps with some relapses; but if they ignore the promptings of conscience, they slip back into the compulsive pattern, and are in some manner responsible for their behavior. But if the homosexual lacks insight into himself, believing or wanting to believe he has no freedom, he is not likely to give up a way of life which gives him some satisfaction, not unmixed with guilt and loneliness.

These reflections are a summary of introspective interviews with homosexuals who would be classified as having a *sexual reorientation disturbance*, while other homosexuals who consider themselves normal remain without such insight. This is one of the ironies of the new nomenclature. Those seeking insight into the nature of their homosexual tendencies are given a new category in psychiatry while those who seek no self-knowledge are regarded as mentally healthy.

The changed nomenclature is both a blessing and a curse. A blessing in the sense that it allows the homosexual to assert his dignity as a human being; and a curse in the sense that it confuses both the young and those who are *not* satisfied to remain overt homosexuals.

CHAPTER FOUR

Definitions

Homosexuality

Before attempting to decide exactly what constitutes homosexuality, it is important to emphasize that until recently practically nothing was known of the *state of being a homosexual*, although there was knowledge of *homosexual acts*. The derivation of the term itself was not known. The term *homo* is from the Greek meaning "same," not from the Latin *homo* meaning "man." Since only *homosexual acts* were known, it led to the belief that all homosexual individuals were perverts. This is not the case. Homosexuals may be perverted, but they are not necessarily so. A *pervert* is an individual, homosexual or heterosexual, who finds his complete sexual satisfaction in a manner which deviates from the usual or accepted way of performing the sex act. It differs, for example, from the way in which the sex act is performed in the society or culture in which the individual lives.

It is important to realize that perversion refers to complete physical satisfaction, not merely to the use of various means of sensory stimulation for sexual arousal which are often employed as preliminaries to sex acts. It is not perversion, for example, when any act which is desired or acceptable to both male and female partners is employed as part of the sex play prior to sexual intercourse. This is true only as long as the act ends with or is intended to end with the deposition of the semen in the vault of the vagina in such a way that there is no interference with penile-vaginal intercourse.

A homosexual, therefore, is not a pervert, unless he performs perverse acts; that is to say, the chaste homosexual should not be considered a pervert. It is important to accept the concept that *homosexuality is a way of thinking and feeling; not merely a way of acting.* The performance of homosexual acts is, therefore, not, in itself, evidence of homosexuality. As I will explain in Chapter 5, homosexuality is not a disease entity but is merely a symptom of a personality disorder. Salzman expresses this same thought:

> A definition in terms of behavior is preferable, since homosexuality is a symptom of underlying personality distortion and not of a single integrated psychiatric syndrome.[1]

More of this later. The condition, however, is sufficiently clear-cut as a behavior disorder that it may be defined and described *per se*.

Definition

As a working definition, *homosexuality may be defined as a persistent, postadolescent state in which the sexual object is a person of the same sex and in which there is a concomitant aversion or abhorrence, in varying degrees, to sexual relations with members of the other sex.*
This aversion and abhorrence should not be understood to mean a total absence of ability to have heterosexual relations on the part of all homosexuals. It is not uncommon to see an individual who is known to be a homosexual pushing a baby carriage. Even in the presence of disgust and revulsion one may carry out an unpleasant task, and although with practice it may become more tolerable, as long as the condition persists it never becomes wholly acceptable. In the case of the homosexual the task may become more acceptable by fantasying a homosexual companion. Disgust and aversion for heterosexual contacts will persist, especially in the male homosexual, as long as he is an invert.
Dr. John F. Oliven emphasizes these feelings of aversion:

> These men are attracted exclusively toward men. Erotic situations involving an attractive woman leave them indifferent or even fill them with repugnance or vague fear.[2]

The term "homosexuality" is often used indiscriminately to include such nonsexual concepts as dependency, aggression, competition, domination, and submission. The term should, however, be restricted only to behavior which has orgiastic satisfaction as its object.[3]

Another definition of homosexuality is given by Anomaly. Since frequent references will be made to this book, I would like to call attention to the fact that the name "Anomaly" is a pseudonym used by the author of a small book called *The Invert*. It was published in 1948 by the Williams and Wilkins Company of Baltimore. Anomaly states that he is a male homosexual who is a Catholic. The book gives excellent insights into homosexuality from the standpoint of a nonprofessional homosexual. It is a book which could be recommended to the homosexual for his own use.

Anomaly gives this definition:

A homosexual person (or invert) is one who, though apparently normal, is entirely unsusceptible to the sexual and emotional attraction of the opposite sex, but is susceptible to the sexual and emotional attraction of his, or her, own sex.[4]

Another definition is that given by the Group for the Advancement of Psychiatry:

Homosexuality is a sexual pattern in which there is an erotic interest in one's own sex, replacing to a greater or lesser degree heterosexual interest and behavior. An individual should be considered to be a homosexual, who after adolescence repeatedly or exclusively prefers sexual activity with the same sex.[5]

Dr. William Tobin, a canon lawyer, offers this definition:

Homosexuality may be described as that condition of psychosexual immaturity characterized by a predominant erotic attraction for a sexual object of the same sex. It constitutes a sexual anomaly that is not an either-or condition but admits of great variations. LeMoal had indicated that erotic attraction for the same sex is the *conditio sine qua non* of this disorder. In its rare, extreme form, this condition includes a complete absence of attraction towards the opposite sex together with a concomitant positive disgust for sexual relations with the opposite sex.[6]

Dr. Oliven emphasizes other aspects of the homosexual state:

> This is a chronic, usually lifelong disorder of the total personality, although in a number of cases its only apparent manifestation is the abnormal direction of the sex drive. Homosexuality is basically a medical (probably chiefly psychiatric) problem. But because of its relative incurability, the fairly frequent tendency of these patients to seduce others, and because of the almost instinctive animosity the homosexual inspires in many normal people, in practice it has remained rather more a social than a strictly medical problem.[7]

Classification of Homosexuality

You may ask, "Is there more than one type of homosexual?" This question is difficult to answer because by the definition given it would appear that homosexuals are an autonomous group. Even within that group we could, however, specify several subgroups; for example:
1. Adolescent pseudohomosexuals.
2. Active adult homosexuals.
3. Passive adult homosexuals.
4. Chaste homosexuals.

Laidlaw describes these psychological types of homosexuals:
1a. Promiscuous: needs a different partner each time he commits the act, and has no use for one after the act.
1b. Faithful to a complete involvement with only one person — comparable to heterosexual love.
2a. Purely physical expression — act is tossed off and forgotten.
2b. Deep feeling and love — really meaningful to the individual.
3a. No conflict in personality.
3b. Violent conflict in personality.[8]

Homosexuals are usually classified as:
1. *True homosexuals*, also called manifest, obligatory, exclusive homosexuals.[9]
2. *Pseudohomosexuals*, sometimes also called bisexuals,

ambisexuals, facultative, substitute, or circumstantial homosexuals.

3. *Constitutional homosexuals.*

True homosexuality or psychosexual homosexuality is the condition defined above. True homosexuals have no real sexual interest in members of the other sex. They may, however, seek them out as intellectual or social companions. This condition is usually considered to be acquired in early life and to be psychogenic in nature. *It is this condition with which we are concerned when discussing the homosexual state.*

Pseudohomosexuality, sometimes erroneously called *bisexuality,* is a condition in which the individual so affected may be sexually interested in members of both sexes. It occurs usually when he is isolated from the preferred sex and, because of a strong, poorly discriminating sex drive, he may sexually accept either sex. This is most likely to occur in prisons, isolated military posts, and similar situations. This is not true homosexuality and resembles it only in its externals. Such individuals usually prefer the heterosexual object if it is available. The term *bisexual* is derived from the biological fact that the urogenital tracts of the two sexes derive from a common embryonic origin. Because the embryo contained cell material from the glands of both sexes it was originally called *hermaphroditic.*

This unfortunate description opened the door to indiscriminate speculation on man's bisexuality and appeared to offer a scientific basis for an explanation of homosexuality. Krafft-Ebing (1840-1902) adopted this idea and introduced it into psychiatry. In 1905 when Freud published his "Contributions to the Theory of Sex," he followed the lead of Krafft-Ebing. Freud later changed some of his ideas, and as late as 1933 he stated that he had merely "carried over the notion of bisexuality into the mental life."[10] This biological concept has withered away and is seldom seriously considered, at the present time, as representative of the genesis of homosexuality (see Ch. 6).

Constitutional homosexuality is a term used by those who feel that the condition is inborn or hereditary. There is little or no scientific proof of this theory.

Definitions

Before proceeding further with a discussion of homosexuality, it is important to pause briefly for the unpleasant but necessary task of defining some terms. These are terms which are requisite for an understanding of our future chapters as well as for an easier comprehension of the books and articles which should be read to extend your knowledge of this subject. These definitions should be committed to memory, but for the time being, until you have done so, they will be listed alphabetically for ease of reference.

Absolute inversion. Freud speaks of those who are "absolutely inverted, i.e., their sexual object must always be of the same sex, while the opposite sex can never be to them an object of sexual longing, but leaves them indifferent or . . . may even evoke sexual repugnance."[11]

Active homosexual. This term refers to the more aggressive homosexual partner who usually assumes the male role, the one who instigates the act, the one who makes the first suggestion.

Amphigenous inversion. Certain individuals are "amphigenously inverted (psychosexually hermaphroditic), i.e., their sexual object may belong indifferently to either the same or to the other sex. The inversion lacks here the character of exclusiveness."[12] These have been described as pseudohomosexuals or bisexuals.

Anomaly, sexual. See *Perversion (sexual)*.

Buggery. A legal term still commonly used in England although archaic in the United States. It refers to the insertion of the penis into the anus or rubbing it between the folds of the buttocks. When the penis is that of an adult, and the anus of a child, the perversion is called "pederasty."

Cunnilingus. The practice of applying the lips, tongue, or mouth to the vulva or to any part of the external genital organs of the female. This may serve as a source of complete satisfaction to the one who employs the practice.

Patient I is a forty-five-year-old American-born, European-educated white male. He is married, but has no children. His best description sexually is that he is a "hard-core homosexual." He is well educated and perceptive. He was given a copy of this manuscript to read and he made some comments about it. In regard to cunnilingus he said:

> I find more and more men indulging in this, until it becomes the whole end in itself of the sex act, and would like to note that these men are very often homosexuals, who from this kind of

relation with women come to men. I suppose the desire to do this is in itself a sign of latent homosexuality. I have so often run into this type who gives one a vivid picture of the pleasure he gets from this act with women, but unfortunately it is not always easy to arrive at, as many women object, but one can do the same with men.

Exhibitionism. Exhibitionism is the derivation of sexual pleasure or gratification from the display of the genitals to another person. In many cases the preference is for this person to be a child. By modification, to make the exhibition more socially acceptable, the tendency may be unconsciously displaced from the genitals to the body as a whole, to clothes, to dramatics, etc. The person to whom the tendency is directed may be either homosexual or heterosexual, depending on the orientation of the exhibitor.

Fellatio. Fellatio (from the Latin *fellare*, "to suck") is the application of the mouth to the penis. The mucous membrane of the lips and mouth were regarded by Freud as a primary erotogenic zone. "An intense activity of this erotogenic zone at an early age thus determines the subsequent presence of a somatic compliance on the part of the tract of mucous membrane which begins at the lips." The original object of the lips and mouth is the nipple. "It then needs very little creative power to substitute the sexual object of the moment (the penis) for the original object (the nipple) or for the finger which did duty for it later on, and to place the current sexual object in the situation in which gratification was originally obtained. So we see that this excessively repulsive and perverted phantasy of sucking at a penis has the most innocent origin."[13]

Fellator. One who practices fellatio.

Fellator, self (autofellatio). The practice of putting the male genital organ into the individual's own mouth. "While he occasionally practices self-irrumination (self-fellatio) to relieve sexual tension that has already been aroused, he more often employs it to stimulate sexual excitement in himself."[14]

Fellatrice. A female who takes the oral part in fellatio.

Fetishism. This is a condition in which the individual gains sexual satisfaction by contact with, or possession of, a part of the clothing or portion of the body of the loved object. This erotic feeling may be heterosexual or homosexual. The fetish may be used as a means of sexual stimulation or as a sexual object in itself. For example, a lock of hair may be held in the same esteem as would be the person from whom it is taken.

Hermaphrodite. A *true hermaphrodite* is an individual who has the complete sex glands of both sexes and frequently the external organs of both sexes as well. A *pseudohermaphrodite* is one in whom, although there may be the external organs of both sexes, the glands of only one sex are present. There is no necessary relation between homosexuality and hermaphroditism.

Homophile. One who looks with favor upon homosexuals.

Homosexual panic (also called Kempff's Disease). An acute schizophrenic-like episode characterized by intense fear, marked excitement, and paranoid ideas, usually of short duration, occurring in individuals whose homosexuality is unconscious.

Incest. A term for sexual relations between persons related within the degrees wherein marriage is prohibited by law. It may be homosexual or heterosexual.

Inversion. A term used for homosexuality indicating that the sex drive has been turned to the self-sex. The expression "sexual inversion" is usually used today in psychiatry in its psychoanalytic sense:

> The popular theory of the sexual instinct corresponds closely to the poetic fable of dividing the person into two halves — man and woman — who strive to become reunited through love. It is, therefore, very surprising to find that there are men for whom the sexual object is not the woman but the man, and that there are women for whom it is not man but woman. Such persons are designated as contrary sexuals, or better, inverts, and the situation of such a relationship is called inversion.[15]

A few writers reserve the words "invert" and "inversion" for a special use: for them, an invert is an individual who desires or seeks homosexual relations and at the same time tries to adopt the complete sex role of a member of the other sex.[16]

> In spite of the work of Kinsey and others there has been an attempt to divide homosexuals into "inverts" and "perverts." This was put forward in the Church of England's *The Problem of*

Homosexuality in 1954, and was used by the counselor in the Montague trial. It was suggested that "an invert is a man who from accident or birth has unnatural desires . . . whereas a pervert is a man who either from lust or wickedness will get desires for either natural or unnatural functions."[17]

The Wolfenden Report comments:

> Some writers on the subject, and some of our witnesses, have drawn a distinction between the "invert" and the "pervert." We have not found this distinction very useful. It suggests that it is possible to distinguish between two men who commit the same offense, the one as the result of his constitution, and the other from a perverse and deliberate choice, with the further suggestion that the former is in some sense less culpable than the latter. To make this distinction as a matter of definition seems to prejudge a very difficult question.[18]

In spite of these comments I shall use the terms "homosexual" and "invert" and "homosexuality" and "inversion" as synonyms.

Kempff's Disease. See *Homosexual panic.*

Latent homosexuality. This term is generally used to indicate a tendency to, or a condition of, homosexuality of which the individual affected is not fully conscious. There has been a good deal of discussion lately as to the real significance of the term which will be discussed later (see Ch. 8).

Lesbian. This term is used for the female homosexual. It derives from the ancient inhabitants of the Island of Lesbos in the Aegean Sea who were said to favor homosexuality.

Masturbation. Masturbation refers to all forms of sexual self-gratification. The impulse to such an act may occur as the result of psychic stimuli, either homosexual or heterosexual, or local physical stimulation of the genital parts. It occurs in both sexes at all ages. Masturbation is not uncommon in small children. Many writers believe that the practice is universal, but there is no proof of this. It is more frequent in boys than in girls. In small infants, the process should not be called masturbation because it has nothing specifically to do with sex but is merely part of the child's exploration of his body. He finds a part which is pleasurable when touched and consequently he tends to touch

45

it repeatedly because of the pleasure involved. Forcible attempts at repression of masturbation may lead to thumb-sucking, nail-biting, tics, or other neurotic disorders, among which might be the development of compulsive masturbation. Masturbation is more frequent in women after middle life and in males during adolescence.

Masturbation may be solitary or be performed with one or more partners. The latter form is referred to as mutual masturbation. It is probably the most common sexual practice between female homosexuals.

Overt homosexuality. A condition in which the individual consciously thinks, feels, and may act in a homosexual manner.

Paraphilia. Another term for sexual perversion (q.v.).

Passive homosexual. This is the partner who is acted upon, who assumes the passive, female role. This term must not be taken to indicate that a homosexual is necessarily always either active or passive. The roles may be interchangeable. An individual may be active at one time and passive at another. A passive homosexual may be more a source of disturbance than the one who is more aggressive, because he is responsive to the demands made on him. Such individuals have a seductive attractiveness while retaining the appearance of innocence.

Perversions, sexual (also called sex deviations, paraphilias, or psychosexual abnormalities). Methods of sex gratification, mainly or exclusively, without penile-vaginal intercourse. Perversion may occur by the individual's selection of an abnormal sexual object or by engaging in abnormal relations with a usual sex object.[19]

Since the term "perversion" carries with it a connotation of serious basic psychopathology, it would be helpful in many cases to employ a term less suggestive of pathology. *Sexual anomaly* is surely a more meaningful term. Behavior in the sexual sphere that deviates rather sharply from the average is not necessarily pathological. The term *sexual anomaly* is proposed as a substitute for "sexual perversion," on the ground that evidence is lacking that perversions are intrinsically pathological and that a less condemnatory term is socially desirable. This term must be distinguished from sex anomaly which refers properly to anatomical deviation.[20]

Sapphism. This term is derived from the name of Sappho, a native of Lesbos. It is a less commonly used term for female homosexuality.

Sodomy. This term is probably derived from Sodom, an ancient Palestinian city which was destroyed, according to Genesis 18 and 19, because of the prevalence there of unnatural sex relations. The term today is most commonly used to designate *coitus per anum,* performed between homosexual partners. It may, however, take place between heterosexual partners, so it is not, therefore, an exclusively homosexual act. If it is performed with a person of the same sex, it is called — by the moralists — perfect sodomy; when it occurs between persons of the opposite sex, imperfect sodomy. In some modern texts the term is used for *coitus of humans with animals.*[21] A better and more commonly used term for this is bestiality.

Transsexualism. An extreme form of transvestism where in addition to cross-dressing, the wish for emasculation is present.

Transvestism. A condition in which the subject prefers to wear the clothes and live the life of the opposite sex. It may be, but is not always, associated with overt homosexuality. In some instances, however, the mere wearing of the clothing satisfies the individual's erotic needs.

Tribadism. A term frequently used to indicate female homosexuality. More specifically it refers to a practice consisting of the mutual friction of the genitals between women.

Voyeurism is a condition in which the individual derives sexual pleasure or gratification by looking at the genitals of another. The *voyeur* is known as a "Peeping Tom." This condition is also known as scopophilia. It may be homosexually, as well as heterosexually, directed.

Although this list is not exhaustive, it includes most of the terms ordinarily used. For other terms, reference should be made to a standard psychiatric dictionary such as that published by Leland E. Hinsie, M.D., and Jacob Shatsky, Ph.D.,[22] from which some of the above definitions were taken.

Homosexual Jargon

In addition to these technical terms, some colloquialisms may be of value for understanding the language used by homosexuals in reference to sex. Alphabetically listed, some of these terms are:

Busted. Arrested.

Butch. Usually used in the sense of "be butch," i.e., to act

47

masculine. Occasionally used to refer to a masculine type of Lesbian.

Camp it up. To act "gay" without inhibitions.

Camping. To flaunt the mannerisms of the other sex.

Cruising. Looking for "pickup," whether because of lonesomeness or for purposes of prostitution.

Dike or *dyke*. A Lesbian.

Drag. Dressed and made up like the other sex.

Drag act. A vaudeville act of female impersonators.

Drag balls. Dances to which guests may come dressed as the other sex.

Fag. A derogatory term for a homosexual.

Faggot. An obvious homosexual.

Fairy. A derogatory term for a homosexual.

Gay. A term frequently used to refer to homosexuality, but it is not necessarily limited to it. Dr. George Weinberg offers the following explanation of what is "gay." "To be homosexual is to have an erotic preference for members of one's own sex. . . . A homosexual person is gay when he regards himself as happily gifted with whatever capacity he has to see people as romantically beautiful. It is to be free of shame, guilt, regret over the fact that one is homosexual . . . to be gay is to view one's sexuality as the healthy heterosexual views his. . . . Being gay means having freed oneself of misgivings over being a homosexual. . . . In essence, it means being convinced that any erotic orientation and preference may be housed in any human being."[23]

Gay trade. One in which many homosexuals may be employed, e.g., hairdressing.

Pansy. A derogatory term for a homosexual.

Pimp. A procurer.

Queen. A transvestite.

Screaming queen. A very obvious queen.

Straight. To act like a heterosexual; to be a heterosexual.

Swish. A derogatory term for a homosexual.

Summary

This is an important chapter. There is so much difference in opinion about homosexuality that there will probably be authors who will disagree with some of the definitions given. Those given, however, should be studied very carefully to understand future chapters.

CHAPTER FIVE

Is Homosexuality a Disease?

What is homosexuality? A disease? A symptom? A neurosis? A personality disorder? Answers to these questions vary. I have myself over the years held different opinions. The belief or opinion which I express at this time probably represents my final conclusion. I believe that homosexuality is not a disease *per se* but represents a defective development of the personality with a fixation of the libido at an early age of development.

Some physicians look on the homosexual as a sick person. If this is so, then the homosexual would constitute only a medical problem. They make this assertion, although they offer no proof that homosexuality constitutes either a physical or psychological disease. Implicit in this opinion is the belief that since the invert is ill, he has little or no control over the developed malady.

In recent years this tendency to regard homosexuality as a disease is being more generally accepted. This is in line with the tendency of some psychiatrists and psychologists to teach that those who habitually break the law, whether moral or civil, are mentally ill.[1] This then would lead to the conclusion that there is no such thing as an immoral person or a criminal, but only a mentally ill or mentally healthy one. As Barbara Wooten says, "The concept of illness expands continually at the expense of the concept of moral failure."[2]

There are also the words of Pope Pius XII, speaking to psychotherapists in April, 1953, to be considered. The Holy Father repudiated the *general* rule that passion excludes subjective guilt and subjective responsibility. He stated at that time: "It cannot be alleged that the psychic troubles and disorders which disturb the normal functioning of a psychic being represent what usually happens."[3]

Such general assumptions as these repudiated by the Holy

49

Father have entered not only the field of civil law in the United States but also the theological writings of at least one French author. The Durham Decision of the U.S. Court of Appeals for the District of Columbia is a case of the former. In this instance an attempt was made to improve upon the "M'Naughton Rule" which has been widely used for over a hundred years as the criterion for determining the responsibility of individuals who were mentally ill (Rex *vs*. M'Naughton, House of Lords Cases, 1843). The danger of the Durham Decision is that it opens the door too wide. It allows a psychiatrist to testify to any theory which he may hold. It then leaves to his persuasive effect upon the jury whether the individual is to be considered irresponsible or not. It offers nothing specific for the jury to consider.

One such opinion in the field of Catholic theology was that of Abbé Marc Oraison whose book, *Vie chrétienne et problèmes de la sexualité*, was placed upon the Index of Forbidden Books less than a year after it was published — although the publication of the fact of condemnation was not made known until two years later (January, 1955). During this time, to the credit of the Abbé, he had withdrawn the book from publication and signified through the press his acceptance of the Church's decision. According to his theory:

> Almost all of mankind is so sexually immature and dominated by passions, that it may be taken as a general rule that sexual sins must be presumed to be only materially grave and thus the person is not subjectively guilty.[4]

From this it is evident that the action and reaction brought about by the teachings of Luther are still being felt within Western culture. It is only in this framework that one can appreciate the convictions that are so evident in the field of modern criminology and psychiatry and almost necessarily in moral theology. Kierkegaard has seen this and put it to use, although it seems that he has reached what might be termed the religion-centered extreme with the conclusion that "only the saint may be called immune against neurosis."[5] The counselor, too, must see this background and be able to judge particular problems accordingly.

Not all share this view that homosexuality is a disease. Father Michael T. Buckley states: "Homosexuality, therefore, is most certainly not a disease."[6]

50

Dr. Clara Thompson, who shared Harry Stack Sullivan's views, regarded the term "homosexual" as "a wastebasket to which all friendly and hostile feelings towards members of one's sex are applied." She considered homosexuality not as a specific entity having characteristic determinants but only as a symptom of a character problem. In this opinion she and Sullivan are not alone.[7]

According to Dr. Thompson:

. . . Homosexuality is not a clinical entity, but a symptom with different meanings in different personality set-ups. One might compare its place in the neurosis to that of a headache in various diseases. A headache may be the result of a brain tumor, a sinus, a beginning infectious disease, a migraine attack, an emotional disturbance, or a blow on the head. When the underlying disease is treated successfully, the headache disappears.

Similarly, overt homosexuality may express fear of the opposite sex, fear of adult responsibility, a need to defy authority, or an attempt to cope with hatred or of competitive attitudes to members of one's own sex; it may represent a flight from reality into absorption into body stimulation very similar to the auto-erotic activities of the schizophrenic, or it may be a symptom of destructiveness of oneself or others. These do not exhaust the possibilities of its meanings.[8]

The Wolfenden Report

The Wolfenden Report was presented to the British Parliament by command of her Majesty Elizabeth II. A work of enormous compassion as well as social and psychological insight, *The Wolfenden Report* was written under the auspices of a committee of public persons drawn from the clergy, medicine, sociology, psychology, and the law, and headed by Sir John Wolfenden, C.B.E. The committee gave the following statement of its purpose:

1. We were appointed on 24th August, 1954, to consider: (a) the law and practice relating to homosexual offenses and the treatment of persons convicted of such offenses by the courts; and (b) the law and practice relating to offenses against the criminal law in connection with prostitution and solicitation for im-

moral purposes, and to report what changes, if any, are in our opinion desirable.[9]

The Wolfenden Report also took the position that homosexuality is not a disease. It pointed out that there is no legal definition of "disease" or of "disease of the mind." The committee also pointed out "ill" health and "good" health are merely relative terms, as are "normal" and "abnormal." The *Report* stated that the mere presence of deviant sexuality in an individual showing no other abnormality was not incompatible with "full mental health." The *Report* further indicated that in those homosexual individuals who showed anxiety or other unpleasant symptoms, the symptoms were not necessarily the result of the condition of homosexuality, but quite likely occurred as the consequence of social attitudes. There is, of course, as the *Report* pointed out, no underlying pathological condition, either organic or psychopathological, which would warrant calling the disorder a "disease." None of the various theories formulated to explain the perversion, the *Report* concluded, is conclusive or specific to it, since the postulated or etiologic factors are also found in other psychopathological states.

> There is a clear-cut situation in which (homosexuality) invariably occurs. It appears as a symptom in people of diverse types of character structure.[10]

The American Psychiatric Association

Unexpectedly, the American Psychiatric Association acted by a vote of its membership to change the previously accepted nomenclature which indicated that homosexuality was a possible mental illness to a new benign name in December, 1973. Except for the fact that "a rose by any name smells as sweet," this change is pleasing to many and is of sufficient importance to devote a chapter to this subject alone. For its historical interest the old classification will be presented here; for the new classification, see Chapter 3.

Personality Disorders

These disorders are characterized by developmental defects or pathological trends in the personality structure, with minimal subjective anxiety, and little or no sense of distress. In most instances, the disorder is manifested by mental or emotional symptoms. Occasionally, organic diseases of the brain (epidemic encephalitis, head injury, Alzheimer's Disease, etc.) will produce clinical pictures resembling a personality disorder. In such instances, the condition is properly diagnosed as a Chronic Brain Syndrome (of appropriate origin) with behavioral reaction.

. . . Although the groupings are largely descriptive, the division has been made partially on the basis of the dynamics of personality development. The personality pattern disturbances are considered deep-seated disturbances, with little room for regression. Personality trait disturbances and sociopathic disturbances under stress may at times regress to a lower level of personality organization and function without development of psychosis.[11]

Personality disorders are divided into three types:
1. Personality Pattern Disturbance.
2. Personality Trait Disturbance.
3. Sociopathic Personality Disturbance.

1. *Personality Pattern Disturbance* (000—x40)
These are more or less cardinal personality types, which can rarely if ever be altered in their inherent structures by any form of therapy. Their functioning may be improved by prolonged therapy, but basic change is seldom accomplished. In some, "constitutional" features are marked and obvious. The depth of the psychopathology here allows these individuals little room to maneuver under conditions of stress, except into actual psychosis. It is subdivided into:
Inadequate Personality (000—x41)
Schizoid Personality (000—x42)
Cyclothymic Personality (000—x43)
Paranoid Personality (000—x44)

2. *Personality Trait Disturbance* (000—x50)
This category applies to individuals who are unable to maintain their emotional equilibrium and independence under minor or major stress because of disturbances in emotional development. Some individuals fall into this group because their personality pattern disturbance is related to fixation and exaggeration of certain character and behavior patterns; others, because their behavior is a regressive reaction due to environmental or endopsychic stress.

53

This classification will be applied only to cases of personality disorder in which the neurotic features (such as anxiety, conversion, phobia, etc.) are relatively insignificant, and the basic personality maldevelopment is the crucial distinguishing factor. Evidence of physical immaturity may or may not be present. It is subdivided into:

Emotionally Unstable Personality (000—x51)
Passive-Aggressive Personality (000—x52)
Compulsive Personality (000—x53)
Personality Trait Disturbance, Other (000—x54)

3. *Sociopathic Personality Disturbance* (000—x60)
Individuals to be placed in this category are ill primarily in terms of society and of conformity with the prevailing cultural milieu, and not only in terms of personal discomfort and relations with other individuals. However, sociopathic reactions are very often symptomatic of severe underlying personality disorder, neurosis, or psychosis, or occur as the result of organic brain injury or disease. Before a definitive diagnosis in this group is employed, strict attention must be paid to the possibility of the presence of a more primary personality disturbance; such underlying disturbance will be diagnosed when recognized. Reactions will be differentiated as defined below.

Antisocial Reaction (000—x61)
Dyssocial Reaction (000—x62)
Sexual Deviation (000—x63)

This diagnosis [Sexual Deviation] is reserved for deviant sexuality which is not symptomatic of more extensive syndromes, such as schizophrenic or obsessional reactions [see pp. 122f]. The term includes most of the cases formerly classed as "psychopathic personality with pathologic sexuality." The diagnoses will specify the type of the pathologic behavior, such as homosexuality, transvestism, pedophilia, fetishism and sexual sadism (including rape, sexual assault, mutilation).[12]

The Kinsey Report

This older opinion of the American Psychiatric Association — that homosexuality in itself provides evidence of a psychopathic personality — is challenged, according to the Kinsey Report on the male, by the incidence and frequency data which they elicited. They comment:

Of the 40 or 50 percent of the male population which has homosexual experience, certainly a high proportion would not be considered psychopathic personalities on the basis of anything else in their histories. It is argued that an individual that is so obtuse to social reactions as to continue his homosexual activity and make it any material portion of his life, therein evidences some social incapacity; but psychiatrists and clinicians in general might very well re-examine their justification for demanding that all persons conform to particular patterns of behavior.

Kinsey adds that there are, of course, some persons with homosexual histories "who are neurotic and in constant difficulty with themselves and not infrequently with society." But he points out that this is also true of heterosexual individuals:

Some homosexual individuals are so upset that they have difficulty in the accomplishment of their business or professional obligations and reach the point where they find it difficult to make the simplest sort of social contact without friction.

He argues, however, that there is a considerable question, as indicated by Bieber, that these persons are neurotic, and that if they are, their neurotic disturbances are the product of society's reaction to them rather than the result of their sexual behavior.[13]

Other Opinions

Allen points out that "homosexuality is not the opposite of heterosexuality — as so many people imagine — but a phase in development which some people find it difficult to pass."[14] This, he states, explains the fact that homosexuality is so often found with other sexual abnormalities which are themselves the residues of earlier developmental phases. The oral and anal interests shown by such individuals are only signs of incomplete evolution of the personality.

According to Ovesey, Freud concluded that homosexuality was not a neurosis. Freud's theory of instincts and the libido theory held that neurotic symptoms represented the repression of perverse infantile sexual impulses. "If no repression occurred, the perverse impulses remained conscious, and found direct expression without displacement." This, Ovesey states, led Freud to one of his earliest conclusions, that "neurosis is the negative of a perversion," a dictum which of necessity excluded homosexuality from the neuroses and also, at least, from the realm of psychoanalytic therapy, "since only neuroses were believed susceptible to psychoanalysis."[15]

To better understand how the sexual impulse becomes deviated from its normal adult heterosexual orientation, an understanding of the Freudian concept of sexuality will be helpful. This is admittedly only a hypothetical construct, but it helps to make understandable how the personality can develop in a way compatible with mental health and yet be associated with deviant sexuality.

Freudian Concept of the Development of Sexuality

The hypothesis for the development of sexuality as described by Freud and his followers is probably the best known and most easily understood. Freud was impressed by the frequency with which his patients' productions had a sexual significance. The more he investigated these, the more he was led to the belief that neurotic manifestations were due to conflicts between sexual impulses and resistance to the acceptance of these impulses. Freud's study of the reasons for repression of sexuality led him back to very early childhood, and he concluded that early sexual traumata formed the basis of later neurotic disturbances. He published these findings in 1905 under the title, *Three Contributions to the Theories of Sex.*[16]

The Freudian concept of sexuality, particularly his ideas on the Oedipal situation, forms an important basis of present thought. It is, therefore, important to discuss this in some detail because it will lead to a better understanding of homosexuality. Freud separated the concept of sexuality from the close association it had previously had with the genital organs. He felt that it included "all of those merely affectionate and friendly impulses to which usage applied the exceedingly ambiguous word 'love.' "

He considered pleasure as the goal of the sexual function and felt that this function existed from the beginning of life. These sexual feelings, he taught, were at first diffuse and their object was the subject's own body (autoerotic), as, for example, in masturbation. These feelings later become localized in certain erotogenic zones, the first of these areas being the lips. He considered that the pleasure the infant gets from sucking (oral stage) was sexual in nature. In adult life, a fixation at this level may lead to fellatio or cunnilingus. Later the erotogenic zone shifts to the anus where the sensation arises first in the pleasure of giving feces (anal-erotic stage) and later in withholding feces (anal-sadistic stage). In adult life this feeling may persist and result, for example, in a desire for sodomy. The next shift is to the genitals where it is at first unorganized (phallic stage) but later develops into the adult or genital stage. Between the phallic stage and the genital phase is a latent period during which the child is interested in children of the same sex. For this reason, the period is sometimes known as the "homosexual phase." It must be clearly understood that although this is a normal stage of development, a fixation at this level may lead to adult homosexuality.

Period of Sexual Latency

This period of sexual latency lasts from about the sixth year to prepuberty. During this period, the child tends to play with children of the same sex. A boy will liberate his aggressive tendencies by playing rough-and-tumble games such as "cops and robbers," whereas the girl tends to play with dolls and keep house and thereby expresses her desire to replace her mother. Parents frequently traumatize their children by forcing them into each other's company during this period. Mixed parties for children are frequently arranged by parents during this period, much before the boys and girls are ready for it. Parents should wait until the children naturally seek each other's company before they force dating upon them. The latter part of this period is frequently considered as a "normal" homosexual period during which children of the same sex seek each other's company. It must be emphasized that this is a normal situation and should, with the appearance of adolescence, give way to a proper heterosexual orientation. Having a "crush," or the development of an attitude of hero worship toward some admired figure, usually a teacher or clergyman, also frequently occurs during this period. This should lead to no difficulty if the adult is mature and well balanced. The "crush" usually passes very quickly (see pp. 106f).

Fixation is a term used to indicate a failure to advance to the next stage of development. For example, a child may become fixated at a homosexual level and fail to progress to a normal heterosexual adjustment. On the contrary, a child may advance to a stage of development and then, by a process of regression due to some traumatic episode, become fixated at a lower level. To explain certain neuroses, Freud stated that the libido (the energy of the sexual instincts) does not move smoothly along with the course of development, but that, as a result of traumatic emotional experience, it may become fixated at any level where pleasure is obtained. The stage of libido fixation, if it occurs, determines the choice of the anomaly. Homosexuality is due, according to this theory, to a fixation at or regression to an earlier level of sexual development.[17]

As may be seen from the above, in accordance with his libido theory, Freud considered unconscious homosexuality as a basic factor in neurosis. More recent analysis, however, has led to the conclusion that inversion is simply a manifestation of a more general personality problem. In a given case, instead of being the causal problem, it is merely one of the symptoms of a character problem and becomes less significant as the more general character disturbance is resolved.

Conclusions

1. Homosexuality is not a disease *per se*.
2. Deviant sexuality, including homosexuality, is a result of a personality or character problem in which the sexual orientation of the individual becomes fixated at an early age.
3. Homosexuality may be a symptom of a neurosis or psychosis, but in such cases it represents the individual's reaction to society or society's reaction to him.

CHAPTER SIX

The Causes
of Homosexuality

Nowhere in the study of homosexuality does the lack of knowledge about it show up as in efforts to explain its origin. The George W. Henry Foundation found that a high percentage of the overt homosexuals it studied had been introduced to the activity by older and more experienced devotees of the practice.[1] Such initiations may have been an etiological factor in the instance of Case X (see p. 197). Those in the older group were looking for fresh material, just as in heterosexual matters the same experience may be sought. One of our patients was introduced to the practice by a valet who was seducing the children in the neighborhood unknown to the parents of the children. There were, however, other factors present. The actual seduction explains the immediate initiation into the practice, but what I want to show now are the more remote causes which predispose the child, or the adolescent especially, toward the initial act.

A number of etiological factors have been advanced. These may be grouped into three classes: (1) organic factors; (2) genetic factors; and (3) psychological factors.

According to the organic viewpoint, homosexuality arises from an imbalance in endocrine secretions or from some defect in the physical constitution. Evidence for this position was sought in studies of the physique of known homosexuals. Among male homosexuals there seemed to be a slight tendency toward a female build, such as broader hips. However, this same tendency was not found in female homosexuals (see below). Another fact which has been used to advance the organic viewpoint is the comparative lack of androgen secretion in males and estrogen secretion in females. If this reasoning were correct, it would seem, then, that a homosexual male should be cured by an increase in androgen. But numerous experiments have shown that the increase of androgen does not decrease the homosexual drive. It only increases the libido in its initial direction. The evidence from physical characteristics has not been validated.

Some authors, like Krafft-Ebing, taught that homosexuality might arise from several sources. In some cases he said it was an acquired evil. In other cases, it arose from a failure of the sexual components of the body to develop completely.

Magnus Hirschfeld maintained that homosexuals were the result of constitutional factors; and he spent most of his life in a defense of homosexuality on this basis.

George Henry took the evolutional viewpoint. He insisted that psychosexual deviations were merely manifestations or by-products of human evolution. His view is similar to that of Maranon who suggested that homosexuality resulted from imperfect development of the human embryo.

Havelock Ellis held for a congenital predisposition toward homosexuality which is activated by environmental influences. Ellis puts more emphasis on the environmental factors than he does on heredity. Ellis says that the most important factors are psychological. In this respect he shares the opinion of the majority of psychiatrists today.

While most students agree that the dispositive influence is psychological, or at least dominantly so, they disagree on whether emphasis should be placed on instinctual or on environmental factors.

Before discussing the theories about the origin of homosexuality, the old wives' tale that homosexuality may be caused by excessive masturbation by an adolescent should be refuted. This notion is as unfounded as that which states that masturbation may lead to insanity. Masturbation is never a cause of anything physical.

Organic Factors

There seems no reason to believe, according to available evidence, that true homosexuality is due either to organic or hereditary factors.[2] Since I have not personally made any investigations in this matter, I shall quote from several sources who have either made investigations or reviewed the literature on the subject.

Allen, for example, speaks quite firmly on this point and states somewhat unwillingly:

60

I am reluctantly driven to the conclusion that there is, so far, no evidence upon which any reliance can be placed that there is any endocrine difference between "normal" and homosexual. This is in accordance with the clinical finding that castration does not cause a man to be homosexual, nor does it even in all cases, cause cessation of heterosexual intercourse. Moreover, injection of female hormones fails to make a man behave homosexually if he has previously been normal. The endocrine factor may be ancillary, but is not the basic cause.[3]

He then concludes:

It would be wearisome to labor the point. No investigations in any sphere indicate an organic basis for homosexuality, whether physical, chemical, cellular, microscopic or macroscopic.[4]

Father Michael Buckley, whose work somewhat suffers from the fact that he largely ignores American sources, in his otherwise careful review of literature finds no evidence in favor of an organic etiology. He concludes:

. . . A cursory examination of the British Medical Association report openly reveals the inadequacy of available medical data to explain homosexuality on a biological or endocrinological basis. The report does not even visualize the possibility that all cases of homosexuality have a medical background.[5]

Physical Constitution

Attempts were made by Weil to determine the physical constitution of 380 male homosexuals in comparison with 1,000 heterosexual males.[6] Weil's findings were that homosexuals had a slightly wider breadth of the hips than heterosexuals. It was 32.36 as compared with 31.41. Weil, however, has been criticized because he did not describe the method of measurement he used in his experiment. He states, for example, that some of the homosexuals he measured were people whom he met socially. He does not state how he determined these people to be homosexual. Nor does he show that he avoided the possibility of unconsciously choosing people who fitted into a pattern he had already designated.

Weil's study, however, is not the only one made on the possibility of physical factors. Henry and Galbraith concluded that there were significant physical characteristics: long legs; narrow hips; large muscles; deficient hair on face, chest, and back; female distribution of pubic hair; high-pitched voice; small penis and testicles; and the presence of the scrotal fold. Sometimes there was excessive fat on shoulders, buttocks, and abdomen. And in some cases the pelvis was exactly the homosexual build which they postulated — very large with unusually wide hips.

Female homosexuals, according to Henry and Galbraith, have "firm adipose tissue, a lack of fat on the shoulders and abdomen, a large amount of hair on the chest, back and legs, male distribution of pubic hair, small uterus, either overdeveloped or underdeveloped labia and clitoris. Moreover the female homosexual body seems to have a shorter trunk, a contracted pelvis, underdeveloped breasts, superfluous facial hair and a low-pitched voice."[7]

Wortis[8] made a study of the measurements of a group of 17 male homosexuals and 16 female homosexuals. This group was compared to a heterosexual control group of 5 males and 10 females. Wortis did not find any significant differences between homosexuals and heterosexuals in this small group. All that Wortis concluded was that the measurements of male homosexuals were somewhat below the average of male university students in Berlin, but the Lesbians were well above the average of female students at the University of Munich. It need hardly be mentioned that Wortis' group is so small that no general conclusions should be drawn from it.

Anthropological investigations help to confirm the opinion expressed by Wortis that there are no physical characteristics of inversion. Coppen, in 1959, stated:

> The androgyny score (i.e. 3 X biacromial = 1 X bi-iliac diameters, in centimeters), however, did not differentiate the homosexuals from the controls any better than did the biacromial diameter, which is less in these patients. It was concluded that homosexuals have a body-build similar to that found in patients with other psychiatric disorders and that it would not be specifically related to their sexual disorder.[9]

The validity of the method of testing was confirmed to some extent by the work of Dixon and Torr. These researchers made oral tests on 260 normal individuals to determine the chromosomal sex. They applied the method to 60 cases of abnormal physical and psychological sexual development. They stated:

> The present series includes cases of true and pseudo-hermaphrodites. The method has been particularly useful in separating out those cases with definite physical abnormalities — for example, Klinefelter's and Turner's syndromes — from those of an essentially psychological nature, without resort to laparotomy. In the psychologically maladjusted group it has been our invariable experience that the physical sex diagnosis is borne out by the chromosomal sex findings.[10]

Pare (1956) by chromatin staining procedures studied 50 homosexual men and 50 control heterosexuals (25 men and 25 women).[11] All male subjects studied were considered biologically male, and all 25 women as female. Other studies by Davidson and Winn confirmed these results.[12]

Barr and Hobbs examined 194 male homosexuals and 5 male transvestites. All of these gave male readings.[13] In any group of homosexuals, the proportion of those having a chromatin sex status inconsistent with their anatomical sex is no greater than among those with normal sexual leanings, according to Raboch and Nedoma.[14]

The possibility of physical factors has been studied in respect to more than body measurements. Studies have also been made on the cell structure of the testes and on the quantity of male and female sex hormones present. Steinach[15] made a microscopic examination of the testes of five homosexuals. His study suggested the possibility of degeneration of the testicles and the presence of certain cells, somewhat like lutein cells in the ovary of a woman. Slotopolsky and Schinz, however, discovered that degeneration in testicles and the presence of these quasi-lutein cells could be found in the testes of heterosexual males as well.[16]

As for the relative quantities of sex hormones, there is evidence that there is relatively less androgen in the urine of male homosexuals than in the urine of male heterosexuals. These were the findings of Glass, Duel, and Wright in 1940.[17] Neustadt and Myerson[18] studied 29 homosexuals in 1940 and found a similar condition and also discovered that there was a higher amount of estrogen present. The studies of Glass *et al.* were later rejected because of technical errors in their work.[19] Sawyer in 1954 stated that hormonal therapy offered no success in the treatment of cases of homosexuality.[20] Apparently the hormonal substances responsible for the develoment of the sexual characteristics play little or no part in the direction of the sexual drive.

Clear evidence seems to have been developed in recent research that androgen, the male hormone, is responsible for the function of sexual arousal in both sexes, although in different degrees.[21] Thus sex identification overrides the effects of the various hormones.[22] After research on the administration of exogenous sex hormones, Waxenburg concluded "that it is the androgens which provide the hormonal basis for the erotic component of human female sexuality."[23]

Margolese and Janiger found that analyses of twenty-four-hour specimens of urine from healthy adult males for androsterone and etiocholanolone produced values which, when calculated as discriminant scores, discriminated between heterosexual and exclusively homosexual individuals. This confirmed a previous study.

No significant differences were found between heterosexuals and homosexuals in parental ages, secondary sex characteristics, genitalia, anthropometry, 17-ketosteroids, and 17-ketogenic steroids.

A significant difference was found between the heterosexual group and homosexual group in the number of homosexual relatives in the immediate and extended families.[24]

Krafft-Ebing[25] believed that there were several sources of origin for homosexuality. He believed that in some cases the determining factor was primarily organic and in other cases it was psychic. According to his organic viewpoint all human embryos have rudimentary male and female sexual organs. Normally one of these sexual organs develops and the other disappears. But in the homosexual there is development of one sexual organ without a complete disappearance of the other. This abnormality in development and disappearance of the organs of the other sex will be accompanied by psychological abnormalities as well. If Krafft-Ebing's theory were correct there would be evidence of bodily abnormalities in all homosexuals. But this is not unanimously conceded.

Laidlaw concluded from his study of male homosexuals in New York City that these tended toward a body-build varying

64

somewhat toward the female; but that female homosexuals had less inclination toward a male body-build.[26]

Some students hold that homosexuality is a natural alternative to heterosexuality; in other words, that the homosexual is of a third sex, between male and female. This theory may be positively rejected on the grounds that: (1) it contradicts revealed truth; (2) it contradicts the conclusions of reality; and (3) it would be contrary to nature.

Father Thomas V. Moore, although he discussed the topic some years ago, gave some conclusions which are still valid on this point:

> The idea of homosexuality as due to some unfathomable force in nature compelling one to act as he does is a creation of the homosexual mind, a parataxis of defense. From an empirical, scientific point of view, the major factors in the occurrence of homosexuality are psychic in their nature rather than organic. From the philosophical and biological point of view, any displacement of the sex drive which makes impossible the attainment of the proper end of the sexual function must of its nature be abnormal. Accordingly, homosexuality and its fruitless acts must be a pathological condition whether the underlying pathology is of a psychic or organic character.[27]

Heredity

Studies have been made on the possibility that homosexuality may be transmitted by heredity. Prior to World War II, Theodore Lang made a study of known homosexuals in Hamburg, Germany, in order to determine whether the relatives of these persons seemed to show evidence of the condition.[28] From this study Lang concluded that the possibility of transmission by genes had to be ruled out. It should be mentioned here that even if he had evidence of homosexuality among the relatives, he would not have been able to rule out the psychological effect.

Since Lang did not see homosexuality as genetic in origin, he considered the possibility of homosexuality as an intersex. According to Lang's final view, the homosexual male is not really a male but a transformed female. That is to say, the homosexual comes about as a result of development just as a new strain of flowers may be developed in a botanical garden. Lang did not derive his ideas from botany but from the work of Goldschmidt[29] who had produced sexual intergrades in butterflies. Lang's fundamental argument, however, is based on a faulty reasoning process which does not give a necessary conclusion. Lang argued as follows: "If it is true that a proportion of male homosexuals are actually transformed females, then an undue preponderance of males must be found among the siblings of male homosexuals."

The normal sex ratio of male-female siblings is 106:100. Lang then attempted to show that there was this undue preponderance in homosexuals. Among the siblings of homosexual fathers, he found a ratio of 121 males to 100 females. His argument falls down, however, when he compares this ratio in the children of homosexual fathers; this turns out to be 106.9 to 100 — which is normal. But this argument is also weak because it does not rule out other possibilities. Therefore, Lang's conclusions should be taken with the possibility of error in mind.

S. Keller has suggested that while Lang's findings are not to be taken conclusively, it might be interesting to make a study of the proportionate number of brothers and sisters among the siblings of homosexuals.[30]

Other studies of the male-female sibling relationship were also inconclusive.[31] Slater studied the families of male exhibitionists, and noted a ratio of 109:144, which he interpreted as an excess of female siblings to form an audience for the exhibitionist brother.[32] Darke studied a small sample consisting of American homosexuals and reported a normal 106:100 ratio.[33]

Franz Kallmann[34] made a study of overt male homosexuality in forty pairs of identical twins. He discovered that whenever one was homosexual, the other was also. And the tendency was moderately increased in brothers or fraternal co-twins of overt homosexuals.

I am recording Kallman's study because it is frequently quoted. His findings, however, are not conclusive. It is just as easy to explain the frequency of homosexuality in these fraternal pairs by "psychic infection" as it is in terms of genetics. In every case these children were subjected to the same family conditions. The possibility of psychic influences would have to be eliminated before any of these studies could be accepted conclusively.

Although Kallman's study must be considered, its reliability is generally held to be doubtful. In the first place, it is too perfect. Clinical investigations seldom work out one hundred per-cent. This is not only my opinion. Berg speaks of the study rather skeptically:

> Since the actual data of his paper is very superficial and sketchy and he gives only three case histories because the patients were still subject to New York laws, one feels that the paper, in spite of the elaborate statistical analysis, is dubious and uncertain. Statistical formulas may be impressive, but the basic clinical facts must be completely determined for them to be of any value at all. Obviously one cannot go up to a man and say, "Excuse me, I understand your twin brother is homosexual; do you mind telling me if you are?" It is here that the perilous part comes and it seems possible that sometimes Kallman went more on hearsay than actual investigation.[35]

Berg concludes: "Kallman's paper, therefore, stands suspect because (1) his clinical material is not satisfactory; (2) it is contradicted by the experience of others; (3) it is unusual in medicine to obtain 100% results and one usually encounters some omission or contradiction; and (4) his work has never been confirmed by anyone else."[36]

I find myself in complete agreement with Berg. There is no conclusive evidence that homosexuality is transmissible hereditarily. This opinion is supported by the studies of Freedman and his associates:

> Kallman (1952) studied 85 homosexuals who were twins, and, although the concordance rates for overt homosexual behavior (5 and 6 on the Kinsey scale) were only slightly higher than normal for the 45 dizygotic pairs, it was 100 per cent for the 40 monozygotic pairs. This finding suggests the presence of a definite and decisive genetic factor in homosexuality, but Kallman's findings have not been confirmed by other investigators. Thus, Kolb (1963) has described 7 monozygotic homosexual twins in which there was no concordance at all with their twin siblings. Moreover, it does not necessarily follow that a higher concordance rate in twins is due to a genetic factor; the powerful identification between them may result in a greater tendency to indulge in preadolescent and adolescent homosexual activities with each other with less inhibiting guilt than exists between other siblings. Given

other facilitating and fixating familial and environmental circumstances, such activities may well result in a greater preponderance of concordant homosexual patterns. Nevertheless, the generally higher incidence of homosexual concordance in monozygotic as compared with dizygotic twins suggests that the possibility of a hidden genetic predisposition interacting with subsequent environmental experiences cannot be entirely ruled out at this stage of knowledge.[37]

A number of European studies have been made which are not too recent but which included larger numbers in their samples than most American surveys.

1. Romer (1906), in a study of 600 male university students in Holland, arrived at a figure of about 2 percent exclusive homosexuality plus 4 percent bisexuality.

2. Hirschfeld (1920), in a survey of 3,665 German men, calculated that 2.3 percent were exclusively homosexual and 3.4 percent bisexual.

3. Friedeberg (1953) studied about 500 men in West Germany and found that 23 percent of them admitted to postpubertal homosexual experiences; he did not obtain figures for exclusive homosexuality.

4. Giese (Schoof, unpublished data, 1967) studied 2,835 male and 831 female college students in North Germany and found that 19 percent of the men and 4 percent of the women reported overt homosexual experiences; but most of these may have been adolescent experiences between the ages of 12 and 18 years of age. Within the previous 12 months, only 3 percent of the men and 1 percent of the women had had a homosexual contact.

5. Schofield (1965) surveyed 1,873 unmarried young people in England, almost equally divided among men and women in the 15-to-19 age group. Although he made no special effort to ascertain the incidence of homosexuality, 5 percent of the men and 2 percent of the women reported homosexual experiences.[38]

The comments of Patient I seem pertinent here:

I am thinking about the case of four brothers, friends of mine in Europe — all four of whom were homosexuals, and the individual life of each was unknown to the others until they were already grown. Was it due to being exposed to the same parental situation? Or the same environmental influences?

Also, have you thought of family histories which show certain sexual aberrations appearing generation after generation, sometimes manifesting themselves in open homosexuality, sometimes in other forms? This has intrigued me in my own family where we have fairly complete information on lives and personalities for some four hundred years. This is not an argument for the hereditary theory of homosexuality, but probably indicates a certain tendency for some form of sexual maladjustment. This does not run like a thread through each generation, and would seem to indicate that there appear some individuals incapable of making an adjustment sexually.

A study of certain royal families will show the reappearance generation after generation of this same thing.

Summary

It is generally held that the possibility of genetic causation of homosexuality rests more on faith than on proof.[39] Much could be said of more recent data on the aspects of etiology but nothing new has been produced.

Psychogenic Factors in Etiology

It seems clear, as I hope to demonstrate, that the basic cause of homosexuality is psychological. It seems also clear that this psychological deviation arises early in life. Although the psychopathology is not always apparent in every case, two factors help to confirm its presence: (a) when a sufficient search in depth is made such factors can usually be detected; (b) there is frequently a good response in psychotherapy.

In approaching the discussion of etiology, I will do so in this order, according to the theories of origin:
1. The Bisexual Theory.
2. The Ishmael Complex.
3. Homosexuality as an Obsessive-Compulsive Neurosis.
4. Lorand's Theory.
5. Fear of the Genitals of the Other Sex.

Bisexuality

So much has been written and said about the role of bisexuality in the development of homosexuality that, although the theory is generally discarded, something should be said about it.

Freud was its greatest exponent, although the idea was not original with him.

Freud's concept of bisexuality was borrowed from a nineteenth-century medical background which was in turn derived from a study of human embryology. It was discovered in the nineteenth century that in both the male and female embryos the sexual organs arose from the same source. It was first debated whether this embryonic source should be considered neutral or hermaphroditic. When it was later discovered that the embryonic source contained elements from the sexual apparatus of both males and females, it was immediately called hermaphroditic. Once the embryonic source was called hermaphroditic, it was easy to extend the theorizing to any field where bisexuality was a matter of concern.[40]

Kiernan[41] was the first to bring the new concept into the field of psychiatry. He was followed by others: Lydstrom, Chevalier, Krafft-Ebing, Ellis, and Magnus Hirschfeld.

Krafft-Ebing[42] began his organic theory of homosexuality on the then new concept of bisexuality. He assumed that if the peripheral structure of the sexual apparatus had a bisexual predisposition, this must be equally true for the brain centers related to sexual activity. From this he concluded that the embryonic cerebrum must also contain male and female centers which ultimately determined the sexual orientation of the human person. Homosexuality, he concluded, therefore resulted when the female brain center developed in an otherwise male body.

Krafft-Ebing was aware that an individual might have a hermaphroditic condition sexually without being bisexual so far as his psychological condition was concerned. Krafft-Ebing was therefore forced to conclude that the sexual centers of the brain and the sexual development of the cell structure of the organs were distinct from one another — that each one had its own autonomous development, and these could be independently subject to aberrations in development. It is maintained by Rado that "not a trace of neurological evidence was then or is now available to give credence to Krafft-Ebing's chain of hypotheses."[43]

Freud[44] eventually took over Krafft-Ebing's hypothesis of the bisexual nature of the human embryo. From this he suggested bisexuality as something generally applicable to all human beings. This early biological explanation of bisexuality seems to be passing from the scientific scene today. The psychogenic explanation is being accepted more widely than ever.

Freud's original theory on homosexuality was that every human being possessed both male and female psychosexual attributes. At the outset these have no genital significance — they merely show up as an attribute of activity or passivity.

It is this early predisposition toward either masculine activity or feminine passivity that fundamentally determines the subsequent sexual development of the child. If the child is male and has been endowed with a strong constitutional diathesis toward passivity then he will adopt the feminine sexual role and nothing can be done for him. On the other hand, if the child is male and has only a weak constitutional tendency toward passivity, he may have this neutralized or doubled in intensity by circumstances in his environment. In the latter case he would become homosexual according to this theory.

Freud described the contributing factors of homosexuality in terms of this constitutional predisposition toward activity and passivity and in terms of his libido theory (see pp. 55ff).

Most authors today would reject Freud's emphasis on the constitutional basis for homosexuality and would place greater emphasis upon environmental factors. This does not mean that Freud ignored all environmental factors. He was well aware that they had a role to play. But he put his emphasis on constitutional factors.

For Freud the most significant environmental factor was the Oedipal situation or complex. It is so named after the tragedy by Sophocles in which the leading character, Oedipus, unknowingly kills his father and eventually marries his mother. Neither Oedipus nor his mother are aware that they are mother and son because Oedipus had been taken away as a child and had been brought up by a shepherd. Freud said that in the normal family development there is a drama similar to this enacted between the small child and the two parents. The child at the outset is narcissistic — that is to say, the child loves itself. Its activities are centered only on its own interests. The child begins to expand its interests to others. The first person the child loves other than itself is the mother. In the course of time the child becomes aware of another individual in the home — if the home has a healthy psychological atmosphere. This second individual is the father of the family. If the child is a boy, he begins to realize that his mother loves not only him but his father as well. The boy begins to see his father as a rival for his mother's affection. This rivalry is not actually hostility. (Hostility in this situation would

71

be indicative of a neurotic element in the family setup.) The rivalry is merely a desire of the boy to have more time with his mother, to have her exclusively with him some of the time. Eventually the boy appreciates that his father is much stronger and more powerful than he is. Anything the boy can do the father can do better (see "Ishmael Complex," below).

When the boy begins to realize this, he gives up an attempt at rivalry and begins to conform himself to his father's pattern of acting. When the boy begins to pattern himself on his father's character, he is said to have resolved the Oedipal crisis. Before he copies his father's attitudes he will probably associate with other boys. Here he is likely to develop an attachment to one or another boy. This is the homosexual stage of development. But the word here refers merely to a direction of affections rather than to genital activity. (It is not until puberty that the flush of hormones through the body concentrates otherwise diffused love interests to actual genital activity.) The boy, under normal circumstances, ultimately patterns himself after his father.

The psychosexual development of the female is similar to this. The female child first centers her affections on her mother and eventually becomes aware of her father. She becomes aware that they are physically different. As she begins to learn the difference between herself and her father, she fantasizes attempts at the incorporation of her father's penis. But she is also aware that it is only for her mother. She sees her mother as a rival for the father. Like the boy, she realizes that she is no competition for her mother, and so she begins to copy her mother with the hope that she too will in time have a male to complement her lack of penis.

The Oedipal complex at first seems wholly fantastic to adults who have no recollection of these stages of development. But these earlier fantasies are often brought out during depth therapy. Sometimes they are not as pronounced as I have indicated here, but they are easily recognizable under similar forms. This statement should not be interpreted to mean that I feel the Oedipal conflict is universal. There is no way of knowing this. It is, however, frequent.

Helene Deutsch[45] and Karen Horney[46] have both asserted that whenever there are difficulties in the Oedipal stage (such as excessive rivalry with the mother or a predominance of castration feelings) there is a more or less marked tendency toward homosexuality in women.

The Ishmael Complex

Helen M. Hacker[47] has suggested an interesting provocative theory on the origin of homosexuality. She feels that too much emphasis has been placed on the importance of the Oedipus complex as an etiological factor in the development of homosexuality. The term "Ishmael" was suggested to her by the opening lines in *Moby Dick*, when the hero exclaims, "Call me Ishmael!" In the course of the story this hero becomes a composite father and mother image to the boy. As with so many names in *Moby Dick* the term "Ishmael" is symbolically significant. Ishmael was the son of Abraham and Hagar, his bondswoman. Because he mocked Isaac, his half brother, he was cast out to wander in the desert.

Hacker points out that in a number of American juvenile classics an interesting situation develops. An American boy finds himself in a primitive and isolated state in association with an older, not too highly civilized, darkskinned man. There is mutual affection and admiration. This affection is strictly nonsexual. The older man in such cases is portrayed as more or less omnipotent in relation to his environment as well as being a loving protector to the boy. This one figure incorporates the main characteristics usually attributed by a child to both his father and his mother.[48]

In American middle-class groups the father-son relationship does not usually follow the Oedipal pattern, according to Hacker. In this group the father shares the authority in the family with the mother so that the supremacy of the father is not present. Hacker also points out that in this group the son is expected to surpass the father socially, financially, and educationally. The child does not, therefore, fear and respect the father as he does in European groups. The American father is more affectionate than the European father. There is therefore a different father-son relationship in the American and European situations. In the American middle-class setup the child does not form an attachment for the father alone but for the mother as well and, consequently, in Hacker's concept of the *Ishmael stage* of psychic development the child has a parent image which fuses the best attributes of both the father and the mother.

Hacker feels that homosexuality results in those individuals who have been unable to resolve the conflicts which arose during the Ishmael stage. This may come about in cases when the boy's desire for affection from the father has been severely frustrated and/or when the boy's mother is markedly deficient in companionable qualities. If the child does not find this Ishmael image fulfilled by his parents he will grow up with a compulsive urge to find some object which will fulfill his dream image. Homosexuality arises when the adult attempts to solidify this image in some individual of his own sex. But the expression of this feeling in overt homosexual behavior spoils that individual as the embodiment of the Ishmael image because according to the ideal image the relationship should remain etherealized. Therefore, the Ishmael myth is not fulfilled in an overt homosexual act and the homosexual goes on in a never-ending search for the idealized Ishmael object.

Homosexuality as an Obsessive-Compulsive Neurosis

This theory has always appealed to the author as having wide application to the etiology of homosexuality. It explains quite satisfactorily most of the facts of homosexuality as we know them and offers a useful therapeutic approach. It was first described by Dr. Erwin O. Krausz.[49] An *obsessive-compulsive neurosis* is one in which the individual affected has an almost irresistible impulse to do something which he knows he should not do. In a negative way this might result in a firm conviction that one is incapable of doing what he ought to do. *Krausz finds the basis for this theory of homosexuality in this negative statement.* The homosexual, he feels, is incapable of imagining himself married or engaging in sexual activity with a person of the other sex; in other words, the male homosexual has an obsessive fear (of the vulva) of women and the Lesbian has an obsessive fear (of the genital organs) of men (see pp. 76ff).

What the homosexual fails to understand is that he will be incapable of loving members of the other sex until he has cleared away the underlying difficulty. According to Krausz, when we probe to see what this difficulty is we find that the homosexual has a fear of being compared with members of his own sex. Proper comparison with members of one's own sex can only be made by members of the other sex. Hence, the homosexual male avoids all women.

At the same time, according to Krausz, the homosexual neutralizes the potential enemies he finds among the members of his own sex by "loving" them. In "loving" members of his own sex, he eliminates them as rivals in the eyes of women. From this, of course, we may conclude that the homosexual "love act" is not an act of love at all, but is really a hostile act of aggression whereby the homosexual emasculates a person who would otherwise be a competitor. The perverse character of homosexuality is not that the homosexual loves a member of the same sex but that he loves what he actually hates. In his homosexual activity the homosexual is doing nothing more than utilizing the technique of reification.

There are several ways in which the homosexual may reify his attitude. He may adopt the "good brother" attitude; that is to say, he acts like a good brother to women. He gets along "fine" with women until they attempt to put the relationship on a sexual basis. In adopting the "good brother" attitude the homosexual is really desexualizing the heterosexual individual. A second attempt at reification may be the depreciation of members of the same sex except those in whom he has a "sexual" interest. The third method of reification — which is the homosexual's masterpiece — is his conviction that he can love only members of his own sex. This is the foundation upon which all else rests. This conviction above all must stand because he believes that if this one fails, he will be left with a crushing feeling of utter nothingness.

Lorand approaches the etiology of homosexuality in a way somewhat similar to that of Krausz. We refer the reader directly to his text.[50]

CHAPTER SEVEN

Other Causes of Homosexuality

Fear of the Genital Organs of the Other Sex
as a Cause of Homosexuality

Although the theory of Krausz has many appealing features, it would seem that if we carry the theory beyond the concept of an obsessive fear of the other sex a more specific and therapeutically useful foundation for the theory may be formulated. In many cases the individual who becomes a homosexual develops a fear of the genital organs of the other sex as dangerous and destructive. This is more clearly seen in cases of male homosexuality than it is in the Lesbian.

The concept is in line with psychoanalysis which accepts castration anxiety as one of the basic etiological factors in male homosexuality. The knowledge, however acquired and however conscious, that a woman has no penis creates in them a fear of castration. In fact, the vulva may be fantasied in oral-sadistic terms as a castrating instrument.[1] The fetishist and the transvestite consciously deny that the female lacks a penis; the homosexual accepts this fact but feels threatened by it. For this reason, although the majority of male homosexuals are interested in women as intellectual companions, they reject them as sexual (genital) partners.

Freud expressed this conception in somewhat similar terms. As described by Freud, the homosexual man is so insistent on the idea of a penis that he cannot accept its absence in his sexual partner. This could also be expressed negatively by saying: homosexual men are so frightened at the sight of a being without a penis, that they reject any sexual reationships with such a partner.

A great many patients quite clearly bring out these fears in

76

therapy, but probably not in sufficient numbers, certainly not in my experience, to make the assertion that such a fear is universally present. Undoubtedly homosexuality has many causes.

It is, however, a useful concept in therapy and one quite generally accepted by those who have written on the subject. For this reason, instead of merely just listing those authors who have commented on the subject, I would like to take time to quote some of their comments. This coverage is not intended to be exhaustive, but only representative.

First, this passage from Berg and Allen:

> Analysis of homosexual men regularly shows that they are afraid of female genitals. . . . The female genitals, through the connection of castration anxiety with oral anxieties, may be perceived as a castrating instrument capable of biting or tearing off the penis.[2]

Sullivan also recognized that the fear of female genitals may exist in men even though they regard women as pleasurable sexual objects — "a fear amounting to a feeling which is literally uncanny, which is quite paralyzing," and which is able to force the male to escape from this "uncanny feeling" into homosexuality. The origin of this fear, he believed, may derive from the "not me," indicating a serious dissociation in the personality.[3]

Rado attributed homosexuality to the following factors:

> Hidden but incapacitating fears of the opposite sex which result in a homosexual adaptation, which through symbolic processes is in fantasy a heterosexual one, or in which problems of rivalry with isophilic partners who represent father are solved.[4]

Bieber:

> This study provides convincing support for a fundamental contribution by Rado on the subject of male homosexuality: a homosexual adaptation is the result of "hidden but incapacitating fears of the opposite sex."

A considerable amount of data supporting Rado's assumption has been presented as evidence that fear of heterosexuality underlies homosexuality, e.g., the frequent fear of disease or injury to the genitals, significantly associated with fear and aversion to female genitalia; the frequency and depth of anxiety accompanying actual or contemplated heterosexual behavior.[5]

Cory:

Briefly summarized, the homosexual is definitely emotionally disturbed, *suffering from fear of the other sex,* puritanical distortions about sexuality, self-abnegation, feelings of inadequacy, self-destructive drives, and compulsive desires.[6]

The aim of therapy is to relieve the hostility toward and fear of relationships, sexual and other, with the other sex, rather than to seek to suppress the homosexual interest. The reasons for this are twofold: (1) to aid the homosexual to get at the root of the problem, and not to attack what is merely a symptom — his problem is not so much that he is attached to males, but that *he is in flight from females. . . .*[7]

Adler:

A. Adler has conceived in these cases the hypothesis of a "fear of the sexual partner." This observation certainly holds true in the case of many homosexuals, but it is *not true of all cases.* Nature does not operate in such simple ways and a single key does not unlock the riddle of homosexuality.[8]

Stekel:

May fear of the sexual partner drive a person into homosexuality? We must answer this question in the affirmative inasmuch as we are able to trace that fear in a number of cases.[9]

Bromberg:

Chiefly, homosexuality develops as a psychological defense against unconscious fear of women with subsequent retreat to men for sexual expression. This is the core of the psychoanalytic theory of homosexuality. The mental mechanisms by which the

78

resultant attitude evolves are complicated. In brief, the boy who is destined to become a homosexual develops a strong unconscious identification with the mother, or mother figure, thus laying the psychological groundwork in early life for a pattern of seeking male love objects. In contrast, the normal boy identifies with the father and hence, in time, seeks a female love object. Early fear of women, in homosexually inclined boys, is observed by their identification with women, the "identification with the aggressor" mechanism. Thus, men become psychologically "safe" for them.[10]

Davidman:

Homosexual relationships in neurotics have the underlying psychological goal of achieving a male-female union in a safe way; that is, *free from the disturbing and terrifying genital of the opposite sex and the heightened responsibilities, expectations, demands and reproductive hazards of normal sexuality.* But each participant preserves in his or her imagination a male-female union with a partner. One partner in fantasy attempts a caricature of one sexual role; the other partner attempts the opposite. Though the reality of the situation is thereby impaired, orgiastic pleasure of a minimal sort is obtained. The individual feels safer emotionally than he would with a "real" sexual partner.[11]

A. Ellis:

In seeing these individuals with severe homosexual problems, an active form of psychoanalytically-oriented psychotherapy was employed, and *one of the main therapeutic goals was to help the patient overcome his fear of heterosexual relations* and, through improved sex-love relations with members of the other sex, to minimize his homosexual interests and activities. The therapeutic goal was not that of inducing the patient to forego all homosexual interests because . . . that would be unrealistic.

The abnormality in homosexuality consists of the exclusiveness, the fear, the fetishistic fixation, of the obsessive-compulsiveness which is so often its concomitant. The aim of psychotherapy, therefore, should be to remove these elements: to free the confirmed homosexual of his underlying fear of or antagonism toward heterosexual relations, and to enable him to have satisfying sex-love involvements with members of the other sex.[12]

Allen:

We thus assume that homosexuals are men who in some way experienced a very deep disappointment which turned them against the female sex.[13]

I find that a large number of timid, shy men who have drifted into homosexual relations have done so because they are afraid of women. They have never developed the male aggressiveness, and literally do not know how to make love to a girl. They feel that if they do so she will be shocked.[14]

Cole:

The male homosexual incurs *fears of the vagina.* Incidentally, it is these same fears which underlie the phenomenon known as premature ejaculation. The man is able to insert the penis into the vagina, but he unconsciously desires to get it out as quickly as possible, so that no matter how he may consciously long to be able to prolong the stimulation, he cannot. The orgasm occurs spontaneously and quickly. Premature ejaculation is a psychological, not a physiological problem. But what is only a partial difficulty with the sufferer from premature ejaculation is virtually a total one for the male homosexual. He cannot stand it even to insert the penis, let alone have an orgasm. This fear of the vagina makes it necessary for him to confine his sexual relations to someone of his own sex, someone without the fearful vagina and with the reassuring penis. A similar attitude prevails in the Lesbian, who fears the penetrating penis and can enjoy sex only with someone who does not possess such a frightening organ. The so-called castration complex seems to play an important role in this process.[15]

Proximate Factors

Psychogenic factors do not produce their trauma in one day. They are not like a sudden automobile accident. They are slow

80

and persistent like some cancerous growths. After all, there are other ways to produce wounds than a quick jab with a knife. It is just as possible to produce a wound by gently scraping back and forth on the surface of the skin with a dull nail.

The factors so frequently mentioned in case reports are more likely to be precipitating, rather than causative, factors in etiology. Some of those to be mentioned are reported quite frequently; others are much less commonly found in the history of homosexuals. A knowledge of these factors is important from several standpoints — e.g., they are part of the natural history of the disorder; such knowledge may be useful in the prophylaxis and treatment of it; and such knowledge may help the counselor in the development of insight into his client. Actually, a knowledge of these proximate factors may be more important to the counselor than the more basic theories. Anomaly expressed this in a different way:

> A study of the prenatal influences which may have contributed to the condition may be interesting and useful to the professional psychiatrist, but an investigation into the present surroundings and friends of the subject is likely to accomplish more immediate good.[16]

These factors will be discussed under these titles:
1. Disturbances in the interfamily relations.
2. Separation of the child from the parents.
3. Sexual immaturity.
4. Mistreatment of one parent by the other.
5. Other situations.

1. *Disturbances in the interfamily relations* frequently lead to deviation. Such disturbances usually follow one of several patterns:

a) Rejection of the child by the parent of the opposite sex. "A tragic proportion — eighty percent — of homosexuals owe their inversion to their mothers. It is those who love us most who are capable of doing us the greatest harm."[17]

b) Seduction of the child by the parent of the same or opposite sex.

c) Rejection of the parent of the opposite sex by the child.

In cases of homosexuality there is almost always a history of unhappy parent-sibling relationships. The homosexual comes frequently from a broken home in which the remaining parent is emotionally unstable, rejecting, or overpossessive. Rejection by the parent may be evidenced in actual neglect or in cruel treatment for real or imagined sexual explorations on the part of the child. Rejection may have a secondary important effect. The rejected child is frequently lonesome and will seek companionship. If the companion he seeks turns out to be an invert there is little doubt that seduction will be the result.

Seduction is a common method of introduction to homosexual practices. Such seduction does not always occur outside the home. According to Johnson and Robinson parental seduction of the growing child is quite common. "It may be extremely subtle or as blatant as incest."[18] A frequent though seldom recognized form of seduction is a lack of modesty in the home.

"Momism" is a frequent source of difficulty. In such cases the undue attachment usually starts with an overpossessiveness on the part of a parent, usually the mother, although "Pop" may also be a "Mom." Soon, however, the child may establish an abnormal dependence on the parent so that a two-way "silver cord" may be established. Such situations may be the beginning of homosexual tendencies. Prolonged attachment of the child to the parent of the other sex may produce an identification which may later cause the male child to act sexually in imitation of his mother or sister. Another result is possible: the child, if a boy, who develops a close maternal attachment may later experience strong feelings of guilt and by identifying all women as maternal figures find sex possible only with individuals of the same sex. An overprotecting parent may interfere more directly with the child's normal sexual development by refusing heterosexual dates to his children. West writes:

Homosexual adaptation occurs when heterosexual adaptation proves too difficult. This is why a too puritanical upbringing can be dangerous. A child instilled with disgust for normal sex is all the more likely to try furtive, substitute outlets. The history of sexual perverts, homosexuals and otherwise, suggests strongly that an overmoralistic upbringing can have a most evil influence.[19]

2. *Separation of the child from the parents* for a long period during early years is likely to lead to confusion in regard to

his proper sexual role, and homosexual seduction is rendered easy. Early entry of children into boarding schools where they associate exclusively with members of their own sex is especially hazardous. Such children, as they grow, will experience the natural biological evidences of developing sexuality. Knowing only the self-sex they are likely to associate this erotic feeling with individuals of the same sex. Even when there is no overt activity there are likely to be strong feelings of guilt and a conviction of inversion. Such feelings, from whatever cause, foster lack of ego strength with consequent feelings of inferiority or inadequacy which may lead to a fear of having one's sexuality subjected to a test and consequent fear of accepting adult responsibilities in marriage. Such feelings might well result in the retention of the already experienced homosexual attraction. Such feelings of inadequacy may foster an already present fear of the other sex (see p. 76) especially if the individual has any physical or emotional handicap.

Absence of the father from the home due to death, divorce, employment, or military service may be interpreted by the child as a rejection. More frequently it leads to a treatment of the child by the mother as a substitute for the father and indirect or even overt seduction is likely to occur. In this respect West commented:

> So one might go on and on, but the point could hardly come out more clearly. Among Henry's cases it is sometimes difficult to categorize the parents with precision, but well over half conform to the pattern of an absent or unsatisfactory father and a mother who dominates the child's life to an unusual degree. But the cases also show how other factors obtrude in even the most clear-cut instances of mother fixation. . . . In matters of sex, the boy normally identifies with his father and takes upon himself his father's manly, assertive approach to life.[20]

3. *Sexual immaturity* with a failure to develop an adequate adult capacity for love as a cause of homosexuality is in accord with the psychoanalytic concept of the development of adult sexuality. According to this hypothesis each individual goes through successive stages in his sexual development (see p. 56). Emotional traumata may cause an individual to become

fixated at any of these levels. Fixation at the homosexual level may result in the development of adult homosexuality. As properly understood, in regard to normal development, the homosexual stage of sexual development means only that during this period boys are interested in boys and tend to play boys' games and girls play with girls at girls' games. There is no implication of latent or of overt sexual activity. In recent years parents have had a tendency to interfere with this phase of development by pushing their children too early into heterosexual associations. This cannot help but have detrimental effects.

4. *Mistreatment of one parent by the other.* Homosexuality may have its beginning in the home where the father is cruel to the mother, and for this reason the boy may hate the father. On the other hand, if the child is neglected, he may come to hate all women. Overprotectiveness on the part of one or the other parent may be a factor in the forming of homosexuality. For the child, heterosexual outlets would mean infidelity to the parent.

5. *Other situations* which various authors have considered significant in specific cases are the following:

a) A very important element of environment is the existence of societies of homosexuals in every large city; a young boy or girl through curiosity may be drawn into these circles.

b) Cruel or excessively strict punishment for sex play in childhood; i.e., a girl may come to believe that only sex activity with boys is taboo.

c) Excessive parental concern for imagined future sexual misdeeds is unwholesome for the child.[21]

d) Poor sexual information. The boy who is inadequately instructed may continue to picture the vagina as a bloody mouth as he pictured it in his early fantasy (castration fear).

e) Gratifying early homosexual experiences.

f) The parent who thinks that sex is "dirty" may transmit this attitude to a child.

g) Lack of effective males in the family. The example of a weak, henpecked father will certainly not inspire the boy with confidence in his relations with the other sex.[22]

h) Fear of loneliness.

i) Parents who want a boy and treat the girl that is born to them as if she were a boy, or want a girl and dress their boy in girlish fashion, letting his curls grow long and polishing his fingernails, and so on.[23]

j) A puritanical view of marital intercourse may be the occasion for the development of homosexuality.[24]

k) The very antithesis of puritanism may lead to homosexual practices, e.g., if the child is reared in a home where the parents are known to be sexually careless and promiscuous. The youngster follows the example of his parents whose affections he has enjoyed but seldom.[25]

l) Sibling jealousy is also worthy of mention; the boy may see his sister preferred (or the other way around) and, feeling rejected in his own sex, may adopt the attitudes and characteristics of the preferred sex in gait, gestures, and behavior to win favor.[26]

m) The rejected child who looks for a protecting being on whom to center affection, finds none such in his home, and finally meets with an adult seeking a homosexual outlet.[27]

n) Adolescent girls may acquire homosexual habits from fear and disgust at the rudeness of men in sexual matters.[28]

o) Both St. Paul and St. Augustine suggest that homosexual sins are the result of a wider sinfulness and an abandonment of moral standards. These views have been strikingly confirmed by contemporary research workers, for, in many, although not all, homosexual "case" histories, there is a background of parental divorce, separation, or estrangement. If homosexual practices are in fact increasing, may not the cause be traced further back to broken homes and the decline in standards of heterosexual morality?[29]

In specific cases it seems quite likely that other factors may play a part — certainly all possible factors have not been enumerated. There was, for example, Fred, who up to the age of fifteen years had his room plastered with pinup girls and who masturbated frequently with heterosexual fantasies. About this age he heard that masturbation and sexual relations with girls were sinful. He turned to homosexuality for sexual relief because no one had told him that this was wrong. He became quite active as a homosexual.

Where the fusion of the sex instinct into the total personality of the individual is either long delayed or only partially, if ever, accomplished, or where the instinct remains fixed at an infantile level of development while its strength increases, there is a danger of the development of sexual perversions. By such sexual perversion, including homosexuality, is meant a deviation of the sex instinct from its natural goal. As the natural instinct becomes more mature, it is normally directed toward a person of the opposite sex. This is in contrast to its less specific activity during the time of childhood and early puberty. During this period of life the sex instinct is more or less undetermined, often turning toward the same sex or to objects not in keeping with its ultimate purpose. If the naturally inclined instinct is so misused in individual actions that it cannot attain its primary purpose of procreation, there may be perverse individual acts, caused through seduction or other lapses.

Homosexuality in the strict sense, the type with which we are primarily concerned in this study, refers to only those sexual deviations which are so deeply rooted in the general personality of the individual that they pervade his whole mental life in all its aspects, not merely those which pertain to sex.

To encourage further research into the literature, I have prepared abstracts of one book and several important articles which I hope will provoke the reader into looking up the originals.

> IRVING BIEBER, editor, *Homosexuality — A Psychoanalytic Study* (New York: Basic Books, Inc., 1962), pp. 303ff.

This book represents the findings of a completed nine-year study by the Society of Medical Psychoanalysts of 106 male homosexuals. In the opinion of the authors the role of the parents in relationship to each other and to the son is of prime importance. All parents of the homosexuals studied had severe emotional problems with each other which in turn created an abnormal environment in which to rear the child.

Here are some of Bieber's conclusions:

> The father played an essential and determining role in the homosexual outcome of his son. In the majority of instances the father was explicitly detached and hostile. In only a minority of cases was paternal destructiveness effected through indifference or default.

> A fatherless child is deprived of the important paternal contributions to normal development; however, only a few homosexuals in our sample had been fatherless children. Relative absence of the father, necessitated by occupational demands or unusual exigencies, is not in itself pathogenic.

A good father-son relationship and a mother who is an affectionate, admiring wife, provide the son with the basis for a positive image of the father during periods of separation.

We have come to the conclusion that a constructive, supportive, warmly-related father precludes the possibility of a homosexual son. . . . Most mothers of homosexual sons were possessive of them.

SANDOR RADO: "A Critical Examination of the Concept of Bisexuality," *Psychoanalytic Medicine,* Vol. II, October 4, 1960, pp. 459-467.

Rado insists at the outset that "there is no such biological entity as sex. . . . Sex of the gametes and sex in bodily structure or expression are two radically different things."

The whole reproductive system of a human being comprises more than his sexual organs. It is composed of a multitude of cellular structures, organic secretions, and functions. Each of these structures, secretions, and functions contributes to the total sexual activity of the individual. No one of these parts may be taken in itself as the sole criterion of sex. Therefore it is absurd to establish "maleness" and "femaleness" simply on the basis of the structure of genital organs or on the relative amounts of androgen or estrogen in the body.

The sex of an individual can only be determined by looking at the reproductive system as a whole. Sex is not merely a small bundle of cells within a larger bundle of cells. We should consider sex more as a group of factors which is part of a larger group of factors . . . a complex biological system which we call the human being.

When we study this human being in his totality we realize that he is more than cell tissue. Besides his cell structure he has drives and activities — all of which are tied into his pleasure system. When we look at human beings from this perspective, we are better able to understand why some become homosexuals. Homosexuality is simply an attempt on the part of some human beings to fulfill the tendencies of their pleasure system when it has been thrown out of line by some other factor in the total integration of the human being.

Human beings will perform acts of sexual intercourse without having any intention of reproduction, and with the sole intention of achieving pleasure. They may even perform acts of sexual intercourse without intending insemination. Their sole intention is to achieve pleasure. We can find this difference between the physical and emotional factors in any heterosexual act. We also observe that in any sexual act the male always achieves a distinctly male pleasure and the female always achieves a distinctly female pleasure.

When we look at the homosexual's activity we find that he has separated the reproductive function from the pleasure function. All sexual activities whether heterosexual or homosexual are eventually oriented toward one goal — the pleasure that results in the orgasm reflex. The homosexual simply is incorporating an abnormal means of stimulation to achieve his pleasure goal.

Besides the sexual pleasure system there are other pleasure systems — oral, anal, and tactile — which are parts of the total pleasure system of the total individual. These pleasure systems interact on one another and together they achieve an integration on a higher level. The integration of these subordinate pleasure systems undergoes a series of changes throughout the life-span of the individual.

It would seem legitimate to conclude from what Rado has said that the pleasure system which is part of the larger entity called the human being is subject to other factors on a higher level of integration. If this is true, then the functioning of the pleasure system as a whole would be partially determined by other systems. We might speak about a logical system in the individual. This would be the whole system of activities by which a man reasons and orients himself to reality. If some block arose in the logical system — suppose that the person judged marriage to be at best a bad risk — then his pleasure system might be adapted in line with this conclusion. In this case, the individual would not derive pleasure from anything he saw as directly related toward marriage. This would block off sex pleasure so far as marriage was concerned — and the pleasure might seek some other outlet. In this case the compromise might be homosexuality.

LIONEL OVESEY: "The Homosexual Conflict," *Psychiatry*, Vol. XVII (1954), pp. 243-250.

Ovesey describes the origins of homosexuality in relation to the concepts of masculinity and femininity and the struggle for supremacy in our culture. One of the dominant factors in Western culture is the exaggerated emphasis put upon all kinds of success. The concept of success is involved with masculinity and femininity because in our culture masculinity is identified with strength, dominance, and superiority, whereas femininity is equated with weakness, submissiveness, and inferiority. In other words the traits of masculinity are associated with success, and the traits of femininity are associated with failure.

Ovesey then goes on to say that a male who fails in any field begins *unconsciously* to have doubts about his masculinity. He says, in fact, that the unconscious process of reasoning can be written out in the following steps:

1. I am a failure, therefore . . .
2. I am castrated, therefore . . .
3. I am not a man, therefore . . .
4. I am a woman, therefore . . .
5. I am a homosexual.

(Ovesey says that if there is any doubt about this unconscious thought process, it may be easily demonstrated with dream material.)

The homosexual conflict contains the aspects of sex, dependency, and power. Only the sexual aspect really has sex as a motivation behind it. The other two — dependency and power — are not truly sexual in motivation but they work with the sexual apparatus in order to achieve their own effects and they determine the kind of sexual activity a homosexual will adopt.

The homosexual who is extremely dependent on others for any feeling of achieving success tends to take a passive role. In each case he symbolically incorporates the masculinity of another male into himself. The active homosexual — that is, the one who assumes the male role in a homosexual relation — is homosexual because he is afraid of sex with women; but he still retains enough independence and power so that he is incapable of seeing himself in the feminine role. This active masculine type attempts a compromise by loving an individual of his own sex. But this loved individual must have feminine characteristics. The masculine type of homosexual may even practice fellatio and anal mount, but in each case is the one acting rather than the one acted upon.

M. Boss: *Sinn und Gehalt Der Sexuellen Perversionen (The Meaning and Content of the Sexual*

Perversions) (Berne: Medizinischer Verlag Hans Huber, 1947). Review in *Psychoanalytic Quarterly,* 17 (1948), p. 106.

Boss is of the opinion that homosexuality, like other sexual perversions, is an attempt at compromise between the urge to love and inhibiting environmental factors. The urge to love seeks to express itself but is unable to do so in a heterosexual manner. Factors in the environment (such as conditioning, learned attitudes, etc.) do not allow this heterosexual outlet.

The homosexual act is an attempt to bypass these barriers and establish some positive kind of emotional relationship with the world around us. This attempt is doomed at the outset. The homosexual tries to be satisfied with only half a loaf rather than with no loaf at all.

CHAPTER EIGHT

Clinical Features

"A diagnosis of homosexuality based solely on physical evidence is not possible."[1]

The comment is frequently heard that an individual "looks" like a homosexual or that two men or two women who live together or are frequently seen together are "probably" homosexual. Such statements are not only uncharitable but, if based on such evidence alone, may result in grave injustice. It should be understood that there is no physical evidence in either the male or female homosexual which would lead to their recognition as sexual inverts. There are, of course, female impersonators who mimic the mannerisms of women for their own purposes, but many of these are not homosexuals; those who are, are usually prostitutes who wish to "flaunt their charms" before other homosexuals. Some are transvestites, the majority of whom are not homosexuals (see p. 114). A few will be transsexualists (see p. 117). Some of these readily adopt feminine characteristics.

Physical Characteristics

In the popular mind homosexuals have distinct physical characteristics. It is important to point out the falsity of this common belief.

In the following statement, Kinsey gives a good summary of what is "commonly believed" on this point:

It is *commonly believed*, for instance, that homosexual males are rarely robust physically, are uncoordinated or delicate in their movements, or perhaps graceful but not strong and vigorous in their physical expression. Fine skins, high-pitched voices,

91

obvious hand movements, a feminine carriage of the hips, and peculiarities of walking gaits are supposed accompaniments of a preference for a male as a sexual partner. It is *commonly believed* that the homosexual male is artistically sensitive, emotionally unbalanced, temperamental to the point of being unpredictable, difficult to get along with, and undependable in meeting specific obligations. In physical characters there have been attempts to show that the homosexual male has a considerable crop of hair and less often becomes bald, has teeth which are more like those of a female, a broader pelvis, larger genitalia, and a tendency toward being fat, and that he lacks a linea alba. The homosexual male is supposed to be less interested in athletics, more often interested in music and the arts, more often engaged in such occupations as bookkeeping, dress design, window display, hairdressing, acting, radio work, nursing, religious service, and social work. The converse to all of these is supposed to represent the typical heterosexual male. Many a clinician attaches considerable weight to these things in diagnosing the basic heterosexuality of his patients. The characterizations are so distinct that they seem to leave little room for doubt that homosexual and heterosexual represent two very distinct types of males.[2]

It should be emphasized that masculinity and maleness are related but are not synonyms. Size of body or genitalia has no relation, for example, to masculinity.

Berg is emphatic in regard to the absence of physical characteristics significant of homosexuality:

> In general the statement I made ten years ago in my book *The Sexual Perversions and Abnormalities* still holds true and is unlikely to be disproved. This is that "we can state with confidence that there is no discernible difference between the physique of the homosexual and heterosexual by any tests, microscopical, macroscopical, biochemical, or endocrine of which we are aware at present."[3]

Cory also emphasizes this lack of specific characteristics in the homosexual: "The ordinary run of homosexuals are not to be distinguished from their fellow citizens by a casual observer."[4]

CHART I

Comparison of Effeminate and Noneffeminate Homosexuals*

		Effeminate	Noneffeminate
1.	Aware of homosexuality by age 11	62%	8%
2.	Knew about homosexuals by age 13	75	50
3.	Knew about heterosexuality by age 13	71	92
4.	First homosexual partner older by at least 6 years	48	33
5.	Repetition of first act in one week	87	50
6.	Repetition of first act with same person	78	50
7.	Passive in first relationship	57	17
8.	Passive relationship preferred in adult life	90	40
9.	First ejaculation due to homosexual act	42	0
10.	Frequency more than 4 acts a month	62	30
11.	Frequency in prison more than 4 times a month	60	15

Effeminate and Noneffeminate Homosexuals

Based on both personal observation and that of others, the author does not believe that there are any physical characteristics which distinguish homosexuals from heterosexuals. There are certain homosexual individuals who from habit or intention have developed traits which give them an effeminate appearance. Although this group is greatly in the minority, there apparently are differences between them which, however, are not physical but psychological. In a study by Holemon and Winokur these differences were described. Chart I, above, was compiled from data in their article.[5]

*Compiled from data contained in "Effeminate Homosexuality: A Disease of Childhood" (this investigation was supported, in part, by the U. S. Public Health Service Grants MH-7081 and MH-5804 from the National Institute of Mental Health), R. Eugene Holemon, M.D., and George Winokur, M.D., Department of Psychiatry, Washington University School of Medicine, St. Louis, Missouri.

Physical Attraction

The physical attraction between homosexuals has many characteristics in common with the erotic attraction of heterosexuals. There is the same yearning for the presence of the loved one, the same physical desires, and the same joy in his presence. In the homosexual relationship, however, there is more suspiciousness, less trust, more selfishness. Homosexual associations are usually full of strife and seldom persist. In such relationships there is usually one partner who assumes a more passive role. Such passivity may not continue into other homosexual relationships and the passive partner of one may be the aggressive member of another. The physical sexual activity of homosexual males is usually more active than that of female inverts and in this respect differs from the activities of Lesbians who are less concerned with overt sexuality and are more often concerned only with companionship. The true homosexual has a genuine aversion to heterosexual relations and although he may associate with members of the opposite sex at an intellectual level he has no interest in them as sexual partners.

The following statement volunteered by Patient II is enlightening on this point:

A homosexual love affair may have all the characteristics of a heterosexual love — the same anticipation, the same delight in the company of the beloved, the joy in receiving a letter, in telephone conversation, in doing things for the beloved or in having things done by the loved one. The relationships possible are as varied as there are kinds of homosexuals, I might even say, as many as there are kinds of human beings. There are homosexuals who are completely faithful to one person throughout their whole life. [I have never known of a case. — *Author*] But these seldom are altogether smooth relationships. They are marked by possessiveness, jealousy, and a struggle for power. After all, the homosexual is never entirely sure of himself, and he is bound to be assailed by doubts when the partner goes away for two or three days — especially if they are living together. And if one of the partners is older, he may become self-conscious about his age. Or the younger man may pick up with someone else just to prove he is not dependent upon an older person. Insecurity is the plague of all homosexual relationships.

The relationship may break up from social pressure. The two homosexuals may attempt to conceal their affection for each other by acting out scenes of cold detachment in the company of other people. The exaggerated detachment is one of those instances in which "the lady doth protest too much." In enacting these scenes the inverts are likely to concretize this cold detachment. Homosexuals are always hypersensitive. It does not take very much to break a love situation.

Homosexual Marriages

Thompson says that homosexual "marriages" are frequently dominated by sadomasochistic feelings, by hate and fear, and sometimes by a child-mother relationship. She asserts that sometimes, however, a great deal of mutual help is afforded to homosexuals by these unions. A timid man, for example, may establish homosexual contact with a stronger man; or a homosexual who is afraid of the world may attach himself to some homosexual who will support him and protect him as a mother does a child. When Thompson speaks about mutual help in these unions she is probably not thinking of them in a long-term view. To merely leave a timid man in his timid condition and to bolster him with false props does not help the man himself.[6]

I have never heard of a homosexual "marriage" that was platonic. And it is no real help to the homosexual to be in the company of another homosexual who will engage him in unproductive sexual acts.

Hans Giese made a five-year study on the sexual relationships among two thousand homosexual men and among one hundred homosexual women. He found that the male relationship was usually an unstable one whereas the female relationship was more frequently permanent and firm. The male homosexual tends to recapitulate his youthful experiences. He plays certain roles and adopts mannerisms.[7]

One of the reasons for this may be found in another study made by Giese wherein he concluded that in the male relationship there was a greater tendency toward actual physical sexual satisfaction whereas in the female relationship there was a great display of tenderness, but not so much a need for physical expression. Giese also pointed out that where there is actual physical expression, it differs in the male and female homosexual relationships. Many homosexuals are content with express-

95

ing themselves physically by caressing the body of the one loved. The mere assurance of being loved is enough.[8]

Although male homosexuals often enjoy feminine company, and women, in turn, enjoy the company of male homosexuals and may even be sexually attracted to them, it is a fallacy to believe that exposure of homosexuals to seduction by attractive women will favorably affect their condition or even arouse them sexually. Nothing is further from the truth. Homosexuals are as unaffected by feminine charms as a heterosexual would be by a fellow male. This must be stressed so as to quash the idea that marriage is a cure for homosexuality. On the contrary, the homosexual-heterosexual marriage is merely a prelude to tragedy (see p. 146).

Not all male homosexuals are attracted to all other males whether they are homosexual or heterosexual. In this respect they resemble the heterosexual individual who similarly is not physically attracted to all members of the other sex.

Some homosexuals are attracted only to adults; others, only to adolescents; still others, to children below the age of puberty; and there are even some who prefer their homosexual relations with old people. Even where an attraction exists they may not seek a physical outlet, but find sexual satisfaction in exhibitionism, transvestism, voyeurism, fetishism, or in other perverse activity.

Ethnic Characteristics

The experience of Patient I will be drawn upon for a description of sexual practice in other cultures. He comments:

I think some note should be made of racial (ethnic) background in sexual habits. Again I can only speak from personal experience and from information gained from others. In the Arab world where homosexuality is a common thing, it is usually in the form of pederasty, or anal relations. Fellatio is almost never indulged in, nor are caresses with the mouth in any form. I have never run into any form of perversion, as you term it, among the Arabs. [It is interesting to notice that Patient I apparently does not regard homosexuality as a form of perversion. — *Author*]

The Latin world has also a very direct approach to homosexual acts — but here fellatio is indulged in, as well as anal forms. But again the thing is very natural, and not tied up with perversions of any kind. I have rarely in many years in Latin countries found perversions among the homosexuals. The French indulge in more complicated forms of sex but, I feel, from viciousness, not because of the need to express themselves sexually in this way.

But it is when one gets into the Nordic countries that one rarely finds homosexuality without complete perversion, masochism, voyeurism, fetishism — the whole gamut is always a preliminary to the sex act, and one rarely finds an individual who wants the simple sex act without all the rest. This is the rule in Germany, and as one gets into Scandinavian countries, it really gets wild — where the most complicated and *recherché* forms are indulged in, these often being more the end of the sex act than sex itself.

The English are in the above class, but then one gets into the Celtic elements where one finds that the mental side of sex, the stimulation of the imagination, not by acts, but by words is absolutely essential to a satisfactory sex act. This kind of lechery that the Celts indulge in as a part of sex is rather peculiar to them. I don't think I have ever run into it in other races than in the Scotch and Irish and Welsh groups.

The Americans, I find, are almost seconds to the Scandinavians in their approach to sex. Perversion is the rule among homosexuals. Sadism and masochism seem definitely to be increasing here. Very neurotic habits are prevalent. I recently met an Air Force officer — a man of forty odd, with no signs of homosexuality, who finally proposed relations with me, but stipulating that he could only indulge in fellatio if his partner smoked a pipe while he was doing the act. Unfortunately, a pipe is inclined to make me ill, so I had to decline his services. I don't know, but if I had a fetish of this sort I would feel some sort of embarrassment about proposing it, but he seemed to feel that this was his normal method of sex, which he could not have without the pipe-smoking business.

One thing I have noted is that the rather flagrant homosexual is more normal in his sex act than the type that one would not suspect of homosexuality as there are no outward signs or physical characteristics that is more apt to indulge in these fantasies and perversions.

Then again I have noted that racial background in these habits tends to continue — the Italo-American, through three generations here, is more natural in his sex act, like his Latin family, than the German-American who follows his racial pattern.

Depressive Features

Many homosexuals are depressed and confused by their sexual relationships. The following autobiographical sketch contained in a letter directed to her therapist reveals quite frankly the emotional reaction of a Lesbian (Patient III) to repeated attempts to establish a homosexual union of some permanence. This is typical of the feelings of guilt, confusion, and suicidal depression which so frequently confront her:

Doubt that I'll have the nerve to mail this — I will have to take a couple more drinks to give me courage, I guess — shouldn't have started drinking the vodka — but I couldn't just keep on thinking — I wanted to just lay down and sleep and not remember — now it's worse than before — and I'm not drunk enough to blame anyone but myself — how can I think something and yet not think it — if I really did think nothing mattered and I didn't care what happened — why am I so digusted now at both of us — mostly at myself — what kind of a person am I really — am I part of the thoughts and beliefs that I have or am I in two parts — what I do and what I feel — am I just a weak immoral person whose desires rule or am I someone with a sense of right and wrong?

All of this is as mixed up here on this paper as I feel — I know for sure I'd never get this told if I were talking to you — I can't even get it down in writing so it makes any sense at all — if I get this written and have the nerve to mail it — what will be your attitude — is a person beyond help who would openly do what I did tonite — I had a couple of drinks hoping to drown out my aching head and all my thoughts — and had reached the stage where I could say nothing is important — I don't care what happens any more — It was the wrong time to have a visitor — and especially one like Jim — anyway we had a drink together — what do I blame the rest on — the drinks — loneliness trying to make myself believe I didn't care what happened — or the thought that at least for a little while I wouldn't be all alone — any of those reasons — or is the truth in another reason — that if I ever did have any integrity or any decency, I'm losing it — I don't know any more how I feel — except confused — Why was I so suddenly sick — and not mentally — at that point — I was physically ill — nauseated — he had only pulled me down on the davenport — put his arms round me and kissed me — all I could think of was that his face was hard, not soft and smooth like a girl's — and then all

I could feel was that I was sick — that I hated him — Even now — after all these hours I still have that feeling of hate — and yet I don't actually hate him — maybe I hate the maleness of him — hate him because he wasn't Mary — he left shortly after that and that should end this sordid tale, but far from it — as the vodka wears off, the whole thing became more of a nightmare.

I wish so much I could put my arms around Mary — and that is a wish without any physical desire — a wish to hold on to something solid in the middle of what seems to be all confusion.

Am I becoming the kind of person I've always disliked — one whose values go no deeper than the first layer of skin — one whose desire today is all important — and tomorrow — a new fact — a new desire — still the ruling force — or have I always been that person — with a veneer — coated with what I thought was decency and self-respect — and now the veneer is wearing off — showing the person hiding under it — and not a pretty picture — the episode with the girl at the post office — no excuse or reason that it happened — reason maybe — my weakness of character — the nurse at the hospital — an unhappy episode that had no beginning and no ending — like something built and hanging in space — no start — no finish — just the middle — and Joan — I guess even the most despicable character would hesitate with a seventeen year old — and who could sort out all the phantoms in a million dreams — and most of all my wild phantasies about Mary — how much decency and self-respect can be left in anyone after all that?

Shocking — illegal — immoral — ridiculous — whatever adjectives may be used by anyone else — I know that the life Mary and I had together was the one nearly perfect thing in my life — and I know that I loved her as deeply as it's possible to love another person — and I also know that she was the one person who has ever loved me completely — and that love was based on something more than physical desire — Mixed up as this is, all I'm trying to say is a big why — why — I'm making a mental shambles of what we had because of the dreams I have of Mary — my desire has become the center of my whole mind — I think — From the dreams I have I wonder if our whole life together wasn't one long sex orgy — why — why should something that was a secondary matter — most of the time — now be so uncontrollable — am I turning into a sex maniac?

It took me so long to forget — or at least bury them below the surface — the things my mother said to me when she found out about Peggy and me — but I finally built up enough confidence — or conceit — to face most people — and even to feel that I was a decent human being with the rights that other people enjoy — but now I feel like all my carefully built fences have fallen — and I'm right back where I started — with all my doubts — maybe I am a "depraved, immoral thing."

If you've read all this, I suppose you think I should be in a mental hospital for sure — maybe you're right — I looked at this gun a long time tonight — and kicked myself for being so damn smart and throwing the box of bullets out — and you told me that anyone who tries that is definitely "ill" — so . . .

Latent Homosexuality

Latent homosexuality has only recently been recognized as an entity. As a consequence it is poorly understood and frequently not diagnosed. It is, however, a serious cause of unhappiness in marriage and frequently leads to its disruption. Since the concept is frequently unrecognized, its importance as a cause of unhappiness in marriage cannot be underestimated.

Definition

Overt homosexuality, as previously defined in Chapter 4, *is a persistent, postadolescent state in which the sexual object is a person of the same sex and in which there is a concomitant aversion or abhorrence, in varying degrees, to sexual relations with members of the opposite sex.*

Latent homosexuality refers to this same condition but, in this case, it exists outside the individual's consciouness. This condition may also be referred to as *unconscious* or *masked homosexuality.* The important element here is that the individual is not aware of his homosexuality as such. It does, however, produce certain conscious attitudes which although they may not appear to be related to homosexuality may puzzle or frighten him. In some cases the manifestation may be, for example, a preference for perverse forms of heterosexual intercourse such as fellatio or sodomy; in other cases, it may show in partial or complete impotence in heterosexual relations. In women it may cause dyspareunia or perhaps frigidity.

There has been extensive discussion as to the real meaning of the term "latent" as it refers to homosexuality. The term apparently has its origins in the writings of Freud. The discussion has revolved around the question as to whether *latent* means *dormant* or *potential*. Dormant would mean that fully developed and matured functions were present unconsciously in an inactive state, whereas *potential* would mean the presence of possible, but undeveloped, functions.[9] A lengthy discussion of this topic is not intended here, but experience leads to acceptance of the belief that the condition represents one which is dormant and not merely potential. This means that the homosexual tendency is repressed and, therefore, out of consciousness, but nevertheless it is dynamic and capable of affecting conscious behavior and attitudes.

Clinical Manifestation of Latent Homosexuality

Clinically, the affected individual may experience only periodic, transient, free-floating anxiety. To the diagnostician, however, the condition may manifest itself in a variety of symptoms which may reveal themselves in different degrees of frequency. The condition occurs in both sexes.

1. There may be a lack of sexual interest in the other sex. This may be manifested by a delayed interest in social dating which may continue until it is commented upon by associates. Even then, if manifested, the interest remains purely platonic. Due to a reaction formation the subject may on occasion display an anti-sexual puritanism.

2. There may be a lack of sexual arousal even when "petting" is undertaken. That is frequently done out of curiosity to see if sexual arousal will take place; at other times, merely because it seems to be expected.

3. A preference for the company of the same sex. This is obviously only significant when the other sex is available.

4. The occurrence of varying degrees of erotic fantasy in regard to the self-sex. This is likely to arouse some anxiety because, although its significance is not understood, it is regarded by its subject as "abnormal." Such fantasy may be associated with masturbation. There is a tendency for such imaginings to be masochistic in nature; if so, they may involve the other sex.

5. Erotic dreams of a homosexual nature, in both their mani-

101

fest and latent content, occur with varying degrees of frequency. They may also be associated with anxiety.

6. There frequently occurs an obsessive curiosity concerning inversion, and in men there may be an excessive interest in physical culture as if there was a need to prove masculinity.

7. In addition to this curiosity such individuals may express a fear of being homosexual without being able to offer an explanation. This may not, however, seem unreasonable to them in view of their recurring thoughts and feelings. Such a preoccupation may be associated with an obsessive tendency to look at the genital area of the self-sex.

8. They may give a history of advances made to them by overt homosexuals. Their reactions to such advances may be quite violent. They may also report being uncomfortable or self-conscious in the presence of known or suspected inverts.

9. Childhood or adolescent experiences may have occurred. These, however, should not be regarded as significant *per se*, but only if related to other, and continuing, manifestations.

10. In some cases there may be present traits which would indicate an identification with the other sex in thoughts or attitudes. Occasionally there may have been present a more or less conscious desire to be a member of the other sex.[10]

11. If such individuals get married, varying degrees of impotence may be manifested. This may reveal itself in an almost total lack of sexual interest; e.g., in one case there was only one act of intercourse in thirty-six years of marriage; in other cases there may be a gradual decrease in sexual interest until it is displayed only on the urging of the heterosexual partner.

12. This disorder is of much greater importance in men than in women. In the man the sex act requires active participation whereas the woman may be passive. The man must give; the woman receives. Impotence and frigidity are unitary in the male; they are not necessarily related in the female.

It must be emphasized that in such cases the individual is not consciously aware of his basic disorder and, except in adolescence, may never have overtly experienced homosexual arousal.

Adolescent Homosexual Activity

Special attention must be paid to adolescent homosexual activity, although it does not necessarily lead to adult inversion.

Patient IV, who is twenty-seven years old, describes his own adolescent experience as follows:

Before I entered the military service I performed a number of homosexual acts. When I was examined for a job, I told them about these, and they seem to think that I am probably a homosexual because of them. I had not given it a thought until they asked me about them. It had been completely out of my mind. I never discussed it with anyone. I wasn't very proud of what I had done, but I regarded it as past. At the time I didn't think anything about it.

I performed my first act when I was 14 or 15 years old — I can't actually remember the first act — I tried to forget it. Right now, I couldn't say exactly how it came about. The first act I can recall was with a boy about my own age. We used to go on camping trips. I probably made the suggestion, but I'm not certain. We performed 69. On other trips we kept this up. It probably went on for two or three years. He was not the only one. There were acts with others such as at summer scout camps. My last homosexual contact was about 8 years ago. That was the end of it. I went into the service and didn't perform any homosexual acts either in the service or since.

I was shy in high school with girls, but I did have some dates. I spent most of my time camping or hunting. I dated a couple of girls I worked with. In the service I didn't date much, but after the service I began to date a couple of girls, quite steady. Right now I'm engaged to get married. I do a fair share of petting which I enjoy, and have relations with other girls every time I have a chance. My sex dreams up to two or three years ago were jumbled up. In the last couple of years, they have been about "making out" with women. In the last six months I haven't had any sex dreams. Before the service I used to dream of men. I want to forget it so bad I don't talk about it and I don't like to hear others talk about it. It upsets me to talk about my early experiences.

I have been engaged to get married for about a year. I have dated this girl over two years. We have both petted and had relations which have been very satisfactory. I was in the service for two years. During this time I had no sexual problems and no temptations — I thought at first maybe I would have because I didn't know anybody. The first heterosexual relations I had were on a weekend pass with a prostitute. I couldn't get aroused — I didn't complete the act. I masturbate about once a week with fantasies of nude or part-way nude women. You get strange ideas of right and wrong — it seemed wrong to do it by rectum.

Discussion of the Case

This is not a clear-cut case of adolescent homosexual experimentation and is presented for that reason. It is only the cases which are not clear that promote discussion, and I hope that this case will do so. On the positive side, in favor of the purely adolescent nature of the sex play are the following:

1. It stopped at the age of 19 years. This is a little late, but there could well have been a delayed adolescence.

2. It occurred under circumstances of isolation in camps and on hikes. It might be argued that the camps and hikes were sought to make opportunities.

3. The subject was shy with girls through high school but did have some dates.

4. Present dreams are heterosexual.

5. He has had no homosexual contacts for eight years.

6. He is petting and having heterosexual relations regularly and plans to get married.

On the negative side are:

1. He states that he performed 69, although there were other acts. This is a type of relationship in which mutual simultaneous fellatio is performed. This is not a common practice in adolescence. On the other hand, he may have read about it in a book and decided to try it.

2. He had sex dreams about men until he was twenty-one years of age, and his sex dreams for several years after this were "jumbled up." He was probably going through a period of sexual confusion.

3. It still upsets him to talk about these experiences.

To help evaluate this subject a series of psychological tests were performed. Most of these were not unusual. Those most suggestive of pathology were the Rorschach and the Thematic Apperception Test which were reported as follows:

Rorschach Personality Test

The out-of-the-ordinary and significant things about this patient's Rorschach test include:

1. Relatively meager number of responses for a person of his intellectual level (a total of twenty-three).

2. Also, especially in relation to his intellectual level, slow responses, indicating a lack of breadth of interests and little evidence of resourcefulness.

3. Frequent inability to accept his responses without qualifications and reservations.

4. Basically introvertive type of personality; indications of inadequacies in handling human relationships.

5. Evidence of inner anxiety, frustrations, and struggle.

6. There are no sex content responses and the "sex-loaded" card (VI) shows nothing out of line with his dealing with the rest of the cards.

7. In general he had much more trouble dealing with the unstructured situation presented by this test than with the more structured situations. He was hesitant, unsure of himself, and seemed insecure in the situation.

8. His Rorschach test generally suggests a rather high degree of drive and ambition, with a somewhat inadequately developed personality to meet all the demands he sets himself.

Thematic Apperception Test

The stories produced by the patient were extremely brief, were generally on some type of human conflict or struggle for attainment situation. Despite instruction to include them, his stories generally lacked outcomes. Sex themes were not prominent.

Opinion

It was my final evaluation that this patient represented a delayed adolescence and that he was not a homosexual.

In the history of many individuals there will occur instances of sexual contacts during adolescence with members of the same sex. These have usually been in the nature of sexual exploration or mutual masturbation. As a rule these acts have not been frequent and have usually occurred before the age of sixteen. The individual giving the history may or may not have been the aggressor. If these experiences occurred over a relatively short period and did not recur as the individual grew older they may usually be disregarded as being significant of homosexuality. They are not usually significant as evidence of the individual's adult sexual orientation. Anomaly agrees with this:

> It is fairly evident that the homosexual acts of adolescence are not necessarily evidence of inversion, nor are they even an inevitable accompaniment of inversion.[11]

For this reason the counselor must be careful never to tell the boy who admits masturbation with his companions that he is a homosexual or in danger of becoming one.[12]

> A priest who in confessing an invert lad pictures in detail the sins and punishments of the Cities of the Plain may drive his penitent out of the Church, or even out of his mind; while a fair and honest facing of the peculiar difficulties of mind, body and conscience which envelop him may turn a potential sinner and criminal into a happy and useful member of society.[13]

These experiences are almost always the result of sexual curiosity which leads to experimentation. They may occur in both sexes. The significant factor is that they have occurred in a circumscribed period of time and have not persisted beyond adolescence.

Particular Friendships — Angelism

Certain types of adolescent love would seem to partake of the character of homosexuality, not because they necessarily result in an overt sex act, but rather because of the thinking behind them, or the emotional immaturity of the parties involved. Some authorities see in exclusive friendships of this sort a phase of homosexuality; but even when these friendships go so far as to manifest themselves in acts which are characteristic of physical love, one should not be too quick to call them homosexual. There are many factors which could be involved, e.g., unhealthy curiosity seeking to satisfy itself, or youthful sexual passion seeking satisfaction under conditions in which there are no persons of the opposite sex available, and so forth. In many cases such disorders are temporary.[14]

There is a danger, however, that true homosexuality may

have its origin at this age and lead to the fixation and inversion of the normal sex instinct. The emotional reactions are very similar to those of the teen-age boy and girl who develop a "crush" on a member of the same sex. Even though the situation may begin with a spiritual bond, it is nonetheless a "particular" bond which may degenerate into physical expression. Such love would have the same characteristics as the personal sex attraction found in heterosexual love.[15] Such a degeneration in an adolescent friendship may come from a false conception of love. As Father John F. Harvey says:

> The youth thinks that he can love with the soul alone another young man who loves him in the same way. This is "angelism," a most apt term coined by the French. For usually these individuals are inclined to regard their love as more noble than that between the sexes. They like to fancy themselves as Davids and Jonathans. They presuppose that there is something angelic about love between man and man, while love for women is simply a means of gratification for the carnal passions of men, and, accordingly, does not evoke from the human heart the noblest sentiments of friendship.[16]

Such individuals feel that only the intellectual is capable of such high-level friendship. They feel that their love for each other is with the soul only. These are, of course, rationalizations, probably unconscious, for a relationship that is outside the realm of natural emotional reaction. A love of man for man is natural, but when it takes on the characteristics of heterosexual love, e.g., exclusiveness, emotional reactions to the other party when separated, etc., the relationship has gone beyond the platonic stage, and entered the realm of angelism and homosexuality.

"The love of angelism does not seek God, but seeks self in neighbor. It is lacking in supernatural motivation which purifies and elevates human love to the level of divine charity."[17] It is a discovering of oneself in another being, and rejoicing in the recognition of one's reflection. "Thus, it is often accompanied by a smug feeling of false superiority."[18]

Dr. Le Moal has underlined the sin of angelism which is found in all homosexuality, a sin so very well defined by Gide in his *Cahiers d'Andre Walter*: "To love with the soul alone a soul who loves you in the same way." And does not love, for the adolescent, ordinarily present itself above all as a union of affection?[19]

An excellent example of angelism which illustrates all of its characteristics is found in the novel, *Compulsion*, by Meyer Levin.[20] Although this book is fiction, it is alleged to be based on fact. It purports to illustrate the personalities of Leopold and Loeb, who were convicted of the murder of Bobby Frank in the 1920s. This murder was the direct result of the superiority these boys felt, and this superiority was to a great measure caused by their angelism, which was also manifested in overt homosexual acts performed by them. A reading of this novel gives a good insight into the emotional and mental processes characteristic of misguided immature love.

Venereal Disease

Promiscuous homosexuals (almost to the same extent as heterosexual prostitutes) are a source of the spread of venereal disease. Syphilis accounts for the highest number of cases with gonorrhea being less frequent. Ketterer says that "the degree of promiscuity of some homosexual persons is significant (W. V. Bradshaw, 'Homosexual Syphilis Epidemic,' *Texas J. Med.*, 57:907-909 [Nov.], 1961). During the prediagnostic period promiscuous persons may have 10 to 20 contacts or more (J. D. F. Tarr and R. L. Lugar, 'Early Infectious Syphilis: Male Homosexual Relations as Mode of Spread,' *Calif. Med.*, 93:35-37 [July], 1960)."[21] Of the contacts named by such individuals venereal disease will develop in 20 to 50 percent.[22] In a letter to the *Journal of the American Medical Association*,[23] Dr. Herman Goodman stated that in a study reported in *Acta Dermato-Venereologica* and in other recent studies, the investigation "began with four male homosexual syphilitics and led to the discovery of 748 exposed persons (735 males and 13 females), plus 243 named by these as suspects (228 males and 15 females)."

The chief of the District of Columbia's Venereal Disease Control Division referred to homosexual venereal disease as "a definite and serious problem in Washington."[24] Homosexual organizations apparently recognize the extent and seriousness of the problem as evidenced by the fact that the Mattachine Society of Washington is working with the Health Department in the District to distribute a pamphlet on "Homosexuality and Venereal Disease." This pamphlet stresses the confidential nature of the information given to the Health Department and stresses the fact that such information will not be handed over to the police. This is recognized as an important factor in epidemiological studies. Ketterer, for example, states:

Indication of homosexuality on confidential reports (Public Health Service form No. PHS-2936) may create problems for patients. The venereal disease offices of the State of California and the USPHS both agree that the epidemiological report should not indicate information identifying the contact as having been exposed to venereal disease through homosexual practices (Venereal Disease Informational Report, State of California, Department of Public Health, Oct. 15, 1962). Even code symbols identifying the informant as homosexual have resulted in employment problems and other personal liabilities.[25]

M. F. Garner, Senior Specialist at the Venereal Disease Laboratory in New South Wales, Australia, found that:

Between July and December, 1973, 340 new cases of syphilis previously unknown to the laboratory were diagnosed on the results of serological tests. The male-female ratio was 2.5:1. Homosexually acquired infections accounted for 34.3% of cases of syphilis in males. The cases were grouped into primary, secondary, latent and late stages of syphilis according to history, clinical signs and serological test results. Cases in each stage were subdivided into age groups. Primary and secondary syphilis (that is, the early infectious stages) occurred in 56 males and 23 females under 29 years of age. In 41 of the males (73.2%) this infection was homosexually acquired. The figures from this analysis show similar trends to those available in the United Kingdom.[26]

In the *Journal of the American Medical Association*, Ritchey and Leff reported:

With the support and participation of area homosexual organizations and a local bar, the City Health Department developed an outreach/education/screening program for venereal disease (VD) control. Venereal disease education and blood testing were conducted during four sequential Wednesday evenings in the bar on a volunteer basis, anonymously if requested.

Of the 118 sera drawn, ten were reactive on serologic testing. Two of these reactive blood tests led to the discovery of two new cases of primary syphilis. No cultures were positive for *Neisseria gonorrhoeae*.

The subject response rate confirms the value of an anonymous reporting method; the discovery of two cases of primary syphilis lends credence to case finding by field-screening a high-risk population.[27]

An important role for the counselor is to urge the homosexual under his care to be aware of his problem. He should encourage him to seek frequent and adequate examination if he is continuing his homosexual activity, especially if he has many or new contacts.

CHAPTER NINE

Differential Diagnosis of Homosexuality

In attempting to establish the presence of homosexuality in an individual there are two basic questions which need examination:

1. Does the individual find himself sexually stimulated by thoughts about members of his own sex?

2. Does he find himself sexually unmoved by thoughts about members of the other sex?

If both of these questions are answered "yes" and the individual is past adolescence there is reason to believe that he is a homosexual. In some cases, of course, these questions are easily answered and it is readily apparent that the individual is a homosexual. In other cases where the condition is less obvious or where it may exist in a latent form or where the individual for some reason wishes to conceal his condition the diagnosis can be less easily established.

Rating Scale for Homosexuals

The late Dr. Alfred C. Kinsey devised a schema or scale which portrayed a heterosexual-homosexual continuum. His seven points for evaluating the degree of sexuality were:

0. Exclusively heterosexual, with no homosexual.

1. Predominantly heterosexual, only incidentally homosexual.

2. Predominantly heterosexual, but more than incidentally homosexual.

3. Equally heterosexual and homosexual.

4. Predominantly homosexual, but more than incidentally heterosexual.

5. Predominantly homosexual, but incidentally heterosexual.

6. Exclusively homosexual.[1]

This scale has several useful purposes: (1) it demonstrates the continuity of sexual feeling and indicates that the homosexual is not a separate sex; (2) it is helpful in establishing a prognosis; and (3) it helps in the evaluation of the results of treatment. Since it is relatively objective, it is even more useful.

Others have suggested the terms "facultative homosexual" for people who are 1 and 2 on the scale, "bisexual" for those who rate 3 and 4, and "obligatory homosexual" for those who rate 5 and 6.[2]

Diagnostic Considerations

Although the diagnosis is obviously dependent in large measure upon the subjective statements of the patient, one is interested in much more than merely an answer to the question, "Is this individual a homosexual?" Other questions which must be answered would include:

a) Where does he stand on the Kinsey scale?

b) Is he sincerely interested in therapy?

c) Based on the background, is he prepared for the long process of therapy?

d) What vocation is most suitable for him?

Many other questions will occur. A psychogram (a complete psychological study) of the patient should be done of sufficient intensity to satisfy the need of the counselor or therapist to understand his patient and his needs. This examination should be systematic and be suited for the purpose for which it is intended. It should include the following:

1. *A careful and thorough history of the subject* which should go as far back into childhood as possible.

It is generally conceded that the homosexual tendency reaches far back into the life history of the individual, and that the critical fixation of the sex drive is usually an accomplished fact well before adolescence, probably even before what we would designate as the *use of reason*. Nevertheless, it is with the coming of adolescence and the first awakening of romantic love that the homosexual is confronted with the painful anomaly of attraction to the same sex. It is then that the self-probings and self-accusations begin, the disillusionments, the inability to comprehend "why God has made me a freak."[3]

Since the homosexual drive may make such an early appearance, careful research in the early life is necessary. In some cases there is a clear-cut attraction to males as early as five years of age; in others the boy has tended to engage in "girlish" games or in some other way shown a feminine identification. In other cases there has been seduction by an older person or by older children. The relationship of the child with his parents should also be carefully explored, as should the many factors considered under the subject of etiology (see Chs. 6 and 7). Careful consideration should also be given to the possibility that the manifestations of the individual are not those of genuine homosexuality but may represent delusions of homosexuality, obsessions of homosexuality, the loss of sexual inhibition due to alcohol, or merely adolescent homosexual activity (see pp. 102ff).

2. *A study of the client's dreams.* Most individuals, especially those who are not leading an active sex life, have sexual dreams periodically. In men these may be associated with nocturnal emissions; in women they may be associated with physical orgastic reactions which occur during sleep. The characteristic content of such dreams reveals the sexual orientation of the individual. Occasional dreams involving homosexuality should not be considered diagnostic, but when most or all of the sexual dreams are indicative of a homosexual orientation, they are important indicators.

3. *Psychological tests* should be performed in many cases. These tests are especially valuable in those cases in which the dynamics are not clear and where the clinical picture may be confused. They may be helpful in the determination of the basic personality pattern. Projective tests are the most useful, such as the Rorschach inkblot test and the Thematic Apperception Test. It must be realized that these tests are no more reliable than the individual administering them. The psychologist who is to perform them should be chosen with care. There are no right and wrong answers to such tests, so that each must be interpreted individually.

It would serve no useful purpose to go into detail on what these tests might show. For details, reference should be made to source material in the bibliography.

It should be remembered, of course, that psychological tests of all sorts are fallible.[4]

4. *The presence of homosexual fantasies*, either alone or associated with solitary masturbation, are quite diagnostic.

5. *Persistent jealousy of self-sex associates* when attention is paid to them by others is a very common manifestation of homosexuality.

6. Keep in mind that *perverse acts are not always evidence of true homosexuality.*

In spite of all the above considerations the diagnosis of homosexuality can be very difficult. Above all, the counselor must carefully distinguish between the act and the actor. Society still tends to condemn the deed without much understanding of the doer, and as such does not treat him with compassion. There is here then a double role for moral education: toward a deeper comprehension of the psychological causes and a clearer condemnation of the evil acts.

Differential Diagnosis

There are a number of disorders in which the part played by homosexuality is not clear. In some of these disorders, e.g., transvestism, some believe that homosexuality is related to its etiology. In others, e.g., the paranoid delusion of the schizophrenic, the part played by homosexuality is debated. Since these conditions sometimes confuse the diagnosis of homosexuality, they will be discussed briefly.

These conditions are:

1. Transvestism.
2. Transsexualism.
3. Pedophilia.
4. Paranoid schizophrenia.
5. Obsessions of being a homosexual.

Also to be considered is the subject of adolescent homosexual acts. These have been considered above on pages 102ff.

Transvestism

The term "transvestite" itself comes from *trans* (a "transference") and *vesta* (the "clothing"). Many individuals are of the opinion that transvestites are basically homosexual. For example, Allen[5] says, "This [homosexuality], I believe with Stekel, is the main or primary root of transvestism." Kinsey[6] states that only a small portion of transvestites are homosexual. Oliven[7] states that there is no connection between primary transvestism and homosexuality. Brown laments the fact that transvestism "is often considered nothing more than a form of *homosexuality*. As a matter of fact, these two phenomena are separate and independent."[8]

From these statements it is clear that there is little agreement among the authors. I have changed my own mind over the years and now do not believe that homosexuality is basic. It would seem to me, rather, that the condition represents a sexual deviation in which satisfaction is derived from the wearing of the clothes of the other sex, or leading their kind of life, rather than through orgasm, although this may also occur. There is no doubt that some transvestites are also homosexuals.

There is also some disagreement among authors as to definition. This definition of Kinsey seems quite satisfactory. I believe, however, that it should also include the comment that there is a certain degree of sexual satisfaction involved.

> An individual who prefers to wear the clothing of the opposite sex, and who desires to be accepted in the social organization as an individual of the opposite sex, is a transvestite.[9]

Since transvestism is not basically homosexually oriented, it has no real place in our chapter. A few comments regarding its general nature, however, may be helpful.

It is more common in men, although its exact frequency is not known. The practice is usually indulged in by the male at home, since, in many localities it is illegal for a man to wear a woman's clothing in public. The opposite is not true. Many male transvestites are married and frequently quite happily so, especially if the wife understands the condition. They frequently have children, and to all outward appearances, under most circumstances, seem to lead a normal life. The condition is, in most cases, quiescent for longer or shorter periods of time. Should the desire to transdress be frustrated, the subject may be moody and not infrequently drinks too much. They are seldom vigorous in their sex life.

As to etiology, there are several suggestions. Probably there is no single etiology for all cases. Idiopathic transvestism must, of course, be differentiated from the cross-dressing of male and female impersonators, of male prostitutes seeking to attract other males, mannish Lesbians, and other allied conditions.

Since this subject is so tangential to our main theme, little time will be spent on its psychopathology. It may be the result of conditioning by parents who raise their children as if they were of the other sex. Parents, for example, who were disappointed in the sex of the child may repeatedly tell the child so and, at least during early childhood, dress him in the clothes of the other sex. *Fetishism* has also been suggested as a basis for transvestism with the clothes of the other sex serving as a fetish. *Exhibitionism* has also been suggested as a factor in etiology. In this case the male, at least, would be seeking affection by the assumption of the clothing of a woman, or perhaps he has "accepted castration" and considers himself a woman.

There is a rare form of transvestism in which the individual dresses in the clothes of an infant or small child. This is referred to as infantosexual transvestism, a regressive phenomenon.

Such cases seldom come to the attention of the counselor or psychiatrist except through the wife who may be startled and anxious when she first discovers the condition. I saw one such patient who was almost literally dragged in by his wife with the comment, "I want him examined. I think he is a homosexual." When the story was elicted it developed that the wife had found, on an upper shelf in the closet, a complete set of woman's underclothing and several pairs of high-heeled shoes. It also developed that the husband was impotent under normal circumstances, although they had three children. Eventually it developed that he was potent only when he wore the woman's underwear and shoes. Since he anticipated his wife's refusal, he would put on the shoes and underwear and masturbate. No attempt at insight therapy was made in this case, but the cooperation of the wife was enlisted, and he was allowed to wear the female clothing during intercourse. This led to a successful sex life, and when last heard from they were both doing well.

An interesting paper on this topic, called "The Disease of the Scythians," or "Morbus Feminarum," was published by William A. Hammond, M.D., in the *American Journal of Neurology and Psychiatry* in 1882 (Vol. I, p. 458). Dr. Hammond blamed the difficulty among the Scythians, which was earlier described by Herodotus, upon excessive horseback riding. He also described a condition of the *mujerados* (men who had changed to women) which he observed among the Pueblo Indians of New Mexico. In both of these instances he appeared to be describing transvestites who had adopted the way of life of a woman.

He closed his article by describing the case of Lord Cornbury, governor of New York during the reign of Queen Anne. He did not seem to recognize the case as one of transvestism, but he did recognize its psychiatric nature. The case he described was reported by Dr. Spitzka in the *Chicago Medical Review* for August 20, 1881, under the title "Historical Case of Sexual Perversion":

> This person was "a degraded, hypocritical and utterly immoral being, devoid of anything remotely resembling a conscience, and so thoroughly mean and contemptible that it required but a short period of his rule to array all classes of the population against him. . . . He was devoid of caution, a spendthrift, and altogether erratic in his behavior. Obtaining his position through nepotism, the Queen was compelled to remove him, although he was her own cousin and the son of Lord Clarendon. On losing his position, his creditors in New York locked him up in a debtor's prison, where he languished until his father died. Then money was sent over to liberate him and to enable him to represent the English people in the House of Lords!
>
> "Unfortunately," continues Dr. Spitzka, "only the most notable feature of his insanity has been preserved in the records. But that single feature demonstrated the character of his mental disease. His greatest pleasure was to dress himself as a woman; and New York frequently saw its governor, the commander of the colonial troops and a scion of the royal stock, promenading the walls of the little fort in female attire, with all the coquetry of a woman and all the gestures of a courtesan. His picture, which is extant, shows him to have had a narrow forehead, an unsymmetrical face, highly arched eyebrows, a very sensual mouth, and a very feminine expression. The painting, of which I have seen a copy, represents him in female dress, with his neck and part of his chest bare, and his hair done up in female fashion."

Transsexualism

In this condition there is a desire to change sex. Allen[10] includes in the definition the delusion that a change of sex is taking place. This would seem to be a manifestation of a schizophrenic delusion rather than transsexualism as usually understood. A few years ago a case of this type was seen in the clinic. This was a young man of about twenty-five years who began to feel that he was changing into a woman. This was his explanation of why he felt attracted to men. He sought psychiatric help but was unable to accept insight. After several months of this feeling, he developed hemorrhoids which began to bleed. He was then quite certain that he was a woman in that he had started to menstruate. He, therefore, went to a secluded spot where he "castrated himself." It must be remembered that in the pschiatric sense "castration" implies removal of the penis, not removal of the testicles as in the surgical sense.

"The term transsexualism has been applied to the person who hates his own sex organs and craves sexual metamorphosis."[11] The term refers to cases such as that of the former American soldier Christine Jorgenson. This case received much publicity as "a man who had been made into a woman." Actually what had happened was that the penis, the testicles, and the scrotum had been removed, followed by plastic surgery to construct a vulva. Following this, estrogenic substances were administered to cause the breasts to develop. Following the publicity given to this case, the surgeons who performed it, Hamberger, Sturup, Herstedvester, and Dahl-Iverson,[12] received 465 letters (forty percent from the United States) from transsexualists asking for similar operations. Three out of four of these letters were from males. According to Allen:

> Hamberger has published an analysis of the letters he received. These show that a desire for a change of sex is most apparent in patients suffering from transvestism. Roughly three times as many men as women wish for the operation. The average age of the men was 28 1/2 and of the women 26 years old. He found that "a homosexual libido plays a considerable part if not a dominant role in the wish to change sex."[13]

The reasons given in the letters sent to Hamberger were:

No information	50
Always wanted to be a girl	NA
Cannot live as a man	NA
Life history like reported case	116
Feminine psyche in male body	NA
Homosexual	75
Other causes (wants admission to Buddhist nunnery!)	1

A more recent case of transsexualism and "sex change" is that of Dr. Richard Raskind, a male opthalmologist, as reported in *Medical World News,* September 6, 1976.[14]

When still Dr. Raskind, the physician, now forty-one, fathered a son before he was divorced. He was a prominent opthalmologist in New York City, specializing in eye muscle surgery.

Dr. Renee Richards (the new name he has taken) was a nationally ranked amateur tennis player as a man. He tried to break into the women's professional circuit after receiving hormone treatments and acquiring the external anatomy of a woman. In July, she won a small tournament in La Jolla, California, and in August, 1976, she was accepted for play in a stronger field in New Jersey. Then she tried to enter the U.S. Open Tennis Championships at Forest Hills, and the women pros resisted.

In a statement on the case, the U.S. Tennis Association decreed, "Persons competing as women in the U.S. Open Tennis Championships will be required to undergo sex-determination tests (a Barr body test, backed up if necessary by a karyotype) as used in the Olympics. While the USTA is sensitive to and respects the rights of individuals to live as they may choose, it believes that the entry into women's events at the U.S. Open, the leading international tennis tournament, of persons not genetically female would introduce an element of inequality and unfairness into the championships."

This would presumably eliminate Dr. Richards, who was born Richard Raskind with a Y chromosome.

Dr. Milton Edgerton of the University of Virginia School of Medicine, who formerly headed the pioneering Gender Identity Clinic at Johns Hopkins Hospital, states:

> There is still dispute about whether this clinical entity (transsexualism) should be classified as a severe variant of transvestism, as a special type of homosexuality, as a form of psychosis involving sexual identity, or as a condition separate from all of these.[15]

Transsexuals, estimated variously at between five thousand and fifty thousand in this country, have a desire from an early age to wear clothes of the other sex but without the sexual thrill experienced by transvestites. Before sex reassignment surgery, a transsexual does not covet homosexual experiences but is attracted to the newly opposite sex afterward. Transsexuals have a lifelong sense of being a member of the other sex.[16]

Pedophilia

Pedophilia is a condition in which there is sexual activity which involves a sexually immature subject. Although the child may be of any age he is usually considered as being below the age of fourteen years. This activity may occur in an individual of any sexual orientation and is not limited to homosexuals, although it is frequently said to be. The condition is sometimes confused with pederasty which refers only to erotic relations between adult males and young boys. Pedophilia refers to activity with either boys or girls. This is made clear in this definition of Oliven:

> Pedophilia is a collective term for any type of abnormal interest in a child on the part of an adult, whether in a nature of infatuation, molestation, abuse, or a pathologic desire to inflict pain. Much overlapping of motives and personality disorders can be found among the abusers of children.[17]

The male pedophile is frequently impotent, at least in his attempt with adult sexual objects. With children he is quite likely to masturbate or merely exhibit himself. Paul Friedman comments that the juvenile object is frequently a fully willing participant in these acts.[18]

Table I (below) shows the frequency of pedophilia in relation to other offenses in 284 sexual psychopaths. Table II (below) shows the variety and sex of the activity of the pedophile. The much higher incidence with girls would seem to rule out homosexuality as the only cause of this disorder.

Classification

Pedophilia may be classified as compulsive pedophilia (*pedophilia erotica*) and symptomatic pedophilia (*pedophilia sexualis*).

1. *Compulsive pedophilia* is a chronic disorder occurring most frequently in men. It manifests itself in a compulsive abnormal fondness for younger children. It may be divided further into two types: (a) tender and (b) aggressive.

The *tender type* of compulsive pedophilia is almost always directed toward young boys by an adult male who may be married although he frequently has difficulty in relating to women of whom, however, he is capable of being fond. His heterosexual drive may be quite deficient but he is usually not completely impotent. Masturbation in such individuals is frequent:

> In some of these deviates the impression prevails that they are vastly "attached to themselves" (narcissism) or rather to their own childhood image of themselves. For instance, they may shave repeatedly all their pubic hair, admire or even kiss their mirror image. Most of these men masturbate a great deal.[19]

The *aggressive type* of compulsive pedophile is more frequently directed against children of the other sex. In this type, instead of showing tenderness, the subject is cruder, crueler, and more aggressive. He may physically harm the child and may occasionally panic and kill, although this is accidental rather than intentional. Not all the conduct of the aggressive pedophiliac is cruel. It may vary from intimate fondling and playful spanking to attempts to have the child masturbate him, masturbating against the child's body, or rape attempts.

TABLE I

Kinds of Offenses in Which 284 "Sexual Psychopaths" Were Involved

	Number	Percent
Pedophilia (under age 14)	148	52
Sodomy	12	4
Other homosexuality (over 14)	35	12
Exhibitionism	40	14
Rape (forcible, attempted, and statutory)	14	5
Incest	4	1
Voyeurism, fetishism, bestiality	10	4
Obscene acts	14	5
Miscellaneous	7	3
Totals	284	100

TABLE II

Pedophiliac Activity (Limited to Children Under Age 14)*

	With Girls	With Boys	Total	Total Percent
Masturbation and/or fondling	86	38	124	84
Oral-genital	7	7	14	10
Intercourse (including intercrural) ...	9	1	10	6
Totals	102	46	148	100

Both types are a serious danger to the community. Chronic alcoholics are frequent in this group. In such cases latent homosexuality may be activated. Neither type tends to change from one sex to the other in succeeding instances.

Both types must be distinguished from *Dorian Love* in which the aggressor is a homosexual who prefers relations with an adolescent male.

2. *Symptomatic pedophilia* may occur at any age past adolescence, and in about ten percent of the cases it occurs in women. The condition differs from compulsive pedophilia in that it is symptomatic of some underlying condition such as mental deficiency or organic brain disease. These individuals are at least as much a danger to the community as the compulsive pedophiliac and less susceptible to treatment.

Paranoid Schizophrenia

In the paranoid type of schizophrenia there is as a rule, a poorly organized delusional system. These delusions are usually of persecution or grandeur but not infrequently are of a homosexual nature. Hallucinations also occur which are of the same nature. The "voices" not infrequently are accusatory and imply that the individual has been guilty of a variety of acts of a homo-

---

*Daniel Lieberman, M.D., and Benjamin A. Siegel, Ph.D., "A Program for 'Sexual Psychopaths' in a State Mental Hospital," *The American Journal of Psychiatry,* Vol. 113, No. 9 (March, 1957), p. 802.

sexual nature. They may respond with an emotional reaction of hostility because of the feeling of being persecuted.

Whether homosexuality is the cause of paranoid schizophrenia or paranoia has been discussed over the years. This discussion was initiated by Dr. Freud's analysis of Dr. Schreber's autobiography in which he suggested that paranoid psychotic symptoms develop as a defense against emerging unconscious homosexual desires. It is not my intention to discuss this subject at length, but Sakel and Winokur offer interesting new opinions on the relationship of homosexuality and schizophrenia.

Sakel doubts whether paranoia is a repressed form of homosexuality:

> The more recent evidence most aptly described and presented by psychoanalysts, of the symptoms of homosexuality and its reversal during the insulin treatment in schizophrenia, seem to obviate this concept and point to the fact that the sexual instincts in paranoia, which is part of schizophrenia, are reversed (as when love becomes hate, etc.). In other words, it seems that the homosexual symptom so much stressed by Freud, far from being a cause of paranoia, is rather a symptom of a schizophrenia disease process.[20]

Winokur comes to this conclusion: "Sexual difficulties in schizophrenia are not proved, and any causal relationship between homosexuality and paranoid schizophrenia must be considered quite tenuous if not totally absent.[21]

The *differential diagnosis* in this case is usually not difficult. Other evidence of a schizophrenic reaction will be present. This is not the type of case for the counselor to handle; the patient shoud be referred to a psychiatrist.

Obsession of Being a Homosexual

An obsession is an overpowering, persistent, and irrational idea accompanied by feelings of tension and fear. From the conscious standpoint of the patient, the obsession is uninfluenced by logic and is distinctly unwanted.

Phobias and obsessions are closely related inasmuch as all obsessions are phobias and phobias are obsessive. The latter adds to the former a note of mental preoccupation with the object feared. The two states are practically inseparable; e.g., those who have a fear of cancer are in reality obsessed with the idea. The thought of cancer is constantly before their minds. The fear element is phobia; the thought element is obsession.

Types of obsessions: As in the case of phobias, almost anything can become the object of an obsession: (a) sexual obsession, i.e., the inability to eliminate thoughts of sex or sexual perversions; (b) irremovable thoughts of blasphemy, sacrilege, and loss of faith (commonly known as religious scruples); and (c) persistent thoughts of murder, suicide, and maltreatment of others or oneself.

In the situation with which we are concerned, the individual for some reason, e.g., seduction, curiosity, while under the influence of alcohol, perhaps even because of a latent homosexuality, or for other reasons, is involved in some way with homosexuality. There may not even have been a complete act. For whatever reason, he became obsessed with the idea that he is a homosexual and, as is typical in obsessions, cannot be dissuaded from this belief. The anxiety displayed by the obsessive individual over his condition is different from the apparent need that the true homosexual has to prove to those who question the validity of his assertions. The obsessive person does, however, seek every possible reason of which he can think to prove that he is *really* a true invert.

With care and patience, such individuals are likely to respond to counseling. A careful differential diagnosis is important, because early stages of schizophrenia are often characterized by such obsessive symptoms.

Summary

In summary it may be said that the diagnosis of homosexuality is usually not difficult. The determination of the prognosis may not be so easily arrived at. There is seldom an urgency for a definite diagnostic formulation. *Festina lente.*

CHAPTER TEN

Female Homosexuality

Female homosexuality is a condition about which little is known. There is confusion even in regard to its incidence. It is certainly less noticeable and less disturbing socially than male homosexuality. "No doubt one reason for the ease with which we can conceal our attitude is that so few people are at all conscious of our existence."[1] The female homosexual is generally referred to as a Lesbian. This relationship between women is sometimes also called "sapphic love." The term "Lesbian" is derived from the Island of Lesbos where the renowned Greek poetess Sappho was born (circa 600 B.C.). The term "sapphic" refers to sensual indulgence associated with Sappho and her followers. St. Paul referred to such activity in his Epistle to the Romans when he condemned the pagan women who "changed the natural use into that which is against nature" (1:26-27).

In spite of the fact that male homosexuals are so involved with the law, there are practically no legal sanctions against Lesbianism.[2] There may be several reasons for this. Lesbians are more concerned with companionship than with sexual activity; perhaps also, because male homosexuality is frequently involved with sodomy which, in the popular mind, is disgusting and degrading. Such acts tended to lower the status of men in the public eye, whereas sex acts between women do not tend to lower either their personal or sexual status. Perhaps also, in the male, the "precious" seminal fluid is lost, whereas in the woman it is not.[3] Male homosexuality is more obvious, whereas women have traditionally shown affection for each other.

The incidence of Lesbianism is disputed. In my experience it has been twice as frequent as male homosexuality. This would mean that if there were approximately 4 percent of male homosexuals in the United States, there would be about 8 percent of female homosexuals. I realize that others disagree with these figures; in fact, reverse them.[4]

In a study of 1,200 women by Katharine Davis, 50 percent had shown evidence of some degree of homosexuality at some time in their lives. About one half of this number had engaged in overt activity.[5] Kinsey, in his report on the female,[6] stated that by age forty-five, 28 percent of women had had some type of homosexual response, but only 20 percent had had actual experience. It is interesting to note that many heterosexual prostitutes are Lesbians. Simone de Beauvoir[7] estimates that 20 percent of the prostitutes in Germany are homosexual.

The Dynamics of Female Homosexuality

According to Brody[8] the pre-Oedipal aggression in such cases is oral-sadistic and its intensification is considered as the central characteristic of homosexuality in women.

Brody also states that the unconscious attitude toward the parents is strongly ambivalent and has been described as a characteristic of homosexual women. In the sexual act, he states, the homosexual woman plays a double role. She is the one who suckles and who is, at the same time, suckled. Not only is the oral system highly charged but urethral eroticism plays a powerful part in the homosexual picture.

Homosexuality, Brody feels, is a syndrome, a mode of behavior. Homosexuals, male and female, are driven to self-degradation, expressed obviously or more subtly and to a more or less marked degree. Unable to tolerate the degraded self, they rationalize that they are so superior that there is no need for them to compete with others (healthy people). The rationalization then continues: Healthy people are so weak and degraded, so afraid of their position in life that they are driven to compete. Homosexual people never show their capabilities and at the same time are enraged that their talents are not recognized. Embittered that they have failed to receive due recognition (for traits they have never shown themselves to possess), they retaliate by refusing to show their capabilities. Homosexuals as seen by the psychiatrist are not individuals who present themselves for treatment because they and society differ as to what mode of sexuality is preferable, but they are neurotic with deep-rooted character disturbances. These people would not be healthy persons even if they lived in a society where sexuality with the same sex was acceptable.

As noted on page 72, both Deutsch and Horney held that difficulties in the Oedipal stage, rivalry with the mother, and predominance of castration feelings always lead to a more or less marked tendency toward homosexuality in women.[9]

In *The Hite Report,* a survey of 3,000 women in the United States, the author commented:

> Besides the increased affection and sensitivity and the increased frequency of orgasm, some women felt that sex with another woman could be better because of the more equal relationship possible. Sex with women can be a reaction against men and our second-class status with them in society.[10]

Clinical Features

Clinically, there is nothing clearly distinctive in the dress or mannerisms of the Lesbian. Traditionally, the active female homosexual is supposed to be dressed in a mannish-cut suit of somber color. This is occasionally, but rarely, true. Most of the Lesbians whom I have treated have not worn clothing which would distinguish them from other women.

One characteristic, while certainly not pathognomonic, is that Lesbians would often come to the office for consultation in pairs — one somewhat older, the younger one perhaps more feminine. Frequently the older woman (by perhaps ten to fifteen years) would have an air of proprietorship, as if to say, "I want you to take good care of this little girl."

Although there are fewer case reports on women than on men, there is little doubt about the type of sexual acts employed between them. To some extent the type of sexual contact depends on the ages of the women involved, although this is not an absolute rule. As a general rule the contacts will start with simple lip-kissing, general bodily contact, tribadism (rubbing the genital areas together),[11] mutual masturbation, manual stimulation of the breasts or genitals, deep tongue-kissing. Obviously, all of these contacts require a partner. Probably the most common sex act performed by the homosexual, whether male or female, is solitary masturbation with homosexual fantasy. In some cases an artificial phallus is employed.[12]

The life histories of Lesbians are remarkably alike, although obviously not identical.[13] Some or all of the following facts are likely to be found in the clinical history:

1. The Lesbian is an only child.
2. She has a normal female appearance physically.
3. She behaves like a normal female in society.
4. She has wanted to play a dominant role with women.
5. She is sexually attracted to girls.
6. She preferred her father.
7. From early life her interests had been masculine; e.g., she liked boys' games, disliked dolls, etc.
8. She is disgusted with the thought of intercourse with a man.

Etiology

The factors concerned in etiology are the same as those which play a part in male homosexuality. Women, however, do not seem to have a tendency to seduce little girls, as frequently as the male pedophiliac does. Kinsey mentions seduction of young girls by older women.[14]

Case Reports

As the following cases are read, reference should be made to the chapter on etiology. Clinically, as one would expect, all female homosexuals do not fall into one class. Some go from one partner to the other. Patient V (see below) was of this type. Two cases will be presented in this chapter. The first case is that of a young, married, psychopathic type of Lesbian. This case is presented for three reasons — to demonstrate, with her words: (1) The behavior and thinking of a Lesbian. (There may be some argument as to which type of homosexual she is. I would put her in the class of the true homosexual instead of the pseudohomosexual group. I would do this principally because of her "total" pattern of behavior, without forming a judgment merely on her early behavior.) (2) The pattern of psychopathic (sociopathic) behavior which she demonstrated. (3) The type of patient who, in my opinion, would not be suitable for psychotherapy.

The second case (Patient VI) is quite different. She was

young and unmarried, and her sexual contacts were less frequent; there seems little doubt that her condition represented a neurotic disorder with true compulsive homosexuality. This case is presented as one which demonstrates many of the psychodynamics of the development of the disorder.

In both cases the patient was instructed to freely associate, i.e., to say the thoughts merely as they came to her mind. This may account for some disconnection between thoughts; other lack of connection may be due to an editing of their productions to condense them and to eliminate duplication.

Patient V

I was born in 1932. . . . I had a very happy childhood. I was strictly Daddy's girl. It seems he and I had more in common, and were more alike than Mother and I. I guess I hurt my mother's feelings a lot. I can remember one time I got mad at Mama, and there was a picture of her and Daddy in my room — so, like the rotten brat I was, I drew a halo around Daddy's head and horns on my mother's head. That afternoon when I got home from the movies, Daddy told me Mother had been crying. I really felt awful about it, and yet sort of shocked. . . . Daddy is uppermost in memories of my childhood. It seems like he spent an awful lot of his time and energy on me. There was always a lot of yelling and contention in our house, even when I was very young, as I recall.

I was unquestionably a spoiled, rotten brat, very difficult and hard to manage. According to Mother, nobody could ever *make* me do anything. I guess that's the way I am now, too. I'm really a hard-headed Irishman.

I was a lousy student in school. I always got caught — never got away with a damn thing. Daddy used to say, "Mary, if you want to skip school, go ahead; but if you're dumb enough to get caught, I'll whip you." It seems like I was always standing in the hall for talking or throwing spitballs or humming, or just anything. I told one teacher to go to hell because he thought I was cheating on a test, and I wasn't, although I have cheated at times. I can remember there was one teacher I dearly loved in the fifth grade — Mrs. White. She was kind of fat, too, and she sort of understood my problem. I guess I was kind of her pet, which was pretty novel for me. I wasn't the type to be anyone's pet. I was pretty bad and uncooperative. When I was real young I used to boss all the kids around, and if they didn't like it, I beat them up; but half the time I was nice. I was a very generous kid and pretty much fun. I always had more nerve than anyone else. I really hated school because I was fat, and the kids always teased me. I did like science, though, when we studied the planets and stars and stuff. I liked music a lot, too, but I hated anything else. I took piano lessons for about a year. But I could hear the song and figure it out, so I had a hell of a time learning to read notes. Then I broke my arm, so that was the end of that. I just never went back to it. I guess I didn't think I could ever really learn to play well like my friends Alice and Jane. Alice and Jane were two little girls I grew up with . . . they lived next door. I was such a devil, though; I, like a lot of other kids, played doctor and patient with the little boys up the street. Alice and Jane never did anything like that. You know, you show me yours and I'll show you mine. I was really pretty bad, I guess. Once I threw a rabbit down the basement steps in a fit of anger. And another time I was having a tantrum — Daddy was going to spank me and I was running around the dining room table. I always ran around the table when he tried to spank me, and I fell on one of my cat's kittens and broke its neck. It was pretty awful. I'll never forget how it ran around the room like a chicken with its head off. Maybe these two things left their mark on me — I don't know.

In Jr. High School I got suspended twice and also once in the first year of high school. I never went past the tenth grade. I got married and quit. Well, actually I quit before I even thought of getting married. I loved my husband very much. But I was married so young that I don't suppose that I really knew what love was. Jim and I lived with Mother and Daddy for a while after he was drafted. I moved from camp to camp with him, and we got an apartment off the post. I had a great deal of respect for Jim. He was very intelligent. He was a very thoughtful, considerate and affectionate person. He was also a very good lover. We lived there for about a year and then Jim was transferred to France. . . . We were in Germany for a week prior to our departure from Europe. When we got home we were fighting like the devil; and then Jim started working for a Senator during his campaign. He ran into a girl he had gone to high school with, Becky, and they had an affair and they eventually got an apartment together. And then I found out that Becky and I were both pregnant. It was a mess. So Jim and I broke up. Becky and I had our babies, and Jim left town a few months after the baby was born. I suffered a great deal over him and my situation, but I lived through it. After the baby was born, I went to business school for about a year and learned typing and shorthand. I also learned that there was another side of my personality, for that was where I met Jackie, my first "gay" lover. My affair with Jackie lasted approximately a year.

My first sexual experience was with a boy named Samuel Jones. I was about 14, and I thought I was madly in love with him. He was about 22 and a real bum. My mother forbade me to see him, so naturally I met him at the corner. He was only interested in one thing, but at my age I didn't realize, and I thought he loved me, I guess. I remember the first time we did it; we were in a big field. There was a big old deserted house that at one time had been a very well-kept mansion. I recall very vividly lying in the grass and Samuel trying to put it in, to no avail. It hurt like the devil and we just couldn't get it in. But the next time I'm afraid we succeeded.

Between the time I broke up with Jim and started to have sex with Jackie, the first girl, there was a period of dating and drinking. I met a guy named Bob Brown and was pretty crazy about him. He was also a bum. I had an affair with him, and his lack of character disgusted me so thoroughly I wouldn't go to bed with him anymore. He was pretty rotten to me. Then one night for no reason at all I had sex with his best friend. I don't know why I did it. I had been out with an awful lot of guys and said "no" before Bob. I guess I figured, what the hell.

Then I met Jackie in school. She was a bitch. I was really crazy about her. It was almost as if I was drunk with her. I think she was the most exciting thing in my whole life. She was mean as hell, though, and slapped the hell out of me all the time. She was a real nut.

But I was just too crazy about her to get her in trouble (after she had more or less kidnapped me and taken me to Florida). They would have sent her back to a mental institution. Finally, after about a month, she brought me back. I continued to see her for a few months, and then I got fed up with her childishness and bully attitude and I left her. I tried going to bed with her after we broke up once, but she just didn't move me.

By the way, I want to mention that I never touched her sexually. It was always one way. She sort of made fun of my attempts to touch her.

After Jackie I met a very nice boy named Bill. We had a wonderful time together. Our personalities really clicked and we laughed all the time. He aroused me pretty much, and after we had gone together about six months, we had sex. This was a mistake. It changed everything in my eyes. Then I found out he went to bed with a girlfriend of mine named Linda, and I called him up and told him off and wouldn't see him any more.

One night Jackie called and asked me to meet her and lend her $5. I did and she told me about a place in Baltimore where all the gay kids went. I had never met anyone gay but Jackie. So I asked her to take me there. She did, and I thought it was terribly exciting. So I started skipping business school and going over in the afternoon, when I was supposed to be in school. I would arrive about 10:30 in the morning and stay until about 2:00 in the afternoon. In that way I could return home at approximately the same time I would have if I had been in school all day. I would sit at the bar and watch all the gay girls, hoping like hell I could meet someone I could be interested in. After a while I started staying until night time; and then one night I met this adorable little singer named Pam. We sort of just looked at each other for a couple of days, and then someone introduced us. Then she took me to get something to eat after the club closed, and then to a couple of parties. We went through the hand-holding stage for about a month before we even kissed. It was a couple of months before we had sex. She was a very nice person. She didn't sing for a living, just for kicks. During the day she worked for a bank. She was, and is, one of the most intelligent people I have ever known. She has a way of seeing everything in the right light, in focus. She always makes me see sides of things I couldn't see by myself. She is steady, reliable, faithful, honest, kind, gentle, affectionate, loving, a good lover, talented, considerate. Everything I can think of, Pam represents to me. I loved her very much. I'm no longer in love with her, but I have a deep respect and love for her, and I will until the day I die.

Pam and I lived in Baltimore for a while, and I could have my child on the weekends. Then I finally talked Pam into moving near my parents. We were very happy all the time. Then we bought a puppy and they didn't allow dogs in the apartment. So we moved into a lovely new apartment which we couldn't afford, even though we were both working at the time. We traded in my old Chevy and bought a new (almost new) white convertible. Then we bought new furniture. Needless to say, we were way over our heads. We had a few unexpected financial mishaps, and that was it. We started getting farther and farther behind in the rent, until we finally had to move out. We had planned to rent a house and for me to take the baby to live with us. So I felt I just couldn't move again and start over without him. I suggested we move in with Mama and Daddy for a couple of months until we got on our feet, but Pam wouldn't do it. Consequently I moved home and she moved in with some friends. This was supposed to be temporary, but one thing after another happened, and we were not getting along. So we never got back together.

I was pretty much of a wreck for a while. I cried all the time and was really miserable. I was alone for about a year after that. Then my sex urge got the best of me and I had an affair with a good-looking French girl named Larry. But she wasn't Pam, so I ended it after about three months, and I started drinking and going to parties and staying out all night and doing nothing. I got about ten traffic tickets and wrecked my car twice — the second time it was a total loss, and I got a few broken ribs and many bruises. I had a couple more affairs.

And then I met Sally, I met her in a bar also, but so what. Bear in mind that during all this, my home life was getting progressively worse. Daddy was drinking more than ever, and Mother was screaming more than ever, and I was withdrawing from my family more than ever, and neglecting the baby more than ever, and losing one job after another. One due to hangovers and insomnia, one due to the accident, one because I hated it, one because they went out of business. And the last because of a personality clash with my supervisor, plus the fact that I was getting more and more depressed, until I slashed my wrists and took off a week — during which I was either drunk or full of sleeping pills. Since then I have done nothing. I have been living partly at home and partly with Sally. Sally and I are so much alike that it is pitiful. I'm very much in love with her. She's a good little thing. She has a wonderful heart. She's overly sensitive and very emotional. She has a terrible temper and is very bossy and jealous and possessive. But she's kind and loving and affectionate and generous. She's steady and reliable in her job, and has many wonderful qualities. But she doesn't believe that I really love her, and I don't believe that she loves me enough to endure time. I think one day she'll leave me. I have to be constantly reassured of her love, and she has to be constantly reassured of mine.

Sexually, I have never met anyone with whom I was more compatible. She's really a wonderful lover. Sally and I fight a lot,

I'm afraid, but three quarters of it is through misunderstanding. The other one quarter is mistrust. We both have to exercise a lot of patience with each other and twice as much self-control. I'm so wrapped up in her that I can't imagine life without her. Maybe if I can make my mind healthier, I can help her.

Patient VI

At the time this patient first came under treatment, she was single and twenty-two years of age; her father was a professional man. This case is presented for several reasons: (1) The patient was anxious about her condition and strongly motivated to overcome it. (2) The material is presented as it was produced in the free associations of the patient. (Obviously, not all the associations are presented, but those selected are complete within themselves. The selections were made to demonstrate etiological factors and emotional reactions. Reference should be made to the chapters on etiology before reading the case.) (3) The patient had a good prognosis and represented a good case for therapy. Important factors in the good prognosis were her youth, her educational level which was postgraduate, her good family background, her good insight, and her feelings of guilt and anxiety. Ultimately she made a quite adequate heterosexual adjustment, and is today happily married with a family.

[Dream] — I was in a restaurant. There was a waitress — full-breasted — wearing a jersey sweater. As she leaned over to take my order, her breast touched my face. I immediately felt content and relaxed. She gave me her phone number. I refused to give my name and number. I wouldn't call because that would prove my perversion.

My thought about any boy is could I sleep with him, could I have sexual relations? I have never found one with whom I could. One night when I was drunk I went up to an apartment with a boy and slept with him. It was unsuccessful. At times I wondered how I could do it. I don't even feel that it is wrong now. I was brought up differently and yet did not feel any guilt. There was another boy who had lived abroad and seemed sophisticated. I deliberately tried to get him interested. Tried again in the back of a car — no pleasure? Why? Can I do it or not do it? Maybe I do feel a little guilty.

. . . I can't imagine spending the rest of my life with any man. I have felt socially insecure as long as I can remember, even as far back as the fifth grade. I can remember being hurt if I were left out of anything. If a friend is not loyal or sincere, I am terribly hurt. It seems that I want to be entirely sure of my women friends before I go out with a man. I was close to a male medical student. In giving myself to a man he must be intellectually above me and worthy of me. The medical student has been the only boy I have really admired. . . . I wish very much I were not an only child. I admired my grandfather a great deal. He was well-liked, did many considerate things, and on the other hand did many inconsiderate things, especially in regard to my grandmother. He kept a mistress whom he later married. She was a source of trouble in the family. My dad and I are not close. I admire him very much. I don't have his push. I take the easy way out. I get good grades, only because of the subjects.

. . . Once we were bathing at Ocean City. Mr. S. got fresh with Mother, and she said, "All men are disgusting . . . except your father." Men who are older always attract me. Intellectual women attract me. I have no attraction to younger, frivolous girls. . . .

. . . At the age of 10 I had a boyfriend. It is amazing how close I was to him. I used to play "footsy" during assembly. I always wanted to kiss him, but I was afraid the other girls would see me. At 12-13 I went out with a large group of boys who were dirty and interested in girls. We went down to the railroad tracks and I let them look at me. I went through a whole period of being a nasty little kid. . . . There has always been a lot of talk about "the other woman" in our family. All the men seem to have other women as a matter of course. I have a great fear of a man dominating me. Yet, I don't want to dominate him; it is not right. Maybe that is the reason I turn to women, because I can dominate them. . . . Betty was in today. Every time I see her, even on the street at a distance, I have a terrific emotional upset. I think I am going to have to concentrate on getting her out of my mind. When Betty would come back for a week and tell me what she had done, I would make up stories because I wanted to do a lot of things, too. I have almost an obsession to be on the go. I don't want to sit still and read and think even for a minute. I have always made such a differentiation between acquaintance and friend. I get a big kick out of people asking my advice and needing me. I think I picked up this idea of being turned down from my mother. I get very afraid when I see these things in her, so I want to stay away. Dad and Mother believe I am not suited for nursing, like you did; they agreed that they would go along with me on social work. I know Mother feels badly about not going to college. Mother and I have always been a source of emotion to each other. If she cries, I cry. I have a great deal of contempt for myself, but also a conceit. Betty has always clung to me. I liked that very much; she depended on me for everything. When I saw her getting away I felt badly. She accepted my friends but I never seemed to accept hers as lightly as I wanted to. I was always embarrassed by our closeness, because I knew it was not right. I don't think that she did. I don't know why it is when I talk about it I have this great emotion. I wish there was someone to take her place. I miss her depending on me.

We made it important that we be with other people. I used to beg her not to leave. I have always had this terrific emotion over Betty. She felt the same thing, I know. The attraction that we seem to have had is the same attraction that a man feels for a woman. I didn't think of a perversion until after I had studied it. I like to have a man around because it is a protection against the things I think of myself. I am weak and selfish. I have really hoped that I could fall in love and marry him. . . . One girl friend in New York said, "You don't seem to want me to have any friends." I seem to recall other evidence of this overpossessiveness before I met Betty. I don't seem to be possessive with men; one of them told me I was not possessive enough. I've never been taught not to show my emotions. . . . Until I met Betty, I was a "touch-me-not" sort of person. After her I became more affectionate at home and with girls but not with boys. In picking friends, I seem to pick those less attractive than myself, always someone who has a problem and may become dependent on me. . . . I was tired and lay down on the bed to go to sleep. Bad week because Betty was turned back to me in part (her father died last week). Having her a little dependent and warmer than she has been has made it rough. Every time I leave her I only live till the next time I can see her and do something for her. I am afraid that when she gets over it she will go away like she did before. I can't eat or sleep; I am jealous of everyone near her, especially boys. There is one boy who has been doing so much for her. Seeing her dependent on him made me jealous. I don't want to be with anyone but her. She has not been as dependent as I would like her to be. I keep wanting to buy her things, to do things

136

for her, anything to bring her back. My friend is here from Maine but I haven't wanted to be with her, even though she is my next best friend. The only time I can have any free thoughts is when I am with her. I can't picture anything in my thoughts without her. The thought popped into my head at home (I had it before) of "this is fine, but wait till they get to know you."

The thought keeps going through my mind, would she come back if I were ill. I think I am doing this to bring her back to me. . . . I associate all upset emotions with my mother and yet Mother has always babied me; we would give in to our emotions together. That is one reason I am so afraid to be around her so much. . . . She turns to me now in her hour of need but nothing compared to the way I would need her if the positions were reversed. . . . Do you pretend when you go to sleep at night? I used to pretend I was a lover to my present crush. My crushes would be of a type, young, tall, full-breasted. Greta Garbo through high school. I dated through high school, but was never much of a "necker." Mother used to say not to park. I can remember a couple of boys I used to like to neck with. There is only one time that I wanted him to kiss me. It became something you had to do. I sort of wished he wouldn't be so honorable. I felt more interested in men when I drank. It all stopped when I became interested in Betty. After that I couldn't wait for the date to be over so I could get home. I've tried to pretend that Betty was with me, but it doesn't work. . . .

Once we lived in a house near the woods where the rats came out on rainy days. I was not allowed to play in the woods because of the rats. At the age of 5-6 years, I was friendly with the boy next door, and we would take off our clothes and compare anatomy. I was never interested in dolls. I would rather have had a catcher's mitt or a train. Grandfather gave me a set of tools which I enjoyed. Grandfather called me Mike. He really wanted me to be a boy. He used to hold me on his lap and tell me the most delightful fairy tales. Those were really good days. . . .

Last night I saw a woman at the Statler. I liked her looks. I felt that I must know her. I began to plan. I decided that the first thing was to get rid of my friend, which I found an excuse for, and I waited around for her to finish her dinner, and my plan was to see if she was alone and then approach her. Fortunately, she and her friend remained together, got in a car and drove off. I even tried to get the number of the car. The idea of approaching people got into my head the other night when David told me about a homosexual approaching him. I don't see how I can be without principles like that. I told myself at the time that no matter how this turns out, I will not tell Dr. C. about it. My uncle and Mrs. B. were sort of neurotic, used to have nervous breakdowns; people used to criticize Grandmother for sympathizing with him. I don't want to be neurotic. I don't want Mother and Daddy to baby me too much. Things are getting better at home; the last few times I have been more relaxed. I can kid with Mother. I am not as strong in my religion as I should be either. There have never been any games or crafts that I could enjoy doing by myself. I never wanted to be alone. When we played house, I would always be the man and put on pants. Mrs. B. said, "You are more like a boy than a girl." Bob and I were pals, and we are still very fond of each other. One thing you asked when I came with Mark stands out in my mind. "When Mark put his arms around you was there an erection?" I am overly conscious of it. Now when I am with David, I am constantly on my guard. I don't want him to get so worked up. . . . I went to a gynecologist at the age of fourteen and had an internal examination. I've had no dreams except vague recollection of shuffling $20 bills around. Just after leaving the office, it occurred to me why the word "erection" means so much to me. Last summer, I was sitting at a window at the university, looking out, and saw a man who had been sunbathing. He had a robe, but when he saw me, he took off the robe and began to masturbate. He kept it up for some time. This sort of thing seems to happen frequently in that neighborhood. I keep going back to sex because I am doing what I shouldn't do [directing her thoughts]. It might not be that at all. I remember my uncle when he used to act improperly with me when I was 5 or 7. He would say, "Doesn't that feel good?" I would lie to him instead of telling my mother, but he really hurt. I would like to get my mind off sex, but when I talk to you, I seem to bring them out because they seem important.

[Dream] — Football game — girls playing — patient playing, caught pass and ran wrong way — one person cheered (girl from New York) — everyone else stood still — changed direction and made touchdown — no emotion. . . .

I enjoy David more the last ten days. I have fun with him. He really is a wonderful boy — everyone comments on what a good-looking fellow he is. He scared me one night — he asked me to marry him — I told him I wasn't ready. He said that I knew his intentions — he put me up on a pedestal. He even gave up smoking. He told me he had had other experiences with girls which he regretted now that he had met me. The fact that he's had experience sort of scared me and I froze up for a while, but I am getting over it. Every man I have ever met seems more affectionate than I am. I have the idea that all a man's mind is on is sex because all the men I've met have been like that.

. . . Girls always discuss the one who wasn't there. Now I have a great urge to find a friend, a woman, who will stick through hell and high water — I have had a lot of men friends who would, but not a woman — there again I think love is mostly sex. Men certainly go through an awfully lot to get what they want.

. . . When I was in my teens and a girl would break a date with me to go with a boy, I always resented it very much. I remember one time. Ann called up to break a date. I felt badly about it. Aunt Mary said this is just the beginning, that a girl will always do that. So now as soon as a man enters the picture with any of my friends I don't trust them as much any more. I don't know whether I have ever done this myself or not — I guess I have and as I recall when I broke a date they took it all right. So now when choosing girl friends, the predominating thought is that they must have no connection with men. The one thing I would like to know is why I have always been closer to girls who are not very popular. Yet when I start going with them I try to build them up. It was the same with Betty and Pat. They turned out to be real cute "gals." Pat wrote recently and said that she was engaged and wanted to thank me. . . .

When I was 9 years old there was a kitten — he didn't belong to us — I was playing with him — I would mistreat him for crawling away. We had a housekeeper — Mother and Daddy were away — the housekeeper brought her daughter with her — I bullied her. . . .

. . . I don't know whether the role of a woman is completely submissive or —.

Talking about a woman being passive — when I am with David I almost have to force him into taking the reins — if he thought I wanted to go — he would go. Lately I have been letting him tell me what to do — but it is like an act because I know I am letting him do it. I have been trying to think if ever in my life I have been really dominated — I don't think I have — ever. I think it would be a good thing if I were.

I know I have one or two friends whom I admire and they do

sort of dominate me — if they mention anything I give it lots of thought — maybe I should be around people like that more. I don't know — David, when I first went with him I don't think I admired him — now I do — as a person. It is amazing the way he is handling me — you can see what he is doing — but it is amazing how he does it. There aren't many men who would have the patience with a woman — certainly not many his age.

There is an emptiness inside of me that I cannot seem to fill. What I think it is, is someone — there is no one who talks my language. This horrible thought occurred to me — whether I *was sexually attracted to my own mother* [tears]. It occurred to me that I am so much stronger than she is. My mother is young — I remember thinking the same thing before — even before I came to you. I am so afraid of my mother — any sign of emotion scares me to death — I guess it is because I want her to be strong. When Mother shows signs of feeling inferior I just freeze up. There is so much I could do for Mother — she has been through a great deal and has no one to understand her. Even in friendly arguments Mother takes my part against my father — when she does I begin to protect my father.

When my father kisses me good-night *I have the most horrible thoughts — let it be a father and daughter kiss —* don't let it go any further — such a horrible thought. I don't know why I have it. *I keep wondering why it is that I don't want to live at home.* I wonder if it is because of my thoughts — I wonder how much of it I put into my own mind. I want to have a good, clean, healthy mind. I get the image of a male organ; of David — all the time I am talking I am picturing it — I often think of it — I can't get it out of my mind.

I told you I never masturbated — that was not true — up until a year and a half ago I did. I told you about the man I saw masturbating. I used to picture him doing it. When I was younger and masturbated I didn't picture anything. I now look on masturbation as a sign of weakness — you must exert your will.

. . . *When a woman belittles a man, all she does is make him not sure of himself and thus deprives herself of something.*

I wish David would say more of what he is thinking — I have an idea that I could trust his judgment more than my own. He is brighter than I am and much more adult. I would be a pushover for him, he could wrap me around his finger if he would assert himself. All I would need is an assurance he would stay that way.

140

I don't have the same attitude toward women I had when I came here at all — I don't know whether I will slip back or not. Maybe I feel that way because I want to — I couldn't imagine myself doing some of the things I once thought I could do. . . . . There is one thing which David does when he kisses me (runs his tongue over my lips) which makes the whole thing repulsive — I've been kissed like that before, but I seem to expect more of David. There is no way to tell him, but I wish he wouldn't. . . .

Male organs always appear as a vivid fantasy. . . . The whole thing is just absolutely repulsive. If David stands too close in kissing me goodnight, I want to push him away. I feel that I could sleep with a complete stranger rather than with David.

When I have been asked by boys to marry them I've often thought I could be their mistress rather than marry them. That is something you can get out of — you are more or less free to do as you please.

If you are really in love, you wouldn't mind being with them all the time. There are times when David is absolutely repulsive to me. He never knows what mood he is going to find me in. I have been trying to keep on an even keel. . . .

It's so strange that the slightest idea of passion on David's part is disgusting to me — why can't I understand it in him when I do in others?

When David kisses me he seems so vulnerable — seems completely in my hands. I feel like shoving him away and telling him not to be a fool — that is an awful attitude. I feel as though I am doing him a favor — it shouldn't be that way at all. I wish I could get over that feeling that any form of sexual relations have to be done because men are men. I know it isn't that way because when you love someone you want to be with him. This is the way I feel about Betty. . . .

Why can I think that the relations I had with Betty were practically spiritual whereas the same relation with a man is sensual. Maybe it is because I think that men look on it as merely physical — maybe they don't. I have no idea.

I can't imagine any man being in love with me for anything but physical reasons.

. . . Other people make changes and take them in their stride — why can't I?

It is horrible to think how close Betty and I were at one time and how the distance is growing and growing. If I just knew how to handle this fear. I seem to be afraid of everything. There are

141

times when I still feel so bitter. I don't think at times like this that I am making any progress. I wasn't able to shake the depression or overcome the feelings. It just shows that when something hits me, I am back where I started from. It is at times like these that I feel so hurt about Betty. I still feel, however, that she has let me down. If I had only been aware a little sooner. I feel as though I was in the middle — too weak to give up but not strong enough to do anything about it.

Yesterday I felt as though I didn't want to do anything but wander around but I didn't want to wander alone — I feel as though I was back where I was 5-6 weeks ago. Maybe I'm not. It's at times like these that I wonder if I shouldn't find what I want in companionship and just stop coming to you at all.

A stranger in the street knows as much about how I am going to react to something as I do. I suppose eventually they won't. Why can't I just say to myself this is a down day and sit it out. I am not even strong enough to settle myself down to study, I have to keep going. . . .

. . . I've been brought up on the belief that men play around — I am going to hurt them before they hurt me.

Am I trying to recapture what I had with Betty? Crushes on movie stars — picture of Mae West in my room, Norma Shearer — attracted to their breasts — they were always in trouble, and I, in the masculine role, was going to get them out of trouble — they were aloof — I could approach them when no one else could — I would have intercourse with them later and that would be the end.

I can't figure out whether I like to dominate people or not. I think I do some people, but I can't figure out which ones — seems to be the weaker, more dependent people when I do. I don't do it at my work. You'd think I'd try to dominate other workers.

I had a desire to beat a horse or dominate a woman. When you ride a horse you are in complete control.

The women in fantasy have never been attractive and did not have much social opportunity — one who was lonely — and I made them happy. . . .

Tuesday night after dinner and cocktails with Dad, I had the sexual urge and the wish to dominate someone. I wanted to see Gerry, but I didn't.

. . . I was wondering tonight if my mother ever loved me — she makes me fill the gap that my father doesn't fill.

I was looking at my father the other night — he seemed so

142

lonely — maybe he isn't at all [tears]. My mother is so cut off from him — I thought I should help him — then I thought of all the years he didn't help me — but the difference is that he wasn't aware of my loneliness, but I am of his. He has no realization at all, but Mother keeps smothering me with love.

. . . I was trying to think the other day about those fantasies I had when I was little — I was both the man and the woman — I was always like the woman — she depended on the man — was lonely — I was the woman, and the man was the way I wanted to be treated.

I don't see any of my mother in me — but I don't know what her expectations are — except to be depending on someone.

Patient I (Commentary)

Because of a dearth of information on female homosexuality and the relations of Lesbians to male homosexuals, these comments of Patient I are included. They represent the observations of only one individual but, as pointed out before, he is an intelligent and perspicacious student of the topic. In spite of this, these comments must be regarded as particular statements and not necessarily universally applicable.

Having known a great many female prostitutes fairly well — I did have a lot to do with them during the war period, when we used them for information — I can confirm your statement that most of them are homosexual. I have talked this subject over with many of them, and feel that they have turned to Lesbian attachments, not from being basically homosexual, but from disgust and repugnance as a result of their experiences in the brothels. Being forced to repress any real pleasure with men clients, they seem to develop their own real and complete sexual orgasms with women.

I have known a few male prostitutes who rented themselves out to women. They were all homosexuals. I was intrigued enough to ask one of them, who had been a soldier of mine during the war, how he managed. He said he was capable of having a continuous erection and could operate as long as the client wanted, but he never had an ejaculation with them. He could only have an ejaculation with a man, orally. From his apparent success in the trade and opulence, he seemed to be very satisfactory and appreciated by women clients.

143

Another bit of brothel lore which I picked up during this time may interest you. A prostitute in Italy told me that the man who comes and pays feels free to ask the woman to do the things for him that he probably would never admit otherwise. Several of them commented to me on the very large percentage of men who wanted some kind of anal stimulus before they were capable of fornication.

I have known over the years fairly well a great many Lesbians and all I can say is that they are on the whole an unpleasant group of individuals, and I avoid them. The male homosexual, and I would say that this is true of at least 90 percent of them, has one redeeming feature. He does have a sense of humor about himself and his life — a quality that I found completely lacking in the Lesbian. The Lesbian by her inversion tends to be antisocial — the contrary of the male "homo" — with a nature turned completely inward — overly intense in everything, no humor, vindictive and generally unpleasant in all her contacts outside of her own friend.

The male "homo," even in his most involved moments, tends to see the whole business with a certain objectivity, and seeing it this way, there is something ludicrous about it, and he can laugh at it, and at himself — which is a saving grace for him and his contacts with the normal world.

I have noted that around the world people tend to exclude Lesbians from their normal social life, while they tend to include homosexuals in it, even though they may not approve, because the average male "homo" is by nature, gregarious, amusing, and really likes and enjoys life, so that he is in general a good companion and fun to have about.

A great many summers in my youth were spent with a cousin of my father's, who was a Lesbian, and the only really enjoyable one that I ever knew. She had been exiled by the family from Wales in the early years of the century, and turned into kind of a remittance woman by the family — paid to stay away, as a result of scandal in the village. She had drifted to Alaska during the Gold Rush, gone to the Pacific Islands, where she had met up with a most feminine creature with whom she had been for many years, at the time I stayed with her.

Jane spent her life with fast cars and boats, and knew every sailor that put into port, and could out-cuss any of them, and tell dirtier stories than they dared. I was taken around this world by Jane, and often wonder if this did not play a role in my own development, for my own sexual tastes have always run to these lower

144

classes — for it introduced me to a world with which I would normally never have had any contact, and I look back on these summers and this strange environment with a certain nostalgia that probably has played a role all my life.

Marriage and the Lesbian*

In the case of the Lesbian the situation in regard to marriage is somewhat different from that of the male. Marriage for her is also not a cure, but women adjust better to family life, and because of the passive role she plays it is easier for the Lesbian to participate in the heterosexual act than it is for her male counterpart. There is some proof of this in the fact that many female prostitutes are homosexual and are able to participate in heterosexual relations without difficulty, although without pleasure. The security offered by marriage and the pleasure of raising a family may balance satisfactorily the loss of sexual pleasure which results from her frigidity in the marriage relationship.

Motherhood does not have the same danger for the children as fatherhood, because the Lesbian is less aggressive and less active in sex than is the male, and the potential harm to the children and family relationships is less. In giving marital advice to the Lesbian the pattern which she has established concerning overt sexual activity must be carefully studied, as well as her adaptability, her ability to accept males socially and sexually, and her maternal capacity. If she knows herself to be a homosexual, she is, of course, morally bound to tell her partner about it before marriage.

Summary

1. Little is known of female homosexuality.

2. Two cases of different types were presented for the sake of contrast and study.

3. Lesbians do not have the same problems in marriage as the male homosexual but they are advised against marriage.

4. In general the prognosis is better than the male homosexual for adjustment and therapy.

---

*See Chapter 11 also.

145

CHAPTER ELEVEN

Marriage and the Homosexual

True homosexuals, whether overt or latent, should not get married. A genuine, obligatory homosexual is personally incapable of entering a valid marriage. Ritty[1] and Oesterle[2] agree with this opinion and give excellent canonical reasons. Excepting the occasional marriage that would work because of an unusual circumstance of personalities, the vast majority of such marriages would fail. In spite of this fact, many such individuals are told by poorly informed counselors to "go ahead and get married. After your marriage it will all work out." This is not so.[3] Marriage should never be a treatment for anything, much less homosexuality. It will not "work out." This statement brings up two questions which require answers:

1. Why will it not work out?
2. What can be done to prevent such marriages?

In answer to the first question — "Why will the homosexual-heterosexual marriage not work?" — one thing is evident from all that has been said in previous chapters: there cannot be a satisfactory operational psychosexual relationship between an obligatory homosexual and a heterosexual person. Whatever physical sexual relationship does occur will be accidental, infrequent, and a counterfeit of the real thing. There is practically no disagreement among psychiatrists with the fact that homosexuality, when present, has existed from early childhood. The reference here is to true homosexuality, not the homosexual acts of the pseudohomosexual sometimes referred to as a bisexual.[4] Such an individual is not actually a homosexual at all, but is one who has a poor sexual identification and will utilize any handy sexual object to satisfy what he considers his needs. There would probably also be agreement that a homosexual individual could perform a sex act with a heterosexual partner if he were to indulge in homosexual fantasies while doing so. One other point of importance about homosexuality is that, except in a small number of strongly motivated cases, complete recovery from the condition is not likely to occur.[5] It is a condition, therefore, which is antecedent and permanent and opposes the very essence of marriage, the conjugal act.

I recognize that marriage enjoys the favor of the law and that the validity of a marriage is to be upheld until the contrary is proved (Canon 1014). This is the way it should be. But speaking as a psychiatrist, with an incomplete knowledge of the law and of theology, I would like to present a brief discussion of those aspects of homosexuality which, in my opinion, render the marriage of such persons a mockery of that sacramental state. This opinion, I believe, is not corroborated by the teaching on marriage given by the Second Vatican Council of which more will be said later. Emphasis in the past has been on the physical aspects of the sex act with little accent on its psychological components.[6] For example, Harrington states the criteria usually accepted canonically for the consummation of marriage in these words:

> In order that a man be considered potent and be apt for contracting a valid marriage, he must have a penis that is capable of erection and of penetrating the female vagina and he must be able to produce, emit and deposit *verum semen* within the vagina. The erection must be maintained and sustained until the vagina has been penetrated and until semination has occurred within it.[7]

Reasons for the Invalidity of Marriage

It would appear that the homosexual-heterosexual marriage is invalid because:

1. The homosexual cannot give the consent necessary to bring into existence the reality of marriage.

2. The homosexual is incapable of the genuine conjugal love required for a proper marriage.

3. The homosexual is psychologically impotent.

1. *The homosexual cannot give the consent necessary to bring into existence the reality of marriage.*

Marriage is frequently regarded as a contract, and there is no question that in some respects it is. But it is so different than most contracts that the term hardly describes its reality. The Canon Law of the Church talks about marriage in terms of a contract, one brought into being by the free act of the will whereby the parties give to and receive from one another the perpetual and exclusive right to the body of the other for the purpose of performing acts suitable of generating new life.[8] When this language is fully understood[9] we can appreciate why the homosexual is incapable of giving the consent necessary to establish a marriage. The teaching of Vatican Council II is significant here.

According to the Second Vatican Council, marriage is not so much a contract as an "intimate partnership of life and love . . . rooted in the conjugal covenant of irrevocable personal consent." It is "a reflection of the loving covenant uniting Christ with the Church and a participation in that covenant."[10] In other words, it is a reality that is brought into being only by the willingness of the partners to give and receive each other in their fullness and by their willingness to promise each other a lasting and abiding love.

By its very nature, marriage is ordered both to the fostering of the full love of the partners for each other and to the "procreation and education of offspring, in whom their love finds its crowning glory."[11] The object of the matrimonial consent is by no means simply a right over the body of the other for the performance of certain sexual acts. It is rather the right "to a life partnership, a *consortium vitae,* a living together that is fully matrimonial."[12]

The marital act is of its very nature intended to foster and to express the love of the spouses, to enable them to share their lives and to complement their differences. So, too, is the marital act of its very nature an act in which the persons who share their lives and love can communicate that life and love to a new human person. In the words of St. Augustine, "to procreate lovingly, to nourish humanely, and to educate Christianly."[13]

Therefore, it is obvious that heterosexuality is a *conditio sine qua non* of marriage. Since the object of the matrimonial consent is the right to a life partnership in which one will share his love with his spouse and, together with his spouse, be capable of communicating life and love to a new generation of human beings, it seems only logical that each partner should expect the other to be capable not only of performing, but also of desiring the marriage act in its full meaning. The capacity to give full personal consent to the marriage act in its total meaning is an essential condition for establishing marriage. The homosexual is not capable of giving full personal consent of this kind.

If one partner reveals his homosexuality and the other persists in a desire to get married, even after such a revelation, the marriage should be actively discouraged.[14] It seems clear that the matrimonial consent necessary to effect the marriage bond must be directed toward the giving and receiving of the right to acts which are truly expressive of an interpersonal conjugal love and capable of bringing that to its "crowning glory," children. This is the real essence of marriage, and an act of the will intending this cannot be complete and free in a homosexual. A homosexual's consent will always be conditional, not an irrevocable personal consent to a sharing of life and a willingness to share that life with children who are to be begotten in acts of loving sexual union. And if "any essential property of marriage" is positively excluded, the marriage is invalid.[15] As Bouscaren and Ellis noted:

> Mere external expression of consent cannot constitute marriage; genuine internal consent on both sides is so necessary that no human power can supply it, and much less can the Church presume it in a case where it is known not to exist (C. 1081, 1).[16]

Therefore, it should be emphasized that a homosexual person cannot give this internal consent.[17]

2. *The homosexual is incapable of the genuine conjugal love required for a proper marriage.*

It has already been noted that the covenant of marriage is a sharing of life that is ordered not only to the loving generation of children but to the intimate partnership of life between the spouses. The spiritual and disinterested love of the spouses for each other must animate the marriage.[18] In the light of the teaching of Vatican Council II on the nature of marriage and of the marriage act as an intimate partnership of life, a covenant that is meant both to mirror and to inwardly participate in the love that Christ has for His Church, it becomes increasingly clear that "where conjugal love is missing, either the consent is not free, or it is not internal, or it excludes or limits the object which must be integral to have a valid marriage."[19]

This teaching of Vatican Council II on the centrality of a genuine sharing of life and love in marriage is a reaffirmation of the meaning of marriage as communicated through the Scriptures. In the oldest account in Genesis of the creation of mankind (the Yahwist account is Genesis 2:18-24) we find the story of the creation of male and female, the creation of marriage as the human reality that God wills it to be.[20] According to this account, it is not good for "the man," that is, the male, to be alone. In other words, the male cannot be fully himself without the help of another. And that help, the only created earthly being equal to the male, is the female, for the love of whom he "leaves his father and mother and clings to his wife and the two of them become one flesh" (Genesis 2:24).[21]

If homosexual love is properly understood, it is apparent that such love is not love as it is usually seen between a man and a woman, but only a sexual love. It is not the love meant by St. Paul when he stated: "You who are husbands must show love to your wives as Christ showed love to the Church when he gave himself up on its behalf" (Ephesians 5:25).[22]

It is also clear, as Dom Massabki has well said, that married love "is the love of a whole person for the whole of another person."[23] The fulfillment of the specifically human sexual act occurs by a union of the whole persons of both husband and wife. It is far more than merely a physical act. It is a mutual compenetration of two human beings who are united body and soul with each other. The sexual act is incomplete unless this physical compenetration of persons is effected with its psychical counterpart. Thus it is not permissible for the partners in a marital act to separate the psychical component of the act from the physical, nor the physical from the psychical. Such separation would be the rule rather than the exception in the case of a homosexual.

According to Jean de Fabregues:

It is true and certain that the kernel of sacramental marriage must be a call of love. And neither the Church nor Christian wisdom has ever refused to recognize in the profound attraction of one being for another, to another, one of the greatest realities in the lives of men, one of those moments when a creature rises almost to the level of his supernatural destiny. Therefore, the Church desires with all her heart that the sacrament should confirm the consent of two beings who are drawn to each other by love, if it really is love.[24]

Such statements could certainly not refer to the narcissistic love of the homosexual.[25] In the absence of true heterosexual

150

love there is a continuous threat to the permanency of the marital relationship.[26]

3. *The homosexual is psychologically impotent.*

Homosexuality is a form of impotency, although at times it may not evidence itself anatomically or completely.[27] Quinn, discussing the impediment of impotence, is one of the few clerical writers on the subject who mention homosexuality as a cause of impotency.

He divides the subject into two classes: (a) organic and (b) functional. The *functional type* occurs, he states, in those individuals who have intact organs which function defectively. He subdivides functional into: (a) nervous type, (b) neurasthenic type, and (c) psychic type.[28]

Under the psychic type he includes sexual perversion, especially homosexuality. He adds that perversion is defined by the Rota as any manifestation of the sexual instinct which does not correspond to the end of nature, which is procreation (for the psychiatric definition see p. 46). He further states that one cannot say without qualification that homosexuality always produces impotence, and, consequently, the Rota insists that each case be judged on its own merits. As a psychiatrist, however, I must insist that the homosexual is psychologically impotent in heterosexual relations. Both the stimulus and the desire for such relations are absent, and there is a positive aversion (in varying degrees) for the act itself. The homosexual lacks capacity for that unselfish love which is necessary for marriage.

We should also remember in evaluating the psychic factor in impotence that man is not a creature composed of a body and a soul, but a body-soul composite. It is true, however, that philosophically considered, the body was made for the soul, not the soul for the body. We could also say that in the hierarchy of values the body occupies a lower level of function than the soul. Psychic values are recognized by common consent as having a high human value. It would seem, therefore, that the exclusively physical, technical requirements as set down by canonists need to be reconsidered in that they ignore a more important aspect of the marriage act.[29]

Proof of Preexistence of Homosexuality

In regard to the preexistence of the homosexual state with its coexistent psychological impotence, there is the interesting possibility that the heterosexual partner could insist on a written statement of the homosexual partner before marriage and before witnesses that he did consider himself a true homosexual.

Would the court accept such a statement or would it require further proof from the spouses? This would raise the question of what are the minimal diagnostic criteria of true homosexuality. These are certainly important but, unfortunately, largely subjective. They were discussed in Chapter 9. From the legal standpoint, witnesses to homosexual acts performed by one or the other spouse could probably be produced, but then how many witnesses and how many acts would be necessary to be acceptable as proof?

The Lesbian

Father John F. Harvey is of the opinion that the true female invert should be advised against marriage. He points out some interesting differences between the male and female homosexual:

> The female differs from the male in such matters as the greater depth of her attachments, her avoidance of erotic transvestism, her ability to keep her anomaly secret, and the alleged deeper sensitivity of her conscience to the guilt of homosexual desires and acts. Perhaps this more sensitive conscience in female homosexuals induces them more readily to seek moral guidance than their male counterparts.
>
> While all sorts of consciences are found among male and female inverts it is noted in pastoral practice that the female is more docile than the male. She is not as likely as he is to defend her way of life by involved arguments of a pseudointellectual stripe, and she is more ready to admit the obviously emotional character of her homosexual attachments, to which she may continue to cling, not as a rebellion against moral principles, but really out of fear of her beloved. In general, in the female there is more weakness and less pride.[30]

I am not sure that I quite agree with Father Harvey in regard to the marriage of Lesbians. I would certainly agree that if they know of this condition, if they are leading an active homosexual life, and wish to get married only for the sake of appearance, then the marriage should be discouraged. On the other hand, the sexual attitude of a woman is different from that of a man, her drive is not as imperative, and many married women are frigid in any case. There is no reason to believe that she could not be a good mother, and that she could show proper interest in and affection toward her husband and children. Father Harvey quotes Henry[31] and Karpman[32] on this subject, both of whom dealt largely with "hard-core" obligatory homosexuals. I do not wish to be misunderstood. I would advise the Lesbian against marriage, but I do not feel that her marriage to a heterosexual male, especially if he had a low sexual drive, would be the catastrophe that is the marriage of a heterosexual woman to a homosexual male.

As for the second question — "What can be done to prevent such marriages?" — serious thought should be given to the prevention and/or relief of the heterosexual partner of such a mixed marriage. Many homosexual individuals do marry, for one reason or other, without informing their prospective spouse of their condition. One of the most flagrant cases with which I have had personal contact was a young man who took his boyfriend on the honeymoon with him. He thoughtfully arranged a lower berth on the train for his bride and got a compartment for himself and his male companion. This couple performed one sex act on their honeymoon, enough to consummate the marriage, and have not lived together since. The young Catholic girl, although normally sexed, is thus condemned to a state of celibacy for the rest of her life, or until the death of her homosexual spouse, or until she renounces her religion. The latter result is unfortunately frequent in this type of case. My purpose in this presentation is to explore the possibility of relief for such tragic situations.

Prevention of the Heterosexual-Homosexual Marriage

We must recognize the right of all individuals to enter the vocation of their choice. We must, however, also recognize that there are qualifications required for each state of life in those who wish to enter it. The canonical impediments to marriage are well known and need not be repeated here. I hope that I have shown that homosexuality is included in these already recognized impediments.[33] If homosexuality is a legitimate impediment, we need not feel guilty for discouraging the marriage of homosexuals.

More knowledge of homosexuality on the part of those giving premarital counsel would be helpful in the prevention of such marriages. This is especially important in view of the prevalent erroneous attitude that marriage is a cure of homosexuality. Canon 1020, paragraph 2, requires the pastor to make certain inquiries concerning the state of mind of the individuals.[34] If he were well informed on this subject, he could judiciously inquire into the possibility of homosexuality in either partner. He could also point to danger inherent in the situation when the partners wish to proceed with the marriage even though aware of the deviant sexuality of the partner.

Conclusions

1. Those concerned professionally with marriage should become increasingly aware of the clinical syndrome of *homosexuality*, both overt and latent.

2. When this condition is present in its true form, the couple should be urged not to get married.

3. Ecclesiastical authorities should give thought to making homosexuality, whether overt or latent, an impediment to marriage because of: (a) the personal incapacity of the genuine homosexual for the married state — for a union that is both valid and happy; (b) his incapacity to give true marriage consent; and (c) the existence of psychological impotency in heterosexual relations.

154

CHAPTER TWELVE

Homosexuality and the Religious Life

Why after 2,000 years, you might ask, does there recently come about this need for the psychiatric screening of candidates for the religious life? There are many who still object to such methods of selection. To require such an examination, they feel, is to naturalize a supernatural vocation. Such individuals feel that the older methods of examination were adequate and that the methods of the spiritual director provided sufficient screening. But those methods did not provide the best results in spite of their use for 2,000 years. Especially in regard to sexual deviation were many spiritual directors inadequately informed and consequently likely to fail in their screening procedures.

Should the presence of perverse sexual conditions be a bar to the acceptance of a candidate for the religious life? There are some who believe they should be. Dr. René Biot is one of these:

At the time of admission, the orientation of the subject's sexuality must have been definitely established for several years. Any persistent deviation of the libido constitutes an absolute counter-indication. We must be inflexible regarding this, else we shall be responsible for a life of unhappiness for the future priest or monk, and greatly imperil the honor of the clergy.[1]

There are others like Father John R. Connery who state: "It seems a little incongruous to demand an attraction for the opposite sex as a requisite for a life of celibacy." Father Connery concludes, however, that "if there have been lapses, a vocation is either out of the question, or should not be considered until a very long trial gives clear proof of control."[2] There seems to be no uniformity of opinion among those who discuss this subject.

155

This may be due in large part to incomplete understanding of the subject and a failure to differentiate between degrees of homosexuality. It is wrong to adopt an "either/or" attitude, a black-and-white concept, in which anyone with any evidence of deviation would be thereby barred from the religious life.

As for the individual concerned, if he contemplates entering the *religious* life, he must give serious thought beforehand to whether he feels that he is able to meet all the obligations of the life. He should in addition consider his ability to cope with situations which will undoubtedly arise in an environment constituted entirely of members of the same sex. The aggressive homosexual should realize that such a step may be inviting serious conflict and possibly immorality. The passive homosexual should realize that under such circumstances he is likely to be a temptation to more aggressive homosexuals if such be present. In the case of pronounced feminine characteristics, he might be a source of temptation to heterosexual members of a community, particularly if it is cloistered. If he is recognized as homosexual he may be faced with the conscious or unconscious aversion or ridicule which may exist, even if in a small degree, in religious communities.

These objections are, of course, purely speculative; as one approaches more proximately to the forming of the final practical judgment, the circumstances of the individual case may overcome the anticipated danger. In an active religious community the individual might find just that proper balance of religious idealism, awareness and stimulation, charity and compassion, satisfying work, etc., which he will perhaps nowhere else encounter, and wherein he can most blamelessly increase in sanctity.

To help clarify misunderstanding, a more complete knowledge of homosexuality in all its aspects should be part of the training of all religious superiors, spiritual advisors, and confessors.

Homosexuality and the Religious Life

Our authority for discussing this matter, which will be limited to homosexuality, comes from many sources of which I shall mention only two. No less an authority than Pope Pius XII directed the exclusion of the homosexual from the religious life:

156

. . . whoever has a special tendency to sensuality, and after long trial has not proved he can conquer it; whoever has no aptitude for study and who will be unable to follow the prescribed courses with due satisfaction; all such cases show that they are not intended for the priesthood.[3]

A private letter of the Sacred Congregation for the Discipline of the Sacraments of December 27, 1955, demands full proof before a given case should receive lenient treatment. And an element of that proof would be thorough examination by a doctor "who is a real expert in psychiatry, known for his skill, morality and practice of religion, advanced in years, free of the tenets of materialism. The doctor, after prolonged examination, should decide whether, having examined the psychic and physical condition of the student, he is fit to carry with honor to the clerical state the burdens of sacred ordination, especially celibacy." The letter goes on to advise the doctor: "If he finds him physically and psychically so disposed as to be considered not qualified for [Holy] Orders, his other qualities, even though outstanding, must be set aside, and he must be counseled in a fatherly but firm manner that he should withdraw from embracing the priesthood."[4]

A Long Trial

How long is a "long trial" as recommended by Pope Pius XII in his encyclical on *The Catholic Priesthood*? Experience would indicate that this should be a period of at least three years or the duration of the individual's stay in the seminary, whichever is longer.

Specific Forms of Homosexual Activity in Relation to the Religious Life

The screening examination should investigate at least the following types of homosexual activity when there is reason to believe that the candidate has perverse sexual tendencies:

1. *Adolescent Homosexual Activity* (see also p. 102). In the history of many individuals there will be noted instances of

157

sexual contacts during adolescence with members of the same sex. These will usually have been in the nature of sexual exploration or mutual masturbation. As a rule these acts will not have been frequent and will have occurred before the age of sixteen. The individual giving the history may or may not have been the aggressor. If these experiences occurred over a relatively short period and did not recur as the individual grew older they may be disregarded as evidence of homosexuality. They are not significant as evidence of the individual's adult sexual orientation:

It is fairly evident that the homosexual acts of adolescence are not necessarily evidence of inversion, nor are they even an inevitable accompaniment of inversion.[5]

The counselor must be careful never to tell the boy who admits such acts with his companions that he is a homosexual or in danger of becoming one.[6]

These experiences are almost always the result of sexual curiosity which leads to experimentation. They may occur in either sex. The significant factor is that they have occurred in a circumscribed period of time and have not persisted beyond adolescence. In general it may be said that if such activity does not persist beyond adolescence it should not in itself be a bar to entering the religious life.

2. *"Surprise" Experiences.* Father John F. Harvey in an unpublished manuscript speaks of homosexual acts, frequently the first, which are "committed more by surprise than by deliberation." If any such act was the first act it is conceivable that through ignorance the passive recipient might have innocently submitted. Such naïveté would, however, be quite rare in these days of sexual enlightenment. If the "surprise" is accompanied by violence or serious threats it would certainly involve no responsibility on the part of the innocent party. If one can accept the statement that the individual was innocently enticed by surprise into an act and this was his only act it should certainly not be a bar to the religious life. His remaining in the religious life should, however, be dependent on a probationary period. Such cases must be quite rare.

When this innocence has been conserved by virtue — I mean through effort, with a struggle on occasion, without ignorance of evil or absolute calm of the senses — evidently we must bless God, and every director has experienced this joy. . . . It is different when innocence does not stem from virtue. Doubtless it remains quite estimable, since it is ordinarily a sign of a suitable temperament. But a certain doubt should arise in the face of this ignorance and this sluggishness of nature; in these cases, it would be necessary besides enlightening the person, to impose a trial before sub-deaconship.[7]

3. *Sexual Arousal During "Contact" Games.* Sexual arousal during physical contact play such as wrestling and rough-and-tumble games may be an indication of homosexuality, although this is not universally true. Such behavior should definitely be avoided by erotically sensitive individuals of whatever sexual orientation. Repeated arousal or rough play sought merely for the purpose of sexual arousal should be carefully evaluated and if there is deliberativeness in it the individual should be accepted only after a period of observation. In cases of premeditated acts the candidate should be dismissed.

4. *Homosexual Experience Under the Influence of Alcohol.* In general homosexual acts committed while under the influence of alcohol have little prognostic significance in the evaluation of sexual inversion. However, when one is evaluating a vocation to the religious life any sexual act or any overindulgence in alcohol assumes a serious significance. How would we view a heterosexual act in the prospective seminarian even under the influence of alcohol? How are we to regard drunkenness in the candidate? If the act occurred before entry into the major seminary and it was not repeated, a sexual act under the influence of alcohol should not be considered as a bar to ordination. If the act is repeated the candidate should be carefully evaluated from the standpoint of both alcoholism and homosexuality. Dismissal or a prolonged period of observation would then be indicated.

5. *Homosexual Dreams.* Everyone from time to time has sexual dreams. In the male these are accompanied frequently by nocturnal emissions. Some individuals who appear to be heterosexually oriented have occasional dreams which seem to have a homosexual connotation. These should be disregarded. If, however, the majority of the sexual dreams are frankly homosexual in nature and are associated with emissions they are most

159

likely evidence of homosexuality. If this is the only evidence of homosexuality and the individual has led an otherwise chaste life the dreams should not be considered a bar to the religious life but should be an indication for an intensive examination of the individual.

6. *Homosexual Attraction Without Homosexual Acts.* This condition is the one that gives rise to the most difficult decisions in regard to the acceptability of the candidate. Homosexuality, of itself, is neither moral nor immoral. If the decision in regard to vocation is based purely on moral considerations then there should be no question of the acceptability of the candidate for the religious life. Many have said that the chaste homosexual should be approved for Holy Orders. If, on the other hand, we consider homosexuality as symptomatic of an underlying personality disorder, then we must evaluate the severity of the condition. Very often homosexuality implies the deification of the ego. "One invert said that God was his ego."[8] There is no doubt that sexual inversion reaches the depths of the personality. The attitude of the individual toward his condition is an important consideration. For instance he must, to be considered acceptable, believe he can overcome his habit, or at least control the tendency. There are other questions which should be answered; e.g., "Does the individual have real insight into his condition? Is he aggressive? Does he resent his condition? Does he feel able to control his impulses? When did he last masturbate? Was this associated with homosexual fantasies? Does he have a fatalistic attitude toward his condition? Is he anxious about the condition or his ability to control it?" There may be individuals in this group who are suitable for the religious life.

7. *Masturbation With Homosexual Fantasy.* Masturbation aside from its other aspects is evidence of sexual and emotional immaturity. In compulsive maturbation there is some diminution of moral responsibility, but since the condition represents a severe disorder it would in itself be a bar to entering the religious life. Chronic masturbation with its associated moral responsibility when combined with homosexual fantasy would be evidence of a psychiatric disorder plus immaturity plus a lack of proper will and motivation. All of these added together would render the individual unsuitable for the religious life. Treatment may be of value in such cases to relieve the masturbatory tendency even though it is effective for the homosexual disorder. If such a habit persists into the major seminary the candidate

should be advised not to continue with his studies. There may be some individuals who, after therapy, may be allowed to proceed but they should be carefully counseled. Masturbation with heterosexual fantasies is another problem, which does not concern us here. It should be understood, nevertheless, that regardless of the sexual orientation of the individual, persistence of masturbation into adult life is evidence of severe emotional and moral immaturity:

> Regarding masturbation, some persons advocate a trial period, since the candidate has a long road ahead of him; but the present writers would be inclined to be severe in this matter. Once relatives and friends have seen a young man wearing the cassock, postponing the decision will make it more painful for all concerned, and prolong the candidate's own suffering.[9]

8. *Homosexual Attraction With Acts in the Minor Seminary.* Some individuals in this category may fall into the class of those who perform adolescent homosexual acts or acts through ignorance. When such acts persist, however, they can hardly be regarded as innocent. The homosexual attraction in some of these young men comes so close to bisexuality that one might be tempted to feel that such a condition was present. A boy going from grammar school into the minor seminary is achieving adolescence and is in a stage of developing sexuality. When sexual arousal takes place in an exclusively male environment as in play or games or even spontaneously from fantasy it is likely to be attributed by the individual to homosexuality, since he knows no other stimulus. Such a fear may lead to scrupulosity associated with a conviction that he is indeed a homosexual.

In more susceptible individuals the homosexual conviction may be accepted without anxiety. Such persons are more likely to yield to seduction by more aggressive students or attempts to seduce others. In spite of these homosexual feelings many students will have strong heterosexual inclinations. In such cases a clear and frank discussion of why they feel as they do is needed — that their sexual arousal under certain circumstances is normal, that they are deceived into believing that they are homosexuals by their exclusively male environment. They should be told that one cannot be a homosexual and have strong positive feelings for the opposite sex. With such an explanation many of these boys straighten out and develop proper control. If the condition persists, i.e., if homosexual acts persist in spite of warning and advice, it is probable evidence of a lack of desire to change or a more deeply seated state of homosexuality. Such individuals should be advised to leave.

9. *Sexual Attraction With Acts in the Major Seminary.* When the condition described in the previous section persists into the major seminary a more serious situation exists. This is especially true if it is associated with particular friendships. Homosexual acts occurring in the major seminary are sufficient evidence of a lack of proper will to conduct oneself in a manner suitable for the religious life and should be cause for asking the individual to leave.[10]

10. *Seduction of Other Individuals to Perform Homosexual Acts.* There may be differences of opinion in regard to certain aspects of homosexuality, but not many would doubt that an individual with a moral attitude which permits the enticement of others to serious sin would be unsuitable for the religious life. Anyone who has been exposed to a proper Christian education knows that sexual acts outside of marriage are sinful. He also knows that it is equally sinful to encourage others to commit sin. Add to this knowledge the fact that the individual who seduces others has a homosexual personality disorder and any doubt of his suitability will vanish.

11. *Sociopathic Personality With Pathologic Sexuality.* There are several varieties of sociopathic personalities which are described in the "Diagnostic and Statistical Manual — Mental Disorders." These were defined on pages 53f. No one would question that such individuals are unsuitable for the religious life, so no further discussion is necessary.

12. *Obsession of Being a Homosexual.* Whether such an obsession is based on latent homosexuality or is an obsessional neurosis is not pertinent to our present discussion. In such a case the individual is most unlikely to perform homosexual acts. He is, however, seriously neurotic and would for that reason be psychiatrically unsuitable for the religious life (see p. 124).

13. Recidivists, psychotic individuals with delusions of homosexuality, voyeurists, exhibitionists, transvestites, fetishists, masochists, sadists, pedophilists are mentioned only for the sake of completeness. They are obviously not suited for the religious life.

162

Father Connery has asked, "Why should heterosexuality be made a prerequisite for the religious life?"[11] This sounds like a good argument when one first reads it, but a little reflection leads one to believe differently. A vocation requires spiritual, physical, psychological, and moral fitness for the life which the subject is about to embrace. The homosexual is not psychologically fit for these reasons, among others:

1. Homosexuality is a personality disorder often associated with other psychiatric disorders (see Ch. 5). Heterosexuality is normal.

2. Homosexuals because of their condition are: (a) narcissistic; (b) fatalistic; (c) likely to submerge reason to emotional forces; and (d) deeply affected in their personality.

3. Although the state of homosexuality in itself is not sinful, the homosexual individual because of his fatalistic attitude frequently yields to the tendency. This is usually due to his "sick will" which is unable or unwilling to rule out such acts. If he is unable, he is too sick for the religious life; if he is unwilling, he is unsuitable.

4. Scandal is an ever-present possibility with the homosexual clergyman. Homosexual conduct reflects discredit on all members of the clergy. It would be rash for a homosexual to venture being responsible for such a danger.

5. For the homosexual to live in a religious community where he is constantly exposed to other males is quite likely to make his sexual problems too difficult for him to handle.

6. If any difficulty does occur, there is no return after ordination. There is the possibility that a homosexual with help may make an adjustment to marriage, but this outlet is closed to a priest. If his resistance fails, then he is likely to escape into sin or alcohol or both.

7. The pastor sets the whole moral tone of his parish, church, and school. The lapse of a homosexual priest could disrupt the whole religious community.

8. The homosexual cannot or can only vaguely understand heterosexual moral and marriage problems. There may be exceptions to this in individuals who make a special effort to understand.

9. If the clergyman slips or his condition becomes known, he may be subject to blackmail.

Conclusion

There are no hard-and-fast rules concerning the entry of the homosexually oriented individual into the religious life. Those concerned with selection should make reference to the suggestions made in this chapter. The homosexual who is giving consideration to the religious life should evaluate himself in this frame of reference. The effect of the grace of the sacrament of Holy Orders in such cases is not determinable. We cannot expect grace to work like magic. *Gratia perficit naturam.*

CHAPTER THIRTEEN

Homosexuality and the Law

The prevailing attitude toward homosexuals in the United States traditionally has been one of revulsion and hostility. This attitude has been reflected in the nation's legal codes. Presently there are thirty-two states where private homosexual acts entered into by consenting adults are punishable by long prison sentences. The person who appears homosexual or who acknowledges his — or her — homosexuality has as much trouble finding a job as a place to live. In the past he has been barred by the federal government from the U.S. Civil Service and Foreign Service; although these guidelines have recently been changed for federal employment, he may still find it difficult to obtain a job in private employment requiring a security clearance. The homosexual still encounters some form of discrimination whether with or without a legal basis.

In recent years, however, many of these laws, rules, and practices have been challenged in the courts and state legislatures. Leading the battle for full legal equality is a group of militant homosexuals rallying under the banner of the "Gay Liberation Movement."

The most recent major report on the rights of homosexuals in the United States is that of the National Task Force on Homosexuality, which was appointed by the National Institute of Mental Health in 1967 and placed under the direction of Dr. Evelyn Hooker, research psychologist at the University of California at Los Angeles. The Task Force observed in its final report two years later:

> Legal penalties relating to homosexual acts mean that the mental health problems of homosexuals are exacerbated by the need for concealment . . . and from the opprobrium of being in

violation of the law. . . . We believe that (a change in the law) would reduce the emotional stresses upon the parties involved and thereby contribute to an improvement in their mental health.[1]

A major argument against laws forbidding homosexual acts is that they are unenforced and almost unenforceable. It is asserted that arrests for private homosexual activity can rarely be made without exceeding the search and seizure limitations of the Constitution. The vast majority of homosexual arrests are for violations of "loitering" and "solicitation" laws. Many legal authorities doubt that these laws help to reduce the incidence of homosexual acts. Robert G. Fisher, associate professor of law at the University of Maryland, contends that "society's social and moral pressures" probably do more to stem homosexual behavior than fear of prosecution.[2]

Gay liberationists are almost unanimous in their condemnation of psychiatrists. They object that the position of such psychiatrists as Edmund Bergler, Irving Bieber, Albert Ellis, Charles Socarides, Lionel Ovesey, and Lawrence J. Hatterer — that homosexuals are emotionally disturbed — has been one of the roots of prejudice toward homosexuals in this country.[3]

It was noted in Chapter 3 that not all psychiatrists agree with the illness concept of homosexuality. "The truth is we really know very little about the origins of homosexuality," states Dr. Martin Hoffman, staff psychiatrist for the Center for Special Problems in San Francisco. "Psychiatrists who claim that all homosexuals are sick . . . apparently forget that members of any group who go to a psychiatrist are there because they are troubled people. . . ."[4] The biggest sign of change by the medical-psychiatric field in its approach to homosexuality was the decision by the American Psychiatric Association to remove homosexuality from its list of psychiatric disorders.

Though far from a vote of confidence, this action by the APA at least hinted at a turn away from discrimination.[5]

More acceptance by society is expected by homosexuals as a result of this change.

For example, when this statement was formulated last June, its author, Dr. Spitzer, foretold that the gay community would

166

draw the conclusion that psychiatry had at long last recognized that homosexuality is as normal as heterosexuality. We now know that is exactly the way the community has responded. As Ronald Gold, communications director of the National Gay Task Force, expressed, "We have won the ball game." Franklin E. Kameny, a lifelong spokesman, added, "This is going to make a big change in public attitudes."[6]

I have little doubt that changes will be made but they are unlikely to occur quickly. The latest edition of the American Civil Liberties Union Handbook[7] lists the following states as having changed their laws in regard to consensual adult homosexual acts:

1. California (1/76)   5. Hawaii
2. Colorado   6. Illinois
3. Connecticut   7. Ohio
4. Delaware   8. Oregon

These should be accurate but the Washington Chapter of Dignity gives seventeen as the number of states.[8]

A more recent figure was given to me by R. Adam DeBaugh, Social Action Director of the Universal Fellowship of Metropolitan Community Churches, which works for the education of the public in regards to homosexuality.[9]

1. Arkansas   10. Maine
2. California   11. New Hampshire (8/75)
3. Colorado   12. New Mexico
4. Connecticut   13. North Dakota
5. Delaware   14. Ohio
6. Hawaii   15. Oregon
7. Illinois   16. South Dakota
8. Indiana   17. Washington
9. Iowa (6/76)   18. West Virginia (6/76)

167

Gay activists feel that many states will continue to outlaw private homosexual acts between consenting adults until the public clearly demonstrates a lack of prejudice toward homosexuals. The states that have repealed or liberalized their laws did so, in most cases, as the result of total revision of their criminal codes rather than as a concerted effort to decriminalize homosexual behavior. In California, where the proposed change had to stand on its own merits in a separate bill in 1971, it was easily defeated in the state assembly. In Idaho, a new penal code adopted in 1971 was later scuttled when public attention focused on its homosexual provisions.[10]

Until recently, homosexuals and lawyers have looked to the judiciary rather than the legislature for relief. The American Civil Liberties Union (ACLU) in 1973 launched a Sexual Privacy Project aimed at attacking all criminal statutes that prohibit consensual sexual activity among adults or discriminate against persons who engage in such activity. The ACLU contends that such laws violate a homosexual's constitutional rights, including:

1. The right to privacy.
2. The First Amendment right of free speech and free assembly.
3. The Eighth Amendment prohibition against cruel and unusual punishment.
4. The due process and equal protection clauses of the Fourteenth Amendment.[11]

The ACLU predicts that in the near future the Supreme Court will rule on the constitutionality of laws restricting the private sexual behavior of consenting adults. Justice Thurgood Marshall already has said that he has "serious doubts whether the state may constitutionally assert an interest in regulating any sexual act between consenting adults."[12]

According to the Social Action Director of Metropolitan Community Churches, there is a bill due to be introduced sometime early in the 95th Congress in the House of Representatives called the "National Gay Civil Rights Bill." This is intended to be an amendment to the Civil Rights Act of 1964, which now only opposes discrimination against the "sex, creed or color" of any individual. Sex in this context refers only to gender. This new bill would be added to include opposition to the discrimination against the "sexual or affectional preference" of an individual. In the last Congress there were twenty-nine congressmen who supported the introduction of this measure; one of these has not been reelected.[13]

"Summary of Forms of Discrimination Against Homosexuals Prohibited by H.R. 166 — the 'Civil Rights Amendment of 1975' " gives the following definition of this term.[14]

> Definition-Section 11 of H.R. 166 defines the term "affectional or sexual preference" to mean "having or manifesting an emotional or physical attachment to persons of either gender, or having or manifesting a preference for such attachment." Therefore, the bill applies to persons maintaining heterosexual as well as homosexual preferences and would prohibit discrimination against either form of preference. However, since discrimination is not usually practiced against persons engaged in heterosexual relationships, the actual effect of the bill would be to protect homosexuals from various forms of discrimination because of their preference.

Sexual Offenses

It is difficult to summarize what is known concerning sexual offenses. There is little agreement among medical men who write on the subject. This is to some extent understandable because the problem is not the offense but the offender. The concern is with the person who committed the offense. Since no two individuals are alike it is important to realize that when one speaks of a sexual offense, he is not describing a definite entity but is speaking of a person who has committed a sexual crime. An exhibitionist, for example, is a person whose sexual disturbance will be conditioned by his basic personality. As one reads through the voluminous literature on the subject of sex and the law, there are many areas which immediately attract attention:

1. Much of the terminology of the law is outdated and confusing. This may lead to misunderstanding.

2. The laws as they are written do not seem to recognize that sexual crimes may be committed by individuals who are not sexual perverts.

3. There seems to be little recognition that pyromania, kleptomania, and similar conditions may be based on sexual pathology.

4. The courts tend to deal primarily with the sexual offense, although this may be, and frequently is, only a surface manifestation of a more deep-seated disorder.

These four points represent only a few of the problems with which a counselor is confronted when he looks at sexual anomalies vis-à-vis the law.

Another disturbing element that becomes apparent as one reviews the literature is that many of the sex laws seem to have been promulgated in anger in response to a public demand which had been aroused by some particularly flagrant sexual crime. Many laws appear to have been written hurriedly. As a consequence, the full implication of the statute was often not fully realized. The penalties imposed by such laws vary widely, some of the penalties being overly severe and others sending too many offenders to mental hospitals. Judges and legislators often decide who should be sent to mental hospitals without consulting psychiatrists who might be considered more likely to understand the value and limitations of such a procedure. As a matter of fact, the mere commitment of an individual to a mental hospital may serve little purpose. Many psychiatrists feel that there are no available techniques for the treatment of the sexual offender (see p. 178). Even if such techniques were available there would not be enough psychotherapists, in most instances, to apply them. Many sexual offenders are sent to the hospital "to remain until cured." This in spite of the fact that there are no criteria of cure. It is conceivable that under such laws the relatively harmless voyeur or exhibitionist could remain in the hospital for life for an offense whose penalty otherwise might be a few days in jail. The editors of *The Mentally Disabled and The Law* look at the problem in this way:

> The reforms that have swept our penal institutions from the eighteenth to the twentieth century have left mental institutions substantially untouched. Physical restraints have departed from the prison but are still standard equipment in many mental institutions. There is no doubt about the legality of sterilizing criminals, but sterilization, lobotomy and electric shock treatment are permissible for sexual psychopaths. Substantial constitutional questions can be raised about the right of a criminal court to expose a defendant to the possibility of sterilization, lobotomy, and electric shock treatment.[15]

One can hardly agree that our mental hospitals have not improved in the past two centuries. Even to one who is not a lawyer, however, the constitutional question which is raised sounds logical.

More study in academic circles needs to be devoted to the sexual offender so that more reasonable laws may be written. Public indignation and public guilt should not play any part in the writing of laws dealing with sexual offenses.

Surprisingly few persons, including attorneys, are aware that the "crimes against nature" can be extended to include married partners. The penalties for such acts may in some jurisdictions be exceeded only by the penalties for murder, kidnapping, and rape. There are court decisions on the applicability of these sodomy statutes, one of which goes so far as to uphold the conviction of a man for soliciting his wife to commit sodomy.[16]

Entrapment

Another aspect of the law which should be reexamined is that which permits entrapment:

> . . . A debatable police practice which reportedly exists in a number of localities is the use of plain-clothes officers serving as "decoys," waiting to be accosted by a homosexual, e.g., in public washrooms ("entrapment").[17]

This practice in itself would not be so bad, but in many instances the officer accosts the homosexual. After the proposition, when the homosexual shows interest, he is arrested and charged. Such practices, to the best of my knowledge, are not permissible in regard to other offenses. This would appear to be the opinion, also, of Clark and Marshall. These authors state:

> Public sentiment, as well as the leaning of the courts, is strongly against the practice of entrapping persons in the commission of crimes by the common detective methods. The practice has frequently been condemned by the courts, and there are reported cases in which it has been held, independently of any question of consent on the part of the person injured, that a criminal act may not be punishable if the accused was induced to commit it by active cooperation and instigation on the part of public detectives.[18]

171

A sound public policy requires that the courts shall condemn this practice by directing an acquittal whenever it appears that the public authorities, or private detectives, with their cognizance, have taken active steps to *lead* the accused into the commission of the act. It is perfectly legitimate and proper, however, to adopt devices and traps for the purpose of detecting crime and securing evidence, provided the device is not a temptation and solicitation to commit it. . . . [19]

As was said by Judge Marston in a Michigan case: "Human nature is frail enough at best, and requires no encouragement in wrong-doing. If we cannot assist another, and prevent him from committing crime, we should at least abstain from any active efforts in the way of leading him into temptation" (*Saunders v. People*, 38 Mich. 218, 222).[20]

I find myself in complete agreement with Judge Marston (see Case X, pp. 197ff).

Following the arrest of a prominent citizen in Washington, D.C., *The Washington Post* reported on February 3, 1965, that the National Capital Area Civil Liberties Union had written the District Commissioners to protest against "peephole" surveillance and the use of police decoys in civilian clothes to apprehend sex offenders. The use of "peepholes," the statement emphasized, is "an unreasonable invasion of the privacy of all members of the public who use" the facilities.

The Civil Liberties Union stated that the right of the public to be free of solicitation and annoyance would be better secured by patrols of uniformed policemen than by secret peeking and "enticement of a special undercover squad."

The *Post* also noted that the police defend their practices and feel they have been unjustly branded by such catchwords as "enticement" and "entrapment." This, the *Post* reported, is how one veteran officer sums up the case for the police:

People can't understand a problem they don't see. We see them — these men are predatory. They hang around theater, store, and public restrooms. It is a question of public decency. We're not interested in the non-predatory ones or acts in private. . . .

Apparently these methods are still being used, at least in the District of Columbia. There have been several arrests of con-

172

gressmen who have solicited (or been solicited) by police officers. Public attention was drawn to some of these because they were congressmen.

It would seem that "to the law, the homosexual offender may be a confirmed, casual, or even one-time homosexual. All are equal in having been caught in the act. The background of the offender makes no difference."

The Wolfenden Report — A Catholic Viewpoint

This is the name given to a proposal in Great Britain which recommended, in effect, that the law should make no effort to interfere in the purely private relations of adult homosexuals, male or female, where the element of seduction or duress is absent.[21] While this report has failed of adoption, the issue raised is of interest to clergymen because their position on such questions is often requested. They are asked whether they as clergymen can accept the recommendations of the report. The briefest and most authoritative statement on this subject was published by the Archbishop of London in the December 2, 1957, issue of the Westminster Cathedral *Chronicle*. The statement is as follows:

In view of the inquiries which have reached Archbishop's House following publication of the report of the House Office Departmental Committee on Prostitution and Homosexuality, His Grace the Archbishop of Westminster has thought it useful to set forth the following principles which should be borne in mind when consideration is given to the proposals regarding homosexual acts between consenting adults:

The civil law takes cognizance primarily of public acts. Private acts as such are outside its scope.

However, there are certain private acts which have public consequences in so far as they affect the common good. These acts may rightly be subject to civil law.

It may be, however, that the civil law cannot effectively control such acts without doing more harm to the common good than the acts themselves would be. In that case it may be necessary in the interests of the common good to tolerate without approving such acts.

It has, for example, invariably been found that adultery or fornication (which, however private, have clear public con-

173

sequences) cannot effectively be controlled by civil law without provoking greater evils.

Applying these principles to the question of homosexual acts between consenting males:

1. As regards the moral law, Catholic moral teaching is:
   a. Homosexual acts are grievously sinful.
   b. That in view of the public consequences of these acts, e.g., the harm which would result to the common good if homosexual conduct became widespread or an accepted mode of conduct in the public mind, the civil law does not exceed its legitimate scope if it attempts to control them by making them crimes.
2. However, two questions of fact arise:
   a. If the law takes cognizance of private acts of homosexuality and makes them crimes, do worse evils follow for the common good?
   b. Since homosexual acts between consenting males are now crimes in law, would a change in the law harm the common good by seeming to condone homosexual conduct? (See p. 167).

Ecclesiastical authority could rightly give a decision on this question of fact as well as on the question of moral law, if the answers to questions of fact were overwhelmingly clear. As, however, various answers are possible in the opinion of prudent men, Catholics are free to make up their own minds on these two questions of fact.

Although this may seem outdated, it is presented for its historical value.

Definition of Terms

A *sexual offense* for purposes of this discussion will be considered to be any act not included in the definition of legal marriage (given below). This may be inexact in terms of the laws of some jurisdictions but it is the consensus of those authors available to me. It will be stressed as the discussion proceeds that many acts which are now offenses could be made legal without harm to the public good, e.g., consenting sexual acts between mentally competent adults. This could decrease the possibility

174

of blackmail and eliminate the need of solicitation and force. The vast percentage of individuals who commit sex offenses which are punishable under our present law are not engaged in behavior basically different from that usual in the population as a whole: such persons are not necessarily to be regarded as psychiatrically ill or as a danger in the community.[22] Sexual acts outside of marriage which involve force or disparity of age should, of course, be regarded as illegal.

Psychiatrically, those sexual offenses which are significant are those which, following a repetitive obsessional fantasy, lead to compulsive acts of forced sexual assault either on adults or children. These may be of the nature of an unresisted urge (irresistible impulse). Such a compulsive sexual act is more often a surface symptom of a more profound psychic disturbance. As a matter of fact, the symptom may be less significant than other psychopathological features of the total personality which can only be detected by a thorough examination. Too, frequently, the more dramatic symptom gets attention because it shocks the public conscience.[23]

Classification of Sexual Offenders

For the sake of the uninformed student the following are some facts relating to sex offenders.

Many attempts have been made to classify sexual offenders into significant groups. Law-enforcement officials attempting to find a behavior classification frequently divide sexual offenders into: (a) those who are a menace, and (b) those who are only a nuisance.[24] The sociologist and the psychiatrist are likely to divide the offenders into: (a) traumatizing, and (b) nontraumatizing.[25]

Both of these classifications have value, but there is much difference of opinion concerning which offenses, except in a few categories, belong to each. It takes little imagination to realize that what would be traumatizing for one individual would not be for another. A neurotic young adolescent girl might be strongly affected by an exhibitionist, whereas a mature married woman might only laugh.

Another classification which has merit is that which divides offenses into those involving physical contact and those not in-

175

volving physical contact. From the legal standpoint, this is a useful classification.

Sexual offenders do not represent discrete types of individuals. Not all things are black or white. This is a fundamental principle of classification. It is the human mind which invents categories and tries to force the facts into manufactured groups. The world of people is a continuum in all its aspects. "We must bear this in mind because the sooner we realize this fact of human sexual behavior the sooner we shall reach a sound understanding of the realities of sex."[26]

Kinsey classified sex acts in regard to the outlet sought; i.e., he described six chief sources of orgasm in the male:

1. Masturbation.
2. Nocturnal emissions.
3. Heterosexual petting.
4. Heterosexual intercourse.
5. Homosexual relations.
6. Intercourse with animals.[27]

Although this grouping includes the vast majority of sexual outlets, it has little use for our present purpose.

Psychiatrists are more inclined to seek the underlying pathology rather than the sexual act which shows on the surface. Psychiatrically, most sexual offenders may be classified in the following categories:

1. Mental defectives.
2. Alcoholics.
3. Personality disorders — this would include most homosexuals.
4. Sociopathic personalities (psychopaths).
5. Psychoneurotics.
6. Psychotics.

From this listing it is apparent that the sexual offender may have one of a great variety of psychiatric syndromes. In reporting the sexual offender to the court, the psychiatrist should be expected to report the basic psychiatric difficulty. If, for example, a schizophrenic is accused of incest, the psychiatric report should list schizophrenia as the primary diagnosis and incest as a secondary one. This is desirable because the individual's responsibility for his offense depends upon his basic mental state, not upon his sexual offense.

For didactic purposes, it is helpful to realize that most sexual offenders have a more serious underlying disorder. In the courtroom this is of primary importance because the proper handling of the patient depends on it. For an insight into sexual offenses, an understanding of the sexual pathology is important (see Ch. 6).

Legally Permissible Sex Acts

A consideration of sex acts which are legally permissible will help to keep this discussion oriented. In most states, only penile-vaginal sexual relations are permissible under the law. These must take place between a man and a woman who are legally married to each other. To be legally married, the couple must be above the legal age for marriage; at the time of their marriage they must have been free to marry each other; and the act must be voluntary on the part of each. In some jurisdictions, both partners must be of the same race since miscegenation is forbidden.[28]

Any other sex act is illegal and as such is subject to punishment. Such a legalistic interpretation fails to take into account certain acts which are employed by many couples as sexually stimulating before intercourse. These include such sexual play as oral stimulation of the genitals, and intromission, spanking, biting, and so forth. These practices are so common, and from the moral standpoint so acceptable, that one cannot find fault with them, as long as they are acceptable to both partners and as long as the act ends properly (or is intended to end properly) with the ejaculation taking place in the vagina.

Legally, however, most such acts are forbidden and punishable. The reality of the situation is that, although such acts are unlikely to come to judicial attention, the possibility that they will do so through pique or anger is always present. This happened in the case of a masochistic woman who could only achieve orgasm if she was spanked or slapped by her husband. He was unable to understand her sexual needs but she could easily provoke him to anger and thus get him to slap her. On one occasion, she provoked him too much and he knocked out two of her front teeth. She swore out a warrant for assault because it was too much for her narcissistic ego to have her self-image distorted by loss of her teeth. A judge issued a peace warrant. Now her sex pleasure is nil because her husband is afraid to give her the sexual stimulus she needs.

177

The sexual psychopath laws are based on a number of assumptions, many of which are not proven. One of the principal assumptions is that there is a high degree of recidivism in sexual offenders. It seems to be assumed not only that the sex offender is more dangerous than other offenders, but that he has a higher rate of recidivism than other criminals. Statistics are incomplete in regard to recidivism but those available do not support this view.

Pacht *et al.,* reporting on their experience with the Wisconsin Sex Crimes Law, state:

> Of 1,065 male offenders examined under this law over a nineyear period, only 783 were found to be in need of specialized treatment. Parole experience with this group has been excellent. Of the 475 individuals granted parole through May 31, 1960, only 81 have violated that parole — a rate (17 percent) considerably lower than that found with parole granted to the general prison population. It is particularly noteworthy that only 43, or 9 percent of the total paroled, violated their parole by commission of a further sex offense. For individuals who have been discharged following a period of institutional treatment and parole supervision, the results are even more outstanding. Through May 31, 1960, 414 individuals were discharged from departmental control: only 29, or 7 percent of this group, committed a new offense following discharge.[29]

The Illinois Commission Report concludes: "Not more than about 5% of convicted sex offenders are dangerous."[30]

Paul W. Tappan reported:

> There are very few aggressive and dangerous sex offenders in the criminal population. Most of the deviates are mild and submissive, more an annoyance than a menace to the community.[31]

He concluded:

> Our sex offenders are among the least recidivous of all types of criminals. They do not characteristically repeat as do our burglars, arsonists, and thugs.[32]

In addition, other studies have concluded that the danger represented by sex offenders is overemphasized.[33] Not all authors agree. For example, Nielson states:

> . . . homosexuality very often is a condition dangerous to society. Well-meaning lay people often believe that homosexuality is an affair between adult responsible persons, who have a right to arrange their sexual life as they like. The fact is that most homosexuals decidedly prefer youngsters, whose mental health and social adaptation may be very much endangered by these assaults. Society has a right and duty to protect immature persons.[34]

Closely related to recidivism is the theory that sex deviates progress from minor sex crimes to major sex crimes of force and violence. The studies undertaken have proved that such is not the case.[35] For example, Guttmacher and Weihofen stated: "It is believed that sex offenders regularly progress from minor sex offenses such as exhibitionism to major offenses like forced rape. Such a gradation is almost unknown."[36]

All students of the subject do not agree on the findings recorded above. Davidson, for example, states that "both the dynamics of sex psychopathy and the actual statistics seem to contradict that optimism (that the sex offender is not a repeater)." Davidson, however, does not present any convincing figures.[37]

My own experience has been that, in offenses involving physical contact with another person, the rate of repetition is low. In those offenses not involving bodily contact, the repeat rate is quite high. Progression from a mild anomaly to a more serious one has not happened in my experience.

Legal Responsibility of the Sexual Offender

Some psychiatrists are reluctant to admit that anyone is "normal," i.e., "responsible," on the theory that no one is free of some personality distortion. They apparently feel that, since the act which has been committed is foreign to their own personality, it is abnormal. This is certainly not true. It is especially not true of sexual disorders. Rather, in many cases the sex offender should be considered responsible because his offense

179

represents absence of control over normal temptations and normal sexual desire.

I find it hard to accept the concept of sexual psychopathy. This concept seems to presume responsibility in all areas of conduct except the sexual.[38] Many of the statutes include the words "not insane." For example, the "sexual psychopath" is defined in the following terms in the District of Columbia Code:

> "Sexual psychopath" means a person, *not insane,* who by a course of repeated misconduct in sexual matters had evidenced such lack of power to control his sexual impulses as to be dangerous to other persons because he is likely to attack or otherwise inflict injury, loss, pain, or other evil on the object of his desires. [Italics are mine.][39]

In the District of Columbia, "insanity" is defined as:

> A condition in which an individual is incapable of managing his own affairs, and is not a fit person to go at large or to go unrestrained, and if permitted to remain at liberty in the District of Columbia, the rights of persons and property will be jeopardized or the preservation of public peace imperiled and the commission of crime rendered probable.[40]

If we substitute this meaning for the word "insane" in the above definition, the latter portion seems redundant. The District of Columbia Code implies that the sexual aspect of personality can be isolated from the rest. This is impossible. Man is a psychosomatic unit. He functions as a whole. The basic problem here is that the sexual manifestation is isolated from the rest of the personality. The individual should not be judged on the basis of symptoms.

If we can accept the statement made above that, psychiatrically, "those offenses which are significant are those which, following a repetitive obsessional fantasy, lead to compulsive acts of forced sexual assault on adults or children," then the problem of responsibility is greatly clarified. A few terms need definition:

Repetitive means frequently repeated.

Obsessional is derived from *obsession* which "is an overpowering, persistent, and irrational idea accompanied by feelings of tension and fear."[41] Such an obsession may, of course, vary in degrees of severity.

Fantasy or daydreaming is "the act or state of dwelling amid people or scenes created by the imagination."[42]

Compulsive is derived from *compulsion* which "is an overpowering, unreasonable urge to perform certain actions and is associated with the development of tension or anxiety if the act is not performed."[43]

Forced means against the wish or will of the individual attacked.

In evaluating responsibility, therefore, the above factors must be considered.

The question of "irresistible impulse" would certainly arise if these conditions are present. Each case must be considered on its own merits and there will quite likely be differences of opinion among psychiatrists. This will result because the degree of compulsion will be a matter of the judgment of each psychiatrist.

Enforcement of many of the present sex laws is impossible. The report of the Group for the Advancement of Psychiatry, for example, comments:

> Moreover, if they were strictly enforced we should be indeed witness to a colossal travesty reaching all levels of American society. Absolute law enforcement would perforce touch about 95% of the total male population. In contrast to the universality of illegal sexual behavior actually only a meager number of persons falls into the law enforcement net to suffer inordinate punishment for the conduct of many. In one category alone recent statistical studies bring to light that 6 million homosexual acts take place each year for every 20 convictions. In the area of extra-marital copulation the frequency to conviction ratio is nearly 30 to 40 million to 300.[44]

Conclusions

An attempt has been made to present in brief outline form the classification and basic psychopathology of sexual anomalies. It is suggested that legal and psychiatric terminology be brought up to date. This would include adopting the term *sexual*

181

anomaly as a substitute for sexual perversion because it is more meaningful. It is also suggested that consenting sexual acts between competent adults be legalized[45] as has already been done in certain states in America. This would bring the law into conformity with the modern knowledge of sex. Most sexual offenders are a nuisance rather than a danger to the community. The recidivism rate is low in offenses involving physical contact but high in noncontact offenses. An enlightened and progressive approach to these problems and the development of enthusiastic communication between the law and psychiatry can only lead to the betterment of society — the end which gives to each science its meaning.

CHAPTER FOURTEEN

Homosexuality and Governmental Agencies

> As long as homosexuals bear the stigma of criminality, not much progress can be made toward removing . . . other disabilities (such as job restrictions).
>
> Professor Walter Barnett[1]

Should homosexuality be a bar to service with the United States government or in the armed services? The homosexual's answer is "no." The *Interim Report* (see below) submitted to the Committee on Investigations stated "yes" in emphatic terms.

Homosexuality is not of itself a condition which would be psychiatrically disabling for employment in the government or elsewhere, unless it is associated with some other disabling psychiatric disorder.

The reason given for this discriminatory federal job policy is that the fear of exposure and possible arrest makes the homosexual particularly vulnerable to blackmail.[2] Gay activists, pointing to the growing numbers of persons who are willing to acknowledge their homosexuality, argue that the professed homosexual cannot be blackmailed with threats of disclosure to family, friends, or employer. With this I would agree if the fact appears on their personnel record. The government counters that he or she may still be subject to criminal prosecution and thus still remain susceptible to blackmail. Law Professor Walter Barnett of the University of New Mexico has observed that if the criminal law were repealed, the potential for blackmail would be eliminated.[3]

Government policy toward homosexual employees has important implications for their employment in other fields. As stated in the *Harvard Law Review:* "The government is a leader in liberal employment policies. As such, its attitude toward a given group is seen as the benchmark liberal evaluation of the group's employability. Hence, government exclusion of homosexual workers significantly jeopardizes their ability to find employment elsewhere."[4]

The first successful challenge to the government's policy of automatically disqualifying homosexuals from employment came in 1969 when the Circuit Court of Appeals for the District of Columbia refused to uphold the dismissal of Clifford Norton, a budget analyst for the National Space and Aeronautical Administration. The court ruled that the government must be able to show some specific connection between an employee's homosexuality and his ability to perform the job before his employment can be terminated. The courts have held in other cases that homosexuality *per se* is not a basis for denying a security clearance, for denying admission to the bar, or for denying an alien citizenship.[5]

Each case, however, should be evaluated on its own merits. A psychiatrist is often called upon to assist in the evaluation and diagnosis of the individual's sexual status. In the presence of sexual deviation the psychiatrist may be expected to give an opinion as to the specific traits of the individual such as his aggressiveness, overtness, and so forth.

Experience or special training may qualify the psychiatrist to give information as to whether the individual is a security risk in regard to a particular job. If the question arises, for example, whether this individual with his particular set of emotional problems is, or will be, a security risk *under certain circumstances,* the psychiatrist may be expected to answer. It should be clear that not all homosexuals are security risks at all times merely *because* they are homosexual. This is quite different from the situation noted in a newspaper article where it was reported that an agency had hired a psychiatrist to review its security regulations. The implication here was that only psychiatrically ill individuals are security risks. This is not true. The individual who needs money or has a grudge to work out is more likely to be a security risk than is the neurotic or even psychotic individual.

In the early 1950s, when there was great concern about Communist subversion among the employees of the executive branch of the federal government, a special investigating subcommittee was created by the U.S. Senate Committee on Expenditures in the Executive Departments to make recommendations concerning the employment of homosexuals by the federal government.

This subcommittee concluded that "those who engage in acts of homosexuality and other perverted sex acts are unsuitable for employment in the federal government. This conclusion is based upon the fact that persons who engage in such degraded activity are committing not only illegal and immoral acts, but they also constitute security risks in positions of public trust." They further stated that the "emotional instability and weak moral fiber" of the homosexual made him untrustworthy.[6]

Because it is impossible to weed out all sexual deviates from the government, some authorities have concluded that the government has made few efforts to purge itself of homosexuals. But during a four-month period in 1950, examination of the sexual behavior and preferences of government personnel resulted in the termination of employment of 382 individuals! This figure should be compared with the less than 200 terminations for sexual deviation in the preceding three-year period. In 1955, the State Department dismissed 104 suspected homosexuals. And, in a three-year period following the report of the Senate subcommittee, 1,700 applications for employment were rejected solely for reasons of homosexuality or other deviant sexual inclination. Such activity would indicate extreme vigilance in following the recommendations of the special subcommittee report.[7]

The United States government is not the only public employer which discriminates against the homosexual. It is the policy of most states and municipalities to deny homosexuals positions in civil service.

As noted in Chapter 3 the recent change in terminology by the American Psychiatric Association may slowly bring about a reevaluation of the place of the homosexual in the government service.

This optimistic view of the future for homosexuals must be taken with a grain of salt bearing in mind that the government moves slowly. In 1969 the U.S. Court of Appeals for the District of Columbia ruled that simple evidence of homosexuality is not sufficient justification for dismissal of a government employee. Speaking for the court, Chief Judge David Bazelon said that the position that the federal government should "enforce the majority's conventional codes of conduct in the private lives of its employees is at war with elementary concepts of liberty, privacy, and diversity."[8]

With this decision of the court in mind, I decided while I was preparing this book that I would contact the U.S. Civil Service Commission and see what information I could receive relative to the employment of homosexuals by the commission. It was not easy. Several calls resulted in being shifted from one desk to another until I finally reached an attorney who knew of a change in the regulations. He did not wish to be quoted verbatim but stated that sometime around December, 1974 (five years after the Court of Appeals decision), the Civil Service Commission changed its suitability and regulation guidelines so that homosexuals are now put in the same eligibility classification as other applicants, to be judged only on their conduct and job performance. This is intended to remove the previous practice that being a homosexual *per se* was sufficient grounds for denying an applicant admission to government service. In order to dismiss a homosexual applicant, according to this new change, one would have to show the nexus between the individual's sex preference and his job efficiency, as has been done in the past with heterosexual applicants.[9]

The *Civil Service News* put out by the U.S. Civil Service Commission in discussing this change stated:

A significant change from past policy — resulting from court decisions and injunction — provides for applying the same standard in evaluating sexual conduct, whether heterosexual or homosexual.

"Court decisions require that persons not be disqualified from Federal employment solely on the basis of homosexual conduct," the guidelines point out. "The Commission and agencies have been enjoined not to find a person unsuitable for Federal employment solely because that person is a homosexual or has engaged in homosexual acts. Based upon these court decisions and outstanding injunction, while a person may not be found unsuitable based on unsubstantiated conclusions concerning possible embarrassment to the Federal service, a person may be dismissed or found unsuitable for Federal employment where the evidence establishes that such a person's sexual conduct affects job fitness."[10]

186

It should be borne in mind that the government does move slowly. An article in *The Washington Star* on January 27, 1977, reported through Joseph Young and headlined "CSC Accused of Aiding Bias, Instead of Curbing It, in Job Promotions," stated in part:

A house report accuses the Civil Service Commission of having dismally failed in its responsibility to eliminate discrimination against minorities and women in government in promotions and upward mobility.

The hard-hitting report by the staff of the House subcommittee on equal opportunities . . . held two years of extensive hearings on the subject, charged that the CSC "has closed its eyes to the employment inequities that prevail in the federal government."

The report asserted that the CSC, instead of fulfilling its mandate in this program, had contributed to a clear pattern of "systematic discrimination" within the federal government. CSC was entrusted with the responsibility for wiping out discrimination in government under the 1964 Civil Rights Act as amended in 1973 and Executive Order 11478.

Blame for these "serious deficiencies was placed directly on the CSC," which the report said, "is primarily responsible for perpetration of discriminatory employment patterns in the federal government."

. . . It has not asserted its authority of Title VII (of the Civil Rights Act) to order agency heads to take the actions necessary to correct these employment inequities.[11]

Points for Government Investigators

In regard to government employment there are a number of facts that should be borne in mind:

1. Sexual disturbance does not *per se* make an individual a security risk. This is especially true if his condition is known and is recorded in his personnel file. I have known professionally many homosexuals who served long and faithfully in government service.

If the condition is known and on file, such an individual is not subject to blackmail or coercion, nor would it be possible for him to form cliques.

2. Many government investigators regard as diagnostically significant adolescent homosexual experiences which are frequently only experimental and investigative. Such experiences have little, if any, significance from the standpoint of adult homosexuality and should usually be discounted. It is only when homosexual tendencies persist into adult life that they become diagnostically significant. Recently some agencies have taken a more realistic view of these experiences and do not give them the significance they once did.

3. Personnel and security officers should bear in mind that homosexuality is a way of thinking and feeling, as well as a way of acting. Many individuals who perform homosexual acts are not homosexuals. They may prefer the acts for variety or thrill.

4. Individual sexual acts performed while under the influence of alcohol are frequently of little significance. There is one trait of homosexuals which seems unusual to the inexperienced. This is the characteristic of being self-accusatory; even when the condition is latent, they may act as if they were anxious to prove that they were genuine homosexuals. Information is offered which is frequently asserted against their own best interest. What has been said of homosexuality is equally true of other sexual deviations — bestiality, sadism, masochism, fornication, and so forth.

Each case must be decided on its own merits. The psychiatrist should not be expected to make moral judgments.

In the government setting, as well as in civilian life, homosexuals have functioned with distinction, and without disruption of morale or efficiency. Problems of social maladaptive behavior, such as homosexuality, therefore, need to be examined on an individual basis, considering the place and circumstances, rather than from inflexible rules.[12]

Attitude of Government to Homosexuality

The *Interim Report* previously mentioned stated the government's attitude on homosexuality quite completely.[13] It will be quoted in part for its historical value. It is quite lengthy, but enough of it will be given to show the attitude of the government when the report was submitted in 1950. There has been no subsequent report and my research turned up nothing more current.

The *Interim Report* stated the purpose of its investigation as follows:

> The primary objective of the subcommittee in this inquiry was to determine the extent of the employment of homosexuals and other sex perverts in Government; to consider reasons why their employment by the Government is undesirable; and to examine into the efficacy of the methods used in dealing with the problem.[14]

The investigation by the committee was apparently precipitated by concern over the number of homosexuals in the State Department. No information is available on the number of such individuals who may have actually been security risks. Interest in the matter was further stimulated by the defection of two alleged homosexuals from the British Foreign Service in 1950[15] and later two employees of the U.S. National Security Agency. Such defections have not knowingly occurred since.

The conclusion of the report is as follows:

> There is no place in the United States Government for persons who violate laws or the accepted standards of morality, or who otherwise bring disrepute to the Federal service by infamous or scandalous personal conduct. Such persons are not suitable for Government positions and in the case of doubt the American people are entitled to have errors of judgment on the part of their officials, if there must be errors, resolved on the side of caution. It is the opinion of this subcommittee that those who engage in acts of homosexuality and other perverted sex activities are unsuitable for employment in the Federal Government. This conclusion is based upon the fact that persons who indulge in such degraded activity are committing not only illegal and immoral acts, but they also constitute security risks in positions of public trust.[16]

Much of the possibility of blackmail and of the report's attitude toward lawbreakers would be eliminated if homosexual acts between mutually consenting adults were made legal and the fact of their homosexuality made known in their personnel record.

A further argument for changing the law is that it is a fertile source of blackmail. The Wolfenden Committee gave some figures for 1950, when thirty-two of the seventy-one cases reported to the police for blackmail were connected with homosexual offenses. Some years earlier, speaking in the House of Lords, Lord Jowitt, a former Lord Chancellor, disclosed that when he was Attorney General, 95 percent of the blackmail cases coming to his attention arose from homosexuality. In the United States the law has also lent itself to blackmail. Judge Ploscowe, in his book *Sex and the Law,* reported that in 1940 the New York District Attorney broke up a blackmailing ring that had been operating for twenty years in and around New York City. Twenty-three members were sent to prison.[17]

Intelligence Services

There are many homosexuals who have commented on how exceptionally well the homosexual adapts himself to intelligence work, how successful he is in the work, and how secure he is. One confirmed homosexual states: "I have found a large percentage of agents of all countries having homosexual tendencies, and I think they naturally gravitate to this form of work."

There are certain characteristics of the homosexual which adapt him for this work:

1. The homosexual by nature of his condition leads a double life, that of his sexual life, which must be kept under cover, and that of his normal relations with the world. The heterosexual person valuing his own dignity and integrity has difficulty leading a double life — unless he is a criminal — but for the homosexual to develop a third, fourth, or fifth personality and a life connected with it is not unusual. He frequently enjoys it, and the necessity of being all things to all men is usually easy for him. As one homosexual said:

> Of course, the danger here lies, as it did with me, that I spread myself out so thin, was so many different people — with a different story for each, that I began to lose touch with reality, losing the core of my own being and hence conflicting stories, attitudes, and so forth resulted. After this experience, in any new assignment I was obliged to keep to one or two targets, and not be a half dozen people, for in that way lies trouble for me, for I had

190

and could lose myself in my own different personalities, till I no longer knew where truth lay.

2. Much of the intelligence work appeals to the juvenile in the homosexual and may involve activity which the average individual would not really enjoy. But because the homosexual maintains certain adolescent attitudes throughout life, he can enter into this type of work fully and enjoy it. "We like the cloak and dagger element, the continuous childhood game of cops and robbers" (see the Ishmael theory, p. 73).

3. The homosexual has by necessity been forced to develop a kind of sixth sense about people — are they, or are they not? He develops a kind of intuitive sense which comes into full play in this type of work. He will go to endless lengths to find out secrets about people, for the power it gives him — this is always an element in the homosexual makeup; since by his nature he feels he cannot meet the world on its own values, he must triumph by this indirect way. The desire for power, channeled into this kind of work, can be of great value.

4. By the nature of his condition the practicing homosexual lives outside the law, and he may thus become a kindred soul with the many others who live outside the law — "the spy," the criminal, the deviate, the pervert.

I remember how well I found myself attuned to these people, murderers, thieves, etc., that I found during the war. It was always the feeling — I am one of you, and I understand you. My own homosexuality not only gave me entry into this group, but sympathy with them, which was of most valuable service during this period. I was one of them, rather than on the other side, and I continuously had the impression during this period that though they may not have known about me, they instinctively felt that I was one of them.

5. As has been pointed out, "fatalism" is one of the characteristics of homosexuality, and in the intelligence work this is important. Most homosexuals have it very strongly.

I found myself taking chances during the war period, rather wild ones, because of it, knowing the odds were against me, yet

191

one went through it with a kind of fatalism that usually led one to success. I found my so-called "normal associates" not able to do this — they wanted too many assurances.

6. The work itself demands a kind of lone-wolf attitude, which the homosexual has already, but which for "normal" people is sometimes very hard to accept. The agent must be able to accept social ostracism, lack of normal social life, lack of close friends, to carry out difficult assignments. Most men with families do not want this, but to the homosexual it is already second nature. Things such as this which are a problem to many "normal" agents never seem to be for the homosexual.

7. Because of his adolescent attitude toward life in general, the homosexual likes constant change, shifting environments, new people, new problems, which the heterosexual person tends to want to avoid as he grows older.

The Armed Forces

The armed forces have always made efforts to keep homosexual individuals out of their ranks.[18] The reason in the past was to prevent the discord which might arise in troops away from female company due to the presence of such individuals. This was particularly true in the Navy where the presence of a homosexual in a small crew at sea for a long time might result in sex acts or even in physical harm to the homosexual. The ultimate result would depend on the mood of the crew. It is only somewhat recently that the concept of danger to the national security has arisen as a bar to the presence of homosexuals in the military service.

What appears to be the latest revision of the regulations dealing with the deposition of homosexuals from the armed forces was made in 1959. Since the regulations in all services are more or less the same, I shall describe only those of the Air Force. *Mutatis mutandis,* what is said of the Air Force will apply with minor changes to the Army and the Navy.

Discharge of Homosexuals From the Air Force

Army Regulation 635-89, Air Force Regulation 35-66, Air Force Manual 39-12, and Secretary of the Navy Instruction 1900.9

proclaim that "homosexuality will not be tolerated" in the services.[19]

Par. 3. *What the Air Force Policy Is Regarding Homosexuality.*

a. Homosexuality will not be tolerated in the Air Force, and prompt separation of known homosexuals is mandatory. Participation in a homosexual act, or attempting to do so, is considered a very serious misbehavior regardless of whether the role of the person in a particular act was active or passive. Members of the Air Force serving in the active military service represent the military establishment 24 hours a day. There is no distinction between duty time and off-duty time as the high moral standards of the service must be maintained at all times. All members of the Reserve Components not serving on extended active duty are required to maintain the same high standards as active-duty personnel throughout the entire period of their military service.

Although Paragraph 3 mentions only acts or attempted acts, Paragraph 6 mentions *tendencies:*

Par. 6. *Who Will Report Acts of Homosexuality.*

It is the duty of every member to report to his commander any facts concerning overt acts of homosexuality or association or tendency by any member which may come to his attention. Any member who makes a false official statement for the purpose of initiating action to obtain a discharge pursuant to the provisions of this regulation or for any other purpose is subject to action under the appropriate articles of the Uniform Code of Military Justice (UCMJ).

West *et al.* point to a serious difficulty for professional people handling such individuals. Under this regulation the medical officer and even the chaplain to whom the homosexual may have gone in confidence is required to inform; if he does not, he violates the regulations:

Any physician or psychologist who learns of the existence in a patient of homosexual tendencies, or a history of a homosexual act at any time in the past, is duty-bound to report it to administrative officials. Needless to say, this requirement is a source of great distress to psychiatrists, and leads to considerable soul-searching.[20]

I cannot imagine either the medical officer or the chaplain making such a revelation, but their failure to do so makes them subject to disciplinary action.

Paragraph 12 of Air Force Regulation 35-66 describes the classification of cases:

Par. 12. *Classification of Cases.*

Cases are generally classified as follows:

a. *Class I.* Those cases where a member of the Air Force has engaged in one or more homosexual acts accompanied by assault or coercion, as characterized by an act in or to which the other person involved did not willingly cooperate or consent, or where consent was obtained through force, fraud, or actual intimidation or where the homosexual act was committed with a minor, regardless of whether the minor cooperated.

b. *Class II.* Those cases where a member of the Air Force has engaged in one or more homosexual acts, or has proposed or attempted to perform an act which does not fall into the Class I category. It is emphasized that no distinction is made in the administrative handling of cases of alleged participation in homosexual acts based upon whether the role of the person in any particular act was active or passive.

c. *Class III.* (1) Those cases where a member of the Air Force exhibits, professes, or admits to homosexual tendencies, or habitually associates with persons known to him to be homosexuals, but there is no evidence that he has, *while a member of the Air Force,* engaged in one or more homosexual acts, or has proposed or attempted to perform an act of homosexuality. (2) Those cases where a member, *prior to becoming a member of the Air Force,* exhibited, professed, or admitted to homosexual tendencies, or habitually associated with persons known to him to be homosexuals, or who engaged in one or more homosexual acts, or proposed or attempted to perform an act of homosexuality, but *there is no evidence that he has, while a member of the Air Force,* engaged in or proposed or attempted to perform an act of homosexuality.

The Class I cases are those generally recognized as criminal acts and which deserve punishment. Any revision of the law

194

would undoubtedly, and should, single out this type of offense as criminal. Class II and Class III involve the danger of including the type of case described on page 197 and create the danger of a gross injustice. In the case of military personnel arrested by civilian authorities, great care must be exercised that their arrest did not come about by a form of entrapment (see Case X, below). It would seem that in Class II and Class III, if the individual is not to be retained in the service, his discharge could be handled at a local level (see pp. 196f).

Par. 4. *Character of Discharge Furnished Members Processed for Discharge Under This Regulation.*

The character of discharge for all classes defined in paragraph 12 will be similar, without distinction as to sex or status.

a. *Class I.* Since trial by general court-martial is usually appropriate for cases in this class, the character of discharge will be that imposed by court-martial action.

b. *Class II.* Discharge Under Conditions Other Than Honorable (undesirable) for airmen or Discharge Under Other Than Honorable Conditions for officers, unless the particular circumstances in a given case warrant a General or Honorable Discharge.

c. *Class III.* Discharge with an Honorable or General Discharge, as appropriate to the particular circumstances in a given case.

I would like to make my own position clear. I do not intend to convey the impression that I believe that the homosexual should usually be retained in the armed forces. This is no place for a homosexual, male or female. My objection is that in so many instances the homosexual is penalized only for *being* a homosexual, not necessarily for *acting* like one. I also feel he should not be penalized by the armed forces for acts which he committed prior to entry into the military service, as happened in Case X (see below).

Drs. West, Doidge, and Williams discuss revision in the present regulations designed to eliminate these injustices. Bowman and Engle have also stated "that the most reasonable view is that in which the homosexual disturbances are seen as problems of individual morality and psychology, and that mutually consenting adults engaging privately in any non-dangerous sexual act should not be considered criminal."[21]

The revisions suggested by West *et al.* are:

1. *Punitive official attitudes should be modified.*
Military law is sufficient to punish acts which might threaten the community; therefore, there is no reason why the individual should be punished because he has homosexual feelings.

2. *Extensive routine investigations should be eliminated.*

The lengthy investigation of the OSI (Office of Special Investigations) required by the present regulations (see Sec. b., Par. 11a) is in most cases unnecessary. It is expensive and keeps the airmen much longer than necessary in the service. This is especially true of self-confessed homosexuals and of those whose acts occurred before they entered the service. In these cases "a man who is unsuitable because of his immaturity (marked only in part by homosexual impulses) can be sent home with a General Discharge soon after his condition is brought to light, just as though he were unsuitable because of enuresis, or stuttering, or lack of physical stamina."[22]

3. *Separations should be on the basis of the primary disorder.*

Certainly within the first 60 days of service General Discharges could efficiently be utilized to separate those immature, passive-aggressive, or inadequate persons who happen to have homosexual symptoms as well as those who haven't.[23]

4. *The special stigma should be eliminated.*
There is no reason for the specification on an individual's discharge that the reason was homosexuality, unless this occurred as a result of a general court-martial.

5. *Investigation should be a benign procedure.*
"Great care should be exercised to guard the dignity and person of the individual being investigated."[24]

6. *Present retention policies should be given a fair trial.*
These policies are not given a fair trial if the retention is decided upon after a long period of investigation during which the individual is removed from his job and kept in detention — Air Force Regulation 35-66, Paragraph 15d (a); also Paragraph 20d (4). By this time the man is likely to be disgusted and discouraged and returns to his outfit with the stigma of having been

under investigation for homosexuality. The local commander could very expeditiously handle most Class II and Class III cases while the individual was in a duty status.

Case X

The subject of this case is twenty-three years of age and is a white male. He is unmarried. His case is presented, among other reasons, to show the element of entrapment.

We are all interested in your case and are all students of the type of problem which you present. Would you, therefore, tell us as completely and frankly as you can why you are seeking help?

I will try to answer your questions. I am here because I was arrested. For this, I was given an undesirable discharge from the military service, and I would like to have that changed.

Tell us what happened.

About four months ago I met a man in the recreation room of a large club. It turned out later that this man was a police officer, but at that time it seemed to me, by his actions and facial expressions, that he was a homosexual. There was no bodily contact between us. The man seemed to be trying by his conversation to get me to make a sexual proposition, but since I thought he had a room in the club, when he asked, "What do you want to do?" I merely said, "Let's go up to your room and find out." Anyway, we took an elevator to the fourth floor. In the corridor he kept asking questions which I now realize were intended to get me to incriminate myself. He finally said, "If you take it in the rear, I'll blow you" (sodomy). After more such remarks were made by the officer I finally said, "Yes, I will." I said "yes" not because I was really intent on doing anything, but because I was lonely and wanted to talk to someone. As soon as I said "yes," the man identified himself as a police officer and "took me into custody." I wasn't sure whether this was the same thing as being arrested, but in any case I went along with him and was brought to a police station and put into a cell. I was quite upset by the whole thing; it was the first time I had ever been "taken into custody" and I wasn't at all sure what was going to happen to me. Confused as I was, I remember that a few hours later, I was questioned by the same officer who was still in plain clothes. I admitted to him that I had had homosexual relations before. I remember that there was at least one other officer in the room at the time I was questioned. I believe that at this time I was fingerprinted and an FBI record was made.

Then what happened?

I spent that night in the police station and the next day I was turned over to the armed forces police who took me to an Army stockade. Here I was questioned by a man whose name I don't remember. He told me that as a homosexual I was a security risk and, therefore, would probably be released from the service. He also told me that I ought to admit to being one now, because it would be easier on me since the psychiatrist would find out anyway. I seem to remember that he also told me that I might stand a chance of being cured of my homosexual tendencies and be allowed to remain in the service. With this promise of a cure, I remember dictating a list of ten or fifteen of my previous homosexual contacts. Of these only two were while I was in the service; these were with civilians, however, and not with military personnel. I remember signing this dictation which, at the time, I did not know was a confession. I remember signing a waiver or some sort of statement which I understood to be my rights under the Fifth Amendment. To the best of my understanding, the story I dictated and signed was not a confession but something which was necessary before I could be referred to a psychiatrist who would cure me so that I could stay in the military. I never saw this man again.

The next day, while still under military arrest, I remember being taken to a military hospital for a psychiatric interview. I remember that no one in the Psychiatric Division seemed to know what to do with me — at least it seemed that way. No one questioned me or counseled me in any way. Later they took me to the MP post at the hospital where I was given a tongue-lashing by an officer. At this point I realized that there was to be no attempt at cure and that I had been tricked into signing a confession.

Someone at the MP post gave me an emergency pass to return to my station, since I was already technically AWOL.

About a month later I was called in by my commanding officer, who told me that he had received notification of my "confession" and that as a homosexual I would be separated from the service. He asked me if I would agree to see the base psychiatrist. He said that this was the procedure in cases like mine. I agreed. I remember repeating the whole story of my homosexual life to two doctors and an enlisted man social worker. I remember being given a Rorschach test by an enlisted man and being interviewed very briefly by a psychiatrist who offered no solution to my problem.

Shortly after this I remember signing a paper whereby I would receive an undesirable discharge and would not have to face a court-martial. Two months later I was released from the service with an undesirable discharge.

This is all I remember. I don't want sympathy — I just feel that what was done was unfair and, since I most probably was mentally unbalanced at the time I signed the confession, that it was illegal. I am willing to return to the service or finish out my two years in the reserves. I do not feel that being a homosexual is moral, but, on the other hand, I do not feel that I ever was or will be a security risk to my country.

The purpose of this examination, then, is to help you get a better discharge from the service or to return to active duty?

That is true.

You have given a good description of the circumstances of your arrest and discharge; now tell us more about yourself. First tell us — do you consider yourself a homosexual?

Well, frankly I must admit that I have had homosexual experiences, if that makes me a homosexual; but I have liked girls, too.

Tell us about your early habits in regard to sex.

I masturbated for about two years — that is, from fifteen to seventeen years of age. At first it gave me a sense of physical

199

pleasure, but around seventeen it stopped having any attraction for me. I started to date girls about this time.

Did you ever have intercourse with a girl?

No, I never did. It seemed wrong to destroy the girl's morals by committing such acts. I went steady with a girl in college — she was about my age. We petted some — I wanted to see what it was like — but I never felt any excitement or pleasure as far as sex was concerned.

When did you perform your first homosexual act?

My first homosexual act was the summer after I finished high school. I met a man in the restroom of a railroad station. I don't remember who made the suggestion. We performed an act of mutual masturbation. I don't recall the next incident exactly, but it consisted only of fondling the genitals of another man. During my first one and one-half years in college, I met some very fine people, and I hoped that I was normal again. However, later in the second year I met a man with whom I performed another sexual act and since that time, I have been both the active and passive partner in quite a few homosexual acts. I don't remember how many.

Tell us more.

When I was ten or twelve years of age, while I was masturbating, I would have fantasies of sex with both men and women. At that time, while I generally thought I would prefer homosexual activity, I hoped I would become heterosexual. My first actual homosexual experience was at the age of seventeen or eighteen. At that time the acts were mostly mutual masturbation with other fellows I happened to meet. I never did have any long affair with any one person. I also had "occasional" experience of oral-genital (fellatio) and anal-genital (sodomy) contact in which I was both the active and the passive partner, but I found these experiences revolting.

200

If you found these contacts so repulsive, why did you continue?

I really don't know, but in spite of the distaste, it seemed that I had a strong tendency in that direction. It never happened before, but since I was in the service I have been teased by the other fellows because of my mannerisms; but none of them knew that I was a homosexual. I never did have any relations with other soldiers, only with civilians.

Thinking back to your early life, can you recall any older man who might have touched your genitals?

When I was very small I can remember being very strongly attached to some man, but I don't recall who it was. It could have been an uncle or someone else in the family. I have always tried to be masculine, but those other "urges" got the better of me at times.

Were there other children?

There were six of us; I was the fourth child. I have three older brothers who are all married. I came next, then I have a fourteen-year-old brother and an eleven-year-old sister who both live with my parents. We got along as well as most families, I suppose; I stayed a bit to myself, but they didn't seem to mind. My family was healthy, except that my mother has a brother who is in a mental hospital. I used to be his favorite before he got sick. I haven't seen him for two or three years now. As far as I know, none of my older brothers had any homosexual experiences.

How old were you when you went to school?

I was five years old when I started in kindergarten. After a year I went to grade school. I got along well with my teachers and classmates and made good grades all through school. In high school I started to realize that there was something twisted inside me, because I was not attracted to girls, but I seemed to be to boys like I thought I should be to girls. Out of curiosity I got some books to find out about homosexuals. These feelings persisted all through college.

When did you enter the service?

I was drafted into the military service in March, 1956, at the age of twenty-one. While in basic I got along very well because I felt that if I could get along in the service, it would prove that I was as much of a man as the next person. On several occasions I withstood more harassment and physical strain than some of the other fellows could. However, because of my effeminate characteristics, particularly my talk and my body, I was constantly teased by the fellows in the barracks. It was all friendly, however. While in the service I made no advances toward any of the men — in fact I had no desire to do so. Since this incident when I was arrested, I don't think the fellows kid me as much. I don't know why they don't, because no one knows what happened.

Is there anything else you would like to tell us?

No. Do you think I can be helped?

Discussion of the Case

Many of the clinical features of this case are fairly typical. No case is really completely typical. It shows the features of early seduction, adolescent puzzlement concerning the direction of the sex drive, heterosexual experimentation, and a military handling of a case of homosexuality. One wonders what would have happened in this case if counseling or therapy had been attempted in adolescence when he "was reading the books on homosexuality." His heterosexual experimentation brings to mind the words of the fictional psychiatrist who commented: "I enjoyed sex with them (girls), I was proud of this, but they couldn't stimulate my mind, nor was I capable of loving them."[25]

The arrest features of this case are in my mind rather typical of entrapment (see p. 171). In this case the police officer does not "catch" the individual in the illegal act, but by his own actions traps him into an illegal act and then arrests him.

202

One wonders also if an undesirable discharge was indicated for a man who had performed no acts with military personnel. It seems, rather, that he was being punished for being a homosexual. As I have indicated before, the military establishment is no place for homosexuals, no more than is a boys' camp, a Turkish bath, or similar all-male establishment. My only point is that too frequently the homosexual seems to be penalized only because he is a homosexual.

A test of these rules was exhibited in a recent case of a Vietnam veteran who was discharged from the Air Force because he is a homosexual. Leonard Matlovich tried to show that a person could be loyal to duty, brave in difficulties, intelligent and capable as well as being a homosexual. He was quoted in the November 17, 1976, issue of *The Washington Post*. He stated in part:

> I want to help people understand that sexual stereotypes are no more valid than racial stereotypes . . . that there are gay people who are virtually celibate and gay people like myself with very traditional moral values. . . .[26]

He was discharged from the service a year earlier than this article appeared after a landmark civil rights case that, at this writing, is still under appeal.

Summary

There is no evidence to show that homosexuals are always security risks. A change of existing laws to make homosexual acts (performed in private between consenting adults) legal would solve most of the objections proposed for their employment in the government. Recently cases indicate this is being done with increasing frequency.

There is no place in the armed forces for homosexuals because of the nature of their sexual drive, not because they are necessarily security risks. Many so-called "fraudulent" enlistments would be avoided if greater assurance could be given that the information supplied at the time of enlistment in regard to sexual tendencies would be treated confidentially.

CHAPTER FIFTEEN

Homosexual Organizations

There has always been a need for homosexual organizations. Over the many years they have varied in their expressed purposes. Several years ago things were likely to be very rough, including torture and death, for persons caught in a homosexual act or for those who were even suspected of being homosexual. Organizations during those times were likely to be minimal and very secretive due to the risks involved to their members. A rather informative history on this period is given in *The Love That Dared Not Speak Its Name*.[1]

A more liberated book, *On Being Different, What It Means To Be A Homosexual*, written by Merle Miller in 1971, indicates relief from this period of fear. He states:

> It took me a long time to do it (admit his homosexuality), but now that I have, I realize how stifling the air has been all these years. I may not be freer, but I'm a lot more comfortable, a lot less cramped.[2]

This solitary nature of the homosexual apparently went on for centuries. But then gay people, as in the case of Mr. Miller, began to "come out of the closet." There were many active homosexual groups which "surfaced." There is no need to attempt to describe them all. I shall only name the more important ones in an effort to portray what is available for the homosexual and the history of homosexual organizations.

Most homosexual organizations seem to have been formed for one or all of three purposes: (1) to improve the social position of the homosexual and support each other; (2) to promote a better public image of the homosexual; and (3) to improve his legal status. It must be emphasized that such homosexual organizations are not only composed of homosexuals but also of their friends and supporters.

Historically, there have been three large groups for homosexuals and their friends:

1. One, Inc.
2. The Mattachine Society.
3. The Daughters of Bilitis.

1. One, Inc. is the oldest active national organization for homosexuals and their friends. It was established on October 15, 1952, around the same time as the Mattachine Society and the Daughters of Bilitis. However, it has lasted longer on a national level and has been known as a powerful and influential group. W. Dorr Legg was its first chairman and still remains an integral person in the organization.

The group is primarily dedicated to educating the public as well as homosexuals on the subject of homosexuality and they have gained the respect of many for developing their thinking on an intellectual level. They appear to be interested in seeking out the truth about homosexuality and in doing so have furthered the cause of homosexuals.

One, Inc. founded the One Institute of Homophile Studies with the stated purpose "to sponsor, supervise and conduct educational programs, lectures and concerts."[3] In line with these goals, speakers are available as well as consultants to set up lectures, supervise programs, and serve on committees in making their expertise and research available to those who wish it. Counseling is also provided.

The institute contains a large reference library and carries out research on all aspects of homosexuality. It has published the *One Institute Quarterly* as well as "One — The Homosexual Magazine of America" which has been described as containing "fiction, poetry, essays, scientific research, legal reports, written for readers of all ages and for acceptance in every home." It also publishes and sells books and other publications on male and female homosexuality.

In a letter to the author, the director of One Institute stated:

> We tend to be highly respectful of biologically oriented approaches, far less so of psychoanalytical methods, highly critical of religiously based counseling.[4]

Since the primary focus of One, Inc. is education and research, as opposed to mutual support of other gays, it does not appear to have local chapters and meetings as in other groups which branch out from its national headquarters in Los Angeles.

As a group it has not adopted the militant or activist techniques of newer groups, but continues to take a more subtle approach to the problems. This could possibly explain why, in recent years, it has not been as influential in the same way as it once was.

2. The Mattachine Society was founded in San Francisco in 1950. It was named after the court jester of the Middle Ages who dared to speak the truth in the presence of his lord and master. The aims and principles of the society were initially set forth as follows in the *Mattachine Society Today*, an explanatory brochure issued by what used to be their national headquarters.

To aid the variant through integration:
1. Since variants desire to be accepted by society, it behooves them to assume community responsibility. They should, as individuals, actively affiliate with community endeavors, such as civic and welfare organizations, religious activities, and citizenship responsibilities, instead of attempting to withdraw into an invert society of their own. For only as they make positive contributions to the general welfare can they expect acceptance and full assimilation into the communities in which they live.

2. The long-term aid is not only to support well-adjusted variants with full integration into society, but to give social aid to maladjusted homosexuals for their own welfare as well as that of the community.

To conduct a program of civil action:
1. To secure the active cooperation and support of existing institutions such as psychology departments of universities, state and city welfare groups, mental hygiene departments, and law-enforcement agencies in pursuing the programs of education and integration.

2. To contact legislators regarding both existing discriminatory statutes and proposed revisions and additions to the criminal code in keeping with the findings of leading psychiatrists and scientific research organizations, so that laws may be promulgated with respect to a realistic attitude toward the behavior of human beings.

3. To eliminate widespread discrimination in the fields of

employment, in the professions and in society, as well as to obtain personal social acceptance among the respectable members of any community.

4. To dispel the idea that the sex variant is unique, "queer" or unusual, but is instead a human being with the same capacities of feeling, thinking, and accomplishment as any other human being.

General aims:

1. To accomplish this program in a law-abiding manner. The Society is not seeking to overthrow or destroy any of society's existing institutions, laws, or mores, but to aid the assimilation of variants as constructive, valuable and responsible citizens. Standard and accepted democratic processes are to be relied upon as the technique for accomplishing this program.

2. The Society opposes indecent public behavior, and particularly excoriates those who would contribute to the delinquency of minors and those who attempt to use force or violence upon any other person whatsoever.

3. The Mattachine Society is a non-sectarian organization and is not affiliated with any political organization. It is, however, unalterably opposed to Communists and Communist activity and will not tolerate the use of its name or organization by or for any Communist group or front.

The society put out a monthly, *The Mattachine Review.* At that time it stated that it "seriously examines and discusses human sex problems, especially homosexuality, with emphasis on legal, medical, social, religious and cultural aspects."

The Mattachine Society was more or less a national organization until 1961. At that time the Washington Mattachine Society was formed in following with other chapters in other large cities which had begun area councils in breaking away from the national headquarters. These area councils are presently independent of each other. They have no national offices or officers. However, they do cooperate with each other and with other gay organizations.[5]

4. The Daughters of Bilitis no longer exists as a national organization. In a current book, *From the Closets to the Courts,* Ruth Simpson states that sometime toward the end of 1971 it "ceased functioning."[6] It appears that they, too, have formed independent groups throughout the country which are offshoots of the original national organization.

The Daughters of Bilitis was founded in 1955 in San Francisco as the first Lesbian organization formed in the United States. It got its name from a collection of Lesbian love poems by Pierre Louys, *The Songs of Bilitis*.[7] To show what the organization was like in its former status, I will quote from a communication with the organization's director of public relations a few years ago.

DOB [The Daughters of Bilitis] is still working with the education of the Lesbian herself rather than the education of the public. We feel that social acceptance will come more easily if the homosexual accepts himself or herself as a human being and is able to work in and with the total societal structure. We have, however, been doing more and more actual public relations work — speaking before groups and appearing on radio and television programs. Our primary means of communication remains THE LADDER which is growing in circulation all the time and is now available in many newsstands, bookstores and libraries throughout the nation.[8]

They published *The Ladder* on a monthly basis. It was regarded as "a sounding board for various points of view on the homophile and related subjects and does not necessarily reflect the opinion of the organization."[9]

"Coming out of the Closets"

On June 28, 1969, the New York police raided a gay bar in Greenwich Village, the Stonewall Inn. This marked the beginning of "gay activism." To quote an observer of the "Rebellion":

It was fantastic. The crowd was a fairly typical weekend crowd, your usual queens and kids from the sticks, and the people that are always around bars, mostly young. But this time instead of submitting to the cops' abuse, the sissies fought back. They started pulling up parking meters and throwing rocks and coins at the cops, and the cops had to take refuge in the bar and call for reinforcements. . . . . It was beautiful.[10]

In 1970, the first anniversary of the "Stonewall Riots," 5,000 to 15,000 gays of both sexes marched into Central Park for a "gay-in." Other smaller demonstrations took place in Chicago and Los Angeles, "men with their arms around men and women kissing women chanting 'Shout it loud, gay is proud,' 'Three-five-seven-nine, Lesbians are mighty fine,' carrying signs that said 'We Are the People Our Parents Warned Us Against,' singing 'We Shall Overcome.' "[11] This incident in particular gave gays courage to "come out of the closet" and fight for their rights.

Regional Homosexual Organizations

Within a month of the "Stonewall Rebellion" the first Gay Liberation Front group was organized in New York City. (The Gay Liberation Front consists of isolated groups in various cities throughout the country who tend to be militant and political with no national headquarters.) To quote from an undated flyer which was passed out on the streets of Washington carrying the caption "Are You Homosexual?":

> Gay Liberation is dedicated to fighting for fair treatment for homosexual men and women, to spreading knowledge of what homosexuality truly is, to opposing discriminatory laws and regulations, and to winning for homosexual men and women decent employment rights. Gay Liberation is here today because we refuse to remain silent any longer. We are determined to win the right to a free, open, loving life.

By the second anniversary of the "Rebellion" other militant homosexual organizations, including the Gay Activists' Alliance, had sprung up across the country.[12] This group has no national office and is at most a loose organization of autonomous groups in the United States. Other such independent groups are the Gay Political Union and the Gay Academic Union, the latter being formed to coordinate activities on several college campuses aimed at: (1) opposing discrimination against homosexuals in academia; (2) supporting individuals on campus in the process of "coming out"; (3) promoting new approaches to the study of gay experience; and (4) encouraging the teaching of gay studies[13] (see p. 25).

Gay Militancy

The emergence of the Gay Liberation Movement brought out many gay militants and activists of both sexes. On May 14, 1970, *The Washington Post,* in an article headlined "Gays and Dolls Battle the Shrinks," reported in part:

> The Gay Liberation and their women allies outshrieked the headshrinkers today and took over an American Psychiatric Association session on sex.
>
> Before the morning was over, the 500 psychiatrists who gathered [in San Francisco] to hear scientific studies on sexual problems, demonstrated that they are as prone to act out antisocial behavior as anyone else.
>
> One distinguished Boston psychiatrist, Dr. Leo Alexander, grabbed a Women's Liberation member who was invited onto the stage. When she denounced his action from the podium, Dr. Alexander lunged on stage after her. He had to be restrained and led back to his front row seat.
>
> The Women's Liberation member, who identified herself as "Judy X," said, "This man wants to put his sadistic hands on me."

Such tactics could hardly be expected to gain mutual understanding. As the article concluded, "The meeting went downhill from there."[14] This was not an isolated instance. Such conduct of disruption was repeated at a theological seminar on homosexuality at the Catholic University of America, held from November 9 to 13, 1970. *The Quicksilver Times,* a local "underground" paper, reported the incident.[15]

> At a session of the week-long conference at Catholic University, about 35 members of the D.C. Gay Liberation Front entered the auditorium in small groups, took seats, and waited until the conference organizer, Dr. John R. Cavanagh, was about 10 minutes into mumbling through a treatise on how latent homosexuality can sometimes cause "marital discord" in heterosexual marriages.
>
> Then one of the gay militants stood up and yelled, "This is a bunch of bullshit." The gay women and men took up the chant,

"Bullshit! Bullshit!" They moved toward the stage where Cavanagh stood glowering and flustered, trying futilely to continue reading his speech.

One of the gay brothers — chosen earlier by lot, to avoid "leadership" hang-ups — read a statement while the other gays stood behind him, with their arms around each others' shoulders.

The gay liberators came down from the stage, banners flying, and paraded around the auditorium. They held hands and chanted such slogans as "Gay power to the gay people," and marched happily out of the room and onto the campus where they chanted some more, to the amazement of a knot of onlookers, and drove off.

The following is the full statement that was read to the conference by the chosen "spokesman" of the gay liberators.

We are homosexuals!

As members of the Gay Liberation Front, we deny your right to conduct this seminar.

It is precisely such institutions as the Catholic Church and psychiatry which have created and perpetuated the immorality myths and stereotypes of homosexuality which we as homosexuals have internalized, and from which we now intend to liberate ourselves.

As homosexuals struggling to be free, we make the following statements:

1. We demand that you stop examining our homosexuality and become homosexual yourselves (later explained as meaning that the participants should examine their own sexuality, and accept any homosexual feelings they had).

2. We do not seek acceptance, tolerance, equality or even entrance into your society with its emphasis on "cock power" (read *male supremacy*). Liberation there would be impossible. For centuries, this system of power, dominance and possession has produced only genocidal wars, the profound oppression of women, and racial minorities, and our own repression as homosexuals.

3. We hold the Catholic Church and the institution of psychiatry responsible for political crimes committed against homosexuals, such as imprisonment, blackmail, beatings, psychological rape, and loss of economic security. We also feel every gay suicide is a political murder!

211

As representatives of the sexist society that daily oppresses us, you are incapable of speaking for or defining the quality of our lives.

ONLY WE AS HOMOSEXUALS CAN DETERMINE FROM OUR OWN EXPERIENCES WHAT OUR IDENTITY WILL BE . . . AND THAT WILL HAPPEN IN THE NEW SOCIETY WHICH WE WILL HELP TO BUILD.

A similar demonstration was reported in the February 3, 1971, issue of *Psychiatric News*. It stated in part:

The National Association of Mental Health at its annual meeting this winter in New York City declared that deviate sexual behavior "does not constitute a specific mental or emotional illness," and urged the elimination of criminal penalties for homosexual acts committed in private.

About 50 members of the Gay Liberation Front disrupted the session at which the statement was approved, and the meeting was adjourned until the hall could be cleared. According to an NAMH official, the disrupters were unwilling to discuss the content of the NAMH position statement insisting instead that a position statement they had drafted be adopted.[16]

There are other incidents which are numerous, but since they are all so similar they will not be presented here. Psychiatrically, I find it difficult to see the value of such conduct in professional meetings.

National Secular Homosexual Organizations

The organizations mentioned previously have either been national groups that have disbanded as such, or regional groups in their formation. There are, however, two secular national organizations that should be discussed briefly because of their objectives and growing influence.

The National Gay Task Force was created by Dr. Robert Brown and seems to function as an activist organization. One of its major aims is to educate the public in areas of homosexuality and the civil rights of homosexuals. It does not basically act as a supportive group for fellow gays. It is a homosexual organization

212

in which both men and women work together. In one gay directory it describes itself as a "national clearinghouse for the gay movement. We promote gay civil rights on the federal, state and local levels, and promote fair and positive representation of gay people in the media."

The Gay Rights National Lobby is also technically a national organization although it as yet has no national office space or staff. It is headed by volunteers from the staffs of other homosexual organizations who have been elected to their office to serve on the board. It is national in the fact that its specific function is to lobby the United States Congress for gay civil rights.

National Religious Homosexual Organizations

A primary goal of the Gay Liberation Movement has been to remove the stigma of religious condemnation. The Council for Christian Social Action of the United Church of Christ (in 1969), the Council of Church and Society of the United Presbyterian Church (in 1970), the Lutheran Church in America (in 1970), and the General Assembly of the Unitarian Universalist Association (in 1970) approved statements opposing criminal punishments for private homosexual acts between consenting adults — *but without asserting that such conduct was sinless.*[17] (Italics are mine.)

The churches' failure to "become in fact, and not merely in word, a home for gay people too,"[18] has contributed to the emergence of a network of gay churches.

At the center of the gay religious movement is the Rev. Troy Perry, a Pentecostal clergyman, who founded his own church. Beginning in Los Angeles in 1968, his gay congregations spread rapidly to Chicago, Dallas, New York, Phoenix, San Francisco, San Diego, and Denver. The Universal Fellowship of Metropolitan Community Churches, more popularly known as MCC, is a separate denomination of gays. It does accept members of other faiths although it is technically not an "ecumenical" church. It has its international headquarters in Los Angeles and, according to its Washington area office, it is currently made up of 120 congregations in the United States and seven overseas.[19] Although these charter churches (commissioned by the national office), study groups (which can stand more or less on their own), and missions have reported a total attendance of 20,000, it should be noted those in attendance are not necessarily members.

Besides the supportive role they seem to extend to their members, they are also actively involved in national civil rights legislation, public education on homosexuality, and the rights of gays. Members of their staff volunteer their time and efforts for Gay Rights National Lobby. They do hold regular religious services as well as social and educational functions for their members.

A second popular denomination for homosexuals and their friends, is the Church of the Beloved Disciple. It was formed by Father Robert M. Clement in New York City. It bills itself as a "Eucharistic Catholic Church" and seems to be an offshoot of the American Orthodox Church. Although it maintains cordial ties with Rev. Troy Perry's denomination, it has a "high church" tone markedly distinct from the evangelical character of MCC.

The first gay synagogue, Temple Beth Chayim Chadashim (The House of New Light), opened in Los Angeles in March, 1972, and a second, Beth Simchat Torah, in New York City opened in December, 1973. Others have formed throughout the country.

There are many gay caucuses that have begun in many other mainline churches and denominations, and they are rapidly forming into national organizations of their own, e.g., Integrity, the national organization for gay Episcopalians and their friends. There are also groups for Quakers, Friends Committee for Gay Concerns and the Committee of Friends on Bisexuality. There is the Lutherans Concerned for Gay People and the Orthodox Episcopal Church of God.[20]

Because this book is oriented basically toward the Catholic viewpoint, I shall devote more time to Dignity, a national organization for Catholic gays which has its national headquarters in Boston, Massachusetts. I have asked Father Robert Nugent, a Salvatorian priest who ministers to gay Catholics and is a chaplain of the Washington, D.C., chapter of Dignity, to describe its origin and purposes. His statements are as follows:

"Dignity is an international organization of gay Catholic women and men who wish to see Christ's love expressed to and among all women and men regardless of sexual preference. Although a lay organization established for gay Catholics, Dignity also welcomes into its membership others concerned with persons who, though not necessarily gay, are concerned with supporting the struggle of gay people in the Church and in society. Individuals from other Christian denominations are welcomed into membership provided they can agree with Dignity's statement of purpose and goals. Priests, sisters, and brothers, both gay and straight, are also members of Dignity either as chaplains or participating members.

"Dignity began in 1968 in San Diego when an Augustinian priest began to gather gay Catholics in small groups for Mass and discussions on being gay and Catholic. In 1973 the group held its first national convention in San Francisco. Since then chapters have grown up in more than fifty cities throughout the country and membership at the present time numbers over 3,000. Each chapter develops a program of spiritual, educational, and social activities to help gay Catholics form a Christian community and grow together in integrating their Catholic faith with a homosexual orientation. For individuals who are not within distance of a local chapter a special 'at large' membership is available. . . . In a relatively short time Dignity has become an important voice in the Catholic community in meeting the pastoral needs of gay Catholics and in helping the Church develop a more sensitive and enlightened theology of sexuality.

"In its statement of purpose, Dignity outlines its official position and program:

> We believe that gay Catholics are members of Christ's mystical body, numbered among the people of God. We have an inherent dignity because God created us, Christ died for us and the Holy Spirit sanctified us in Baptism making us His Temple, and the channel through which the love of God might become visible. Because of this, it is our privilege, our right and our duty, to live the sacramental life of the Church, so that we might become more powerful instruments of God's love working among all people.

"In speaking of sexuality and gay persons Dignity believes that 'gays can express their sexuality in a manner that is consonant with Christ's teachings' and that 'all sexuality should be exercised in an ethically responsible and unselfish way.' In responding to the Vatican document on sexual ethics in January, 1976, Dignity reiterated and strengthened this position:

> Dignity continues to maintain that, in the light of recent findings by both Church and scientific scholars and in the light of the

gay person's own experience, constitutional homosexuality is a natural, irreversible variation of sexual behavior, evidenced consistently throughout history and in every species of mammal. We maintain, further, with many competent theologians and Scripture scholars that it is intrinsically good when it is expressed in an ethically responsible, unselfish, and Christian manner, as all sexuality must be.

"Dignity attempts to work in three major areas: the Church, society, and individual gay persons. Its responsibility to the Church includes working for the development of its sexual theology and for the acceptance of gays as 'full and equal members of the one Christ.' In society Dignity works for 'justice and social acceptance through education and legal reform.' And it helps individual gays 'reinforce their self-acceptance and their sense of dignity' and aids [each of] them in becoming 'a more active member of the Church and society.'

"In fulfilling its program to the Church, society, and individual gays the Dignity community works in four main areas:

"1. Spiritual development — striving to achieve spiritual growth through the Mass, sacraments, personal prayer, and active love of neighbors.

"2. Education — informing members in matters of the Christian faith and issues relating to gay people in order to develop maturity needed to live fulfilling lives 'in which sexuality and spirituality are integrated.'

"3. Social involvement — leading a life of service to others, working with other gay groups to promote justice in society and helping religious and secular groups understand the plight of gay people.

"4. Social events — providing gay people an alternative to gay bars and an atmosphere where friendships can develop and mature and where a spirit of community can be fostered so that gay people can maintain and develop a sense of acceptance both personal and communal.

"Through its varied programs of spiritual direction, sacramental celebrations, retreats, counseling, community building, educational materials, out-reach programs to the Church and society, personal renewal, and social justice ministry, Dignity has touched the lives of thousands of gay Catholics and others with a spirit of hope and a sense of healing reconciliation. Each chapter has developed a program based on the model from the interna-

216

tional office in Boston but with individual modifications depending on the particular circumstances of the local situation. New programs such as a pen-pal group of members at large, a prison ministry, educational resources (bibliography for Catholics, discussion booklet, theological/pastoral articles, tapes, books, etc.) are constantly being developed and implemented on the international level, while each chapter is also free and encouraged to pursue similar projects which will help the Catholic community come to a better understanding and Christian acceptance of gays as persons with human needs and rights. The international newsletter is an especially important tool in keeping members informed of events relating to gays both in society and the Church. Usually each local chapter also publishes a newsletter for activities in the chapter's own region.

"Since its beginning as an international organization Dignity has striven to maintain cordial and open relationships with the Church hierarchy on both the national and diocesan levels. Following the 1973 national convention the Dignity officers sent 'An Affirmation and Appeal' to the Catholic bishops of the United States in which they urged the bishops to continue to expand their apostolate to gay people noting a concern about 'the alarmingly large number of gay Catholics who constantly leave the Church to find the spiritual consolation in other religious bodies more open to their needs.' In the same letter Dignity professed a need for the bishops' leadership, love and concern and apostolic guidance 'for the Catholic clergy and laity alike to a better understanding of and compassion for our lifestyle.' Reminding the bishops of the 1971 International Synod's call to all members of the Church 'to be prophetic in championing the rights of individuals and groups that are treated unjustly,' the letter asked the bishops for justice in keeping with the Church's growing insistence on justice as a constitutive element in preaching the Gospel.

"Several events in the past few years have provided great hope and encouragement to Dignity that its ministry is making a great deal of progress on many levels:

"1. An increasing number of articles in journals, magazines, and newspapers (both secular and Catholic) highlighting Dignity and its call for pastoral care for homosexuals.

"2. Several major theological articles by prominent theologians urging the Church to reconsider its traditional teaching on homosexuality.

"3. Talks and workshops on ministry to gays for diocesan priests, religious, and specialized groups such as teachers and counselors.

"4. A Mass of Reconciliation and a dialogue with the American Catholic bishops at their annual meeting in Washington, D.C., in November, 1975.

"5. The appointment of priests to work with gay Catholics and other sexual minorities in several dioceses.

"Official statements by individuals or groups in the Catholic community have also spurred Dignity's ministry to gay Catholics and to the larger community."

In the Call to Action meeting recently held in Detroit by the bishops, several resolutions affirming the rights of homosexuals were entered where the needs of gay people were addressed in four documents pertaining to personhood, the family, work, and the Church. In one document the delegates recommended that "the Church encourage and affirm the pastoral efforts of Dignity, the organization of gay and concerned Catholics, to reconcile the Church with its homosexual brothers and sisters."

Father Nugent points out that while in some dioceses "the relations between the local Church hierarchy and Dignity chapters have been less than amicable, in most places Dignity has received active acceptance and encouragement or at the least a passive tolerance. In several instances the Dignity chapter meets in Catholic facilities such as parish churches or Newman Centers. From time to time Dignity provides active assistance to diocesan officials in formulating workshops for priests or counseling referrals. One bishop has appointed a priest as official Dignity chaplain. In Baltimore an auxiliary bishop celebrated a Dignity liturgy, and in the same diocese the education committee of the Priests' Senate passed a resolution supporting the Dignity ministry in the diocese.

"Dignity continues to grow both in numbers and in influence as it reaches out to touch and heal the lives of people where sexual orientation and deep commitment to the Church has caused much pain and confusion. Dignity continues to maintain strongly that 'our document does not express positions that are contrary to the official teachings of the Catholic Church, that it does not and cannot speak on these theological issues, which are the proper domain of Catholic theology.' "

Father Nugent adds: "Dignity's primary concerns are pastoral, and it is on this level that it continues to exercise great influence not only on individual gay Catholics but on the whole Catholic community as it challenges it to rethink its teachings on sexual morality in all areas in light of new developments especially as a new understanding of the Church begins to emerge among Catholics."

These are Father Nugent's words. Dignity is not, according to my sources, an official Catholic organization. In fact, the *National Catholic Reporter* (April 9, 1976) stated that it is not. It is also not listed in the current *National Directory of Catholic Organizations*. It is indeed an organization of Catholics, but not an *official* Catholic organization.

It is difficult to disagree with the purposes and aims of Dignity as stated above. However, their activities, publications, and "crusades" obviously seem to support, in sometimes less than subtle ways, the practice of overt homosexuality. If this is true, it not only disagrees with my philosophy of pastoral counseling, but also with the current teachings of the Catholic Church which has recently addressed itself to this issue in its "Declaration on Certain Questions Concerning Sexual Ethics" of January, 1976 (see p. 238).

Membership in Homosexual Organizations

Sasha Lewis-Gregory, reporting on the responses to a survey of homosexual organizations, commented:

> If any single finding of the *Advocate's* 1976 survey of gay organizations is indisputable, it is that gay people may go to church, but the overwhelming majority of them do not belong to any secular gay community organization.
>
> Nearly 375 organizations responded to the *Advocate* survey. About a third were religious groups (with a combined membership of more than 20,000), and another third were student groups. The remaining third were secular gay community organizations and commercial enterprises. When we eliminated the commercial enterprises, we were left with 110 secular, non-student gay organizations that reported a combined membership of 9,873 — about the same number claimed by the Polish Army Veterans Association of America. And more than a quarter of these members belonged to a single organization: the National Gay Task Force, which reported 2,500 members.
>
> In all, we estimate that we heard from more than one third of the existing gay organizations.

219

The survey also showed that gay organizations aren't very wealthy. The total annual revenue they reported was $869,993, with the seven wealthiest organizations accounting for $775,000 of this total — most of which came from government or foundation grants. Organizations not among the top seven averaged annual expenditures of $2,000, derived mostly from dues, donations and small fund raisers.[21]

Homosexual Publications

Although there are many homosexual publications, they are too numerous to mention. *The Advocate* is the most widely read publication of its kind. Although it is referred to by some gays as not necessarily the best gay publication currently available, it is the best known one which is published regularly on a national level. It is printed biweekly by Liberation Publications in San Mateo, California.

Another gay publication which is mentioned because it is relatively new but rapidly gaining in popularity is *NewsWest*, which is also published biweekly in Los Angeles, California. It was established in the Spring of 1975 and carries the same type of advertisements and homosexual focus as *The Advocate*. It has adopted a more newspaper type of format in its content as opposed to *The Advocate* which tends to be more subjective in its approach.

Gay directories are also available on local and national levels. The *Gayellow Pages* is printed twice a year in April and November on a national level by Renaissance House in New York. It is a directory of "baths, bars, businesses, churches, organizations, accommodations and publications."

There are many other newspapers, newsletters, books, pamphlets, and magazines published regularly throughout the country. In my experience, the ones I have mentioned are indicative of the others available.

What Do Homosexuals Want?

The aims stated in the official publications of the homosexual organizations are not always those of the "unorganized" homophile. According to Masters, who asks the question — "What do homosexuals (say they) want?":

Most basically — and most obviously — what homosexuals want is to be regarded as ordinary citizens who differ from the rest of the population only in terms of their sex object-choices (which they would wish to have regarded as, for them, natural); and they would wish to be accepted on the basis of their worth as individuals (apart from their sexual inclinations and behavior). Almost equally basically and prerequisite to social acceptance, they want to be freed from the laws that brand them criminals even though, as is usually the case, their prohibited sex acts occur between consenting and responsible adults.[22]

More specifically, Masters then summarizes some of the demands made by homosexual spokesmen. How many homosexuals want any or all of these demands satisfied one could never know. They are listed here after the order of Masters, but they are a paraphrase of his summary:

1. The homosexual, both male and female, wants the right to serve in the armed forces.

2. The homosexual does not feel that he should be excluded from government service for "security reasons."

3. Marriages between homosexuals should be legalized and the various consequences of this should follow, such as joint ownership of property and income-tax deductions.

4. Married homosexuals should be allowed to adopt children.

5. Realistic presentation of homosexual life should be allowed in movies, on TV, and in literature. Such presentations should be subject only to the good taste applied to present heterosexual themes.

6. Homosexual marriages should be accepted by the various religious groups.

7. Homosexuals should be allowed to wear such clothing, makeup, and perfumes as their personality dictates.

8. The homosexual press should enjoy the same freedom as that of the heterosexual press in the matter of pinups, etc.

9. Homosexuals should be allowed to display their affection for each other as openly as do heterosexuals within the limits of good taste.

It seems unlikely that many of these objectives will be achieved. It is obvious that through their organizations homosexuals are making their demands heard. How long it will take for some or all of them to occur no one could say.

CHAPTER SIXTEEN

Contemporary Theological Views

(John F. Harvey, O.S.F.S.)

In this chapter a critique will be given of major theological views currently being proposed by Roman Catholic theologians that are at variance with the authentic teaching of the Church regarding the objective morality of homosexual acts. In the first part of the chapter the views of Father John McNeill, S.J., and of Gregory Baum will be considered, inasmuch as they are regarded by gay Catholics as offering an attractive alternative theology to that of the Church on the nature of homosexual acts.[1] In the second part of the chapter the views of Father Charles E. Curran on the subject will be examined.

The Position of John McNeill, S.J.

In this recently published book, *The Church and the Homosexual,* which is basically an expansion of his address given at the first national convention of Dignity (see Ch. 15) held in September, 1973,[2] Father McNeill makes a distinction between "genuine" and "non-genuine" homosexuals. "Genuine" homosexuals are those whose "permanent psychological condition" is erotic orientation toward the same sex. This "permanent psychological condition" can serve as a basis for constructive human love, involving genital relationships, which help each partner grow as a person.[3] Furthermore, genital expression becomes a form of human play in which the procreative value of sexuality is negated.[4] On the basis of this distinction he claims that homosexual acts performed out of love by a "genuine" homosexual are good, whereas sexual acts performed by a heterosexual or by a homosexual out of lust would be immoral. On the psychological level he offers no real proof that "the permanent psychological condition'' must remain permanent; there is evidence to the contrary, as I have indicated elsewhere.[5]

Father McNeill's effort to distinguish good and bad homosexual acts purely on the basis of motivation and intention leads him into dualism. The way in which he justifies homosexual actions should be noted.

When homosexuals use their genital organs to express love, these actions *become* good, because of their psychic disposition; but if the person performing the homosexual action is heterosexual, the action *becomes* evil, because his psychic disposition is contrary to the homosexual action. Thus, the physical action has no meaning in itself, but derives its entire meaning from the psychic disposition and intention of the agent. Instead of confronting the meaning of the physical act, McNeill superimposes meaning. For example, he says that love makes the physical act good.[6]

His thesis about the goodness of "holy unions" raises the objection that the homosexual act is not, by its nature, situated in a family history. It is without future. Heterosexual activity, on the other hand, is meant to lead to procreation as well as to foster love between two persons. It leads to family and history. It makes two persons performing the heterosexual act of intercourse responsible to society in a way that homosexual activity cannot. Little wonder that homosexual liaisons do not tend toward permanency and fidelity, but to relatively brief encounters. Equally vague is McNeill's argument that a "genuine" homosexual can have an ethically responsible relationship. The task of describing such a relationship would be left to the communal discernment of Christian homosexuals.

Father McNeill overlooks the truth that humans can attain intimacy with other humans, or at least a few humans in the course of a lifetime, with or without genital activity. He simply assumes that deep friendship between two homosexuals or between a homosexual and a heterosexual is practically impossible without genital activity. He would say that such chaste friendships are not viable excepting when the vows of religion or celibacy grant a charisma.

Going beyond the position of Father Charles Curran, who seeks to justify faithful homosexual unions by his principle of compromise (on this, see below), McNeill does not consider homosexual actions wrong in themselves. It is not surprising then, that Dignity, a national organization of gay Catholics affirming that "gays can express their sexuality in a manner that is consonant with Christ's teaching" makes frequent use of his statements.

McNeill's major arguments treat (1) the various texts in Holy Scripture concerning homosexuality and conclude that none of the texts contains a clear condemnation of faithful homosexual union (see Ch. 1); (2) that man's radical freedom enters into the formation of man's sexual orientation in such a way that biological givens, such as the sex in which one is born, should not be determinative of sexual activity. First, let us consider his use of Scripture.

1. Cautioning that the Scriptures are historically and culturally limited, McNeill makes reference to the Genesis account of the creation of male and female. He cites the traditional view that genital human sexuality derives its meaning exclusively in terms of the relationship of male and female in a procreative union. Then he questions whether this traditional view is really an expression of God's will, or merely the reflection of the needs of the primitive human community. He suggests that with some theologians we should read Genesis with a new perspective: The Genesis account of the origin of man and woman and marriage is a myth, expressing an ideal for the future rather than an event of the past.

> The Garden of Eden in which man found himself perfectly at one with himself and his sexuality, his fellow man, nature, and God represents primitive man's primordial dream of what ought to be in the future which he projected into the past as a state he once possessed and lost and now must work to regain. From this perspective, ideal human sexual relationships are not to be sought in the past, but must be created for the future. And the key to that future is man's ideal human nature which represents not so much a static given from the past but a dynamic ideal process of growth and development.[7]

2. McNeill believes that the Genesis account represents various aspects of the then monogamous agrarian family unit: (a) it reflects the need of a paternalistic society to reflect male superiority; (b) like other accounts of sexuality in the Old Testament and New, it is fearful of Canaanite and other idolatrous sexual practices.

Turning to the Code of Leviticus' condemnations of homo-

224

sexual acts, McNeill sees it as an expression of the Jewish horror of the meaning of sodomy, namely, it was the common practice in the Middle East to submit a captured foe to sodomy. (Homosexual activity then was an expression of domination, contempt, and scorn.) The Jewish male population undoubtedly suffered this indignation, and because the dignity of the male was of prime importance to this society, it would follow that "any activity necessarily associated with the degradation of the male was a serious offense."[8]

McNeill finds problematical "that what is referred to in Scripture as homosexuality is either not the same reality at all, or that the Biblical author did not manifest the same understanding of that reality as we have it today. Therefore it can be seriously questioned whether what is understood today as the true homosexual and his activity is ever the object of explicit moral condemnation in the scriptures."[9]

After all, he continues, biblical writers were not familiar with the distinction between homosexual orientation and homosexual activity, and could not have reasoned to the conclusion that a homosexually oriented person should be allowed to engage in homosexual activity. For this reason, even in the one passage which McNeill finds in the New Testament (Romans 1:26-27) as referring clearly to homosexual activity, he sees no condemnation of contemporary homosexual unions. He believes Paul understood the Greeks who indulged in homosexual activity to be heterosexuals involved in homosexual activities, probably forms of the sacred prostitution so often condemned in the Old Testament.

From his study of biblical scholars on human sexuality McNeill concludes that the primary message of the Old Testament is that "love, including sexual love, requires respect for the other person as well." The sin which man can commit in his sexual conduct with another consists in dishonoring the person of a fellow human being. In the New Testament the writers teach the need to integrate sexual powers into one's total personality within the context of free, interpersonal love.

While I believe that the Scriptures are not the only source of our teaching on homosexuality, they are important for our understanding of sexuality in general and homosexuality in particular. McNeill's use of Scripture presents many difficulties. Were one to grant for the sake of the argument that the Genesis account was an ideal representation of a future condition, an ideal

225

to be striven for, it is significant that the biblical account is concerned with the man-woman relationship. The Genesis accounts (chapters 1 and 2) have been regarded as both an ideal and norm of sexual behavior, and the sexual behavior is heterosexual. Matthew's reference to this norm strengthens the argument that Genesis taught a heterosexual norm of sexuality in permanent marriage; in this passage (Matthew 19:1-6) the author quotes both Genesis 1:27 and 2:24 when he says: ". . . He [Jesus] replied, 'Have you not read that at the beginning the Creator made them male and female and declared, "For this reason a man shall leave his father and mother and cling to his wife, and the two shall become as one"? Thus they are no longer two but one flesh. Therefore, let no man separate what God has joined.' "

Again, in Genesis accounts it is said that man was created as male and female (Genesis 1:27) and that it was not good that man should be alone. At this point, however, God did not create another man but a woman. Surely, the Genesis account says something about the complementary nature of man and woman, something stressed quite strongly by such scholars as John L. McKenzie, Pierre Grelot, and Edward Schillebeeckx.[10]

Another argument used by McNeill throughout his discussion of scriptural references is that sexual norms are determined exclusively by culture factors: Jewish and Christian marriages were structured to assure male domination. Homosexual acts were condemned because they were forms of prostitution rites, or painful reminders of humiliation by the captors of the Israelites. And so forth. It can be argued against this kind of speculation that the authors of the sacred books, beginning with Genesis' account of marriage, intended to affirm certain transcendental principles concerning human sexuality and marriage. If this were not so, how could the author of Matthew (19:1-9) refer back to the pristine integrity of marriage? On another occasion why would Jesus say that divorce was not prevalent in the beginning, but was a concession due to the hardness of men's hearts? (Cf. Mark 10:2-12.)

This is not to say that everything which is said about sexuality in the Old Testament is of permanent value. One recognizes the prescriptions of Leviticus (15:19-30) concerning the menstruating woman as a purely cultural determinant. In accepting the cultural milieu of Genesis and other books of the Bible we do not deny that they also contain certain perennial principles, such as the norm of heterosexual marriage.[11]

It would be a mistake to demonstrate the heterosexual norm of marriage from individual texts when the context of both the Old and New Testaments stresses the complementary relationship of man and woman.[12] Nowhere in Holy Scripture is the homosexual person condemned, but always the action is condemned. Nowhere is there any approval of homosexual unions, but the heterosexual union of man and wife is confirmed from Genesis to Ephesians as a perennial principle. While Holy Scripture does not say the last word about homosexuality, it gives no support to such actions.

As already mentioned, McNeill interprets all the specific texts referring to homosexual activity in terms of a relationship to prostitution cults. Prescinding from the Leviticus texts in the Old Testament, and the other references in the New, one wonders how one can prove that in Romans 1:26-27 homosexual acts were condemned *only* because they happened in the background of deliberate repudiation of God, or because it happened to be Greek heterosexuals performing homosexual activities. He draws the conclusion that the men were heterosexuals because of the active aorist participle, *aphentes*, men *giving up* their natural relations with women. He does not explain St. Paul's reference to women making use of other women. This is hardly a convincing proof. It cannot go both ways.

In one place he argues that biblical authors condemn homosexual actions, because of their association with prostitution rites, while they do not condemn the interior disposition toward homosexuality; but on the other hand, McNeill argues on the basis of a grammatical phrase (*aphentes*) that Paul was condemning heterosexual Greeks performing homosexual actions. It has been assumed by McNeill that biblical authors knew nothing about the interior dispositions of the homosexual.

In summing up his understanding of Scripture and homosexuality McNeill asserts correctly the primacy of love in both Testaments, and hence the need for mutual respect. But his attempt to show that a faithful homosexual couple fulfills these ideals of Scripture is weak in the absence of any supporting scriptural texts dealing with the matter at hand.

Personal Uniqueness

3. In his treatment of human nature and human freedom, McNeill stresses the point that every individual is more than the

species, and that each human being has a personal uniqueness. If a loving action takes the form of a sexual gesture it must be directed to the other person as unique, and as an end in himself or herself. Too much emphasis on procreation can lead to a dehumanizing form of sexuality. As he puts it, "There is something more to the question of the moral quality of sexual behavior than purely the objective legal question of marriage or the objective rational question of openness to procreation — that something else is love."

McNeill posits that human sexuality, like all human reality, participates "in the radical freedom of man" precisely because it is human.

Many theologians ignore the fact that sexuality is not a totally instinctive determined phenomenon. Human freedom, however, cannot receive its total explanation in terms of causal determinancy, but only in terms of ideal goals and purposes. Since man can project ideal goals, man can allow these goals to be the ultimate determining factor in his behavior.

He goes on to argue that man can use his bodily organs in many creative ways. He uses his mouth, which is obviously intended for eating, in order to communicate his innermost sentiments; likewise, he can use his sexual organs, designed by nature for procreation, in order to give the most intimate personal expression of his drive for union in love with a fellow human. The point is that man has the freedom to decide how he will use his powers.

McNeill explains how man's freedom enters into the formation of his sexual orientation. Biological givens (one's physical sexuality) do not determine human behavior precisely as it exists on the human level. What we are in our society, is a free cultural creation. For each culture creates its own ideal identity images from the masculine and feminine roles. That is why the young undergo a process through which they adapt themselves to the prevailing cultural images and expectations, which are in agreement with their biological identity. Although in the past, theologians have mistakenly identified such cultural images as divine givens, in more recent times they have been able to identify such images as determined purely by particular cultures.

In this context Jesus is seen as the great liberator from sexual taboos. (McNeill does not identify these taboos, nor does he show how Jesus liberates us from them.) He concludes that the sexual identity images which concretize heterosexual relationships at any point in human history are human creations, and to assert that they come forth from God's will is to raise a human creation to the level of idolatry. Theologians then should make a critical investigation of sexual identity images. If they do so, they will find that as a result of our identifying with the heterosexual identity images, we have accepted as the form of heterosexual relationships that of the master-slave, in which the male seeks to dominate, and the female seeks to be dominated.

Such a relationship is contrary to ideal Christian love, which can exist only if both persons see themselves as equals. The primary goal, then, of human sexual development is that "we should fashion cultural identity images that make it possible for human beings to achieve the fullness of a true personal relationship in the process of conforming to the images provided by society."

According to McNeill, then, ideal human nature lies in the future; and to the development of this ideal, man must be directed: a free, mature person living in a mature, interpersonal community. Then a homosexual relationship will be viewed as a truly constructive and mature expression of human love.

Following Carl Gustav Jung's analysis of positive traits in the homosexual, McNeill concludes:

> Each of the special qualities Jung attributes to the homosexual community is usually considered as a striking characteristic of Christ — the qualities which distinguished him from the ordinary man. The ability to meet the individual as a person apart from stereotypes and cultural prejudices, the refusal to establish his identity and accomplish his mission by means of violence, the image of himself as the loving servant of all humanity.

McNeill asks that we be prepared to meet every individual person on his or her own merits without allowing ourselves to be blinded by stereotypes. The tendency of both heterosexuals and homosexuals to define themselves in contrast to one another leads to a "narrow and impoverished self-image for both parties." Man should be free to develop all the qualities belonging to the fullness of person.

McNeill's Concept of Freedom

To understand McNeill one needs to examine his concept of freedom, which he derives from Blondel. In several other articles [13] he contrasts the traditional notion of freedom with that of Blondel. In the traditional concept man exists and then he acts. "All actions are considered as functions which can only influence that unchanging reality on the phenomenal or accidental level of substantial determination."[14] In the Blondelian conception, however, man's freedom must be understood beyond all particular actions as the radical self-positing of his own reality. Man must exist at every moment as a consequence of his freedom. "If in the depths of his own subjective being man meets with any determinism whatsoever — biological, psychological, social and even a determinism springing from the divine will, a determinism which lies radically outside his free ability to determine himself — then one must be forced to accept the conclusion that the existence of an individual human being as such is an illusion."[15] The law is within us, and we cannot escape it, whether we conform to it freely or oppose it freely.

McNeill accepts as a first principle of moral activity Blondel's understanding of freedom, which he quotes: "There is no being where there is only constraint. If I am not that which I will to be, I am not. At the very core of my being there is a will and a love of being or there is nothing. If man's freedom is real, it is necessary that one has at present or at least in the future a knowledge and a will sufficient never to suffer any tyranny whatsoever."[16]

McNeill logically accepts the Blondelian principle of immanence:

> Nothing can impose itself on a man, nothing can demand the assent of his intellect or the consent of his will, which does not in some way find its source in man himself.[17]

Thus, accepting these premises, McNeill draws the conclusion that whatever we are as men in this present society is a free cultural creation. In the circumstances of his life and culture man creates his own freedom. At the same time McNeill admits the strong cultural influences which shape a child from earliest years. He also acknowledges that his freedom is "dependent upon a transcendent truth, to which it must conform and is directed to values which, far from being his exclusive creation serve him as guide, norm, and sanction."[18] Referring to Blondel, he resolves the relationship between transcendence and immanence by the philosophy of action:

Action has its own *a priori* structure from which the totality of thought derives its meaning and structure. . . . Accordingly, he changed the central structure of philosophy from thought as analytic to action as synthetic. . . . His search for moral principles is therefore an endeavor to discover the all-encompassing dialectical law that immanently governs the evolution of human life.[19]

One exercises his freedom by responding to ideals, which are not imposed from without, but arise within consciousness:

The metaphysical order is not outside the will as an extraneous end to be attained, but is contained within the will as a means to move beyond. It does not represent a truth already constituted in fact, but presents to thought what one wishes to will, that is, an ideal object. . . . Man is thereby free from all predeterminism.[20]

In the free action one synthesizes the real and the ideal, and thereby discovers his moral principles. A communion with God is possible through union with Jesus Christ. Man can make a free commitment to both God and fellowman.[21]

Once one has grasped McNeill's acceptance of Blondel's thought, he can see why McNeill rejects the traditional position of the Church on objective standards of morality. Any sexual action by a loving person is a unique action not measurable by any *extrinsic* norm. Sharing in the radical freedom of man, this action derives its morality from the ideals which arise within the will of the person himself. Thus, as long as a sexual act is free, loving, and creative, it is good; the biological and instinctive elements of the sexual act determine *in no way* its moral goodness or evil. This is quite dualistic.

McNeill then holds that all moral authority comes from within the person himself as he reaches out to grasp transcendental truth. This presupposes a process in all areas of development including the sexual. In the homosexual, according to McNeill, it often begins with promiscuous sex and advances over a long period of time to a mature, loving relationship, which is characterized by love and trust. Implicitly, contrary to his own theory of freedom, however, McNeill presupposes that the homosexual has been *determined* in his orientation toward his own sex by myriad influences in early life. He regards this

231

learned inclination as connatural to him; and so he seeks the same kind of fidelity from his chosen beloved as a man and woman should do in marriage. Just as sexual intimacy between two heterosexual persons is considered as an expression of union, so sexual actions between two homosexual lovers is meant to be an expression of their committed love.

In contrast to traditional Christian teaching McNeill makes the homosexual union the alternative to marriage. It is meant only for those homosexually oriented. It presupposes an earlier experimental period (promiscuity) followed by faithful union. Apart from Roman Catholic teaching on marriage, the homosexual community by and large does not accept even the ideal of faithful homosexual union.

The Position of Gregory Baum

In presenting his views on homosexuality, Gregory Baum also tends to vary with the Church's theology. He contends that the Catholic theologian has become suspicious of the old arguments about human nature. Perhaps what a particular culture calls "human nature" is merely the self-understanding of the dominant class; and the perpetuation of that self-understanding tends to extend the power of the class. For this reason, "the theologian must try to discern in the inherited, historically constituted human nature the possible structures of oppression, legitimating various forms of what Hegel has called master-slave relationships."[22]

Baum speaks of God's judgment enabling him to discern the structures of evil in this world. This judgment rests upon man's historically constituted nature, which appears to be mutuality: "What is normative for normal life is the human nature to which we are divinely summoned, which is defined in terms of mutuality. This, at least, is the promise of biblical religion."[23] Further in his discussion Baum describes mutuality as friendship. He sets down a new norm by which to evaluate the morality of homosexual relationships, namely, mutuality. This means that a homosexual relationship is good if it is grounded on a friendship which "enables the partners to grow and to become more truly human. . . . For the structure of redeemed life is mutuality."[24]

Baum realizes that there are damaged forms of sexuality which do not admit of mutuality: sadism, masochism, and pedophilia. They do not fulfill the ideal of mutuality to which God summons us. While recognizing that some psychiatrists and psychologists do not believe that a homosexual relationship can fulfill the norm of mutuality, Baum holds that theologians should take seriously "the witness of homosexual men and women who have struggled for self-knowledge and transcended the weight society has put on them and who tell us that their lives are based on mutuality." From the specific witness of Catholics and other Christians who have sustained lasting homosexual relationships the theologian may draw the conclusion that constitutive homosexuals "must accept their orientation and live accordingly. Homosexual love, then, is not contrary to the human nature, defined in terms of mutuality, toward which mankind is summoned."[25]

Some Unproven Assertions

Before evaluating Baum's position it is profitable to note some of his unproven assertions. When he speaks of a historically constituted human nature, he is asserting that human nature at any given time is constituted exclusively from the elements of a particular culture; he asserts also that human nature as generally understood by scholastic philosophy is so entangled with dehumanizing elements which have been woven into our culture that it is no longer an operative moral norm. Yet the only example he gives of these dehumanizing elements is the tradition affirming the superiority of the male, or the master-slave relationship. He also asserts that the long-standing tradition against homosexuality is an example of the cruelty of the heterosexual culture. The consequence of the hostility of the majority is the placing of an unspeakable burden on homosexuals. The burden takes the form of self-hatred. The homosexual learns to hate himself in the same way he feels society hates him, and he becomes full of self-loathing. Theologians, then, should seek new ground for moral norms, because the traditional arguments arise from a cruel culture.

Baum is aware of the distinction between temporary and constitutive homosexuality. He refers to the former "as a *phase* to be passed through" and the latter as "a *constant* to be lived with." (Italics are mine.) He is concerned with the question whether the constitutive homosexual should be allowed to

233

express himself genitally. He is convinced that such an expression cannot be proven to be immoral, because the concept of human nature and the relationship between man and woman have become problematic in the writings of some theologians, who are not specified. Thus, he seeks a new norm to evaluate morally homosexual relationships, and he finds it in mutuality, or true friendship.

As already pointed out, Baum does not prove sweeping assertions about the constitution of human nature. He presupposes that society's attitude toward homosexuals is the major cause of whatever neurosis the person may have. This is contrary to sound psychiatric opinion.[26] This is not to deny that the self-hatred found in the homosexual is in part a reflection of the attitude of hatred found in society toward the homosexual. Baum's choice of mutuality as a norm of human sexuality ignores other varied and complex aspects of sexuality, such as procreative longing, motherhood, fatherhood, and family stability. He does not treat the scriptural teaching on sexuality or homosexuality. On the basis of his own understanding of the interplay between human nature and the prevailing culture, he chooses the norm of mutuality for sexual actions. Since his norm is not comprehensive enough to take in all the known elements of sexuality, and does not give an account of scriptural teaching, it is inadequate.

Summary

There is a series of weak points in the reasoning of McNeill and Baum: (1) If the norm is purely subjective, and divorced from the history of man, it will not be able to see the full reality of man as he has learned from historical experience. Why should Baum's perception of morality as mutuality displace more nuanced norms which take into account not only man's subjective condition, but also the structure of human society, the structure of human acts, one person in relationship to another person and to society? (2) On the scriptural question Baum does not really treat it; McNeill interprets the pertinent passages on the condemnation of homosexuality in such a way as to render them all non-applicable to the homosexual in the faithful union. (3) The concentration of both McNeill and Baum on the situation of the faithful homosexual union is quite disproportionate when one considers that the vast majority of homosexuals do not desire

234

and do not seek this kind of union. Moral theology is supposed to evaluate *per se* situations more than it does *per accidens* problems. Granted theologians consider both kinds, but more attention should be given to the typical behavior of the typical homosexual. (4) In psychiatry the idea of the constitutive homosexual, that is to say, the person who is permanently oriented in this direction is not universally accepted.[27] It is premature to say that there is very little hope that future study will not reveal ways of helping some homosexuals to change the direction of their sexual instincts. (5) No consideration is given to the alternative lifestyle of perpetual continence, motivated by the love of God, and expressed in service to neighbor.

The Position of Charles E. Curran

In a thorough review of the problem of homosexuality Father Charles E. Curran advocates a mediating position, which recognizes that homosexual acts are wrong, but does not believe that all such acts fall under total condemnation.[28] Here I repeat the substance of the argument. Curran accepts the conclusions of H. Kimball Jones, who feels that in certain circumstances homosexual behavior can be morally acceptable, because the person has no other alternative.[29] Jones had recommended that the Church recognize "the validity of mature homosexual relationships" without an "endorsement of homosexuality."[30]

Curran approaches the problem in a different way, because he does not agree with the reasoning or the methodology of Jones. For Curran there is a "basic meaning of human sexuality in terms of maleness and femaleness which sin neither eradicates, neutralizes or reduces to the same ethical significance as homosexual relations."[31] A solution to the dilemma of the homosexual is to be found, however, in the theory of compromise, which is described best in Curran's own words:

> In the theory of compromise the particular action in one sense is not objectively wrong, because in the presence of sin it remains the only viable alternative for the individual. However, in another sense the action is wrong and manifests the power of sin. If possible, man must try to overcome sin, but the Christian knows that the struggle against sin is never totally successful in this world.[32]

Curran applies his theory of compromise to the apparently confirmed homosexual who has little hope of change in instinctual direction through therapy and who has settled into a "somewhat stable" homosexual union. After all, Curran states, such unions are better than homosexual promiscuity. They are a middle ground between celibacy and promiscuity. In this situation, then, the individual may come to the conclusion that a somewhat permanent homosexual union is the best and sometimes the only way for him to achieve some humanity.[33]

Critique of Curran

Since I have already evaluated Curran's theory of compromise in other publications,[34] I shall summarize my views as briefly as possible. Implicitly, the theory of compromise denies the element of freedom in sin, because it holds that in certain situations one must perform the "sinful" act, which in one sense is good, since it is the best one can do, and in another sense is bad, because it is an expression of a sin-filled situation. In effect, Curran teaches that one *must freely* sin, and this is a contradiction in terms. For, in the formal sense, an act cannot be sinful unless it is truly free. It should be noted in this problem that we are not concerned with the truly compulsive homosexual who is presumed to have suffered a significant diminution of his freedom, but with a person who has sufficient freedom to act virtuously or to sin.

In traditional moral theology recognition has always been given to the difficult life situation, and guidance has been offered to help the person practice heroic virtue, if need be. It was assumed that God gave sufficient grace to each individual to fulfill the law of God.[35] The principle of compromise is really a denial of this principle of the sufficiency of divine grace for the "too hard" case.

In his pastoral sympathy it would seem that Father Curran has posited an untenable principle, which, when it is applied to heterosexual persons, deprived of the fullness of genital pleasure for a variety of reasons, would allow them to indulge in some form of genital relationships. In the language of the world, "bad sex is better than no sex." Implicit also in his principle, although never clearly enunciated, is the belief that complete abstinence from all genital pleasure is possible only to those who have the charism of celibacy through vow or promise. The homosexual, the divorced and unremarried, the unwilling singles, the deprived married, and various others, should be allowed to have some genital indulgence as part of their intimate relationships with partners of the same or other sex.

Another weak point in Curran's theology of homosexual activity is the inadequate treatment of the virtue of chastity. He says that "celibacy and sublimation are not always possible or even desirable for the homosexual."[36] At the root of this opinion is the idea that the homosexual will not be content without some genital fulfillment. A somewhat stable union is the best and sometimes the only way the homosexual can achieve humanity.[37]

What Curran has missed is the basic truth that humans do not need genital intimacy to be fully human. They do need psychological intimacy in the form of deep friendship with at least one other human,[38] and, preferably, more than one close friendship. Each person needs a community of close friends.

In short, Curran does not give serious attention to the viability of chastity for the homosexual because he settles for the principle of compromise. I should like to respond to this question of the viability of chastity in presenting my own view.

Personal View

The elements of my approach to the pastoral problem of homosexuality are implied in my critiques of McNeill, Baum, and Curran.[39] Since I have written on this subject so extensively, I believe it is best at this point to summarize both my moral and pastoral views. Morally, homosexual actions cannot be reconciled with the chaste intercourse of the married; pastorally, homosexual actions may never be approved, while at the same time every effort is made to help the homosexual person live chastely. The impression must not be given that such is an impossible task; rather, he should be encouraged to transcend his genital desires in the pursuit of the more basic need of intimacy.

Like other humans, the homosexual needs real personal relationships to develop himself in all his human powers. This truth is usually addressed in a different way. It is said that man wants to know and to be known; to love and to be loved. He cannot affirm himself until he has been affirmed by others; he cannot love himself until he experiences love from others. Unfortunately, however, he confuses his need to love and to be loved with the need for genital intimacy and pleasure. He has been told by the culture that he is not completely human until he has engaged in some form of genital activity with members of his own or the opposite sex. It is something he must do; and, given his strong impulses in this direction, he needs no further persuasion.

Hence, the difficulty which the counselor must face in re-educating this person in all the meaning of love and intimacy. Nothing is more important than to lead the homosexual person into an examination of the different forms of positive real relationships which he can form to develop himself as both a lovable and loving person, indeed as a sexual person, but without the need of genital intercourse.

Positive Chastity

Principles to Guide Confessors in Questions of Homosexuality[40] and the Vatican's "Declaration on Certain Questions Concerning Sexual Ethics," Paragraphs 11 and 12, stress the positive values of chastity for the development of the whole person. This virtue is more than the mere avoidance of faults, it is an interior attitude of mind and a way of life, adaptable to all the different conditions of life. "It is a virtue which concerns the whole personality as concerns both interior and outward behavior."[41] Significantly, the "Declaration" underlines the fact that chastity is appreciated as a result of fidelity, that is to say, that men and women in every state of life understand it better when they are faithful to its practices.[42]

That one *can* lead the chaste life happily, and that many do, is the conclusion of Bishop Francis J. Mugavero's pastoral letter.[43] At the same time, it is a long and demanding process of growth in which there may be many relapses, and much pain and confusion. Like Bishop Mugavero, I pledge my willingness to help persons of homosexual orientation in bearing their burdens and in finding Christ. I respect them in their struggle.

238

CHAPTER SEVENTEEN

Treatment

The treatment of homosexuality has been regarded with pessimism in the past. This difficulty arose partly from a failure of the therapist to define his objectives and partly from an inadequate concept of the proper therapy for the condition. A rational therapy for homosexuality requires a solid etiological foundation. Until recently even a rational hypothesis has been lacking. Even today, although the psychic origin of the disorder is generally recognized, it is most likely that the causative factors which lead to the various forms of homosexual adaptation are not all the same. The treatment, therefore, must be flexible and the therapist must be willing to alter his method to suit the case. For each case, after a preliminary diagnostic survey (see p. 111), the therapist should discuss with the patient what he hopes to accomplish. This is necessary because the direction of the therapy is related to the aim which is sought.

Many of the following forms of treatment are presented more for their historical value than practical use to counselors.

The Aim of Therapy

Confusion concerning the results of the treatment of homosexuals has frequently followed from a failure on the part of the therapist to state what he hoped to achieve by his therapy. The professional counselor or psychiatrist should aim at "cure," not merely "acceptance." The ends of therapy should be:

1. A new orientation on the part of the homosexual so that he adopts a completely heterosexual attitude.

2. A new orientation which would include an acceptance of heterosexuality but with no basic change in his homosexuality.

3. An acceptance of his condition with the decision to remain abstinent.

Cory, with other therapists, has adopted complete change of orientation as the ideal:

> The present writer, following Freud and being under certain misapprehension, misunderstandings, and limited experience, formerly urged but no longer espouses an orientation toward adjustment within the framework of homosexuality, rather than an expenditure of energy in the effort to effectuate a change. This preference for adjustment seems to have been mistakenly chosen by many modern therapists (particularly Freudians, such as Dollard), and is also espoused, for entirely different reasons, by most homosexuals.[1]

In defining his goals the therapist must also determine his prognosis of two factors: (1) Will the patient persist in his treatment? (2) Is he likely to achieve the goal decided upon?

In regard to his persistence in the treatment, the following factors are important:

1. *Not likely to persist*
   a) No concern over problem.
   b) Threat of punitive measures is present.
   c) Lack of strong personal motivation.
   d) Pressured by relatives to seek help.
   e) Less than high school education.
   f) No previous heterosexual acts (Bieber).
   g) Chronically established pattern.
   h) Men less likely to persist than women.

2. *More likely to persist*
   a) Anxious, fearful, or ashamed over his condition.
   b) Strongly motivated with a sincere desire to change.
   c) No firmly established pattern.
   d) Previous heterosexual acts.
   e) Better than high school education.
   f) Women more likely to persist.
   g) Loneliness.
   h) Desire for normal marriage and children.

The financial factor must always be borne in mind. The treatment is expensive because of its duration. Age must also be considered — the younger the individual at the time he seeks treatment, the better the prognosis. Two factors play a part here: the shorter duration of the pattern and the greater adaptability of youth.

In planning treatment the therapist cannot hope for success of his therapy if it includes techniques which are morally unacceptable to the patient. One should not, for example, suggest heterosexual intercourse to the unmarried patient. Heterosexual petting attempts certainly cannot be recommended to the priest-homosexual. Moll, for example, suggested a form of treatment which he called "association therapy." His aim was to shift the sexual attention from boys to boyish-looking girls.[2] This has rather clear-cut moral drawbacks.

Treatment may be divided into two types:
1. That involving some physical method.
2. That in which the method is purely psychological.

Physical Methods

1. Imprisonment

Imprisonment as a method of treatment of homosexuality has failed over the years because the homosexual was sent to prison more often for punishment than for treatment. In many instances, at least until very recent years, no treatment was given in the prison setting. No means were provided for rehabilitation.

Homosexuality in prisons. There have been many misconceptions concerning homosexuality in prisons. Next to the belief that all homosexuals are effeminate, the most common misconception about inversion is that homosexuality is rampant in prisons. There is a reason for this misconception. It is the confusion of homosexuality with criminality. Since acts committed by the overt homosexual are subject to criminal prosecution, the argument runs: If homosexuals are criminals, then criminals are homosexuals — at least they are homosexual by the time they come out of prison because they have been too long removed from the company of women, and they must have had their sex some way.

Facts refute these erroneous concepts. Suppose we look at the reports of two men who have been intimately associated with psychiatric work in prisons.

Robert Lindner, Ph.D., states that no criminal, homosexual,

sexual psychopath, or sexual pervert of any kind ever becomes one as a result of his prison confinement. What actually happens is that these repressed tendencies come to light during confinement because of the very nature of prison life. In Lindner's own words, there is "an unmasking rather than a fashioning."[3] By this Lindner means that prisoners have their lives regulated so completely that they lose any characteristics of adult maturity they might have had, and they regress to more infantile stages. That is why, he adds, it is a "kind of lunacy" for the general public or prison officials to be surprised when prisoners begin adopting infantilistic modes of adjustment in all fields, including sex. To confuse the homosexual with the criminal and to confuse the criminal with the homosexual is to display a lack of understanding about homosexuality and a naïve grasp of the nature of sex.

There is perhaps a lower percentage of criminals among homosexuals than in any other group of human beings. In any particular prison the number of true homosexuals is approximately the same as for the general population.

Perhaps another reason why prisons are thought to be crowded with homosexuals is because homosexuals, when they are present in the prison population, stand out so prominently that their presence cannot be overlooked. Prisons are close quarters, and life in a prison is like life in a goldfish bowl. Almost anything that happens is noticed. It is practically impossible for two prisoners to engage in any kind of relationship without being observed by either prison officials or fellow prisoners.

When Kinsey reports that thirty to eighty-five percent of prisoners perform some kind of homosexual acts he fails to distinguish between homosexual acts and the acts of a homosexual. For example, Kinsey fails to make this distinction in this statement:

> The judge should bear in mind that the penal or mental institution to which he may send the male has something between 30% and 85% of its inmates engaging in the sort of homosexual activity which may be involved in the individual case before him.[4]

For this reason, as I have indicated before, Kinsey's figures cannot be accepted without great reservations.

Lindner remarks that the real troublemaker in a prison is not the homosexual but the sexual psychopath.

242

Charles E. Smith, M.D., studied 100 homosexual prisoners in the federal penitentiary at Springfield, Missouri.[5] Only 15 out of the 100 were sentenced for offenses directly connected with their homosexuality; 9 were cases of sodomy; the other 6 were sentenced for misuse of the U.S. mails for solicitation. The specific violation was that the letters were obscene. Among the remaining 85, one was a pimp and another was a middle-aged man who had raped a 13-year-old girl. Most of these homosexuals were sentenced for crimes that are frequently committed on impulse.

Only 6 of the 100 prisoners were free of any mental deviation other than homosexuality; 42 were diagnosed as psychopathic personalities (on the subject of sociopathic personality disorder, see p. 53); 21 were diagnosed as schizoid personalities; 17 had some form of neurosis; 7 suffered from a schizophrenic psychosis; 1 suffered from an involutional psychosis; and 6 were mentally deficient.

Most prison officials find it necessary to segregate homosexual prisoners because they so frequently either seek out other prisoners for sex contacts or are sought out. In many instances the homosexual is resented by the other prisoners and physical violence is often inflicted on him. Homosexual murders are not infrequent in prison.

Psychotherapy of Prisoners. In recent years, psychotherapy, both group and individual, has been introduced in some prisons. This is especially true in those states which have adopted "Sexual Psychopath Laws." Although these laws do not apply specifically to homosexuality, they do include it.

Pacht, who has worked with the Wisconsin Sex Crimes Law, is cautiously optimistic after nine years of experience with psychotherapy in a prison setting. The reeducative therapy described by Pacht and his co-workers may be broken down into three phases. Keep in mind that all of their subjects were in confinement with an indeterminate sentence. According to Pacht:

> The *initial phase* is devoted to creating a climate which allows the establishment of a therapeutic relationship. This period may encompass several months to a year. Only after the development of such a relationship can the individual begin to examine his behavior without resorting to defensiveness or intra-punitive mechanisms.

> The *second phase* in this system is employed in working through nuclear conflicts. "During this period, therapy focuses

upon those factors in the background of the individual that have contributed to the development of deviant trends." The day-to-day behavior of the subject in the prison setting is carefully observed and correlated with the therapy.

The *last phase* of therapy is devoted to problems of separation from the prison and planning for the future.

> This is often a very complicated process. Returning to the free world from a closed institution presents an additional burden to the stresses of community attitude, vocational problems, family attitudes, and separation from the therapist.[6]

2. Castration

Castration as a treatment of sexual deviations is not new. Denmark was apparently the first country to enact a special castration law. This law was first passed in 1925 and revised about ten years later.

Considerable interest was displayed concerning castration as a treatment of sex offenders in Europe during the 1930s. This was exemplified by resolutions adopted at the Berlin meetings of the International Penal and Penitentiary Congress in 1935 where the section on prevention of crime held, *inter alia,* that:

> The favorable preventive-therapeutic results from castration achieved relative to sexual disorders in cases involving a leaning toward criminality, ought to cause all States to amend or supplement their respective laws, so as to facilitate the performance of such operations upon demand or with the consent of the person concerned in order to free that person from a disordered sexual inclination which might bring in its train the committing of sexual crimes. (Compulsory castration is also provided for.)[7]

In general the attitude in the United States is strongly opposed to castration. In some sporadic cases it has been employed, however, in different sections of the country:

> Castration has been proposed to some of the legislative commissions seeking more effective policy in the handling of sex offenders, but nowhere has it been taken seriously in this country.[8]

The use of the procedure is not likely to become widespread in the United States.

244

From the psychiatric standpoint castration is not likely to produce its desired effect unless the patient recognizes the desirability of the procedure and the likelihood of its beneficial results. If the procedure is imposed against the subject's will, it is more likely to be harmful than helpful. If consent to the procedure is required, it would serve to minimize possible abuses in the administration of the law in this regard. Even so, certain pressures are inevitable, even though these be of a psychological nature and applied by the patient on himself.

3. Behavior Therapy

A number of psychotherapeutic methods known as "Behavior Therapy" have been developed in recent years. Based on a common theory, the procedures themselves vary from aversion conditioning to desensitization: [9]

> A brief account of this rationale may be stated as follows: the position adopted by this theory is that neurotic behavior is acquired. The process of acquisition implied in the theory is derived from modern learning theory. If neurotic behavior is regarded as being acquired, then it must follow that such behavior will be subject to the established laws of learning. Current knowledge about the learning process concerns not only the acquisition of new habit patterns but also their elimination. The elimination of learned responses occurs either by the extinction process or by inhibition. [10]

Rachman, reporting in 1961 from England, described the use of behavior therapy in a small number of cases. He felt that the method might prove valuable but emphasized that the treatment must stress positive sexual behavior and not merely attempt to eliminate the abnormal.

Stevenson and Wolpe[11] reported the use of the method in two cases of homosexuality.

The largest series of cases was that of Freund and Srnec, who reported forty-seven cases in all. Unfortunately, they had no control series.

Freund's treatment consisted of two phases. Phase I involved the administration of "an emetic mixture by subcutaneous injection." While the unpleasant effects of the injection were being experienced the patient was shown slides of dressed and undressed males. In Phase II of the treatment the patient was shown films of nude and semi-nude females approximately seven hours after the administration of testosterone. Follow-up studies after three and six years indicated that 51 percent of the patients showed no improvement, 14.9 percent showed temporary improvement, and only 25.5 percent were permanently improved; the remaining 8.5 percent were not adequately documented and were excluded from the final analysis.[12]

Feldman and McCulloch, also reporting from England, described their method of aversion therapy. They aimed to develop in their patients an aversion to previously attractive males and to develop an attraction to previously unattractive females. They described the treatment of twelve patients with a follow-up of nine months in their longest case.[13]

Their technique consisted in showing the patient a series of photographs of attractive males. If he did not put aside the picture in eight seconds, an electric shock was given until he did remove the picture. When the picture was put aside the shock ceased. They would then introduce female pictures after the male picture was removed. These would then be associated with the relief of anxiety after the shock.

They state that McGuire and Vallance[14] were the first to use Faradic current for this purpose.

Feldman et al. report one case in which eight booster sessions were given over nine months. Before treatment this patient had a Kinsey rating (q.v.) of 4 to 5; after treatment this rating was reduced to 1.

Dr. Marcel Saghir, assistant professor of psychiatry at the Washington University School of Medicine, in discussing this method of treatment, stated:

> Various modifications of this aversion technique have been developed. The patients who respond most successfully to this treatment method start with no significant personality disorder and with a high degree of motivation. Furthermore, there is a tendency for those under 30 and for those with some past heterosexual interests to respond more favorably. The usual number of treatment sessions is about 20. Each session lasts for 20 to 30 minutes during which about 20 stimulus presentations are made. During follow-up, reinforcement might be given by occasionally repeating the therapy. Two thirds of homosexuals so treated, and followed for two years or more, showed improvement.[15]

4. Hypnosis

Hypnosis has been tried through several generations. R. Krafft-Ebing,[16] A.P.F. von Schrenck-Notzing,[17] and A. Meares[18] all felt it had very limited and short-lived value. The danger of transference is very great and for the passive homosexual there may be considerable erotic satisfaction from the therapy. It is not a recommended form of therapy.

5. Shock Therapy

Owensby in 1940 reported on the use of pharmacological shock therapy in the treatment of inversion:

> Of a series of 15 homosexuals of both sexes successfully treated with the pharmacologic shock therapy during the past three years, only two have resumed their former practices. These relapses occurred in patients who did not remain under observation for a sufficient period of time to complete the psychiatric measures believed essential for the success of any method employed in an attempt to correct homosexuality. Many years will have to elapse before a correct evaluation of this method of treatment can be made but certainly its employment has been followed by remission of three years' duration in 13 patients.[19]

I know of no series of cases in which electroshock was used. There is no reason why electroshock should have a beneficial effect on this condition. It might possibly have an effect on some of the depressive manifestations associated with homosexuality as in Patient III (see p. 98).

6. Drug Therapy

No drug has been found that is specific for the disorder. Various hormones have been tried. Their effect, however, was to accentuate the prevailing sexual drive rather than to divert it. Drugs have been used principally by those who accepted a constitutional genesis.

Primarily Psychogenic Therapies

Hirschfeld suggested what he called "adaptive therapy."[20] By this he meant that the subject was aided in adapting to his condition and learning to live with it. Ellis suggested sublimation.[21] Aside from these early suggestions, Freud's rejection of psychoanalysis did much to delay the adoption of psycho-therapeutic depth techniques. His much quoted letter of 1935 in which he expressed marked pessimism about the results of psychotherapy in homosexuality did not encourage others to try. The letter, which was written to an American woman who had sought advice about the treatment of her homosexual son, was as follows:

Dear Mrs. _____

I gather from your letter that your son is a homosexual. I am most impressed by the fact that you do not mention this term yourself in your information about him. May I question you, why you avoid it? Homosexuality is assuredly no advantage, but it is nothing to be ashamed of, no vice, no degradation, it cannot be classified as an illness; we consider it to be a variation of the sexual function produced by a certain arrest of sexual development. Many highly respectable individuals of ancient and modern times have been homosexuals, several of the greatest men, among them (Plato, Michelangelo, Leonardo da Vinci, etc.). It is a great injustice to persecute homosexuality as a crime, and cruelty, too. If you do not believe me, read the books of Havelock Ellis.

By asking me if I can help, you mean, I suppose if I can abolish homosexuality and make normal heterosexuality take its place. The answer is, in a general way, we cannot promise to achieve it. In a certain number of cases we succeed in developing blighted germs of heterosexual tendencies which are present in every homosexual, in the majority of cases it is not more possible. It is a question of the quality and the age of the individual. The result of treatment cannot be predicted.

What analysis can do for your son runs in a different line. If he is unhappy, neurotic, torn by conflicts, inhibited in his social life, analysis may bring him harmony, peace of mind, full efficiency whether he remains a homosexual or gets changed. If you make up your mind he should have analysis with me!! I don't expect you will!! He has to come over to Vienna. I have no intention of leaving here. However, don't neglect to give me your answer.

Sincerely yours with kind wishes,
Freud[22]

Today, intensive psychotherapy or psychoanalysis is the method of choice. Results with this method are the most satisfactory so far, but even here the results leave much to be desired.

Albert Ellis reported on the treatment of 28 male and 12 female homosexuals. These patients were seen in from 5 to 220 psychoanalytic sessions. It was found that in terms of the ability to engage in satisfactory "sex-love" relationships with members of the other sex, 36 percent were "distinctly" improved and 39 percent were "considerably" improved; 33 percent of the Lesbians were "distinctly" improved and 66 percent were "considerably" improved. In this series he gave no Kinsey rating either before or after treatment.

In commenting on these results Dr. Ellis felt that the following aspects of his technique were important in bringing about the improvement:

1. The therapist was quite accepting and noncritical in relation to the patients' homosexual desires and acts in themselves, but at the same time insistent on unmasking the neurotic motivation behind exclusive, fetishistic, and obsessive-compulsive homosexuality.

2. The therapist did not insist that the patients overcome all their homosexual tendencies, but accepted many of these tendencies as normal or idiosyncratic. He emphasized the patients' becoming more heterosexual rather than less homosexual.

3. The therapist showed, by his manner and verbalizations, that he himself was favorably prejudiced toward heterosexual relationships.

4. Special attention was usually concentrated on the patients' general antisexual attitudes and an active attack was made on his feelings of sexual guilt and shame.

5. In every instance there was as much focusing on the individual's general feelings of inadequacy as on his sex problems. A major goal of therapy was always the achievement of general ego-strengthening, on the assumption that exclusive homosexuality often follows from, and is in turn the further cause of, severe feelings of worthlessness.

6. Wherever possible, the patients were persuaded to engage in sex-love relationships with members of the other sex and to keep reporting back to the therapist for specific discussion of and possible aid with these love relationships.[23]

Others reporting on the results of treatment (for example, Woodward,[24] Knight,[25] and Curran and Parr[26]) gave a guarded and not too optimistic prognosis. Allen was more hopeful. He felt that the condition was durable.[27] A more favorable prognosis was given by Hadfield,[28] Hadden,[29] Poe,[30] Ovesey,[31] and Bieber.[32] All of these authors expressed the opinion that psychotherapy offers promise.

Curran and Parr reported that there was no significant difference between their therapy cases and their controls. Only three out of thirty-eight homosexual cases studied showed some change toward heterosexuality after psychotherapy.[33]

Knight reported that two of twelve treated cases were considered cured.[34]

Hadden employed group therapy with homosexual patients. He was unwilling to think in terms of cure "because we regard homosexuality as only a symptom and its suppression without definite personality reorganization is of little value. . . . We should aim at personality reorganization rather than symptom control."[35] In such group efforts it is desirable to have patients of a similar age and without too rigid a pattern.

The most recent figures on the results of psychoanalytic treatment are those given by Bieber *et al.*:

Of 106 homosexuals who undertook psychoanalysis, either as exclusively homosexual or bi-sexual, 29 (27 percent) became exclusively heterosexual:
    (a) Of the 72 H-patients who began treatment as exclusively homosexual, 14 (20 percent) became heterosexual.
    (b) Of the 30 H-patients who began treatment as bi-sexual, 15 (50 percent) became heterosexual.

In this study it was felt that results depended to some extent on the length of treatment. The results of treatment as related to duration were as follows:

1. Only 2 patients of 28 (7 percent) who had fewer than 150 hours became heterosexual.

2. Nine of 40 (23 percent) of those patients who had 150-349 hours of analysis became heterosexual.

3. Eighteen of 38 (47 percent) of the patients who had 350 or more hours of analysis became heterosexual.[36]

Prevention

In view of the multiplicity of factors involved in the etiology of inversion, prophylaxis is difficult. A look at the variety of possibilities of psychiatric traumata listed in Chapters 6 and 7 helps to some extent in seeing the size of the problem. Certainly a happy marriage and a happy homelife where children are wanted and treated equally, lovingly, and with proper attention to their sexual upbringing would be important contributory factors in prevention. One finding of Bieber and his group is of special importance:

> We have come to the conclusion that a constructive, supportive, warmly-related father precludes the possibility of a homosexual son. . . . Most mothers of homosexual sons were possessive of them.[37]

Improved knowledge of proper parent-child relations, although not easily obtained, would be useful, since parents could then at least avoid some of the more obvious mistakes (see Ch. 7). Better education of the public and especially of adolescents would help to alleviate the possibility of seduction. This type of instruction has been avoided until recently. In fact the whole subject of sex education has only been treated with any degree of adequacy in recent years. Education of the general public, including professional people, on the subject of homosexuality has been lacking and is still inadequate.

It seems inadequate, too, to sum up the prevention of homosexuality in these terms: that what is required is a happy marriage, a happy home with children who are contented, accepted, and loved. Yet this is the environment which produces citizens who are mentally and physically healthy and who perpetuate these things in their children.

CHAPTER EIGHTEEN

Pastoral Counseling
of Homosexuals

Although some knowledge of the general principles of counseling are presumed in the reader, it might be well to summarize some general considerations. It is first important to make a distinction between types of counseling.[1]

Pastoral counseling is a comparatively new term. In its technique it partakes of some of the elements of all forms of counseling. It is essentially eclectic in its methods and its practitioner is not bound to any one school. It is pragmatic and expedient in its approach, elastic and adaptable in its method. It would be called "guidance" by some, but depending on circumstances it may at times use a counseling approach. It differs from other methods of counseling in that instead of the counselor-counselee approach of the directive-nondirective counselor, it specifically includes God in the counseling relationship. It is clear that the counselor-God-counselee relationship would differ in many respects from the one-to-one "secular" counseling relationship. The term *secular counselor* is used to distinguish the counselor with specialized training, whether he be clerical or lay, from the pastor without such specialized training. The pastor, although he may not aim at being a specialist in counseling, does need knowledge and insight beyond his theological training before he can consider himself more than an amateur in the field.

Pastoral counseling differs from "secular" counseling in its aims, in its methods, and in its techniques. It is a three-way relationship of which God is the third member. "Consequently," according to Father Charles Curran, "pastoral counseling, as I conceive it, is a unique kind of relationship between the person and the counselor, a relationship which implies and introduces God as a third party."[2] As stated above, pastoral counseling is essentially eclectic. It accepts the best from all other methods.

It may at times be directive, authoritarian, and nonpermissive, although at others it may be permissive, nondirective, and accepting. It must always have in mind the pastor's primary religious goal.

It is clear that the pastor's primary function is the salvation of souls and that his primary duties are of a religious nature. His counseling activities, therefore, will be secondary to these purposes and will be aimed primarily at making his parishioners more accessible to his pastoral ministrations. There will therefore be, for the pastor, two aspects of counseling: (a) Primary — that directly aimed at the accomplishment of his pastoral function. (b) Secondary — that which indirectly aids his parishioner and thus makes him more accepting of the pastor's primary ministrations.

Father William C. Bier, S.J., says that pastoral counseling must be related to the pastor's overall aims if it is to be distinct from secular counseling.[3]

The Pastor as Counselor

The pastor, as counselor, must be prepared to listen with all available patience, he must direct with all available wisdom, he must correct and admonish with kindness, he must delve into a difficulty with diligence and prudence. The pastoral counselor must extend his field beyond the confessional to the rectory parlor and office whenever it becomes necessary. When the pastor extends his interests from the purely religious field into the area of general living, he enters the counseling field, if, in doing so, he refrains from offering solutions to the problems brought to him; in renouncing "the imparting of advice in favor of an attempt to get people to understand themselves, he begins to adopt what is essentially a counseling approach."[4]

From this brief description we can deduce that very frequently, in contrast to the "secular" counselor, the pastor offers guidance or direction rather than counseling. The pastor, as pastor, frequently cannot be nondirective, completely permissive, or indiscriminately accepting. The relationship between the pastor and the parishioner frequently cannot be client-centered or counselor-centered, but must be theocentric. Only by stepping out of his priestly role can the pastor practice secular counseling. *He may wear two hats; he may be a profes-*

sional (secular) counselor, and he may be a pastor. He cannot be both simultaneously.

Ordination by the grace of office does not make the pastor a counselor. His purpose is to shepherd the souls entrusted to his care. He uses the customary pastoral means to achieve this end, e.g., teaching revealed doctrine and doctrines connected with revelation, offering the sacrifice of the Mass, and administering the sacraments. His main duty is not helping people in emotional or mental trouble, but rather the salvation of souls. The pastor may use specific techniques which he has acquired from the mental health field, but he does so only in order to reach an individual and help him through pastoral means.

Though the pastor can, and should frequently, be permissive — he may, for example, urge his client to discuss any matter whatsoever, in whatever way he wishes to do so — he must also at times, however, have an attitude of authority in pointing out the Church's laws and teachings as applied to the client's problem. The pastor must bear in mind that he is primarily a clergyman, and, though some knowledge of mental illness and its treatment will be helpful to him, this is not his primary concern. His conviction must be that he counsels, not primarily mentally disturbed persons who happen to be members of his congregation, but members of his congregation who happen to be emotionally or mentally disturbed.

With these general principles clear, I shall now discuss specific aspects of counseling the homosexual.

Counseling the Homosexual

Because of the numerous demands for counseling the homosexual, the pastor must learn early that only those homosexuals who are genuinely concerned over their condition *per se* are likely to benefit from his services. The homosexual who seeks advice because he has gotten into the hands of the police is seldom looking for more than a temporary refuge. This is also true of the homosexual who, although he seeks help, persistently continues to maintain his homosexual friendships and to perform sex acts. The best candidate for counseling and/or psychotherapy is the individual who is in conflict with his homosexuality and who has developed enough anxiety as a result of the conflict that he is likely to persist in his therapeutic efforts (see p. 240).

Provided he accepts his position philosophically and mixes with others of like mind, the homosexual can leave behind the emotional turmoil that originally drove him away from women. Neurotic conflict only remains evident in those who do not fully accept either homosexual or heterosexual adjustment.[5]

The best test of sincerity is the willingness to forgo sexual activity. It is possible, even in some cases in which the individual was poorly motivated in the beginning, to awaken a desire for a change. In most cases it is necessary to combat a fatalistic attitude on the part of the homosexual which produces a feeling that nothing can be done to change the direction of his sex drive and that because of this he is justified in persisting in his sexual activities.

The fact that all homosexuals have a feeling of isolation from their fellows, which produces a feeling of loneliness, brings about the need for a confidant. Since, by the very fact of his office, the clergyman is more inclined to view the moral rather than the psychological aspects of the case, he must be careful, as a rule, not to actively condemn the individual's activity before good rapport is established.

The Pastor Is the First Contact

The pastor is looked upon by many of his parishioners as having a ready solution for almost any problem. To most people the pastor is the one most available for a discussion of the problems which they hesitate to take to others because of their personal nature. The pastor is frequently, therefore, the first to come in contact with these troubled individuals. Dr. Robert Felix, director of the National Institute of Health in the U.S. Public Health Service, estimated that perhaps forty percent of people take their personal problems first to a clergyman.[6]

An effective spiritual rapprochement often rests in the initial *greeting*. It is a very difficult moment for the homosexual when he faces up to admitting his emotional problem, especially if it is for the first time. The counselor must, therefore, be understanding, but discreet and considerate, in his first questions. He must awaken confidence before going on to speak of spiritual remedies. "With many homosexuals, the fact of being able to

255

speak of it openly for the first time without seeing a pharisaic look or the look of naïve astonishment on the face of the listener, is the beginning of rapport. The clergyman should aim, therefore, at creating to the fullest possible extent an atmosphere of confidence."[7]

There is, perhaps, no other admission so painful to make as that of being homosexual; to admit that one is hyper-erotic is at least to state *ipso facto* and sometimes even with a touch of satisfaction, that one's instinct is normally oriented.[8]

Homosexual Acts Are Objectively Immoral

It has been established that homosexual acts are objectively immoral; they are directly opposed not only to the divine positive law, but also to the natural law. Granted this fact, there is still the need for pastoral counseling. Before any further discussion is ventured on the point of counseling, a correction of the following statement should be made:

It requires a voluntary act on the part of the homosexual to perform a homosexual act. The homosexual has the same ability, and should be expected to abstain from sexual activity outside of marriage in the same manner that the heterosexual person is expected to abstain from sexual activity outside of marriage.[9]

I said this in *Fundamental Marriage Counseling* in 1963. Since then I have changed my mind slightly. It is still true that it takes a voluntary, conscious, and deliberate action to perform a homosexual act. It is still true that the homosexual should be altered only to the extent that *all* homosexuals do not have the same ability as *all* heterosexuals to abstain from the sex act outside of marriage. On reflection and additional experience, I am now convinced that *some* homosexuals have *some degree* of decreased responsibility for *some* of their acts.

The counselor may find that the homosexual client believes he has no control over his desires, that he must take pleasure in them, and that they necessarily lead him, willy-nilly, to commit overt homosexual acts. In such a situation it should be explained to him that merely because he is a homosexual his sex drive is not necessarily stronger than that of any "average" heterosexual his own age. Rather, just as chastity is morally and practically possible for a heterosexual, so with divine help it is possible and absolutely necessary for the homosexual. If the homosexual client has goodwill, is otherwise mentally well balanced, and really wants to obey the law of God, then the counselor has real ground for confidence that, if his client keeps away from the people with whom he has committed acts, before long he will be living a chaste life.

The counselor should not hesitate to communicate this confidence which, given the above qualification, is not merely a pietistic optimism, to his homosexual client. Whatever habits of solitary acts and acts with others the client may have contracted, if he has goodwill, honesty, and love of God he can, in most instances, overcome them and lead a celibate life.

When the client is otherwise seriously neurotic the counselor will have less hope for his client's spiritual care, but he may have the opportunity to suggest that, along with his own work, the homosexual consult a psychiatrist. When the client is not firmly persuaded of the undesirability of overt homosexuality, the counselor should warn him that, though he is not responsible for being a homosexual — for his abnormal sex drive — he is responsible for what he allows himself to do with it. In a word, the counselor should so talk to him that he will reach a determination to give up homosexual acts and any inner complacency he might have had about homosexual desires.

Psychiatric Care Should Be Advised

Because of the emotional pressures that often accompany homosexuality there is undoubtedly a high incidence of deep psychological disorders among homosexuals. In such cases a pastor would best fulfill his role by recognizing such disorders and encouraging the client to seek psychiatric treatment. He should not, however, discontinue his own help of a spiritual nature to aid the homosexual in controlling his tendencies.

Certainly it is not the job of the pastoral counselor to attempt a thorough probing of the homosexual's problems. Since he is not trained for "depth psychology" there is a real danger that he may do more harm than good. Writers on the clergyman's guidance of homosexuals agree that the counseling situation should be a supportive one. The understanding attitude of the clergyman will go a long way in helping the homosexual overcome the feeling that his condition has made him a social outcast and in establishing some hope where previously there may have been only despair.

Often, however, psychiatrists are met who distrust this collaboration. To understand their reserve, you must first of all appreciate the instability of the first therapeutic results and the obligation of keeping the full confidence of the subject. But the distrust of the physician may also arise from unfortunate experiences in which the pastoral counselor, ignorant of psychic and especially of psychoanalytical therapeutic techniques, has thwarted, sometimes unconsciously, the therapeutic plan. Mutual collaboration has become easier as knowledge of depth psychology and the problems of the human mind have become more current among the clergy.

In this regard Dr. William Tobin commented:

> The priest or spiritual counselor often will play an ancillary, auxiliary role in the therapy of homosexual individuals. Spiritual values may help to develop and sustain the proper motivation for treatment.[10]

Westwood, however, was not too sure about the favorable effect of religion. He noted that 61 percent of his contacts had turned at one time to their church for help.[11] Yet, only 6 percent reported that they had obtained help with their homosexual problem from their religion, while 5 percent more stated that their religious beliefs had afforded them some comfort. Unfortunately, 87 percent reported no help or comfort from religion[12] and, furthermore, 88 percent had adjusted to their condition.[13]

The Aim of Pastoral Counseling

What should a priest hope to accomplish in his guidance of the homosexual? Father Michael Buckley puts it this way:

> The aim of all pastoral care of the homosexual should be ultimately his re-orientation to heterosexuality and where this is impossible an adjustment to his condition in the only way acceptable to Catholic moral theology — a life of chastity.[14]

It is generally agreed that there is little hope of sexual reorientation for a true homosexual through pastoral counseling. A clergyman should be content to set as his ultimate aim the adjustment of the homosexual to a life of chastity. A more immediate aim and one which is a means to this adjustment should be to help the client understand his own conflicts. A lack of this self-knowledge, an inability to see outside of his narrowed emotions, is the cause of a great many difficulties involved in homosexuality. Regarding this more immediate aim, Father Bier says: "The generic aim of counseling of whatever kind is to help people to help themselves by gaining understanding of their inner conflicts."[15]

Lest any clergyman become discouraged with recidivism while counseling the homosexual, let him keep in mind these words of Father Leo Trese:

> Indeed it is quite conceivable that one might be a homosexual and become a saint, since it is by the conquest of temptation that sanctity is developed, under God's grace. Since "the greater the temptation the greater the merit," the homosexual who achieves self-discipline is doubly admirable, since he must do so despite the lack of safeguards which shelter the person of normal impulses.[16]

The Qualities of the Counselor

Not everyone is equipped to counsel. Since, however, the pastor by his office is forced into counseling situations, there are certain qualities which he must seek to develop. Among these would be the ability to accept individuals professionally, regardless of their personalities, with patience and self-confidence. He must be accepting without condemning or condoning. He must be prepared to be empathetic and not sympathetic. He must be prepared to distinguish between the homosexual who wishes to use the clergyman for his own purposes and the one who is genuinely seeking help. He must be prepared to make a differential diagnosis between true homosexuality, the obsession of being a homosexual, and the homosexual delusions of the schizophrenic (see p. 124).

In addition he must be able to reassure the normally sexed girl who fears that because she dated a male homosexual this proves she is also a homosexual. He must be prepared to accept the fact that many homosexuals have no desire to be cured and that, even in those who do, there is a marked tendency to recidivism. He must be prepared to recognize his own professional deficiencies and to make prompt referrals to others more qualified than himself if he gets beyond his depth.

Homosexuals who turn to a pastor should be able to expect at least to be heard and treated in a spirit of Christian charity. There is no justification for regarding them as a class to be abhorred, as depraved and degenerate.[17] They, like all people, deserve to be understood and to be given the same sympathetic assistance that is willingly given to other types of people. Scorn, contempt, and undue severity will only increase the feeling of inferiority that predominates in many homosexuals despite an outward appearance of self-satisfaction or defiance. Kindness does not mean weakness on the part of the pastor, who should insist on the giving up of all homosexual practices and relations. Unless the client shows definite signs of his intention to do so, the case is well-nigh hopeless; but even then the counselor should try to form in the client the right intention, particularly by educating him to the use of supernatural means. When natural means fail, divine grace may still prevail.

The clergyman is in a position to help remove the undue fear and guilt which are often an integral part of the homosexual's mental outlook. Especially consoling would be the assurance that the client need feel no guilt because of his homosexual inclinations since they are ordinarily beyond the scope of responsibility. A clergyman can help the homosexual regain a sense of his own individual worth which may have been lost over the years.

Basic Tenets of Counseling

For the professional counselor no hints on how to conduct his interview are necessary. Because, however, many clergymen are forced into counseling situations without previous training, I would like to set up some basic ground rules for the untrained counselor. This is not intended as a shortcut to the achievement of counseling skill. It is merely an attempt at "self-help" for those who must counsel because of the office they hold, even though they have had no training.

1. Treat the client as a person with dignity.

2. Bear in mind that many homosexuals do not want to be cured.

3. Do not raise false hopes as to the value of treatment.

4. Accept the client as he is.

5. Do not be surprised if the client seeks to avoid discussing the real problem.

6. Do not interrupt the efforts of the client to tell his story.

7. Ask questions only if necessary.

8. Be flexible in your approach.

9. Encourage the client to discuss himself rather than his symptoms.

10. Encourage the client to discuss his feelings.

11. Do not moralize, criticize, or blame until you have heard the whole story.

12. Be slow in offering advice.

13. Make no promises.

14. The untrained counselor should avoid long and frequent personal interviews with a true homosexual.

Specific Counseling of the Homosexual

There are some specific points about counseling the homosexual which should serve as guidelines for the pastoral counselor. It is important to bear in mind the distinction between counseling and therapy:

> Counseling is a definite dynamic interpersonal relationship in which the counselor, who should be more mature, more educated, and more experienced, applies common sense in assisting another individual who is troubled to reach a beneficial self-solution of a mutually defined problem which is within the "normal" range of behavior, thinking, or feeling.[18]

Therapy is defined in Webster's *New International Dictionary* as: "Treatment of disease; therapeutics; now used chiefly in compounds [compound words]." Psychotherapy is the application of a remedy for emotional or mental illness. Crotty makes this distinction between psychotherapy and counseling:

> Counseling should be distinguished from psychotherapy; the latter being a term referring to techniques employed by persons

261

working with the mentally ill, those persons with deep, difficult to uncover, emotionally laden psychological problems; the former concerned with procedures employed with relatively normal people who have personal problems which they feel are beyond self-solution.[19]

No clergyman, unless he has adequate training, should attempt therapy. This is beyond his capability. In making referral of cases in which he feels such treatment is necessary or desirable, he must be careful to recommend a psychiatrist of whom he has assurance that his principles and practice do not offend against morality. Above all, it would be inadvisable for any clergyman who may have either latent or overt homosexual tendencies of his own to counsel those with similar inclinations.

The good judgment of the counselor must be the guide to procedure as the situation unfolds. There are certain recommendations, however, which will serve to guide his counsel.

1. The first step is that the *individual must be urged to admit to himself that he is a true homosexual.* This step must never be omitted because without such a frank admission further steps in treatment are quite likely doomed to failure. This also gives the counselor an opportunity to make his own prognosis which will include an estimate of the individual's sincerity.

As a rule there is little doubt in the mind of either the counselor or the client that homosexuality exists in the subject. The homosexual merely does not express it in words. As in Alcoholics Anonymous where the first step consists in the admission by the individual that he is powerless in the face of his adversary, so too in homosexuality the individual must admit: "I am a homosexual and I find myself in need of help in the face of my perverse sex drive." The counselor should dwell on this point — "Are you a homosexual?" — until the client has decided he is or is not. If the subject refuses to come to a conclusion about his condition, there is nothing to treat.

This is a *sine qua non* to successful or even relatively profitable treatment. Most homosexuals do not want to recover. Many of them are only looking for a chance to prove their inability to behave otherwise and so to be accepted as they are. . . . The patient must become convinced that he can get well. Furthermore, one must show him moral, social, and psychological reasons *why* he should get well.[20]

2. An early concern of the counselor will be to *break down gradually in the client the idea of the deterministic nature of his condition,* an idea with which he is often obsessed. "It is stronger than I am; I can do nothing against it." The pastor must exercise patience, as was said before (but cannot be said enough), for he is faced with a will that cannot yet exercise itself until the counseling process shall have given back to the subject a little of his autonomy. However, some instruction of the homosexual on the supernatural action of grace may be of help to him. The pastor may, then, systematically remove from him all false, childish conceptions of the "magic power" of grace; if not, the faults which still continue for a time to burden his life will occasion doubts of the efficacy of spiritual aid, such aid being thought of too frequently as a "psychological remedy."

While the counselor is concentrating on relieving the fatalistic attitude, he must at the same time avoid overoptimism. If, for example, assurance of the nonfatalistic nature of homosexuality is followed by informing the homosexual that his sexual deviation is not so difficult to control, there is danger that he will lose confidence at the first lapse. Rather, he must be told that cure is not instantaneous and that a fall does not mean abandonment by God or impossibility of change. He must be assured that with God's grace not only a cure but even sanctity can be attained, since it is by conquest of temptation that sanctity is developed under God's grace.

When the homosexual makes the objection that his is an abnormal drive, Dr. Robert Odenwald may be quoted as saying, "His abnormal drive is probably no stronger than an exaggerated heterosexual drive."[21] Furthermore, we know as a matter of fact that the alcoholic and other addicts have proved that abnormal urges can be controlled. The counselor must be careful in discussing the defenses of the homosexual patient never to permit his own attitude to suggest that the homosexual cannot help himself nor control himself. Such an attitude, however slight or unwitting, would give the homosexual sufficient excuse for considering himself incurable and thus not responsible.

3. *All homosexual activity must stop.* Falls from grace will occur in many cases, but not in all. The homosexual must be

persuaded that he has the ability to remain continent. He will frequently argue that, since he is a homosexual through no choice of his own and since he can never in the nature of things have a normal sexual outlet, therefore he is different and homosexual activity is permitted him. The answer to this is obvious. The homosexual, just as the heterosexual, is not permitted sexual activity outside of marriage. Just as we expect the heterosexual person to be continent outside of marriage, so, too, the homosexual.

4. *All of his previous homosexual companions must be avoided.* This is of the utmost importance because these individuals are a real source of temptation. In forming new friendships, individuals who are sexually attractive should be avoided. The homosexual should live alone. He should not work with boys and, if possible, should avoid entry into the military service. The question of entry into the religious life has been discussed in Chapter 12.

One of the principles of conduct that a homosexual should formulate is that, because of his special condition, there is no value in allowing himself to form or to continue romantic friendships (i.e., those in which sexual attraction is a determining element) with people of his own sex, no matter how chaste the relationship may be. Even if the homosexual is continent in these friendships, it is, nevertheless, a human love which can never be fully realized or satisfied licitly. It will, therefore, inevitably lead to anxiety and repression. Meanwhile, he dissipates energy on frustrated emotion which he could fruitfully apply to some other area of his daily life.

Even if the homosexual's romantic friendships do not lead him into sin, they are still imprudent in that they orient him to unachievable goals. He should, therefore, give them up, as depressing as this may be. The counselor should explain to his homosexual client the virtue of perfect Christian chastity, that is, "for love of God to abstain for the rest of one's life from sexual pleasure,"[22] and that even though he is himself incapable of marriage, his wholehearted obedience to the commandment of chastity (according to one's state in life) will be meritorious.

This is the theory, but what can be done from the practical point of view? The unity of willpower and determination to give up the practice should urge him to give up the persons, places, and things which for him are occasions of sin. He must refuse any contact at all with his former associates. If this cannot be done for some grave reason, then the homosexual must take every means available to render that occasion of sin as remote as possible.

The void that results from such a severance should be filled with new interests, new work, new hobbies, works of charity for others. He should be advised to make new friends of those who view life healthily, to get into fields that will allow a release for his energies in a healthy manner. He should live and work with others who will help him to get over his feelings of inferiority. Such help will increase his courage and confidence when he sees an improved ability to accomplish.

Complete withdrawal from accepted social circles may, on the other hand, also be damaging for the homosexual. Thus:

> The uninformed confessor has a tendency to demand that the invert avoid every contact which might possibly be a source of stimulation for him, e.g., swimming, sports, stag society, artistic circles, male friendships. In many cases such involvements help to drain off a more basic urge for physical contact. To stifle these outlets could very well precipitate the penitent into more frequent and more overt homosexual activity.[23]

The client then should not be discouraged from his social activities but avoid only those persons or places which are for him a proximate occasion of sin.

The counselor must remember in his efforts to seek safe, social activity for his client that male company should be suggested cautiously because it may increase anxiety, tension, and frustration. Professor Jean Lhermitte has said:

> Is it possible, however, to attempt the cure of this tendency by the cultivation of female company without going, be it clearly understood, to the extent of having sexual relations? Certainly, because the experience carries no risks; but in spite of his efforts, the real homosexual experiences only disgust for and aversion to women.

The professor is of the opinion that the prohibition need be less strict for the woman homosexual. Not because he thinks the woman will change, but because "it is legitimate to think that maternity will develop her sentiments of attachment to home, and thus effect a union which the abnormal man is certainly incapable of realizing.''[24]

5. *The homosexual should be urged to keep silent about his condition.* The counselor should urge the homosexual to keep his handicap to himself, and never let himself be tempted to talk about it to anyone, even to his closest friends or to members of his family. It should be discussed only with professionals who have a need to know. On this point Anomaly is firm.[25]

Don't . . .

- Write admissions to inclinations.
- Masquerade in women's clothes.
- Be too meticulous in clothing, wear jewelry, etc.
- Allow voice or intonation to be feminine.
- Stand with hand on hip or walk mincingly.
- Be identified with groups.
- Believe love is the same as friendship.
- Become involved in marked intimacies with men.
- Let enthusiasm for certain males become noticeable.
- Occupy self with pastimes that are feminine.

Do . . .

- Hold frank conversations with suitable persons, avoiding mental repression.
- Encourage every symptom of sexual normalization.
- Cultivate self-esteem.
- Become deeply engrossed in a congenial occupation or hobby.
- Observe discretion and practice self-restraint.

The homosexual can never be sure that if he and his confidant have an argument in the future the information he once imparted will not be held over his head or thrown back at him as a taunt, or that, even if no such rift occurs, the confidant will not let it slip out to a third person. Even if he deliberately indulges in

266

impure thoughts that have as an object a person of his own sex, he need not say more in confession (unless he is asked) than that he had impure thoughts, without describing their precise species; in a word, for his own good he should keep the fact of his sexual misdirection to himself, except when he needs to tell a counselor or a psychiatrist.

6. *A search must be made for psychological factors and an effort made to develop insight into them.* Even if the counselor succeeds in giving the client an insight into the acquired nature of his condition and into his own potentialities, there is still a long road for him to travel because insight alone will not be enough to make him discontinue his homosexual tendencies, which may be deeply ingrained through many years of habit formation.

One of the reasons for tracing the psychological development of the disorder is to establish insight into the acquired nature of the illness and into the client's own capabilities of self-control. The client should be shown the relationship of his psychic tendencies toward members of his own sex, once it is discovered after a discussion of his development. Once the client begins to become more and more convinced of the accidental rather than essential nature of his illness through this development of insight, he is ready for further insight.

> The patient may well be convinced of the acquired nature of his illness, of the possibility of a cure, and the desirability of a cure . . . but he is still faced with the problem of breaking this long-existing habit of homosexual practices.[26]

7. *The part the will plays must be stressed continually.* Only the homosexual who sincerely desires to be cured is likely to persist in the counseling. It should be made clear that while he may not be able to control his indeliberate desires, he can control his actions and deliberate desires by an act of the will. Further, the counselor must make an effort to arouse in the homosexual a desire for normality. He must be persuaded that with effort he can change his sexual orientation which is psychogenic and not the result of heredity or other physical causes.

After pointing out the part of the will, the counselor must inspire in his client supernatural motivation. He must be urged to adopt a new attitude (provided he does not already have it) which includes a love of God and a dedication to his service. In this way he may find a new incentive, a new inner peace, and a stronger desire for normality. Homosexuals who have this attitude may not find their way to counselors.

8. The homosexual should *avoid alcohol,* which tends to limit his control and may lead to relapses.

9. The counselor must help to *supply a socially and morally acceptable sublimation.* Since the only course open to the homosexual until he develops a heterosexual orientation is that of celibacy, St. Augustine's ideas on this reorientation may be useful to him. These may be summed up briefly as follows: "(1) the realization that chastity is a supernatural gift, (2) the achievement of unity of purpose in his own will, (3) the decision to devote his life to an ascetical ideal, (4) constant prayer for healing grace."[27]

The client must be convinced of God's love for him and persuaded that he can live with his inclination in a life of peaceful self-control and sublimation. The priest should encourage sublimation by providing opportunities for works of charity and personal sacrifice.

> The priest can help his penitent focus his perspective so that his whole life is not clouded and colored by the one problem. The invert can be helped to develop the many positive talents he is sure to have, and be proud of them. In doing so he can actually minimize the obsession with sexuality which can so poison the mind with guilt, fear and helplessness that all other creative and compensating activities become stifled or sterile.[28]

Comment

The pastoral counselor has an important role to play in helping the distressed homosexual. He is literally on the front line and should, therefore, be well informed on "spiritual first aid." A good basic knowledge of the natural history of the homosexual is an important part of such training. Actual therapy should be left to the professional counselor.

The following pages are quoted from *Principles to Guide Confessors in Questions of Homosexuality* (National Conference of Catholic Bishops, 1973) and are republished with permission.

This paper has been approved by the Bishops' Committee on Pastoral Research and Practices for distribution to priest-confessors who deal with the moral and pastoral problems of homosexuals.

In the Committee's judgment, the paper contains a valuable digest of traditional and contemporary theological thought on this complex question. It is made available in the hope that homosexuals who seek the Church's aid may find in the priests they consult an ever more effective channel of Christ's grace and mercy.

In increasing numbers Catholic homosexuals ask whether they can be involved in an overt homosexual relationship and receive regularly the Holy Eucharist. To reply to this question the confessor must seek some principles concerning sexuality which will guide him in the direction of homosexuals. He must also seek an understanding of the homosexual condition and the viable alternatives to living in an overt homosexual relationship. The term homosexual is understood to designate an adult person whose sexual inclinations are orientated predominantly toward persons of the same sex. While fully aware that individuals manifest a whole spectrum of sexual behavior, from extremely heterosexual to the opposite pole, our concern is with the individual whose attraction to his* own sex has made him aware of a moral problem, namely, whether the genital expression of his inclinations is seriously sinful for him; and, if it is, what viable ways of living are open to him.

The *objective* morality of sexual acts is based upon the teaching of the Church concerning Christian marriage: Genital sexual expression between a man and a woman should take place only in marriage. Apart from the intentions of the man and of the woman, sexual intercourse has a twofold meaning. It is an act of union with the beloved, and it is procreative. Neither meaning may be excluded, although for a variety of reasons, the procreative meaning may not be attained. By their nature homosexual acts exclude all possibility of procreation

---

*It is understood hereafter in this chapter that the pronouns are intended to apply equally to male and female, except where the context makes it evident that only one sex is intended.

of life. They are therefore inordinate uses of the sexual faculty. It is assumed, moreover, that the only ordinate use of the sexual faculty must be oriented toward a person of the opposite sex. Sexual acts between members of the same sex are contrary not only to one of the purposes of the sexual faculty, namely, procreation, but also to the other principal purpose, which is to express mutual love between husband and wife. For these reasons homosexual acts are a grave transgression of the goals of human sexuality and of human personality, and are consequently contrary to the will of God.

The goals of human personality and sexuality demand that the exercise of the sexual faculty should take place within the family framework. The procreation and education of children is at least as important a goal in marriage as the expression of mutual love. But homosexual acts make the attainment of this goal impossible.

Homosexual acts are also a deviation from the normal attraction of man for woman, which leads to the foundation of the basic unit of society, the family. Two homosexuals cannot complement one another in the same way as male and female. Not surprisingly, lasting and fulfilling homosexual relationships are not found very often. Both Old and New Testament teaching confirms the heterosexual union of man and woman in procreation. Genesis' description is concerned with man and woman forming a new family. In Ephesians man and woman are compared with Christ and his Church. Whenever homosexual acts are mentioned, they are condemned. (See John F. Harvey, O.S.F.S., "Homosexuality," *NCE*, Vol. 7, pp. 116-119 at p. 118.) Six references are found in Sacred Scripture, five to male and one to female: Leviticus 18:2 and 20:13; Romans 1:27; 1 Corinthians 6:9-10; 1 Timothy 1:9-10 (male); Romans 1:26-27 (female). The clearest reference is Romans 1:26-27: "For this cause God has given them up to shameful lusts; for their women have exchanged natural intercourse for what is against nature, and in the same way men, too, having given up natural intercourse with women, have burned in their lusts toward one another, men with men practicing that well-known shamefulness and receiving in their own persons the fitting punishment of their perversity" (Kleist-Lilly translation).

That homosexual practices are a grave violation of the law of God is clear from the context in which St. Paul writes. Because the pagans had refused to worship the true God, God had given them up to the practice of vices, including unnatural forms. God had withdrawn his grace from them in punishment for their idolatry (cf. Romans 1:24-25).

The *subjective* morality of homosexual acts must be considered under two aspects, the origin of the tendency, and the manner in which the person controls it. Concerning the origin of the condition in a given person it can be said safely that man or woman does not will to become homosexual. At a certain point in life, the person discovers that he is homosexual and usually suffers a certain amount of trauma. Sometimes he is young enough to seek professional treatment to reorientate his sexual desires; sometimes he feels too old to benefit by such treatment, or cannot afford to pay for it. In every case he discovers an already existent condition.

Because a deeper knowledge of the possible causes of homosexuality may help both the counselor and the homosexual to understand the condition and to act with greater freedom it is of value to state briefly some of the prevalent theories concerning its origin. The term possible is used advisedly, inasmuch as the etiology of inversion demands further badly needed research. There is hardly a more difficult problem unless it is the conversion of developed homosexual tendencies into normal channels. Mindful of our ignorance, it is better to speak about factors which contribute to the genesis and growth of homosexuality rather than to speak about causes in the strict sense. With these reservations one may say that the theory which attributes homosexuality to psychogenic causes enjoys wide acceptance.

In a summary of research on heredity and hormonal factors Father Michael J. Buckley concludes that there is little available evidence that either factor contributes significantly to the formation of the homosexual. While some studies may suggest that homosexuality may run in families among brothers, as a genetic factor, other studies do not point in the same direction: "Even if a high familial incidence could be demonstrated, a genetic conclusion would be vitiated in many cases by the identity among brothers of environmental conditions, which might also be the sole cause, or a contributory cause, of their homosexual condition.

"*The hormonal theory as a whole* affords little or no basis on which to construct moral principles, and it is beyond question that the general pattern of homosexuality is chiefly due to something other than hormonal imbalance."

Recent studies focus more attention on the father than the mother in the development of the male homosexual, and more stress on the mother than the father in the growth of the female homosexual. Homosexual boys usually have too possessive mothers and too unconcerned fathers, and it is the unconcerned fathers with whom they fail to identify. Homosexual girls, on the other hand, usually have mothers who belittle the femininity of their daughters, and fathers who allow their wives to domineer over the family. In the development of both male and female homosexuals a weak father figure is typical — indeed in many cases a neglectful and alcoholic character. Very often repressed memories of sexual brutality of the father towards the mother shape the little girl's concept of men.

A neglected factor in the genesis of homosexuality is the preschool boy's inability to form effective peer relationships. Perhaps of sickly disposition, and unduly sheltered from the other boys by his mother, this youngster yearns to play with his peers, but is not allowed to do so. He sees other boys romping and playing and experiencing a kind of rough but warm relationship with companions. He feels left out. As a result of this feeling, he may never develop normal peer relationships, and eventually he will tend to seek physical fulfillment with peers whom he regards as more masculine. He will offer himself as a sexual object so as to be accepted and embraced by peers or other males. Basically, he has failed to identify with his own sex either in terms of father or of peers, and, consequently, he identifies with a female way of viewing reality.

Others hold that homosexuality represents arrested emotional development; for example, the adolescent who fails to get beyond a phase of homosexual attraction remains emotionally fixed at this level. The child who does not outgrow an earlier narcissistic stage may be capable of loving only a person as much like himself as possible, and very probably a person of the same sex. He may meet this person during adolescence. It seems that "learning experience" may precipitate a youngster into homosexual practices who otherwise might have passed through the adolescent phase without any overt acts. By "learning experience" is meant a form of seduction which induces the youth into seeking the same pleasure again.

The initiating factor may be unconscious fear of the opposite sex or lack of opportunity to contact such. In a broader sense, the future homosexual has "learned" from his or her early childhood *attitudes* towards the opposite sex which become the seed ground of adolescent seduction. While early childhood attitudes formed toward both parents and towards self do not make adolescent seduction inevitable, they certainly predispose the youngster toward inversion.

Other factors in the development of the homosexual person include: deprivation of normal family life (for example, institutionalized children); antisexual puritanism, which regards woman as "untouchable." This idolization of woman may be a disguised fear of her. At any rate, such a person tends to regard actions with his own sex as innocent, or only slightly serious, thus forming a habit of homosexual practices out of which it is difficult to withdraw. Also, early unconscious seduction of a child by his parents in circumstances of extreme immodesty. Another factor is fear of inadequacy in fulfilling the role of male or female; a bad case of acne, deep shyness, the habit of stammering, may cause a boy to seek companionship and affection exclusively among his own sex. If the ordinary early adolescent seeks his own sex until he is sure of himself, all the more so will the very shy youth tend to find a refuge in the company of his own sex for a longer period of time with risk of homosexual seduction. Similar patterns are found among female inverts. Also, rigid, loveless family life: in his study of 106 homosexuals, Dr. Irving Bieber concluded that not one of them had a relationship with either parent that could "by any stretch of the imagination be called normal." Some see the origin of homosexuality in the child who perceives the lack of love between his or her parents.

From this summary of the multiple factors involved in the development of the homosexual person it is clear that one cannot pinpoint precisely the decisive factors in the history of any homosexual. "Probably no single factor alone is present in all instances, and possibly no single factor is exclusively responsible in one individual, but to a greater or less extent many of the causes . . . are found as a thread of continuity in most instances of exclusive or overwhelming homosexual development."

Responsibility for controlling the homosexual tendency, however, is another matter — indeed a complex question.

Homosexuals vary in the *degree* of freedom which they possess in controlling their sexual desires. At one extreme are homosexuals who have as much control over their tendencies as normal heterosexuals; and at the other extreme are homosexuals who are as compulsive as alcoholics. Each homosexual has the obligation to control his tendency by every means within his power, particularly by psychological and spiritual counsel. A special word should be said about the compulsive homosexual. Compulsion may be described as a narrowing of consciousness concerned either with a fascination for some object or with obedience to an impulse regarded as intolerable unless accepted. In a broader sense, the term also includes a conviction, both of failure to control it, that a particular urge is irresistible. The compulsive nature of many homosexual acts may be surmised from the squalid circumstances, coupled with risk, in which many meetings take place. Reciprocal masturbation in a public washroom is hardly the sort of thing which would appeal to a normally free agent.

Since there are so many kinds and degrees of compulsion, it is practically impossible to say that an action was the result of a compulsive urge. Before one can say that an action was compulsive, one must know the whole person. Although the person may be regarded as a compulsive homosexual, he is not hopeless if he seeks professional help, which can help him either to live with the compulsion without giving voluntary consent to its movements, or to rid himself of it by therapy. It should be noted that heterosexuals also apparently have hopeless compulsions of various kinds, including self-abuse, alcoholism, drug addiction, and the like. In sexual compulsions, particularly, the real problem is not the strength of the sexual instinct, which usually is no stronger than in normal persons, but rather the individual's inability to adjust to tensions within his personality.

In assessing the responsibility of the homosexual the confessor must avoid both harshness and permissiveness. It is difficult for the homosexual to remain chaste in his environment, and he may slip into sin for a variety of reasons, including loneliness and compulsive tendencies and the pull of homosexual companions. But, generally, he is responsible for his actions, and the worst thing that a confessor can say is that the homosexual is not responsible for his actions.

This does not mean that in most instances the homosexual

has full freedom of will. Very often freedom is diminished, more in some situations than in others. One may speak of a weakened *voluntarium,* but at the same time one must be careful not to excuse the homosexual for past behavior. His or her responsibility is to discover ways of strengthening the power of the will through renewed vision and fresh motivation. It is the confessor's task to help the person work out an ascetical plan of life so that he or she realizes that one can draw motivation from many sources for leading a Christlike life. The person with homosexual tendency should be made aware that, despite the resolution to begin a new life, very probably there will be relapses because of long-standing habit, but this must not be allowed to be an occasion for sterile self-pity.

PASTORAL APPROACHES: Since the teaching of the Catholic Church on sexuality does not permit homosexual acts, it is necessary to propose to individuals who have homosexual tendencies some alternatives, alternatives which will vary contingent upon the age and state of life of the person. The fact that there are so many degrees of homosexuality should also be noted. The first category may be called *temporary* homosexuals.

Temporary Homosexuals: A teen-age boy or girl or young adult confesses actions with members of his own sex. This may be only a passing experience, and it should be treated with prudence. The confessor must seek to know more to determine whether he is dealing with a person who is predominantly homosexual. He should encourage the young person to seek professional help and to return to the confessor for further guidance. The younger the person, the greater the chance that therapy can redirect his sexual inclinations. The confessor should encourage the person to form stable relationships with persons of both sexes. He should treat the person with this difficulty in the same way as he would help the heterosexual.

Some specific directives for the apparent adolescent homosexual. If prevention is better than cure, then counselors should make extraordinary effort to help the adolescent (or even young adult) with apparently homosexual tendencies. Such a person must avoid obvious homosexual groups with their affectations of dress and speech; prowling in those areas of the city where sexual deviates congregate, usually in bars; conversations with strangers loitering in public lavatories, physical culture magazines and weight-lifting clubs; impassioned letters, while destroying all received; situations where immunity from adult observation is combined with a high degree of physical exposure (private swimming pools, summer camp cabins, dressing rooms for athletes). As these directives indicate, modesty is necessary in the individual's relationships with members of his own sex as well as the other. (See John F. Harvey, O.S.F.S., *Continuum*, "Morality and Pastoral Treatment of Homosexuality," pp. 279-297 at p. 296.)

A similar approach is advisable with older persons who occasionally, particularly under the influence of liquor or drugs, lapse into homosexual acts.

While prisoners frequently submit to homosexual acts under terror, they are not entirely inculpable. Their culpability, however, is reduced significantly, and, once returned to society, the homosexual condition usually disappears. The confessor can help them best by seeking to remedy the total situation of the prison.

Apparent Permanent Homosexuality: The older person may come to argue with the confessor that the sole relationship in which he can find fulfillment is a homosexual one; or he may come to seek help to avoid the homosexual environment in which he finds himself regularly. If the person comes to argue the merits of faithful homosexual unions, he should be given time to express his feelings on the matter, but advised that only by lengthy discussion outside the confessional can the priest respond to his argument and to his need for direction.

The priest should do more than outline the arguments which we have indicated above; he should show the person that he can live chastely in the world by means of a plan of life, which will include personal meditative prayer, spiritual reading, reception of the sacraments, and some specific work of charity in the world. Two other elements which should be stressed are regular access to spiritual direction and the formation of a stable friendship with at least one person. One of the greatest difficulties for the homosexual is the formation of such a friendship.

Sometimes the individual seeks the confessor's help to break out of his homosexual environment. He does not need any persuasion concerning the morality of his way of living. He needs motivation to move out of a situation in which he has had a measure of human affection and support from others in the same condition as himself. While he should be encouraged to reintegrate himself into the heterosexual culture, he should seek to form stable friendships among both homosexuals and heterosexuals. On the surface, this may seem like placing the homosexual in "the proximate occasion of sin," but other elements in his plan of life, and spiritual direction, can temper this danger, which is justified, considering his need for deep human relationships, and the good which will come from them in the future. A homosexual can have an abiding relationship with another homosexual without genital sexual expression. Indeed the deeper need of any human is for friendship rather than genital expression, although this is usually an element in heterosexual relationships.

The confessor need not insist that the longtime homosexual seek psychiatric treatment, although it may be beneficial. Unfortunately, many homosexuals have a hang-up about psychiatry, and will seek the aid of a clergyman instead. It is a mistake for the confessor to refuse to help such persons. When it is clear to the confessor that the person does not hope for any change in sexual orientation, the confessor should accept this fact and continue to provide an ascetical plan of life.

If a homosexual has progressed under the direction of a confessor, but in the effort to develop a stable relationship with a given person has *occasionally* fallen into a sin of impurity, he should be absolved and instructed to take measures to avoid the elements which lead to sin without breaking off a friendship which has helped him grow as a person. If the relationship, however, has reached a stage where the homosexual is not able to avoid overt actions, he should be admonished to break off the relationship.

The Married Homosexual: The first point to be determined by the confessor is whether the penitent is homosexual, bisexual, or basically heterosexual with occasional homosexual relapses. Usually, this cannot be determined immediately, and may call for professional counseling. If it is clear that the person has been homosexual for a long time, it would be better for the penitent to disclose this information to his wife, or vice versa, rather than to remain in a union which is doubtfully valid. The canonical aspects should be referred to the diocesan marriage tribunal, provided, of course, the penitent is willing to transfer the matter to the external forum. If, however, as is usually the case, the person has manifested the capacity to be husband or wife, despite relapses into homosexual activities on certain occasions, and if the person wants to save his marriage, the confessor should encourage him to do so, provided the individual is willing to seek regular spiritual guidance and to make use of the various means already mentioned. Whether the husband or wife of such a person should be told by the person himself is a question which can be resolved by the ordinary rules of prudence. Where the person's behavior has the earmarks of compulsion, it is generally better that the spouse be told, and his or her help sought. In these circumstances secrecy itself increases the tension of the compulsive person.

The Seminarian, Religious, and Priest: In regards to seminarians who suspect this tendency in themselves the confessor should seek counsel from professional sources so as to distinguish between passing homosexual proclivities, known as "crushes," and a real homosexual orientation. If there is a real homosexual orientation, the individual should be advised to seek psychiatric help, because, generally speaking, the person has other problems besides the homosexual condition, and the related question, whether this person should continue his studies for the priesthood, will have to be examined. While a confessor should have no hesitation in refusing absolution to a student who has regularly indulged in homosexual activity unless he leaves the seminary, there are other situations which are too complex for immediate solution. The teen-ager or young adult in the minor seminary who has failed seriously on one occasion in this regard should be guided differently from another individual who masturbates frequently with homosexual fantasy. It is very probable that the latter should leave the religious life or the priesthood, because the prognosis for a healthy religious or priestly life is poor. Homosexual fantasy leading to masturbation is symptomatic of deep-seated problems. In the case of seminarians the basic question is whether the person will have such great difficulties in the practice of complete chastity that he will be constantly unhappy in the priesthood or in religious life. Doubts ought to be resolved in favor of the Church and really of the individual himself, because his departure very probably will avoid subsequent spiritual and emotional harm to himself and scandal to those who would be affected by his behavior in the future. In this area our hindsight can become foresight.

When it comes, however, to those already perpetually committed to religious life or the priesthood, the problem should be handled differently. As already mentioned, there are many different degrees of the homosexual condition. For the priest who *occasionally* slips into homosexual actions what is necessary is that he examine the KIND of occasion in which he is wont to fail. Oftentimes it is a combination of frustration and depression, need to escape, alcohol, and cruising in homosexual (gay) haunts. Just as the heterosexual priest under similar motivation may commit sins of unchastity, so the occasionally homosexual priest should be induced to see that in both cases persons tend to fall when they lose sight of their motives for the life to which they have committed themselves. Under guidance, then, the priest who slips only on occasion can learn to practice complete chastity.

Unfortunately, however, there are priests who are deeply steeped into a homosexual way of life and who usually do not make it a matter of confession, if they go at all. One reason why they do not mention homosexual activity is that they have convinced themselves that it is either not sinful for them, or that it is not a serious sin. These individuals need a complete spiritual rehabilitation in which both psychologists and spiritual directors take part. The problem is both psychological and spiritual. [At this writing] an institute whose objective will be the rehabilitation of such priests and religious is in the process of formation. Meanwhile the confessor or spiritual director should encourage persons in this condition to pray and to hope that they can rise above their situation. Despite verbal rationalizations these priests really want to be chaste.

Lesbians: The confessor should become acquainted with some of the traits of the Lesbian. Female homosexuals differ from male inverts in the depth of their attachments and in the relative permanency of their relationships. This means that the priest will encounter Lesbians who are living in a kind of faithful union more often than he will meet male homosexuals living together. Homosexual women have a better chance to express themselves, yet their relationship is less physical, and in some cases the physical action is very infrequent. Those who come for counsel are generally more receptive than male homosexuals to another point of view. She is more willing to admit the obviously emotional coloring in her attachments, to which she will cling, not so much in rebellion against moral principles, but rather from fear of the vacuum which she foresees as consequent upon her renunciation of the beloved. Finally, the social pressures to marry are greater in the life of the female homosexual. These differences have pastoral significance. First of all, female homosexuals do not feel the same need for physical expression as their male counterparts. If they could maintain an intimate relationship with another woman without passionately physical expression, they would settle for it in order to avoid serious sin. Some Catholic women do maintain such a relationship. The emotional reward which they derive from such a relationship more than compensates for the lack of genital expressions. Again, the Lesbian does not engage in rationalizations like the male homosexual. She seeks some form of intimate relationship, but has not been able to find it in heterosexual contacts. Now she prefers an intimate friendship with another woman. If she sees it as a question of conscience she is willing to try to sublimate her sexual desires.

Many homosexual women did not accept this way of life until they had been engaged to marry or already married; many are able to engage in both heterosexual and homosexual relationships. On the whole, they are more fluid and open to the possibility of conversion into heterosexuality. Unfortunately, however, they are under greater social pressure to marry than their male counterparts. As in the case of the married male homosexual, a canonical cause for invalidity can be posed, but it is more difficult to prove.

The Overt Homosexual and the Reception of the Eucharist: One of the results of recent literature on the subject, coupled with the Gay Liberation Movement, has been an increased demand by Catholic overt homosexuals that they be allowed to receive the Holy Eucharist. Usually the argument runs that homosexual actions are normal for them; and that just as the heterosexual person can enter into a faithful union with a person of the opposite sex in order to complete himself, so the homosexual should be allowed to form an analogous union with one of his own sex. He may have to go through a period of promiscuity before he arrives at such a stable relationship, but in this respect he is not significantly different from many heterosexuals who are involved in more than one passionate affair before marriage.

These concepts are championed by Catholic organizations composed of homosexuals and homophiles who are dedicated to helping the Catholic homosexual to develop a healthy respect for himself and to realize that his manner of sexual expression does not exclude him from full participation in the sacraments of the Church. Some Catholic homosexuals argue that as long as the person is trying to serve God and neighbor, the fact of his sexual deviation is of no major consequence. One looks to the fundamental way of living of the person, and not to the sexual aberrances, which oftentimes the person himself does not see as abnormal.

To these relatively new arguments the confessor should respond with firmness, showing how erroneous is the idea that each person has the right to variety in sexual expression contingent upon his sexual orientation. The confessor, however, should provide the person with a viable alternative, however difficult the chaste life may be. Already mentioned are various elements in the plan of life which can be proposed to the homosexual. If possible, he should be encouraged to change his sexual orientation. He should seek to form at least one stable human relationship, if not more. He should not be surprised by periodic tensions and some relapses. He should sublimate repeatedly his sexual desires in the pursuit of service to God and neighbor. In short, the confessor helps him to live as a Christian in the world and in religion.

Chapter Notes

Chapter 1

1. Martin S. Weinberg and Alan P. Bell, *Homosexuality: An Annotated Bibliography* (New York: Harper and Row, Publishers, Inc., 1972).

2. Henry V. Sattler, "Sex: A Christian View," *New Catholic Encyclopedia* (New York: McGraw-Hill, 1967), Vol. 13, p. 147.

3. Bernard Häring, C.S.S.R., *The Law of Christ* (Westminster, Md.: The Newman Press, 1966), Vol. 3, p. 269.

4. *Ibid.*

5. Francis W. Carney, "Reproduction and the Whole Man," *America,* Vol. 12, No. 8 (February 20, 1965), p. 246.

6. John F. Harvey, O.S.F.S., "Morality and Pastoral Treatment of Homosexuality," *Continuum,* Vol. 5, No. 2 (Summer, 1967), pp. 289-290.

7. Häring, *op. cit.,* p. 268.

8. Derrick S. Bailey, *Homosexuality and the Western Christian Tradition* (London: Longmans, 1955), pp. 1-28.

9. Raymond E. Brown, S.S., John A. Fitzmyer, S.J., and Roland E. Murphy, O. Carm. (eds.), *The Jerome Biblical Commentary* (Englewood Cliffs, N.J.: Prentice-Hall, Inc., 1968), Vol. I, pp. 21, 78-79, 297.

10. John F. Harvey, O.S.F.S., "Homosexuality," *New Catholic Encyclopedia* (New York: McGraw-Hill, 1967), Vol. 7, p. 117.

11. Häring, *op. cit.,* p. 273.

12. Charles E. Curran, *Catholic Moral Theology in Dialogue* (Notre Dame: University of Notre Dame Press, 1972), pp. 209ff.

13. John J. McNeill, S.J., *The Church and the Homosexual* (Kansas City: Sheed Andrews and McMeel, Inc., 1976).

14. *The Washington Post,* February 2, 1971, editorial page.

15. Häring, *op. cit.*

16. C.A. Tripp, Ph.D., *The Homosexual Matrix* (New York: The New American Library, Inc., 1975).

Chapter 2

1. Karl Bowman and Bernice Engle, "A Psychiatric Evaluation of the Laws of Homosexuality," *The American Journal of Psychiatry,* Vol. 112, No. 8 (February, 1956), pp. 577-578.

2. Derrick S. Bailey, *Homosexuality and the Western Christian Tradition* (London: Longmans, 1955), p. 33.

3. George Hagmaier, C.S.P., and Robert Gleason, S.J., *Counseling the Catholic* (New York: Sheed and Ward, 1959), p. 94.

4. Charles Berg, M.D., and Clifford Allen, M.D., *The Problem of Homosexuality* (New York: The Citadel Press, 1958), pp. 20-21.

5. Magnus Hirschfeld, *Die Homosexualität des Mannes und des Weibes,* 2nd ed. (Berlin: L. Marcus Verlagsbuchhandlung, 1920). Quoted by Alfred C. Kinsey *et al., Sexual Behavior in the Human Male* (Philadelphia and London: W.B. Saunders Co., 1948), p. 619.

6. Kinsey *et al., op. cit.,* p. 624.

7. The British government in 1954 appointed a "Committee on Homosexual Offences and Prostitution." This committee, which published its report in 1957, was known informally as the Wolfenden Committee.

8. Alfred M. Freedman *et al., Comprehensive Textbook of Psychiatry,* Vol. II, 2nd ed. (Baltimore: Williams and Wilkins Co., 1975), pp. 1510-1511.

9. Shere Hite, *The Hite Report, A Nationwide Study on Female Sexuality* (New York: The Macmillan Co., 1976), p. 261.

10. John F. Oliven, M.D., *Sexual Hygiene and Pathology* (Philadelphia and Montreal: J.B. Lippincott Co., 1955), pp. 430-431.

11. Laud Humphreys, *Out of the Closets: The Sociology of Homosexual Liberation* (1972), p. 10. As quoted in *Editorial Research Reports* (Washington, D.C.: Congressional Quarterly, Inc., 1974), p. 184.

Chapter 3

1. Robert L. Spitzer, M.D., "A Proposal About Homosexuality and the APA Nomenclature," June, 1973. The press release of December 15, 1973, was based on this document, p. 4.

2. *Ibid.*

3. *Roche Report: Frontiers of Psychiatry,* "Deleting homosexuality as an illness, a psychiatric challenge to values," Vol. 4, No. 3, February 1, 1974.

4. National Institute of Mental Health, *op. cit.,* No. 43, pp. 20-21.

5. San Francisco, October, 1973 *(S. I. R. and Hickerson* vs. *Hamppon);* Washington, D.C., December, 1973 *(Baker and Rau* vs. *Hamppon).*

6. Jack Roth, "Nationwide Ring Preying on Prominent Deviates," *New York Times,* March 3, 1966.

7. Arthur J. Silverstein, "Constitutional Aspects of the Homosexual's Right to a Marriage License," *Journal of Family Law,* Vol. 12, No. 4 (1973), pp. 607-634.

8. John F. Russell, Interview, manuscript in preparation on the subject, December 3, 1976.

9. *Psychiatric News,* April 3, 1974, pp. 2, 19.

10. Milman, *ibid.,* p. 19.

11. John F. Harvey, O.S.F.S., "Counseling the Apparent Adolescent Homosexual," *Bulletin of the Guild of Catholic Psychiatrists,* Vol. 10, No. 4 (October, 1963), pp. 204-214.

12. *Documents of Vatican II,* "The Church in the Modern World," Walter Abbott (ed.), Nos. 47-52, pp. 249-258.

13. "The American Confessor and Homosexuality," *Dignity,* April, 1974, p. 9.

Chapter 4

1. Leon Salzman, "The Concept of Latent Homosexuality," *American Journal of Psychoanalysis,* Vol. XVII, No. 2 (1957), p. 167.

2. John F. Oliven, M.D., *Sexual Hygiene and Pathology* (Philadelphia and Montreal: J.B. Lippincott Co., 1955), p. 431.

3. Lionel Ovesey, "The Homosexual Conflict," *Psychiatry,* Vol. XVII, No. 3 (August, 1954), p. 245.

4. Anomaly, *The Invert* (Baltimore: Williams and Wilkins Co., 1948), p. 6.

5. "Report on Homosexuality With Particular Emphasis on This Problem in Governmental Agencies," compiled by The Group for the Advancement of Psychiatry (3617 W. 6th Ave., Topeka, Kans.), Report No. 30, January, 1955.

6. Rev. William J. Tobin, *Homosexuality and Marriage* (Rome: The Catholic Book Agency, 1964), pp. 22-23.

7. Oliven, *op. cit.,* p. 430.

8. Robert W. Laidlaw, "A Clinical Approach to Homosexuality," *Marriage and Family Living,* Vol. XIV, No. 1 (February, 1952), p. 42.

9. Oesterle states that homosexuality is such that in relation to persons of the opposite sex the subject is absolutely impotent (Gerald Oesterle, "De Relatione Homosexualitatis ad Matrimonium," *Revista Española de Derecho Canonico,* X [1955], No. 28, p. 23). The term will not be used in this sense in this text. It will be considered as a synonym of "true" inversion.

10. Sigmund Freud, *New Introductory Lectures on Psychoanalysis,* Lecture 33 in volume on *The Major Works of Sigmund Freud* in *Great Books of the Western World* (Chicago: Encyclopaedia Britannica, Inc., 1952), p. 854.

11. Sigmund Freud, *The Basic Writings of Sigmund Freud,* A.A. Brill (ed.) (New York: Random House, Inc., 1938). Quoted by Leland E. Hinsie, M.D., and Jacob Shatsky, Ph.D., *Psychiatric Dictionary* (New York: Oxford University Press, 1953), p. 304.

12. *Ibid.*

13. Sigmund Freud, *Collected Papers,* Vol. III, trans. A. and J. Strachey, London: Leonard and Virginia Woolf, 1952, quoted by Leland E. Hinsie, M.D., and Jacob Shatsky, Ph.D., *Psychiatric Dictionary* (New York: Oxford University Press, 1953), p. 222.

14. E. Kahn and E.G. Lion, *American Journal of Psychiatry,* Vol. XCV (1935), p. 132.

15. *The Basic Writings of Sigmund Freud,* quoted by Hinsie and Shatsky, *op. cit.,* p. 304.

16. *The Encyclopedia of Sexual Behavior,* Albert Ellis and Albert Abarbanel (eds.) New York: Hawthorn Books, Inc., 1961, Vol. I, p. 485.

17. Clifford Allen, *A Textbook of Psychosexual Disorders* (London: Oxford University Press, 1962), p. 172.

18. *The Wolfenden Report,* authorized American edition with Introduction by Karl Menninger, M.D. (New York: Stein and Day, 1963), pp. 35-36.

19. Ellis and Abarbanel, *op. cit.,* Vol. II, p. 802.

20. English and English, *A Comprehensive Dictionary of Psychological and Psychoanalytical Terms* (New York: Longmans, Green and Co., 1958), p. 498.

21. Hinsie and Shatsky, *op. cit.,* p. 493.

22. *Loc. cit.*, fn. 11.

23. George Weinberg, *Society and the Healthy Homosexual* (1972), quoted in *Educational Research Reports*, March 8, 1974, p. 185.

Chapter 5

1. Robert G. Gassert, S.J., and Bernard H. Hall, M.D., *Psychiatry and Religious Faith* (New York: The Viking Press, 1964).

2. Barbara Wooten, "Sickness or Sin," *The Twentieth Century*, May, 1956.

3. *The Linacre Quarterly*, Vol. XX, No. 4 (November, 1953), p. 99.

4. In John Ford, S.J., and Gerald Kelly, S.J., *Contemporary Moral Theology* (Westminster, Md.: The Newman Press, 1958), Vol. I, p. 175.

5. Rudolph Allers, *The Homiletic and Pastoral Review*, April, 1942, p. 642.

6. Rev. Michael J. Buckley, *Morality and the Homosexual* (Westminster, Md.: The Newman Press, 1959), p. 153.

7. Irving Bieber *et al.*, *Homosexuality* (New York: Basic Books, Inc., 1962), p. 9.

8. Clara Thompson, "Changing Aspects of Homosexuality in Psychoanalysis," *Psychiatry*, Vol. X (1947), p. 186.

9. *The Wolfenden Report*, authorized American edition with Introduction by Karl Menninger, M.D. (New York: Stein and Day, 1963), p. 19.

10. Thompson, *op. cit.*, p. 184.

11. *Diagnostic and Statistical Manual of Mental Disorders*, prepared by the Committee on Nomenclature and Statistics of the American Psychiatric Association (Washington, D.C.: A.P.A. Mental Hospital Service, 1952), pp. 34-35.

12. *Ibid.*, pp. 38-39.

13. A.C. Kinsey *et al.*, *Sexual Behavior in the Human Male* (Philadelphia and London: W.B. Saunders Co., 1948), p. 660.

14. Clifford Allen, "The Meaning of Homosexuality," *International Journal of Sexology*, Vol. VI, pp. 207-212 at p. 209.

15. Lionel Ovesey, "The Homosexual Conflict," *Psychiatry*, Vol. XVII, No. 3 (August, 1954), p. 243.

16. In *The Basic Writings of Sigmund Freud*, A.A. Brill (ed.) (New York: Modern Library, 1938).

17. John R. Cavanagh, M.D., *Fundamental Pastoral Counseling* (Milwaukee: The Bruce Publishing Co., 1962), p. 140.

Chapter 6

1. Father Buckley agrees with the findings of the Henry Foundation and states that "acquired homosexuality by initiation and indulgence must be admitted as the main causative factor in a large number of homosexual cases" (Rev. Michael Buckley, *Morality and the Homosexual* [Westminster, Md.: The Newman Press, 1959], p. 114). On the contrary, Father Harvey, a longtime student of this disorder, comments: "It has not been proven that a real homosexual tendency is *mainly* the result of initiation" (John F. Harvey, O.S.F.S., *Theological Studies,* Vol. XXI, No. 3, September, 1960, p. 493).

2. John R. Cavanagh, M.D., and James B. McGoldrick, S.J., *Fundamental Psychiatry,* 2nd rev. ed. (Milwaukee: The Bruce Publishing Co., 1958), pp. 552-553.

3. Clifford Allen, *A Textbook of Psychosexual Disorders* (London: Oxford University Press, 1962), p. 169.

4. *Ibid.,* p. 170.

5. Buckley, *op. cit.,* p. 151.

6. A. Weil, "Concerning the Anatomical Fundamentals of the Congenital Homosexual," *Arch. Frauenck-Eugen.,* 10, pp. 23-26. See also: A. Weil, "The Substance of the Expression of Homosexuals About Their Specific Constitution," *Arch. f. Entwicklungsmechanik der Organismen,* 49 (1921), p. 538; J. Vague, G. Favier, and J. Nicolino, "Somatic Aspects of Male and Female Homosexuality," *Sessuologia,* Vol. IV, No. 3 (July-September, 1963), pp. 124-149; L. Muscardin, "Research Into Some Morphological Features in a Group of Homosexuals," *Sessuologia,* Vol. IV, No. 3 (July-September, 1963), pp. 124-149; L. Muscardin, "Research Into Some Morphological Features in a Group of Homosexuals," *Sessuologia,* Vol. IV, No. 3 (July-September, 1963), pp. 150-154.

7. Quoted in Dom Thomas V. Moore, *The Nature and Treatment of Mental Disorders* (New York: Grune and Stratton, 1951), p. 321.

8. J. Wortis, "Intersexuality and Effeminacy in a Male Homosexual," *American Journal of Orthopsychiatry,* 10 (1940), pp. 567-569. See also: J. Wortis, "Note on Body Build of Male Homosexuals," *American Journal of Psychiatry,* 93 (1937), p. 1121.

9. A.J. Coppen, "Body Build of Male Homosexuals," *British Medical Journal,* Vol. II (1959), pp. 1443-1445.

10. A.D. Dixon, and J.B.D. Torr, "Chromosomal Sex and Abnormal Sex Development," *British Medical Journal,* Vol. I (1948), pp. 222-228. See also: G. Lapponi, "Determination of Nuclear Sex. Technical Note and Findings Obtained From a Large-Scale Survey," *Sessuologia,* Vol. IV, No. 3 (July-September, 1963), pp. 120-123; F. Brambilla, "Endocrinal and Chromatinic Pictures of Male Homosexuality," *Sessuologia,* Vol. IV, No. 3 (July-September, 1963), pp. 170-174.

11. C.M.B. Pare, "Homosexuality and Chromosomal Sex," *Journal of Psychosomatic Research,* 1 (1956), pp. 247-251.

12. W. Davidson and S. Winn, *Postgraduate Medical Journal,* 35 (1959), p. 494.

13. M.L. Barr and G.E. Hobbs, *Lancet,* L (1954), p. 1109.

14. J. Raboch and K. Nedoma, "Sex Chromatin and Sexual Behavior: A Study of 36 Men With Female Nuclear Pattern and of 134 Homosexuals," *Psychosomatic Medicine,* Vol. XX (1958), p. 55.

15. Steinach is mentioned only because of his historical interest. His work of rejuvenation of the aging and the treatment of homosexuality by the transplantation of testicles created quite a furor in 1918-1919. For example, in Volume 6 (1921) of the Cumulative Medical Index of Periodical Literature, there were 28 articles listed by different authors. In spite of the interest the results were illusory and the method is no longer employed. A typical article of Steinach on this subject is the following: E. Steinach and R. Lichtenstein, "Umstimmung der Homosexualität durch Austausch der Pubertätsdrusen," *Munchener medizinische Wochenschrift,* Vol. 65 (1918), I, pp. 145-148.

16. Referred to in Moore, *op. cit.,* p. 329.

17. S.J. Glass, H.J. Duel, and C.A. Wright, "Sex Hormone Studies in Male Homosexuals," *Endocrinology,* 26 (1940), pp. 590-594.

18. R. Neustadt and A. Myerson, "Quantitative Sex Hormone Studies in Homosexuality, Childhood and Various Neuropsychiatric Disturbances," *American Journal of Psychiatry,* 97 (1940), pp. 524-551.

19. Cf. Alfred C. Kinsey, *Journal of Clinical Endocrinology,* I (1941), p. 424.

20. G.I.M. Sawyer, "Homosexuality: The Endocrinological Aspects," *The Practitioner,* 172 (April, 1954), pp. 374-377. Cf. also: G.I.M. Sawyer, *Lancet,* 2 (December 12, 1959), p. 1077; L.A. Lurie, "The Endocrine Factor in Homosexuality," *American Journal of Medical Science,* 208 (1944), pp. 176-186.

21. Cf. John Money, "Components of Eroticism in Man. I: The Hormones in Relation to Sexual Morphology and Sexual Desire," *Journal of Nervous and Mental Diseases,* 132 (1961), pp. 239-248; "II. The Orgasm and Genital Somesthesia," 132; pp. 289-297; *idem,* "Sex Hor-

mones and Other Variables in Human Eroticism," in W.C. Young (ed.), *Sex and Internal Secretions*, 3rd ed. (Baltimore: Williams and Wilkins Co., 1961), Ch. 22.

22. John Money, *art. cit.*, p. 32. Cf. also: G.I.M. Sawyer, *op. cit.*, pp. 374-377; J. Tudor Rees and Harley V. Usill (eds.), *They Stand Apart* (New York: The Macmillan Co., 1955), pp. 71-72; L.A. Lurie, *op. cit.*; "Endocrine and Disordered Sexual Behavior," *British Medical Journal*, 1 (March 9, 1957), p. 574.

23. Sheldon E. Waxenburg, "Some Biological Correlatives of Sexual Behavior," in George Winokur (ed.), *Determinants of Human Sexual Behavior* (Springfield, Ill.: Charles C. Thomas, 1963), p. 57. Cf. also: U. Teodori and F. Morabito, "Endocrinological Aspects of Homosexuality," *Sessuologia*, Vol. IV, No. 3 (July-September, 1963), pp. 156-164; M. Tocca and F. Micheli, "The Validity of Hormonal Exploration in the Diagnosis of Homosexual Conditions," *Sessuologia*, Vol. IV, No. 3 (July-September, 1963), pp. 165-169; F. Brambilia, *op. cit.*; A. Marcozzi, "Value of Homosexual Behavior in Adolescence," *Sessuologia*, Vol. IV, No. 3 (July-September, 1963), pp. 175-177; A. Marcozzi, P. Pomini, and N. Caprioli, "Determination of Urinary 17-Ketosteriods in Females With Homosexual Tendencies," *Sessuologia*, Vol. IV, No. 3 (July-September, 1963), pp. 178-179.

24. M. Sydney Margolese, and Oscar Janiger, "Androsterone/Etiocholanolone Ratios in Male Homosexuals," *British Medical Journal*, July 28, 1973, p. 207.

25. R. v. Krafft-Ebing, *Psychopathia-Sexualis* (New York: The Physicians and Surgeons Book Co., 1934), pp. 282ff.

26. Robert W. Laidlaw, "A Clinical Approach to Homosexuality," *Marriage and Family Living*, Vol. XIV, No. 1 (February, 1952), pp. 39-45.

27. Dom Thomas V. Moore, O.S.B., "The Pathogenesis and Treatment of Homosexual Disorders," *Journal of Personality*, Vol. XIV, No. 1 (September, 1945), pp. 49-50.

28. Theodore Lang, "Studies on the Genetic Discrimination of Homosexuality," *Journal of Nervous and Mental Diseases*, Vol. XCII (1940), pp. 55-64.

29. R. Goldschmidt, *The Mechanism and Psychology of Sex Determination* (London: Rd. Methuen, 1924).

30. See Moore, *The Nature and Treatment of Mental Disorders, loc. cit.*, p. 325.

31. K. Jensch, "Zur Genealogie der Homosexualität," *Archiv fur Psychiatrie und Nervenkrankheiten*, 112 (1941), pp. 527-540, 679-696.

32. Eliot Slater, "The Sibs and Children of Homosexuals," in *Symposium on Nuclear Sex* (New York: Interscience Publishers, 1958).

33. R.A. Darke, "Heredity as an Etiological Factor in Homosexuality,"*Journal of Nervous and Mental Diseases,* 107 (1948), pp. 251-268.

34. Franz J. Kallman, "Comparative Twin Studies on the Genetic Aspect of Male Homosexuality," *Journal of Nervous and Mental Diseases,*115 (1952), pp. 283-298. Cf. also: L. Gedda, "Genetic Aspects of Homosexuality," *Sessuologia,* Vol. IV, No. 3 (July-September, 1963), pp. 108-119.

35. Charles Berg, M.D., and Clifford Allen, M.D., *The Problem of Homosexuality* (New York: The Citadel Press, 1958), p. 39.

36. *Ibid.,* p. 40.

37. Alfred M. Freedman *et al., Comprehensive Textbook of Psychiatry,* Vol. II, 2nd ed. (Baltimore: Williams and Wilkins Co., 1975), p. 1512.

38. *Ibid.*

39. Allen, *op. cit.,* p. 166.

40. Referred to in Sandor Rado, "A Critical Examination of the Concept of Bisexuality," *Psychosomatic Medicine,* II, No. 4 (October, 1940), p. 460.

41. See Rado, *op. cit.,* pp. 460ff.

42. Krafft-Ebing, *op. cit.,* pp. 282ff.

43. Rado, *op. cit.,* p. 460.

44. Sigmund Freud, *Three Contributions to the Theory of Sex in The Basic Writings of Sigmund Freud,* A.A. Brill (ed.) (New York: Modern Library, 1938).

45. Helene Deutsch, "Homosexuality in Women," *Psychoanalytic Quarterly,*October, 1932, pp. 484-510.

46. Karen Horney, "On the Genesis of the Castration Complex in Women," *International Journal of Psychoanalysis,* Vol. V (1924), p. 50.

47. Helen Mayer Hacker, "The Ishmael Complex," *The American Journal of Psychotherapy,* Vol. VI, No. 3 (July, 1952), pp. 484-513.

48. The first footnote to Hacker's article in the *American Journal of Psychotherapy* gives the names of other novels in which she sees elements of the Ishmael complex; for example, *Moby Dick, Huckleberry Finn, Two Years Before the Mast,* and *The Leatherstocking Tales.*

49. Erwin Krausz, notes distributed as "ditto" copies after the

paper was read at a meeting of the American Psychiatric Association. I have not seen it published subsequently.

50. Sandor Lorand, M.D., and Michael Balint, M.D. (eds.), *Perversions, Psychodynamics and Therapy* (New York: Random House, Inc., 1956), pp. 92-94.

Chapter 7

1. See O. Fenichel, *The Psychoanalytic Theory of Neurosis* (New York: Norton, 1945); Karen Horney, "The Problem of Female Masochism," *Psychoanalytic Review,* 22, (1935), p. 241.

2. Charles Berg, M.D., and Clifford Allen, M.D., *The Problem of Homosexuality* (New York: The Citadel Press, 1958), p. 143.

3. Harry Stack Sullivan, *The Interpersonal Theory of Psychiatry,* Helen Swick Perry and Mary Ladd Garvel (eds.) (New York: Norton, 1953). Quoted by Irving Bieber *et al., Homosexuality* (New York: Basic Books, Inc., 1962), p. 9.

4. Quoted by Bieber, *op. cit.,* p. 10.

5. *Ibid.,* p. 303.

6. Donald W. Cory, "Homosexuality," in *The Encyclopedia of Sexual Behavior,* Albert Ellis and Albert Abaranel (eds.) (New York: Hawthorn Books, Inc., 1961), Vol. I, p. 491.

7. *Ibid.,* p. 492.

8. Quoted by William Stekel, M.D., *The Homosexual Neurosis* (New York: The Physicians and Surgeons Book Co., 1934), p. 15.

9. Stekel, *op. cit.,* p. 15.

10. Walter Bromberg, M.D., "Homosexuality," in the *Encyclopedia of Mental Health,* Albert Deutsch and Helen Fishman (eds.) (New York: Franklin Watts, Inc., 1963), Vol. III, pp. 751-752.

11. Dr. Howard Davidman, "What You Should Know About Homosexuality," *State of Mind* (published by CIBA, Summit, N.J.), Vol. II, No. 4 (April, 1958), pp. not indicated.

12. Albert Ellis, "The Effectiveness of Psychotherapy With Individuals Who Have Severe Homosexual Problems," *Journal of Consulting Psychology,* Vol. XX, No. 3 (1956), p. 191.

13. Clifford Allen, *A Textbook of Psychosexual Disorders* (London: Oxford University Press, 1962), p. 176.

14. *Ibid.,* p. 185.

15. William G. Cole, *Sex and Love in the Bible* (New York: Association Press, 1959), p. 358.

16. Anomaly, *The Invert* (Baltimore: Williams and Wilkins Co., 1948), p. 130.

17. Paul Le Moal, "The Psychiatrist and the Homosexual," in *New Problems in Medical Ethics,* Dom Peter Flood (ed.) (Westminster, Md.: The Newman Press, 1955), Vol. I, p. 82.

18. Adelaide M. Johnson, M.D., and David B. Robinson, M.D., "The Sexual Deviant," *Journal of the American Medical Association,* 164 (1957), pp. 1559-1565.

19. Donald J. West, M.B., *The Other Man* (New York: Whiteside, Inc., and William Morrow and Co., 1955), p. 152.

20. *Ibid.,* pp. 148-149.

21. Johnson and Robinson, *op. cit.*

22. "The Hidden Problems," *Time,* December 28, 1953, p. 29.

23. Dom Thomas V. Moore, O.S.B., "The Pathogenesis and Treatment of Homosexual Disorders," *Journal of Personality,* Vol. XIV, No. 1 (September, 1945), p. 79.

24. John F. Harvey, O.S.F.S., "Homosexuality as a Pastoral Problem," *Theological Studies,* Vol. XVI, No. 1 (March, 1955), p. 90.

25. *Ibid.*

26. James H. VanderVeldt, O.F.M., and Robert P. Odenwald, M.D., *Psychiatry and Catholicism* (New York: McGraw-Hill, 1957), p. 429.

27. Moore, *op. cit.,* p. 79.

28. VanderVeldt and Odenwald, *op. cit.,* p. 429.

29. Norman St. John-Stevas, *Life, Death and the Law* (Bloomington, Ind.: Indiana University Press, 1961), p. 215.

Chapter 8

1. John F. Oliven, M.D., *Sexual Hygiene and Pathology* (Philadelphia and Montreal: J.B. Lippincott Co., 1955), p. 435.

2. Alfred C. Kinsey *et al., Sexual Behavior in the Human Male* (Philadelphia and London: W.B. Saunders Co., 1948), p. 637.

3. Charles Berg, M.D., and Clifford Allen, M.D., *The Problem of Homosexuality* (New York: The Citadel Press, 1958), p. 43.

4. Donald W. Cory, *Homosexuality: A Cross Cultural Approach* (New York: The Julian Press, Inc., 1956), p. 386.

5. R. Eugene Holemon, M.D., and George Winokur, M.D. "Effeminate Homosexuality: A Disease of Childhood," mimeographed notes distributed after the talk delivered at the annual meeting of the American Psychiatric Association, May, 1964, Los Angeles, Calif.

6. Clara Thompson, "Changing Concepts of Homosexuality in Psychoanalysis," *Psychiatry,* 10 (1947), p. 188.

7. Hans Giese, M.D., *Jahrbuch Psychol., Psychother.,* 1 (1953), pp. 223-225.

8. Hans Giese, M.D., "Differences in the Homosexual Relations of Man and Woman," *International Journal of Sexology,* May, 1954, pp. 225-227.

9. Leon Salzman, "The Concept of Latent Homosexuality," *American Journal of Pscyhoanalysis,* Vol. XVII, No. 2 (1957), pp. 161-169.

10. Irving Bieber (ed.), *Homosexuality — A Psychoanalytic Study* (New York: Basic Books, Inc., 1962), pp. 257-258.

11. Anomaly, *The Invert* (Baltimore: Williams and Wilkins Co., 1948), p. 143.

12. Dom Peter Flood, O.S.B. (ed.), *New Problems in Medical Ethics* (Westminster, Md.: The Newman Press, 1955), p. 115.

13. Anomaly, *op. cit.,* p. 130.

14. John F. Harvey, O.S.F.S., "Homosexuality as a Pastoral Problem," *Theological Studies,* Vol. XVI, No. 1 (March, 1955), p. 87.

15. Gerald Kelly, *Modern Youth and Chastity* (St. Louis: The Queen's Work Publishing Co., 1941), p. 18.

16. Harvey, *op. cit.,* p. 88.

17. *Ibid.*

18. *Ibid.*

19. Rev. Charles Larere, "Passage of the Angel Through Sodom," in *New Problems in Medical Ethics,* Vol. I, p. 111.

20. Meyer Levin, *Compulsion* (New York: Simon and Schuster, 1956).

21. Warren A. Ketterer, M.D., "Venereal Disease and Homosexuality," special communication in the *Journal of the American Medical Assocation,* Vol. 188, No. 9 (June 1, 1964), pp. 811-812.

22. See W.J. Daugherty, "Epidemiological Treatment of Syphilis Contacts," *Journal of the Medical Society of New Jersey,* 59 (November, 1962), pp. 564-567. See also W.V. Bradshaw, "Homosexual Syphilis Epidemic," *Texas Journal of Medicine,* 57 (November, 1961), pp. 907-909.

23. *Journal of the American Medical Association,* Vol. 185, No. 5 (August 3, 1963), p. 415.

24. Reported in an article by Jean M. White in *The Washington Post,* Feb. 3, 1965, p. 1.

25. Ketterer, *op. cit.*

26. M.F. Garner, M.B., B.S., M.R.C. Path., F.R.C.P.A., "An Analysis of 340 Cases of Syphilis Diagnosed in the Laboratory in Six Months in 1973," *The Medical Journal of Australia,* May 15, 1976, p. 735.

27. Michael G. Ritchey and Arnold M. Leff, M.D., "Venereal Disease Control Among Homosexuals: An Outreach Program," *JAMA*, May 5, 1975, Vol. 232, No. 5, p. 509.

Chapter 9

1. Alfred C. Kinsey, *et al., Sexual Behavior in the Human Male* (Philadelphia and London: W.B. Saunders Co., 1948), p. 638.

2. Alfred M. Freedman *et al., Comprehensive Textbook of Psychiatry,* Vol. II, 2nd ed. (Baltimore: Williams and Wilkins Co., 1975), p. 1511.

3. Radcliffe Hall, *The Well of Loneliness* (New York: Covici, 1928).

4. D. Riccio and A. Petiziol, "Psychological Examinations in Homosexuality," *Sessuologia,* Vol. IV, No. 4 (October-December, 1963), pp. 215-218.

5. Clifford Allen, *A Textbook of Psychosexual Disorders* (London: Oxford University Press, 1962), p. 245.

6. Kinsey, *op. cit.,* p. 679.

7. John F. Oliven, M.D., *Sexual Hygiene and Pathology* (Philadelphia and Montreal: J.B. Lippincott Co., 1955), p. 397.

8. Daniel G. Brown, "Transvestism and Sex-Role Inversion," in *The Encyclopedia of Sexual Behavior,* Albert Ellis and Albert Abarbanel (eds.) (New York: Hawthorn Books, Inc., 1961), Vol. II, p. 1017.

9. Kinsey, *op. cit.,* p. 679.

10. Allen, *op. cit.,* p. 252.

11. Karl M. Bowman, M.D., and Bernice Engle, M.A., "Medico-legal Aspects of Transvestism," *The American Journal of Psychiatry,* Vol. CXIII, No. 7 (January, 1957), p. 583.

12. C. Hamberger, G.K. Sturup, and E. Dahl-Iverson, "Transvestism," *Journal of the American Medical Association,* Vol. 152 (1953), pp. 391-396.

13. Allen, *op. cit.,* p. 253.

14. "MD tennis star's sex surgery spotlights transsexualism," *Medical World News,* September 6, 1976, pp. 26-27.

15. *Ibid.*

16. *Ibid.*

17. Oliven, *op. cit.,* p. 409.

18. Paul Friedman, "Sexual Deviation," in *The American Handbook of Psychiatry,* Silvano Arieti (ed.) (New York: Basic Books, Inc., 1959), p. 605.

19. Oliven, *op. cit.*, p. 410.

20. Manfred Sakel, *Schizophrenia* (New York: Philosophical Library, 1958), p. 177.

21. George Winokur, "Sexual Behavior: Its Relationship to Certain Effects and Psychiatric Diseases," in *Determinants of Human Sexual Behavior,* George Winokur (ed.) (Springfield, Ill.: Charles C. Thomas, 1963), p. 98.

Chapter 10

1. Quoted from *The Homosexuals,* A.M. Kirch (ed.) (New York: The Citadel Press, 1954), p. 3.

2. Kinsey *et al., Sexual Behavior in the Human Female* (Philadelphia and London: W.B. Saunders Co., 1953), p. 484:

"[34]There are specific statutes against female homosexuality only in Austria, Greece, Finland, and Switzerland."

"[36]The states in which the statutes apparently do not apply to female homosexuality are: Connecticut, Georgia, Kentucky, South Carolina, and Wisconsin. Heterosexual cunnilingus has been held not 'the crime against nature' in Illinois, Mississippi, and Ohio, and the decisions would supposedly apply to homosexual cunnilingus. In Arkansas, Colorado, Iowa, and Nebraska there is also some doubt as to the status of female homosexuality."

3. See Derrick S. Bailey, *Homosexuality and the Western Christian Tradition* (London: Longmans, 1955), p. 164.

4. In Kinsey, *op. cit.,* pp. 475-476, fns. 19 and 20 give these references:

"[19]For instance, Clark (Clark, W. E., ed., *Two Lamaistic Pantheons,* Cambridge, Mass.: Harvard University Press, 1937, Vol. I, p. 70) and Bergler (Bergler, E., *Neurotic Counterfeit-Sex,* New York: Grune and Stratton, 1951, p. 317) feel that the incidence of homosexuality among females exceeds that among males. Others differentiate various types of homosexuality, and feel that incidental or temporary homosexuality is commoner in the female, as in: Bloch (Bloch, I., *The Sexual Life of Our Time in Its Relations to Modern Civilization,* trans. by M.E. Paul, London: Rebman, 1908, p. 525) and Hirschfeld (Hirschfeld, M., *Sexual Anomalies and Perversions,* London: Francis Aldor, 1944, p. 281). Others who estimate that homosexuality is equally common in both sexes include: Havelock Ellis (*Studies in the Psychology of Sex,* 3rd ed., Philadelphia: F.A. Davis Co., 1915, Vol. II, p. 195); Krafft-Ebing (*Psychopathia Sexualis,* trans. by F.J. Rebman, Brooklyn, New York: The Physicians and Surgeons Book Co., 1922, p. 397); Freud (*Collected Papers,* trans. by J. Riviere and A. and J. Strachey, London: Hogarth Press and the Institute of Psychoanalysis, 1924, Vol. II, p. 202); Kelly (*Sexual Feeling in the Woman,* Augusta, Ga.: Elkay Co., 1930, p. 143); and Sadler (Sadler, W.S. and L.K., *Living a Sane Sex Life,* Chicago and New York: Wilcox and Follett Co., 1944, p. 92).

"[20]All specific studies have arrived at incidence figures for the male which exceed those for the female: Hamilton (Hamilton, G.V., *A Research in Marriage,* New York: Albert and Charles Boni, 1929, pp. 494ff.) (57 percent male, 37 percent female); Bromley and Britten (Bromley, D.C., and Britten, F.H., *Youth and Sex,* New York and London: Harper and Brothers, 1938, pp. 117, 210) (13 percent male, 4 percent female); Gilbert Youth Research 'How Wild Are College Students?' [Unsigned article on survey by Gilbert Youth Research], *Pageant,* November, 1951, pp. 10-21) (12 percent male, 6 percent female)."

5. Cited in *They Stand Apart,* His Honor Judge Tudor Rees and Harley V. Usill (eds.) (New York: The Macmillan Co., 1955), p. 69.

6. Kinsey, *op. cit.,* pp. 452-453.

7. Simone de Beauvoir, *The Second Sex* (New York: Alfred A. Knopf, 1953), p. 561.

8. Morris W. Brody, "An Analysis of the Psychosexual Development of a Female — With Special Reference to Homosexuality," *Psychoanalytic Review,* 30 (1943), pp. 47-58.

9. Helene Deutsch, "Homosexuality in Women," *Psychoanalytic Quarterly,* October, 1932, pp. 484-510; Karen Horney, "On the Genesis of the Castration Complex in Women," *International Journal of Psychoanalysis,* Vol. V (1924) p. 50.

10. Shere Hite, *The Hite Report* (New York: The Macmillan Co., 1976), p. 275.

11. Preuss (J. Preuss, *Sexuelles in Bibel und Talmud,* Allg. med. Zentral-Zeitung, 1906, pp. 571ff.) quotes a few passages from the Talmud which show that tribadism was known, but it is not mentioned in the Bible. The usual expression for it is *soledeth* ("moving towards each other with a springing or hopping movement"). Only a few schools fancied that such women should be treated legally as prostitutes; the others declared such doings to be "unmoral," but attached no legal consequences to it.

12. The following is from Hermann Heinrich Ploss, Max Bartels, and Paul Bartels, *Woman* (London: William Heinemann, Ltd., 1935), pp. 74-76:

"In England the word *dildo* is usually employed. The O.E.D. states that it is 'a word of obscure origin, used in the refrains of ballads.' It was, however, used for other purposes; the word may be connected with the Italian *diletto*. Thomas Nash sang the praise of this object, 'attired in white velvet or in silk,' which indeed 'maie fill, but never can begett,' and for the pleasure it gives 'no tongue maie tell.' Such playthings were amongst the miscellaneous assortment of objects hawked by pedlars which trade Boucher has painted (see 'Bilder-Lexikon,' I, 245), and Shakespeare has mentioned when he speaks of the 'delicate burthen of dildos and fadings' ('Winter's Tale,' Act IV, sc. 4). . . .

"Here may also be mentioned the Madigo of the Hausa women, a contrivance made in imitation of the male organ, which women strap on in order to gratify other women, and which was employed especial in very large harems. Before England took possession of the country a woman found with such an instrument was severely punished: She was buried alive and her partner was sold into slavery. (For further details see Mischlich, *Bilder-Lexikon,* I, p. 419; and for the same customs among the women of Lake Chad, see Bouillez). . . .

"In classical antiquity, especially in Greece, as Knapp illustrated with several examples, the use of an instrument called 'Olisbos,' knowledge of which apparently came from Asia Minor, was for a time very widely spread so that even the authorities took severe measures against it. Passages in Aristophanes, Herondas, Lucian, as well as certain pictorial representations, which Knapp discusses in greater detail, give full particulars."

13. Radcliffe Hall (pseudonym) in *The Well of Loneliness* gives a sensitive and artistic appraisal of the pathos of the homosexual conflict within a female homosexual though the etiology suggested is oversimplified and perhaps naïve; furthermore, the solution suggested seems to be a rather pessimistic acceptance of a *fait accompli.*

14. Seduction by older females: A. Moll, *The Sexual Life of the Child* (New York: The Macmillan Co., 1912), p. 314. H. Ellis, *Studies in the Psychology of Sex; op. cit.,* Vol. II, p. 322. M.F. Farnham, *The Adolescent* (New York: Harper and Brothers, 1951), p. 167.

Chapter 11

1. Charles J. Ritty, J.C.L., "Possible Invalidity of Marriage by Reason of Sexual Anomalies," *The Jurist,* Vol. XXIV, No. 4 (October, 1963), pp. 394-422.

2. Gerard Oesterle, "Welchen Einfluss hat die Homosexualität

auf die Ehen," *Oesterreichesches Archiv fur Kirchenrecht,* Vol. XII (1961), pp. 305-334. See also Monsignor Vincent P. Coburn, "Homosexuality and the Invalidation of Marriage," *The Jurist,* Vol. XX, No. 4 (October, 1960), pp. 441-459.

3. John F. Oliven, M.D., *Sexual Hygiene and Pathology* (Philadelphia and Montreal: J.B. Lippincott Co., 1955), p. 450:

"The exclusive homosexual, as a rule, should be strongly advised against marriage, no matter how greatly he seems to long for the comforts of a conventional home or for a child. The belief that marriage can cure true homosexuality in any way is a fallacy. It matters little if the prospective bride is aware of his abnormal tendencies; such marriages almost always lead to sorry complications for all parties. Permissible exceptions are marriages of convenience with a woman who is totally anhedonic or a Lesbian herself, or considerably older than the patient. In these cases he may obtain some of the companionship and ordered life of marriage without its sexual obligations."

Rev. James H. VanderVeldt and Robert Odenwald, M.D., *Psychiatry and Catholicism* (New York: McGraw-Hill, 1957), p. 434:

"Is marriage indicated as a solution in cases of homosexuality? For pseudo-homosexuals, as we have defined them, marriage or a return to regular marital life will often be the best and only solution. But it would be disastrous to advise marriage to a genuine homosexual as long as he has not been changed into a heterosexual by some method of therapy, regardless of whether his condition is supposed to be organogenic or psychogenic. Marriage does not cure the genuine homosexual of his deviant inclinations, and because he does not feel any real psychic attraction toward the other sex, his condition will cause his partner untold grief. Should a homosexual, before being cured, insist upon marriage, he is morally bound to reveal his condition to his partner."

4. John F. Harvey, O.S.F.S., "Homosexuality and Marriage," *Homiletic and Pastoral Review,* December, 1961, pp. 227-234; "Counseling the Homosexual," *Homiletic and Pastoral Review,* January, 1962, pp. 328-335. It would seem to me that Father Harvey does not clearly state the nature of the "bisexual" individual. In my opinion, as stated in this book, the individual usually referred to as "bisexual" is one who will accept relations with either sex. He is not really a homosexual, but merely an "opportunist" (see p. 41 of this book).

5. See also John F. Harvey, "Homosexuality as a Pastoral Problem," *Theological Studies,* Vol. 16, No. 1 (1955), p. 98.

6. A great deal of emphasis has been put on the psychological

components of marriage, other than the sex act, for quite some time. Every effort is made to safeguard the freedom of the parties from force and fear, stimulated consent, mental disorders, psychic impotency, etc. However, the law by its very nature tends to stress the licitness and validity of acts. It leaves other aspects of marriage to dogmatic and pastoral literature.

7. Rev. Paul V. Harrington and Charles J.E. Kickham, M.D., "The Impediment of Impotency and the Condition of the Male Impotence," *The Linacre Quarterly,* Vol. XXV, No. 3 (August, 1958), p. 108.

8. *Code of Canon Law,* Canons 1012 and 1081. See T. Lincoln Bouscaren, S.J., and Adam C. Ellis, S.J., *Canon Law,* 3rd ed. (Milwaukee: The Bruce Publishing Co., 1957), pp. 453-454, 553-554.

9. Thus, in speaking of marriage as a contract, Bouscaren and Ellis stress that it is a very special kind of contract, a sacred contract. *Ibid.,* pp. 453-455.

10. *Gaudium et Spes,* par. 48.

11. *Ibid.*

12. Roman Rota, *Coram I. Anne,* Feb. 25, 1969, cited by Paul Palmer, "Marriage," *New Catholic Encyclopedia: Supplement* (New York: McGraw-Hill, 1972), p. 279.

13. St. Augustine, *De bono conjugali,* 5, 12.

14. In the case of a person desiring to marry a confessed homosexual, the law does give the ordinary of the diocese or archdiocese the power forbidding the marriage (C. 1039, 1).

15. Canon 1086, 2: "But if either party or both parties by a positive act of the will exclude marriage itself, or all right to the conjugal act, *or any essential property of marriage,* the marriage contract is invalid."

16. Bouscaren and Ellis, *op. cit.,* p. 551.

17. Ritty, *op. cit.,* p. 409: "Here there is no question of a diriment impediment, there is no question of insanity; but there is a basic incapacity of the subject to give full and free consent to the substance of the contract of marriage. Is it not conceivable, therefore, that one who is afflicted with one of the sexual anomalies, by reason of an obsessive compulsion to perform unnatural and perverted acts, could also be considered in the same category as the nymphomaniac, who has an invincible sexual instinct contrary to the substance of marriage?"

18. In the opinion of Dom Boissard the immediate end, that is, the one first achieved, "is to give the couple through close, complete and final union of the lover's person with that of the beloved, that completion which is his natural desire: a deeply valued support — material, bodily, sensual, emotional and spiritual all at the same time — which is

for the majority of human beings the providential means to their moral progress and of their sanctification" (*Questions theologique sur le mariage,* p. 17).

19. Roman Rota, *Coram v. Fagiolo,* Oct. 30, 1970, in Palmer, *art. cit.,* p. 279.

20. See E. Schillebeeckx, *Marriage: Human Reality and Saving Mystery* (New York: Sheed and Ward, 1965), Ch. 1; and John L. McKenzie, S.J., *The Two-Edged Sword* (Milwaukee: The Bruce Publishing Co., 1956), Ch. 4.

21. *Ibid.*

22. De Fabregues, *op. cit.,* p. 23: "Can we conclude from a text such as this that an absolute parallel exists between the relation of the husband and wife and the relation of Christ and the Church? There is no question of this, and the reasons are obvious, the first one being in the very nature of a relationship between creatures and the fact that it is realized through the senses, physically, even though it is rooted deeper and grows higher. Yet St. Paul himself goes further, saying that the bride is the completion of the bridegroom as Christ is completed by the Church which 'is His body, the completion of Him who in all things is complete' (Ephes. 1:23). And again: 'You who are husbands must show love to your wives, as Christ showed love to the Church when he gave Himself up on its behalf' (Ephes. 5:25). We can see more clearly here the meaning that we should learn from this symbol. It is the greatness of an absolute giving which is here envisaged."

Ibid., p. 54: "The Church measures love by the fullness of the meaning given to that 'yes,' by the completeness of that consent which is a promise quite different in standard from those that are exterior and purely emotional. Marriage is a 'society of love, that is, one in which its members are required to love each other,' writes Dom Massabki, who among recent defenders of Christian love has given it the highest place."

23. *Ibid.,* p. 54.

24. *Ibid.,* p. 53.

25. See fn. 18.

26. A sampling of the literature in reference to "homosexual love" shows a universality of opinion that he cannot experience true love: "In contrast to them stands another 'love' which is *sui generis* — a love between man and woman which seeks fulfillment in the establishment of a 'one flesh' *henosis,* the creation of an unique common life in marriage and the building of a family. This, too, has its chastity, but of a different order for it is a love in which the sexual organs have their proper and necessary uses, both in its consummation and in the fur-

therance of its relational and conceptional ends; chastity here, therefore, relates to the due employment of the sexual faculties for their appointed purposes.

"It will be evident *ex hypothesi* that such a love as that last described and the union in which it results cannot possibly have any parallel in homosexual relationship. While, therefore, we may not deny that homosexual love can be a true and elevated experience, we must insist that it is one to which expression may not be given in sexual acts — a limitation which it shares with all forms of heterosexual relationships except one" (Judge Tudor Rees and Harley V. Usill, *They Stand Apart* [New York: The Macmillan Co., 1955], pp. 51-52).

"Male homosexuals often enjoy feminine company and are liked by women, but it is a common fallacy to believe that if they are introduced to sufficiently seductive members of the opposite sex, they will arouse them. Nothing is further from the truth. They are as unaffected by the charms of a bevy of chorus girls as the normal man would be by a platoon of guardsmen. It is most important to stress this, and to contradict the common belief that marriage will cure homosexuality. On the contrary, it is merely a recipe for tragedy" (*Ibid.*).

" 'All the world loves a lover' — but he must be a normal lover and a natural lover. This the invert cannot be" (Anomaly, *The Invert* [Baltimore: Williams and Wilkins Co., 1948], p. 31).

"There is also a question as to whether it is ethically justifiable to ask any woman to give herself into the keeping of a man who is, and who will be tempted, at least, to seek expression for his radical passion in the society of his own sex. The idea is hideous" (*Ibid.*, p. 97).

"The honest invert will admit — perhaps with regret — that he does not know what it means to experience normal desire and that, while he may, or may not, be peculiarly passionate, he feels that whatever potential romances lie sleeping in his heart, they will never be awakened by a woman" (*Ibid.*, p. 53).

"There are inverts for whom feminine society has platonic attractions and who go sometimes even so far as to practice a little lovemaking for convention's sake. On the other hand, many inverts brought to frank admission will tell you that women bore them, while some regretfully admit that in the presence of women they are physically distressed' (*Ibid.*, p. 103).

"These men are attracted exclusively toward men. Erotic situations involving an attractive woman leave them indifferent or even fill them with repugnance or vague fear" (Oliven, *op. cit.*, p 431).

"The essential feature of this strange manifestation of the sexual life is the want of sexual sensibility for the opposite sex, even to the extent of horror, while sexual inclination and impulse toward the same sex are present" (R. v. Krafft-Ebing, *Psychopathia Sexualis* [New York: The Physicians and Surgeons Book Co., 1934], p. 335).

"I am now speaking not of actual homosexuals who, as pathological figures are *incapable of a real friendship* and, therefore, find no particular sympathy among normal individuals, but of more or less young people who feel such an enthusiastic friendship for each other that they express their feeling also in a sexual form" (C.G. Jung, *Contributions to Analytical Psychology* [London: Routledge and Kegan Ltd., 1948], p. 274).

"More common than this automonosexualism are the cases of homosexuality, in which persons of the opposite sex can cause no sort of desire or erection at all" (Magnus Hirschfeld, *Sexual Pathology* [New York: Emerson Books, Inc., 1940], p. 274).

27. Canon Law does not define impotence, though Canon 1068 refers to it:

"1. Impotence antecedent and perpetual, whether on the part of the woman, or on the part of the man, whether known to the other party or not, whether absolute or relative, invalidates marriages by the law of nature itself.

"2. If the impediment of impotence is doubtful either in law or in fact, the marriage is not to be hindered.

"3. Sterility neither invalidates marriage nor renders it unlawful" (cf. James R. Risk, *The Law of Catholic Marriage* [Chicago: Callaghan and Co., 1957], p. 60).

28. Rev. Joseph J. Quinn, *Rotal Jurisprudence With Regard to Functional Impotence in the Male* (Washington, D.C.: The Catholic University of America, 1956), p. 11.

29. Oesterle argues that a marriage with a homosexual can be annulled on three grounds: (1) *exclusio matrimonii ipsius:* there is no intention of entering a real marriage; (2) *exclusio fidelitatis;* (3) *exclusio iuris ad coniugalem actum.* He attempts to prove the invalidity of marriage on homosexual grounds by stating that homosexuality is in its essence imcompatible with marriage. Even though homosexuals may have the wish to break off their prior relationships, they often are unable energetically to fight against their inclinations and, consequently, at the time of the marriage they are lacking in good faith (*op. cit.,* p. 305).

30. *Op. cit.,* pp. 231-232.

31. Benjamin Karpman, *The Sexual Offender and His Offense* (New York: The Julian Press, Inc., 1954), pp. 314-315.

32. See Ritty, *loc. cit.,* and Oesterle, *loc. cit.*

33. "Canon 1020.2. He must ask the man and woman even separately and cautiously, whether they are under any impediment, whether they are giving their consent freely, especially the woman, and whether they are sufficiently instructed in Christian Doctrine, unless in view of the quality of the persons this last question should seem unnecessary."

34. Ritty, *op. cit.*, p. 417: "The arguments that homosexuality is incompatible with marriage may be summed up as follows:

"1. According to canons 1081 and 1086, the homosexual could not have the will to enter a true marriage; under the outward appearance of marriage he desires to continue his homosexual relationships.

"2. On the basis of canons 1081 and 1086, the person before the marriage proposes to sin against matrimonial fidelity, and this can sometimes be established by evidence before and after the marriage.

"3. On the basis of canon 1081, matrimonial consent is not had in the sense that the man and the woman reciprocally hand over and receive forever the exclusive right (*ius in corpus*).

"For these reasons the marriage is invalid: (1) because the homosexual is incapable, as a result of the homosexual relation, even if he had the intention of giving true matrimonial consent, of restraining himself from the homosexual relationship (often there results a true impossibility of normal intercourse with the spouse); (2) because the homosexual not only does not permit the exclusive right to marital intercourse, but often excludes it entirely. The conclusion is that homosexuality is incompatible with the essence of marriage."

Chapter 12

1. René Biot, M.D., and Pierre Galimard, M.D., *Medical Guide to Vocations* (London: Burns and Oates, 1955), p. 135.

2. John R. Connery, S.J., "Notes on Moral Theology," *Theological Studies,* Vol. XVI, No. 4 (December, 1955), p. 586.

3. Pope Pius XII, *The Catholic Priesthood* (Washington, D.C.: National Catholic Welfare Conference, undated), p. 47.

4. "Thorough Examination of Candidates for Orders Strongly Emphasized" (S.C. Sacr., December 27, 1955); Bouscaren-O'Connor, *Canon Law Digest* (Milwaukee: The Bruce Publishing Co., 1958), Vol. IV, p. 312.

5. Anomaly, *The Invert* (Baltimore: Williams and Wilkins Co., 1948), p. 143.

6. Dom Peter Flood, O.S.B. (ed)., *The Problems in Medical Ethics* (Westminster, Md.: The Newman Press, 1955), p. 115.

7. Biot and Galimard, *op. cit.*, p. 144.

8. John F. Harvey, O.S.F.S, private communication.

9. Biot and Galimard, *op., cit.,* p. 135.

10. *Canon Law Digest,* p. 312, Section 11.

11. Connery, *op. cit.,* p. 586.

Chapter 13

1. "Final Report of the Task Force on Homosexuality," October 10, 1969, National Insitute of Mental Health, Dr. Evelyn Hooker, Chairman.

2. Quoted in *Education Research Reports,* Vol. 1, No. 10, March 8, 1974, p. 186.

3. See Edmund Bergler, *Homosexuality: Disease or Way of Life* (1957); Irving Beiber *et al., Homosexuality* (1962); Albert Ellis, *Homosexuality: Its Causes and Cure* (1964); Charles Socarides, *The Overt Homosexual* (1968); Lionel Ovesey, *Homosexuality and Pseudohomosexuality* (1969), and Lawrence J. Hatterer, *Changing Homosexuality in the Male* (1970).

4. Martin Hoffman, "Homosexuality," *Today's Education,* November, 1970, p. 47.

5. *Medical World News,* January 25, 1974.

6. John F. Harvey, O.S.F.S., "The Controversy Concerning Nomenclature Vis-à-Vis Homosexuality," *Linacre Quarterly,* August, 1974, p. 187.

7. E. Carrington Boggan *et al., An American Civil Liberties Union Handbook: The Rights of Gay People* (New York: Avon Books, 1975), p. 138.

8. Personal communication, November 15, 1976.

9. Personal communication, December 3, 1976.

10. *Educational Research Reports, op. cit.,* p. 195.

11. *Ibid.*

12. Dissenting opinion in California v. LaRue (1972), quoted by Walter Barnett, *Sexual Freedom and the Constitution* (Albuquerque: University of New Mexico Press, 1973), p. 67.

13. Personal communication, December 3, 1976.

14. Memorandum from the American Law Division of The Library of Congress, Congressional Research Service, December 11, 1975, p. CSR-9.

15. Frank T. Lindman and Donald M. McIntyre, Jr. (eds.), *The Mentally Disabled and the Law* (Chicago: University of Chicago Press, 1961), p. 310.

16. Alfred C. Kinsey *et al., Sexual Behavior in the Human*

Female (Philadelphia and London: W.B. Saunders Co., 1953), p. 370.

17. John F. Oliven, M.D., *Sexual Hygiene and Pathology* (Philadelphia and Montreal: J.B. Lippincott Co. 1955), p. 441.

18. Saunders v. People, 38 Mich. 218; People v. McCord, 76 Mich. 200, 42 N.W. 1106; State v. Hayes, 105 Mo. 76, 16 S.W. 514, 24 Am. St. Rep. 360; State v. Dudoussat, 47 La. Ann. 977, 17 So. 685; Love v. People, 160 Ill. 501, 43 N.W. 710.

19. William L. Clark and William L. Marshall, *A Treatise on the Law of Crimes* (Chicago: Callaghan and Co., 1912), pp. 226-227.

20. *Ibid.,* p. 227, fn. 213.

21. Charles Berg and Clifford Allen, *The Problems of Homosexuality* (New York: The Citadel Press, 1958). This book has a complete text of the Wolfenden Report on "Homosexuality and Prostitution."

22. Group for the Advancement of Psychiatry, *Psychiatrically Deviated Sex Offenders,* Report No. 9, New York, February, 1950.

23. *Ibid.,* p. 1.

24. Henry Davidson, *Forensic Psychiatry* (New York: The Ronald Press, 1952), p. 111.

25. *Ibid.,* p. 112.

26. Alfred C. Kinsey *et al., Sexual Behavior in the Human Male* (Philadelphia and London: W.B. Saunders Co., 1948), p. 638.

27. *Ibid.,* pp. 193-194.

28. This is likely to change under new desegregation laws. Some thirty states [at this writing] now have antimiscegenation laws (Harper, *Problems of the Family* [1952], p. 268). Almost half of the states are in the North and West. Most laws prohibit intermarriage between members of the Caucasian race and Negroes. In the states having these laws, Negroes comprise from 50 percent or more of the population to less than 1 percent ("Intermarriage with Negroes — A Survey of State Statutes," 36 Yale L.J. 858, 1928). the prohibition in other states is extended to Mongolians, Malayans, Hindus, Indians (Harper, *op. cit.,* pp. 266-268; see note, 58 Yale L.J. 472, 480, 1949). Some statutes specify "Negro or Mulatto" (for example: Idaho Code [1947], Sec. 32-206) or "perhaps possessed of one-eighth or more" Negro blood (for example: Mississippi Constitution, Art. 14, Sec. 263; Code, 1942; Secs. 4-459, 11-2002, 11-2234, 11-2339; Missouri Revised Statutes [1942], Secs. 3361, 4651). All such states make the prohibited marriage void and most of them characterize the offense as a felony subject to severe penalties (Charles W. Lloyd [ed.], *Human Reproduction and Sexual Behavior* [Philadelphia: Lea and Febiger, 1964], p. 542).

29. In *Current Psychiatric Therapies,* Jules H. Massermann (ed.) (New York: Grune and Stratton, 1962), Vol. II, p. 179.

30. Report of the Illinois Commission on Sex Offenders to the Sixty-Eighth General Assembly of the State of Illinois, 11 (1953).

31. Paul W. Tappan, "Sentences for Sex Criminals," *Journal of Criminal Law, Criminology and Police Science,* Vol. 42 (1951), pp. 332-336.

32. *Ibid.,* p. 336.

33. *The Mentally Disabled and the Law,* p. 304, fn. 48.

34. Nils Nielson, "What is Homosexuality?" *International Journal of Sexology,* Vol. VI, No. 3 (February, 1953), p. 188.

35. *The Mentally Disabled and the Law,* p. 304, fn. 51.

36. M.S. Guttmacher and H. Weihofen, *Psychiatry and the Law* (New York: Norton, 1952), p. 111.

37. Davidson, *op. cit.,* p. 114.

38. *The Mentally Disabled and the Law,* p. 318.

39. D.C. Code 22-3503 (1951).

40. *Ibid.,* Code 21-311.

41. John R. Cavanagh and James B. McGoldrick, *Fundamental Psychiatry* (Milwaukee: The Bruce Publishing Co., 1958), p. 264.

42. *Ibid.,* p. 122.

43. *Ibid.,* p. 265.

44. Group for the Advancement of Psychiatry, *op. cit.,* p. 2.

45. Paul Friedman, "Sexual Deviations," Ch. 29 in *American Handbook of Psychiatry,* Silvano Arieti (ed.) (New York: Basic Books, Inc., 1959), Vol. I, p. 605: "The fact that sexual perversions are punishable by law is meeting with increasing opposition based upon the view that sexual morality is a private matter and should be subject to public regulation only if (1) the acts are carried out in public places, (2) one of the partners is a minor, or (3) violence or coercion is involved."

Chapter 14

1. Walter Barnett, *Sexual Freedom and the Constitution* (Albuquerque: University of New Mexico Press, 1973), pp. 8-9.

2. See "Homosexuality and Security," *Editorial Research Reports* (Washington, D.C.: Congressional Quarterly, Inc., 1963), pp. 507-524.

3. Walter Barnett, *op. cit.*

4. "Government-Created Employment Disabilities of the Homosexual," *Harvard Law Review,* Vol. 82 (1960), p. 1739.

5. "Homosexual Legal Rights," *Editorial Research Reports,* Washington, D.C.: Congressional Quarterly, Inc., 1974), p. 196.

6. Roger S. Mitchell, *Homosexuals and the Law* (New York: Arco Publishing Co., Inc., 1969), p. 54.

7. *Ibid.,* p. 55.

8. *Psychiatric News,* August, 1969, p. 22.

9. Personal communication, December 6, 1976.

10. *Civil Service News,* U.S. Civil Service Commission, July 3, 1975, p. 1.

11. *The Washington Star,* January 27, 1977, p. B-2.

12. "Report on Homosexuality With Particular Emphasis On This Problem in Governmental Agencies," formulated by the Committee on Cooperation with Governmental (Federal) Agencies of the Groups for the Advancement of Psychiatry (3617 W. 6th Ave., Topeka, Kans.), Report No. 30, January, 1955, p. 6.

13. "Employment of Homosexuals and Other Sex Perverts in Government," interim report submitted to the Committee on Expenditures in the Executive Departments by its Subcommittee on Investigations pursuant to S. Rec. 280 (81st Congress), December 15 (legislative day, November 27), 1950 (United States Government Printing Office).

14. *Ibid.,* p. 1.

15. For a complete report on this defection see *The Great Spy Scandal* by John S. Mather and Donald Seamon (London: Purnell and Sons, Ltd., 1956).

16. "Employment of Homosexuals and Other Sex Perverts in Government," *loc. cit.,* p. 19.

17. Norman St. John Steves, *Law and Morals* (Vol. 148 of the Twentieth Century Encyclopedia of Catholicism) (New York: Hawthorn Books, Inc., 1964), p. 121.

18. Roger S. Mitchell, *op. cit.,* pp. 49-53.

19. *The Armed Services and Homosexuality* (San Francisco: Society for Individual Rights, undated), p. 3.

20. Louis J. West, William T. Doidge and Robert L. Williams, "An Approach to the Problem of Homosexuality in the Military Service," *The American Journal of Psychiatry,* Vol. 115, No. 5 (November, 1958), p. 393.

21. Karl M. Bowman, M.D., and Bernice Engle, "A Psychiatric Evaluation of Laws on Homosexuality," as submitted to the *Temple Law Quarterly,* Spring, 1956. This article was subsequently published in *The American Journal of Psychiatry,* Vol. 112, No. 8 (February, 1956), pp. 577-583. Quoted at p. 583.

22. West *et al., op. cit.,* p. 399.

23. *Ibid.*

24. *Ibid.*

25. Rodney Garland, *The Heart in Exile* (London: The Camelot Press, 1954), p. 40.

26. *The Washington Post,* November 17, 1976, p. B-1.

Chapter 15

1. H. Montgomery Hyde, *The Love That Dared Not Speak Its Name* (Boston: Little, Brown and Co., 1970).

2. Merle Miller, *On Being Different: What It Means To Be A Homosexual* (New York: Random House, Inc. 1971), p. 64.

3. *One,* October, 1965, p. 2.

4. Personal communication, March 1, 1965.

5. Personal communication, January 17, 1977.

6. Ruth Simpson, *From The Closets To The Courts* (New York: The Viking Press, 1976), p. 160.

7. *Ibid.,* p. 150.

8. Personal communication, February 13, 1965.

9. *The Ladder,* Vol. LX, No. 3 (December, 1964), p. 3.

10. Miller, *op. cit.,* p. 35.

11. *Ibid.,* p. 36.

12. "Homosexual Legal Rights," *Editorial Research Reports* (Washington, D.C.: Congressional Quarterly, Inc., 1974), p. 183.

13. *The Chronicle of Higher Education,* December 10, 1973, as reported in *Editorial research repor ts, op. cit.,* p. 189.

14. *The Washington Post,* May 14, 1970, front page.

15. *The Quicksilver Times,* November 24-December 4, 1970, p. 5.

16. *Psychiatric News,* February 3, 1971, p. 1.

17. *Editorial Research Reports, op. cit.,* pp. 192-193.

18. Peter E. Fink, "Homosexuality: A Pastoral Hypothesis," *Commonweal,* April 6, 1973, p. 110.

19. Personal communication, January 17, 1977.

20. *Editorial Research Reports, op. cit.,* pp. 193-194.

21. *The Advocate,* December 1, 1976, p. 7.

22. R.E.L. Masters, *The Homosexual Revolution* (New York: The Julian Press, Inc., 1962), p. 130.

Chapter 16

1. John McNeill, S.J., *The Church and the Homosexual* (Kansas City: Sheed Andrews and McMeel, Inc., 1976); and Gregory

Baum, O.S.A., "Catholic Homosexuals," *Commonweal,* February 15, 1974, pp. 8-11.

2. See *National Catholic Reporter,* October 5, 1973, pp. 7-8, 13-14.

3. McNeill, *op. cit.,* p. 194.

4. *Ibid.,* p. 23.

5. "The Controversy Concerning the Psychology and Morality of Homosexuality," *The American Ecclesiastical Review,* November, 1973, p. 624.

6. McNeill, *op, cit.,* pp. 65, 102, 104, 164 and *passim.*

7. McNeill, "The Homosexual and the Church," *National Catholic Reporter,* October 5, 1973, pp. 7-8, 13-14. (Where no reference to McNeill is given, the source is the *National Catholic Reporter* article.)

8. Lionel Ovesey believes that the master-slave relationship is still present in actions which are not homosexual in *motivation.* He cites examples of the *pseudohomosexual* elaboration of the power struggle among men and among women: *Homosexuality and Pseudohomosexuality* (New York: Science House, 1969,) pp. 58-61, 84-96, 104-106.

9. *National Catholic Reporter,* October 5, 1973, pp. 7-8, 13-14.

10. John L. McKenzie, *The Two-Edged Sword* (Milwaukee: The Bruce Publishing Co., 1956), Ch. 6, "Human Origins"; Pierre Grelot, *Man and Wife in Scripture* (New York: Herder and Herder, 1964); Edward Schillebeeckx, *Marriage: Human Reality and Saving Mystery* (New York: Sheed and Ward, 1965), Ch. 1. See also Roger Shinn, "Homosexuality, Christian Conviction and Enquiry" in *The Same Sex,* Ralph Weltge (ed.) (Philadelphia: Pilgrim Press, 1969), p. 26: "The Christian tradition over the centuries has affirmed the heterosexual, monogamous faithful marital union as normative for the divinely given meaning of the intimate sexual relationship."

11. On this see Schillebeeckx, *op. cit.,* pp. 27-30.

12. Grelot, *op. cit.* The author develops the theme of marriage from all the books of the Old Testament and the New which treat the matter.

13. "Freedom and the Future," *Theological Studies,* Vol. 33 (1972), pp. 503-530; and "Blondel on the Subjectivity of Moral Decision Making," proceedings of the American Catholic Philosophical Association, Vol. 48 (1974), pp. 208-217.

14. "Freedom and the Future," *loc. cit.*

15. *Ibid.,* p. 507.

16. "Blondel on the Subjectivity . . .," ACPA Proceedings, Vol. 48

(1974), p. 209. McNeill takes this quotation from *L'action* (1893): *Essai d'une critique de la vie et d'une science de la pratique.*

17. Taken from Blondel's *The Letter of Apologetics* (New York: Holt, Rinehart and Winston, 1964), pp. 60-61.

18. "Blondel on the Subjectivity . . .," *op. cit.*, p. 211.

19. *Ibid.*, p. 221.

20. *Ibid.*, p. 212.

21. *Ibid.*, pp. 212-217.

22. Baum, *op. cit.*, p. 9.

23. *Ibid.*

24. *Ibid.*, p. 10.

25. *Ibid.*

26. See Harry Gershman, "Reflections on the Nature of Homosexuality," *American Journal of Psychoanalysis* XXVI (1966), pp. 46-58. (See my article in *Continuum,* "Morality and Pastoral Treatment of Homosexuality," Summer, 1967, pp. 279-297 and 282-284.)

27. Samuel Haddon, M.D., interview, October 19, 1975.

28. "Homosexuality and Moral Theology: Methodological and Substantive Considerations," *Thomist* (1971), pp. 447-481, particularly pp. 471-481; reprinted under the title "Dialogue With the Homophile Movement" in Curran's *Catholic Moral Theology in Dialogue* (South Bend: Fides, 1972). I have offered a critique of Curran's position in *The American Ecclesiastical Review,* "The Controversy Concerning the Psychology and Morality of Homosexuality," November, 1973, pp. 613-624.

29. *Toward a Christian Understanding of the Homosexual* (New York: Association Press, 1966), p. 98.

30. *Op. cit.*, p. 108.

31. *Op. cit.*, p. 474.

32. *Op. cit.*, p. 478.

33. *Op. cit.*, p. 479.

34. "The Pastoral Implications of Church Teaching on Homosexuality," *Linacre Quarterly,* August, 1971, pp. 157-164; "The Morality Conference in St. Louis Revisited," *Homiletic and Pastoral Review,* October, 1968, pp. 35-42; *The American Ecclesiastical Review, op. cit.,* pp. 620-621; "Law and Personalism," *Communio,* Spring, 1975, pp. 70-71.

35. Thus Pius XII refers to the Council of Trent and St. Augustine in support of the position that at times extended continence may be required of the married: "In confirmation of this argument we have the Council of Trent which, in its chapter on the observance, necessary and possible, of the commandments, teaches us that, as St. Augustine

said, 'God does not command impossible things, but when He commands, He warns us to do what can be done and to ask what cannot and gives you help so that you can.' " The quotation is taken from the Sixth Session of the Council of Trent, "Married Questions Affecting Married Life," Ch. 2, p. 16, par. 40 (Washington, D.C.: National Catholic Welfare Conference, 1951).

36. *Op. cit.,* p. 479.

37. *Ibid.*

38. Jacob Dominian, "Helping the Homosexual," *St. Anthony Messenger,* June, 1973, pp. 14-19.

39. The views of John Dedek who justifies homosexual activity of a stable kind as the best confirmed homosexuals can do are practically similar to those of Curran: cf. *Contemporary Medical Ethics* (New York: Sheed and Ward, 1975), p. 86.

40. National Conference of Catholic Bishops, Washington, D.C., 1973.

41. Vatican's "Declaration on Certain Questions Concerning Sexual Ethics," par. 11.

42. *Ibid.*

43. "Pastoral Letter: The Gift of Sexuality," *Origins:* NC News Service Documentary Service 5, No. 37 (March 4, 1976), pp. 581-586.

Chapter 17

1. Donald M. Cory, "Homosexuality," in *The Encyclopedia of Sexual Behavior,* Albert Ellis and Albert Abarbanel (eds.) (New York: Hawthorn Books, Inc., 1961), Vol. I, p. 492.

2. A. Moll, *Libido Sexualis. Studies in the Psychosexual Laws of Love Verified by Clinical Sexual Case Histories* (New York: American Ethnological Press, 1933).

3. Robert Lindner, "Sex in Prison," *Complex,* Vol. VI (Fall, 1951), p. 6.

4. Alfred C. Kinsey *et al., Sexual Behavior in the Human Male* (Philadelphia and London: W.B. Saunders Co., 1948), p. 664.

5. Charles E. Smith, "The Homosexual Federal Offender: A Study of 100 Cases," *Journal of Criminal Law and Criminology,* Vol. XLVI, No. 5 (January-February, 1954), pp. 528-591.

6. Asher R. Pacht, Ph.D., Seymour L. Halleck, M.D., and John C. Ehrmann, Ph. D., "Psychiatric Treatment of the Sex Offender," in *Current Psychiatric Therapies,* Jules H. Masserman, M.D. (ed.) (New York: Grune and Stratton, 1962), Vol. II, p. 177.

7. Quoted by Paul W. Tappan, Ph.D., "Treatment of the Sex Offender in Denmark," *The American Journal of Psychiatry,* Vol. CVIII, No. 4 (October, 1951), pp. 244-245.

8. Tappan, *op. cit.,* pp. 244-245.

9. See S. Rachman, Ph.D., "Sexual Disorders and Behavior Therapy," *The American Journal of Psychiatry,* Vol. CXVIII, No. 3 (September, 1961), pp. 235-240.

10. *Ibid.,* p. 235.

11. I. Stevenson and J. Wolpe, *American Journal of Psychiatry,* Vol. 116 (1960), p. 737.

12. K. Freund, in *Behavior Therapy and the Neuroses* (London: Pergamon Press, 1960). See also Freund and Srnec in *Sbornik Lekarsky,* officialni Publikancni Organ Lekarske Fakulty University Karlovy V. Praze (reported in the *International Journal of Sexology,* Vol. VII, No. 2 [November, 1953], pp. 92-93).

13. M.P. Feldman, Ph.D., and M.J. MacCulloch, M.B., "A Systematic Approach to the Treatment of Homosexuality by Conditioned Aversion: Preliminary Report," *American Journal of Psychiatry,* Vol. 121, No. 2 (August, 1964), pp. 167-171.

14. R.L. McGuire and M. Vallance, *British Medical Journal,* 1 (1964) p. 151.

15. Marcel Saghir, M.D., "The Homosexual Dilemma," pp. 42-43, 1970.

16. R. v. Krafft-Ebing, *Psychopathia Sexualis, with Special Reference to the Antipathic Sexual Instincts. A Medico-Forensic Study* (New York: Rebman, 1906).

17. A.F.F. von Schrenck-Notzing, *Therapeutic Suggestions in Psychopathia Sexualis (Pathological Manifestations of the Sexual Sense) with Especial Reference to Contrary Sexual Instincts* (Philadelphia: Davis, 1895).

18. Ainslie Meares, M.D., *A System of Medical Hypnosis* (Philadelphia and London: W.B. Saunders Co., 1961).

19. Newdigate M. Owensby, M.D., "The Correction of Homosexuality," *The Urologic and Cutaneous Review,* Vol. XLV (August, 1941), p. 496.

20. M. Hirschfeld, "Homosexuality," in *Encyclopaedia Sexualis: A Comprehensive Encyclopaedia-Dictionary of the Sexual Sciences,* V. Robinson (ed.) (New York: Dingwall-Rock, in collaboration with *Med. Rev. of Rev.,* 1936), pp. 321-324; see also *Sexual Anomalies and Perversions: Physical and Psychological Development and Treatment* (New York: Emerson Books, Inc., 1944).

21. H. Ellis, *Studies in the Psychology of Sex,* Vols. I and II (New York: Random House, Inc., 1942).

22. Paul Friedman, "Sexual Deviation," in *American Handbook of Psychiatry,* Ch. 29, pp. 606-607. Friedman gives as his source of this letter: E. Jones, *The Life and Work of Sigmund Freud, The Last Phase:* 1919-1939, Vol. III (New York: Basic Books, Inc., 1957).

23. Albert Ellis, "The Effectiveness of Psychotherapy With Individuals Who have Severe Homosexual Problems," *Journal of Consulting Psychology,* Vol. XX, No. 3 (1956), p. 194.

24. Mary Woodward, "The Diagnosis and Treatment of Homosexual Offenders," *British Journal of Delinquency,* 9 (July, 1958), pp. 44-59.

25. R.P. Knight, "Evaluation of the Results of Psychoanalytic Therapy," *American Journal of Psychiatry,* 98 (1941), pp. 434-436.

26. Desmond Curran and Denis Parr, "Homosexuality: An Analysis of 100 Male Cases Seen in Private Practice," *British Medical Journal,* 1 (1957), pp. 797-801.

27. Clifford Allen, M.D., *Homosexuality* (London: Staple Press, 1958), p. 111.

28. J. Hadfield, "The Cure of Homosexuality," *British Medical Journal,* 1 (June 7, 1958), pp. 1323-1326.

29. Samuel B. Hadden, "Attitudes Toward and Approaches to the Problem of Homosexuality," *Pennsylvania Medical Journal,* 60 (September, 1957), p. 1195; also "The Treatment of Homosexuality by Individual and Group Therapy," *American Journal of Psychiatry,* 114 (March, 1958), p. 810.

30. J.S. Poe, "The Successive Treatment of a 40-Year-Old Passive Homosexual," *Psychoanalytic Review,* 29 (1952), pp. 22-23.

31. Lionel Ovesey, Willard Gaylin, and Herbert Hendin, "Psychotherapy of Male Homosexuality," *Archives of General Psychiatry,* 9 (July, 1963), pp. 19-31.

32. Irving Bieber *et al., Homosexuality: A Psychoanalytic Study* (New York: Basic Books, Inc., 1962), p. 300.

33. Curran and Parr, *op. cit.,* pp. 797-801.

34. Knight, *op. cit.,* pp. 434-446.

35. Samuel B. Hadden, "Homosexuality: Observations on Its Psychogenesis and on Its Treatment by Group Therapy," paper read at the Third International Congress of Group Therapy, Milan, Italy, July 20, 1963, p. 9.

36. Bieber *et al., op. cit.,* p. 301.

37. *Ibid.,* pp. 311, 315.

Chapter 18

1. Some parts of the next few pages are paraphrased from *Fundamental Pastoral Counseling* (John R. Cavanagh, M.D. [Milwaukee: The Bruce Publishing Co., 1962], pp. 8-22).

2. Rev. Charles A. Curran, "A Catholic Psychologist Looks at Pastoral Counseling," *Pastoral Psychology,* February, 1959, p. 13.

3. William C. Bier, S.J., "Goals in Pastoral Counseling," *Pastoral Psychology,* February, 1959, pp. 10-11.

4. *Ibid.,* p. 9.

5. Donald J. West, *The Other Man* (New York: Whiteside, Inc., and William Morrow and Co., 1955), p. 154.

6. Quoted by William C. Bier, S.J., *op. cit.,* p. 9.

7. Rev. Charles Larere, "Passage of the Angel Through Sodom," article in *New Problems in Medical Ethics,* Dom Peter Flood, O.S.B. (ed.), Vol. I (Westminster, Md.: The Newman Press, 1953), p. 116.

8. Paul Le Moal, M.D., "The Psychiatrist and the Homosexual," article in *New Problems in Medical Ethics,* Vol. I, p. 70.

9. John R. Cavanagh, M.D., *Fundamental Marriage Counseling* (Milwaukee: The Bruce Publishing Co., 1963), p.196.

10. Dr. William J. Tobin, *Homosexuality and Marriage* (Rome: The Catholic Book Agency, 1964), p. 73.

11. Gordon Westwood, *A Minority: A Report on the Life of the Male Homosexual in Great Britain* (London: Longmans, Green and Co. Ltd., 1960), p. 51.

12. *Ibid.,* p. 52.

13. *Ibid.,* p. 61.

14. Rev. Michael J. Buckley, *Morality and the Homosexual* (Westminster, Md.: The Newman Press, 1960), p. 184.

15. William C. Bier, S.J., *op. cit.,* p. 10.

16. Leo Trese, "Muted Tragedy," *The Commonweal,* 51 (February 17, 1950), p. 512.

17. John F. Harvey, O.S.F.S., in *Theological Studies,* Vol. XVI, No. 1 (March, 1955), p. 86.

18. John R. Cavanagh, M.D., *op. cit.,* p. 17.

19. Charles Crotty, "Marriage Counseling and Psychology," *Bulletin of the Guild of Catholic Psychiatrists,* Vol. VI, No. 4 (October, 1959), p. 12.

20. Robert Odenwald, M.D., "Counseling the Homosexual," *Priest,* Vol. IX (December, 1953), p. 941.

21. *Ibid.,* p. 944.

22. Pope Pius XII, *On Holy Virginity,* an encyclical, Rome, March 25, 1954.

23. George Hagmaier, C.S.P., and Robert Gleason, S.J., *Counselling the Catholic* (New York: Sheed and Ward, 1959), p. 102.

24. Jean Lhermitte, "Problems of Sexual Morality," *New Problems in Medical Ethics,* Vol. I, p. 67.

25. Anomaly, *The Invert* (Baltimore: Williams and Wilkins Co., 1948), p. 133.

26. Odenwald, *op. cit.,* p. 942.

27. Harvey, *op. cit.,* p. 99.

28. Hagmaier and Gleason, *op. cit.,* p. 110.

Bibliography

Abbott, Walter M., S.J. (ed.), *The Documents of Vatican II* (New York: The America Press, 1966).

Air Force Regulation No. 35-66: "Discharge Processing Where Homosexual Acts or Tendencies Are Involved (Effective April 14, 1959)," (Washington, D.C.: Department of the Air Force, March 17, 1959).

Allen, Clifford, M.D., "On the Cure of Homosexuality," *International Journal of Sexology,* (1952), 5, 148-150.

——, *Homosexuality* (London: Staple Press, 1958).

——, "The Meaning of Homosexuality," *International Journal of Sexology,* Vol. VI, 207-212.

——, *The Sexual Perversions and Abnormalities: A Study in the Psychology of Paraphilia* (London: Oxford University Press, 1949).

——, *A Textbook of Psychosexual Disorders* (London: Oxford University Press, 1962).

Allers, Rudolph, M.D., *The Homiletic and Pastoral Review* (April, 1942).

——, *The Psychology of Character* (New York: Sheed and Ward, 1943).

——, "Sex and Morals," *Commonweal,* LIII (December, 1950).

"The American Confessor and Homosexuality," *Dignity* (April, 1974), 4.

American Psychiatric Association, *Diagnostic and Statistical Manual of Mental Disorders,* 2nd ed. Prepared by the Committee on Nomenclature and Statistics (Washington, D.C.: A.P.A. Mental Hospital Service, 1968).

Anomaly, *The Invert* (Baltimore: Williams and Wilkins Co., 1948).

Arieff, A.J., and Rotman, D.B., "Psychiatric Inventory of 100 Cases of Indecent Exposure," *Archives of Neurology and Psychiatry,* 47 (1942), 495-498.

Arieti, Silvano (ed.), *American Handbook of Psychiatry,* 3 vols. (New York: Basic Books, Inc., 1959).

The Armed Services and Homosexuality (San Francisco: Society for Individual Rights, undated).

Armon, V., "Some Personality Variables in Overt Female Homosexuality," *Journal of Projective Techniques,* Vol. 24 (1960), 292-309.

"Artificial Insemination" (editorial), *Justice of Peace and Local Government Review,* Vol. 109 (1945), 194, 448ff.

Attwater, Donald, *A Catholic Dictionary,* 3rd ed. (New York: The Macmillan Co., 1961).

Bailey, Derrick S., *Homosexuality and the Western Christian Tradition* (London: Longmans, 1955).

Bancroft, J.H., "Homosexuality in the Male," *British Journal of Psychiatry,* No. 9, (1975), 173-184.

Barahal, H.S., "Testosterone in Psychotic Male Homosexuals," *Psychiatric Quarterly,* 14 (1940), 319-330.

Barcroft, J., "Homosexuality and the Medical Profession: A Behaviorist's View," *Journal of Medical Ethics,* Vol. 1, No. 4 (December, 1975) 176-180.

Barnett, Walter, *Sexual Freedom and the Constitution* (Albuquerque: University of New Mexico Press, 1973).

Barr, Murray L., and Hobbs, G. Edgar, "Chromosomal Sex in Transvestites," *Lancet* (1954), 1109.

Barton, G.A., "Sodomy," *Encyclopedia of Religion and Ethics,* XI (New York: 1921), 672.

Bauer, J., "Homosexuality as an Endocrinological, Psychological, and Genetic Problem," *Journal of Criminal Psychopathology,* 2 (October, 1940), 188-197.

Baum, Gregory, O.S.A., "Catholic Homosexuals," *Commonweal,* (February 15, 1974).

de Beauvoir, Simone, *The Second Sex* (New York: Alfred A. Knopf, 1953).

Benda, Clemens E., "Existential Psychotherapy of Homosexuality," *Review of Existential Psychology & Psychiatry,* 3 (May, 1963), 133-152.

Bendel, R., "The Modified Szondi Test in Male Homosexuality, I," *International Journal of Sexology,* Vol. 8 (1955), 226-227.

Bender, L., and Paster, S., "Homosexual Trends in Children," *American Journal of Ortho-psychiatry,* 11 (1941), 730.

Berg, Charles, M.D., "The Problem of Homosexuality. Part 1," *American Journal of Psychotherapy,* Vol. II (1957), 65-70.

Berg, Charles, M.D., and Allen, Clifford, M.D., *The Problem of Homosexuality* (New York: The Citadel Press, 1958).

Berg, C., and Kirch, A.M. (eds.), *Homosexuality* (London: Allen, 1958).

Bergler, Edmund, *Homosexuality: Disease or Way of Life* (New York: Hill and Wang, 1957).

————, "The Myth of a New National Disease, Homosexuality, and the Kinsey Report," *Psychiatric Quarterly,* Vol. 22, No. 1 (1948), 66.

————, *1000 Homosexuals* (Peterson, N.J.: Pageant Books, Inc., 1959).

Bergler, E., and Kroger, W.S., *Kinsey's Myth of Female Sexuality* (New York: Grune and Stratton, 1954).

Bergmann, M.S., "Homosexuality on the Rorschach Test," *Bulletin, Menninger Clinic,* Vol. 9 (1945), 78-93.

Beukenkamp, C., "Phantom Patricide," *Archives of General Psychiatry,* Vol. 3 (1960), 282-288.

Bieber, Irving, *et al., Homosexuality* (New York: Basic Books, Inc., 1962).

Biegel, Hugo (ed.), *Advances in Sex Research* (New York: Harper and Row, Publishers, Inc., 1963).

Bier, William C., S.J., "Goals in Pastoral Counseling," *Pastoral Psychology* (February, 1959), 10-11.

Bills, N., *The Personality Structure of Alcoholics and Paranoids As Revealed by Their Responses to the Thematic Apperception Test,* unpublished thesis (Western Reserve University, 1953).

Biot, René, M.D., and Galimard, Pierre, M.D., *Medical Guide to Vocations* (London: Burns and Oates, 1955).

Birk, L., "Group Psychotherapy for Men Who Are Homosexual," *Journal of Sex and Marital Therapy,* Vol. 1, No. 1 (Fall, 1974), 29-52.

Blondel, *The Letter of Apologetics* (New York: Holt, Rinehart and Winston, 1964).

"Blondel on the Subjectivity of Moral Decision Making," Proceedings of the American Catholic Philosophical Association, Vol. 48, 1974.

Boggan, E. Carrington, *et al., An American Civil Liberties Union Handbook: The Rights of Gay People* (New York: Avon Books, 1975).

Boss, M., M.D., *Sinn and Gehalt der Sexuellen Perversionem* (The Meaning and Content of the Sexual Perversions) (Berne: Medizinischer Verlag Hans Huber, 1947). Reviewed in *Psychoanalytic Quarterly,* Vol. XVII (1948), 106.

Bouscaren, T. Lincoln, S.J., and Ellis, Adam C., S.J., *Canon Law,* 3rd ed. (Milwaukee: The Bruce Publishing Co.,1957).

Bouscaren-O'Connor, *Canon Law Digest,* Vol. IV (Milwaukee: The Bruce Publishing Co., 1958).

Bowman, Karl M., M.D., "The Problem of the Sex Offender," *The American Journal of Psychiatry,* Vol. 108, No. 4 (October, 1951), 250-257.

Bowman, Karl M., M.D., and Engle, Bernice, M.A., "Medicolegal Aspects of Transvestism," *The American Journal of Psychiatry,* Vol. CXIII, No. 7 (January, 1957), 583-588.

⸺, "The Problem of Homosexuality," *Journal of Social Hygiene,* Vol. 39 (January, 1953), 2-16.

⸺, "A Psychiatric Evaluation of the Laws of Homosexuality," *The American Journal of Psychiatry,* Vol. 112, No. 8 (February, 1956), 577-583.

Bradshaw, W.V., "Homosexual Syphilis Epidemic," *Texas Journal of Medicine,* 57 (November, 1961), 907-909.

Brambilla, F., "Endocrinal and Chromatinic Pictures of Male Homosexuality," *Sessuologia,* Vol. IV, No. 3 (July-September, 1963), 170-174. Translated Summary, *Sessuologia,* Vol. IV, No. 4 (October-December, 1963), xii.

Brill, A.A. (ed.), *The Basic Writings of Sigmund Freud* (New York: Modern Library, 1938).

British Medical Association, *Homosexuality and Prostitution,* (London, 1955).

British Medical Association and Magistrates' Association, *The Criminal Law and Sexual Offenders* (London, 1949).

Brody, Morris W., "An Analysis of the Psychosexual Development of a Female — With Special Reference to Homosexuality," *Psychoanalytic Review,* 30 (1943), 47-58.

Bromberg, Walter, M.D., "Sex Deviation and Therapy," *Journal of Social Therapy,* Vol. 1, No. 4 (October, 1955), 203-210.

Brown, D.G., "The Development of Sex-Role Inversion and Homosexuality," *Journal of Pediatrics,* 50 (1957), 613-619.

Brown, Raymond E., S.S., Fitzmyer, John A., S.J., and Murphy, Roland E., O. Carm. (eds.), *The Jerome Biblical Commentary,* Vol. I (Englewood Cliffs, N. J.: Prentice-Hall, Inc., 1968).

Buckley, Rev. Michael J., *Morality and the Homosexual* (Westminster, Md.: The Newman Press, 1960).

Buki, Rudolph A., M.D., "The Use of Psychotropic Drugs in the Rehabilitation of Sex-Deviated Criminals," *The American Journal of Psychiatry,* Vol. 120, No. 12 (June, 1964), 1170-1175.

Bullough, Vern L., *et al.*, *An Annotated Bibliography of Homosexuality*, 2 Vols. (New York: Garland Publishing Co., 1977).

Burridge, William (trans.). *Twentieth Century Encyclopedia of Catholicism*, Vol. 143 (New York: Hawthorn Books, 1961).

Carney, Francis W., "Reproduction and the Whole Man," *America*, Vol. 12, No. 8 (February 20, 1965), 246.

Cavanagh, John R., M.D., *Fundamental Marriage Counseling* (Milwaukee: The Bruce Publishing Co., 1963).

————, *Fundamental Pastoral Counseling* (Milwaukee: The Bruce Publishing Co., 1962).

Cavanagh, John R., M.D., and McGoldrick, James B., S.J., *Fundamental Psychiatry* (Milwaukee: The Bruce Publishing Co., 1958, 1966).

Chang, J., and Block, J., "A Study of Identification in Male Homosexuals," *Journal of Consulting Psychology*, Vol. 24 (1960), 307-310.

Chapman, A.H., and Reese, D.G., "Homosexual Signs in Rorschachs of Early Schizophrenics," *Journal of Clinical Psychology*, Vol. 9 (1953), 30-32.

Chesser, Eustace, *Live and Let Live* (New York: Philosophical Library, Inc., 1958).

————, "Society and the Homosexual," *International Journal of Sexology*, Vol. VII (1954), 213-216.

Choisy, Maryse, *Psychoanalysis of the Prostitute* (New York: Philosophical Library, 1961).

Clark, T.R., "Homosexuality and Psychopathology in Nonpatient Males," *American Journal of Psychoanalysis*, Vol. 35, No. 2 (Summer, 1975), 163-168.

Clark, William L., and Marshall, William L., *A Treatise on the Law of Crimes* (Chicago: Callaghan and Co., 1912).

Coates, S., "Homosexuality and the Rorschach Test," *British Journal of Medical Psychology*, Vol. 35 (1962), 177-190.

Coburn, Monsignor Vincent P., "Homosexuality and the Invalidation of Marriage," *The Jurist*, Vol. XX, No. 4 (October, 1960), 4441-4459.

Cole, William G., *Sex and Love in the Bible* (New York: Association Press, 1959).

Connery, John R., S.J., "Notes on Moral Theology," *Theological Studies*, Vol. XVI, No. 4 (December, 1955), 586.

"The Controversy Concerning the Psychology and Morality of Homosexuality," *American Ecclesiastical Review* (November, 1973).

Coogan, Matt J., "Wisconsin's Experience in Treating Psychiatrically-

Deviated Sexual Offenders," *The Journal of Social Therapy,* Vol. I, No. 2 (January, 1955), 3-6.

Coppen, A.J., "Body Build of Male Homosexuals," *British Medical Journal,* Vol. II (1959), 1443-1445.

Cory, Donald Webster, *The Homosexual in America* (New York: Greenberg, 1951).

————, *The Homosexual Outlook* (London: Peter Nevill, 1953).

————, *Homosexuality: A Cross Cultural Approach* (New York: The Julian Press, Inc., 1956).

————, "Homosexuality in Prison," *Journal of Social Therapy,* Vol. I, No. 3 (April, 1955), 137.

Crotty, Charles, "Marriage Counseling and Psychology," *Bulletin of the Guild of Catholic Psychiatrists,* Vol. VI, No. 4 (October, 1959), 12.

Curran, Rev. Charles, *Catholic Moral Theology in Dialogue* (Notre Dame: University of Notre Dame Press, 1972).

————, "A Catholic Psychologist Looks at Pastoral Counseling," *Pastoral Psychology* (February, 1959), 13.

Curran, Desmond, and Parr, Denis, "Homosexuality: An Analysis of 100 Male Cases Seen in Private Practice," *British Medical Journal,* Vol. 5022 (April 6, 1957), 797-801.

Darke, Roy A., "Heredity as an Etiological Factor in Homosexuality," *Journal of Nervous and Mental Disease,* Vol. 107, No. 3 (March, 1948), 251-268.

David, H.P., and Rabinowitz, W., "Szondi Patterns in Epileptic and Homosexual Males," *Journal of Consulting Psychology,* Vol. 16 (1952), 247-250.

Davidman, Dr. Howard, "What You Should Know About Homosexuality," *State of Mind,* Vol. 2, No. 4 (Summit, N.J.: CIBA, April, 1958).

Davids, A., "Rorschach and TAT Indices of Homosexuality in Overt Homosexuals, Neurotics and Normal Males," *The Journal of Abnormal and Social Psychology,* Vol. 53, No. 2 (1956), 161-172.

Davidson, Henry A., *Forensic Psychiatry* (New York: The Ronald Press, 1952).

Davidson, W., and Winn, S., *Postgraduate Medical Journal,* 35 (1959), 494. "A Delicate Problem," *Newsweek* (June 14, 1954), 99.

David, K.B., *Factors in the Sex Life of Twenty-Two Hundred Women* (New York: Harper, 1929).

"Deleting Homosexuality as an Illness, a Psychiatric Challenge to Values," *Roche Report: Frontiers of Psychiatry,* Vol. 4, No. 3 (February 1, 1974).

"Depravity and Unbelief," from a legal correspondent, *The Tablet,* Vol. 202 (December 19, 1953), 606.

Deutsch, Albert, and Fishman, Helen (eds.), *Encyclopedia of Mental Health,* 6 Vols. (New York: Franklin Watts, Inc., 1963).

Deutsch, Helene, "Homosexuality in Women," *Psychoanalytic Quarterly* (October, 1932), 484-510.

Devereaux, G., "Retaliatory Homosexual Triumph Over the Father," *International Journal of Psycho-Analysis,* Vol. 41 (1960), 157-161.

Dickinson, R.L., and Beam, Laura, *The Single Woman* (New York: Reynal, 1934).

Dinerstein, Russell H., and Glueck, Bernard C., "Sub-Coma Insulin Therapy in the Treatment of Homosexual Panic States," *Journal of Social Therapy,* Vol. 1, No. 4 (October, 1955), 182.

Dixon, A.D., and Torr, J.B.D., "Chromosomal Sex and Abnormal Sex Development," *British Medical Journal,* Vol. I (1948), 222-228.

Dougherty, W.J., "Epidemiological Treatment of Syphilis Contacts," *Journal of the Medical Society of New Jersey,* 59 (November, 1962), 564-567.

Drummond, Isabel, *The Sex Paradox* (New York: Putnam's, 1953).

Duhamel, Joseph, S.J., and Hayden, Dom Jerome, O.S.B., *Theological and Psychiatric Aspects of Habitual Sin.* A paper copresented at the Eleventh Annual Convention of the Catholic Theological Society of America, June, 1956. Published in the Proceedings.

Ellis, Albert, "On the Cure of Homosexuality," *International Journal of Sexology* (1952), 5, 135-138.

————, "The Effectiveness of Psychotherapy With Individuals Who Have Severe Homosexual Problems," *Journal of Consulting Psychology,* 20, No. 3 (1956), 191-195.

————, "A Homosexual Treated With Rational Psychotherapy," *Journal of Clinical Psychology,* 15 (1959), 338-343.

————, "Are Homosexuals Necessarily Neurotic?" *One* (1955), 3(4), 8-12.

Ellis, Albert and Abarbanel, Albert (eds.), *The Encyclopedia of Sexual Behavior,* 2 Vols. (New York: Hawthorn Books, Inc., 1961).

Ellis, H., *Studies in the Psychology of Sex,* 2 Vols. (London: Heinemann, 1950).

"Employment of Homosexuals and Other Sex Perverts in Government," Interim Report Submitted to the Committee on Expenditures in the Executive Department by Its Subcommittee on Investigations pursuant to S. Res. 280 (81st Congress), December 15 (legislative day, November 27), 1950. United States Printing Office.

English, Horace B., and English, Ava C., *A Comprehensive Dictionary of Psychological Terms* (New York: Longmans, Green and Co., 1958).

English, O. Spurgeon, and Finch, Stuart M., *Introduction to Psychiatry* (New York: Norton, 1954).

Epstein, Louis, *Sex Laws and Customs in Judaism* (New York: Block, 1948).

de Fabregues, Jean, *Christian Marriage* (New York: Hawthorn Books, Inc., 1959).

Farnham, M.F., The Adolescent (New York: Harper and Brothers, 1951).

Federal Bureau of Investigation (ed.), *Crime in the United States* (Washington, D.C.: United States Department of Justice, 1961).

Fein, L.G., "Rorschach Signs of Homosexuality in Male College Students," *Journal of Clinical Psychology,* Vol. 3 (1950), 248-253.

Feldman, M.P., Ph.D., and MacCulloch, M.J., M.B., "A Systematic Approach to the Treatment of Homosexuality by Conditioned Aversion: Preliminary Report," *American Journal of Psychiatry,* Vol. 121, No. 2 (August, 1964), 167-171.

Fenichel, O., *The Psychoanalytic Theory of Neurosis* (New York: Norton, 1945).

"Final Report of the Task Force on Homosexuality," National Institute of Mental Health (October 10, 1969), Dr. Evelyn Hooker, Chairman.

Finger, F.W., "Sex Beliefs and Practices Among Male College Students," *Journal of Abnormal and Social Psychology,* Vol. 42 (1947), 57-67.

Fink, Peter E., "Homosexuality: A Pastoral Hypothesis," *Commonweal* (April 6, 1973).

Fink, P.J., "Homosexuality — Illness or Life-Style?" *Journal of Sex and Marital Therapy,* Vol. 1, No. 3 (Spring, 1975), 225-233.

Finney, Joseph Claude, M.D., Ph.D., "Homosexuality Treated by Combined Psychotherapy," *Journal of Social Therapy,* Vol. 6, No. 1, First Quarter (1960), 27-34.

Fisher, Robert G., "The Sex Offenders Provisions of the Proposed New Maryland Criminal Code: Should Private, Consenting Adult Homosexual Behavior be Excluded?" *Maryland Law Review,* Vol. 30, No. 2 (Spring, 1970).

Flood, Dom Peter, O.S.B. (ed.), *New Problems in Medical Ethics* (Westminster, Md.: The Newman Press, 1955).

Ford, Clelland S., and Beach, Frank A., *Patterns of Sexual Behavior* (London: Eyre and Spottiswoode, 1952).

Ford, John, S.J., and Kelly, Gerald, S.J., *Contemporary Moral Theology,* 2 Vols. (Westminster, Md.: The Newman Press, 1958).

————, "Psychiatry and Moral Responsibility," *Theological Studies,* 16 (1955), 86-108.

Foster, Jeannette H., *Sex Variant Women in Literature* (New York: Vantage Press, 1956).

Freedman, Alfred M., *et al., Comprehensive Textbook of Psychiatry,* Vol. II, 2nd ed. (Baltimore: Williams and Wilkins Co., 1975).

"Freedom and the Future," *Theological Studies,* Vol. 33 (1972).

Freud, Anna, "Clinical Observations on the Treatment of Manifest Male Homosexuality," *Psychoanalytical Quarterly* (1951), 20, 337-338.

————, "Problems of Technique in Adult Analysis," *Bulletin of the Philosophical Association of Psychoanalysis,* 4 (1954), 44-69.

Freud, Sigmund, *New Introductory Lecture on Psycho-Analysis* (New York: Norton, 1933).

Freund, K., *Behavior Therapy and the Neuroses* (London: Pergamon Press, 1960).

Freund, K., *et al.,* "Heterosexual Interest in Homosexual Males," *Archives of Sexual Behavior,* Vol. 4, No. 5 (September, 1975) 509-518.

Freund, K., and Pinkave, V., "Homosexuality in Man and Its Association With Parental Relationships," *Review of Czech Medicine,* Vol. 7 (1961), 32.

Freund, Dr. K., and Srnec, Dr. J., *International Journal of Sexology,* Vol. VII, No. 2 (November, 1953).

Friedberg, R.L., "Early Recollections of Homosexuals as Indicators of Their Life Styles," *Journal of Individual Psychology,* Vol. 31, No. 2 (November, 1975), 196-204.

Fromm, E.D., and Elonen, A.S., "The Use of Projective Techniques in the Study of a Case of Female Homosexuality," *Journal of Projective Techniques,* Vol. 15 (1951), 185-230.

Garland, Rodney, *The Heart in Exile* (London: The Camelot Press, 1954).

Garner, M.F., M.B., "An Analysis of 340 Cases of Syphilis Diagnosed in the Laboratory in Six Months in 1973," *The Medical Journal of Australia* (May 15, 1976).

Gassert, Robert G., S.J., and Hall, Bernard H., M.D., *Psychiatry and Religious Faith* (New York: The Viking Press, 1964).

Gedda, L., "Genetic Aspects of Homosexuality," *Sessuologia,* Vol. IV, No. 3 (July-September, 1963), 108-119. Translated summary, *Sessuologia,* Vol. IV, No. 4 (October-December, 1963), ix.

Gemelli, A., *Artificial Insemination* (Milan, Italy: Catholic University of the Sacred Heart, undated).

Gershman, Harry, "Consideration of Some Aspects of Homosexuality," *American Journal of Psychoanalysis,* 13 (1953), 82-83.

———, "The Effect of Group Therapy on Compulsive Homosexuality in Men and Women," *American Journal of Psychoanalysis,* Vol. 35, No. 4 (Winter, 1975), 303-316.

———, "Reflections on the Nature of Homosexuality," *American Journal of Psychoanalysis,* XXVI (1966).

Gide, A., *Corydon* (Paris: Gallimard, 1925).

Giese, Hans, M.D., "Differences in the Homosexual Relations of Man and Woman," *International Journal of Sexology* (May, 1955), 225-227.

———, *Jahrbuch Psychol. Psychother.* (1953), 223-225.

Gilby, Thomas, O.P., "Not All That Anomalous," *Blackfriars,* Vol. XLI, No. 486 (November, 1960), 402-408.

Glass, S.J., Duel, H.J., and Wright, C.A., "Sex Hormone Studies in Male Homosexuals," *Endocrinology,* Vol. 26 (1940), 590-594.

Gleason, Robert W., S.J., "Homosexuality: Moral Aspects of the Problem," *The Homiletic and Pastoral Review,* Vol. LVIII, No. 3 (December, 1957), 272-278.

Glick, B., "Homosexual Panic: Clinical and Theoretical Considerations," *Journal of Nervous and Mental Diseases,* Vol. 129 (1959), 20.

Glover, E. (ed.), *The Problem of Homosexuality* (London: Institute for the Study and Treatment of Delinquency, 1957).

Glueck, B.C., "Psychodynamic Patterns in the Homosexual Sex Offender," *The American Journal of Psychiatry,* Vol. 112 (1955-1956), 584-590.

Goldberg, S., "What is 'normal'? Logical aspects of the question of homosexual behavior," *Psychiatry,* Vol. 38, No. 3 (August, 1975), 227-243.

Goldschmidt, R., *The Mechanism and Psychology of Sex Determination* (London: Methuen and Co., Ltd., 1924).

Gough, H.P., "Diagnostic Patterns on the M.M.P.I.," *Journal of Clinical Psychology,* Vol. 2 (1946), 23-47.

"Government-Created Employment Disabilities of the Homosexual," *Harvard Law Review,* Vol. 82 (1960).

Grams, A., and Rinder, "Signs of Homosexuality in Human Figure Drawings," *Journal of Consulting Psychology,* Vol. 22 (1958), 394.

Graner, D., "Homosexuality and the Paranoid Psychoses as Related to the Concept of Narcissism," *Psychoanalytical Quarterly,* Vol. 22 (1955), 516.

Graver, D., "Homosexuality in Paranoid Schizophrenics as Revealed by the Rorschach Test," *Journal of Consulting Psychology,* Vol. 18 (1954), 459-462.

Greco, M.C., and Wright, J.C., "The Correctional Institution in the Etiology of Chronic Homosexuality," *American Journal of Orthopsychiatry,* 14 (1944), 295.

Greenspan, H., and Campbell, J.D., "The Homosexual as a Personality Type," *American Journal of Psychiatry,* Vol. 101 (1945), 682.

Greenspan, Jack, "Sex of the Persecutor in Female Paranoid Patients," *Archives of General Psychiatry* (September, 1963), 217-223.

Grelot, Pierre, *Man and Wife in Scripture* (New York: Herder and Herder, 1964).

Group for the Advancement of Psychiatry, *Psychiatrically Deviated Sex Offenders,* Report No. 9, New York (February, 1950).

———, "Report on Homosexuality With Particular Emphasis on This Problem in Governmental Agencies," Report No. 30 (January, 1955).

Grygier, T.G., "Psychometric Aspects of Homosexuality: A Pilot Study in Psychological Measurement," *The British Journal of Delinquency,* Vol. 9, No. 1 (1958), 59-61.

Guttmacher, Alan F., "The Role of Artificial Insemination in the Treatment of Human Sterility," *Bulletin of the New York Academy of Medicine,* Vol. 19 (1943), 590.

Guttmacher, M.S., and Weihofen, H., *Psychiatry and the Law* (New York: Norton, 1952).

Hacker, Helen Mayer, "The Ishmael Complex," *The American Journal of Psychotheraphy,* Vol. VI, No. 3 (July, 1952), 494-513.

Hadden, Samuel B., "Attitudes Toward and Approaches to the Problem of Homosexuality," *Pennsylvania Medical Journal,* 60 (September, 1957), 1195-1198.

———, "Homosexuality: Observations on Its Psychogenesis and on Its Treatment by Group Psychotherapy." Paper read at the Third International Congress of Group Therapy, Milan, Italy (July, 1963).

_____, "The Treatment of Homosexuality by Individual and Group Therapy," *American Journal of Psychiatry,* 114 (March, 1958), 810.

Hadfield, J.A., "The Cure of Homosexuality," *British Medical Journal,* Vol. I (1958), 1323-1326.

Hagmaier, George, C.S.P., and Gleason, Robert, S.J., *Counselling the Catholic* (New York: Sheed and Ward, 1959).

Haines, William H., M.D., "Homosexuality," *Journal of Social Therapy,* Vol. I, No. 3 (April, 1955), 132.

_____, "The Sex Offender in Illinois," *Journal of Social Therapy* (double issue), Second Quarter, Vol. 3, No. 2, and Third Quarter, Vol. 3, No. 3 (1957).

_____, "Some Sexual Deviations," *Journal of Social Therapy,* Vol. 3, No. 1, First Quarter (1957), 39-45.

Hall, Radcliffe, *The Well of Loneliness* (New York: Covici, 1928).

Hamberger, C., Sturup, G.K., and Dahl-Iverson, E., "Transvestism," *Journal of the American Medical Association,* Vol. 152 (1953).

Hamilton, Gilbert V., *On the Cause of Homosexuality* (two essays, the second in reply to the first) (New York: G. Legman, 1950).

_____, *Research in Marriage* (New York: A.C. Boni, 1929).

Hammond, W., "The Disease of the Scythians (Morbus Feminarum)," *American Journal of Neurology,* Vol. 3 (1882), 339.

Häring, Bernard, C.S.S.R., *The Law of Christ,* 3 Vols. (Westminster, Md.: The Newman Press, 1966).

Harmon, L.R., and Wiener, D.N., "Use of the M.M.P.I. in Vocational Advisement," *Journal of Applied Psychology,* Vol. 29 (1945), 132-141.

Harper, Robert A., "Psychological Aspects of Homosexuality." Paper delivered at the meeting of the Society for the Scientific Study of Sex, New York (May 22, 1959).

Harrington, Rev. Paul V., "Indications and Proof of Non-Consummation," *The Linacre Quarterly,* Vol. 19 (August, 1952), 61.

Harrington, Rev. Paul V., and Kickham, Charles J.E., M.D., "The Impediment of Impotency and the Condition of Male Impotence," Part I, No. 3. *The Linacre Quarterly,* Vol. 25, No. 3 (August, 1958), 100-110. Part II, Vol. 25, No. 4 (November, 1958), 143.

Harvey, John F., O.S.F.S., "The Controversy Concerning Nomenclature Vis-à-Vis Homosexuality," *Linacre Quarterly* (August, 1974).

_____, "Counseling the Apparent Adolescent Homosexual," *Bulletin of the Guild of Catholic Psychiatrists* (October, 1963), Vol. 10, No. 4, 204-214.

———, "Counseling the Homosexual," *The Homiletic and Pastoral Review* (January, 1962), 328-335.

———, "Homosexuality and Marriage," *Homiletic and Pastoral Review* (December, 1961), 227-234.

———, "Homosexuality as a Pastoral Problem," *Theological Studies,* Vol. XVI, No. 1 (March, 1955), 86-108.

———, *The Moral Theology of the Confessions of St. Augustine* (Washington, D.C.; Catholic University, 1951).

———, "Morality and Pastoral Treatment of Homosexuality," *Continuum,* Vol. 5, No. 2 (Summer, 1967), 289-290.

———, *Proceedings of the Second Institute for Clergy on Problems in Pastoral Counseling,* Fordham University (1957).

———, "Review of Morality and the Homosexual by Michael J. Buckley," *Theological Studies,* Vol. XXI, No. 3 (September, 1960), 491-495.

Hayden, Dom Jerome, O.S.B., "Theological and Psychiatric Aspects of Habitual Sin," *Proceedings of the Eleventh Annual Convention,* Catholic Theological Association (June 25 through 27, 1956).

Helmer, William J., "New York's 'Middle-class' Homosexuals," *Harper's Magazine* (March, 1963), 85-92.

Henry, George W., *All the Sexes* (New York: Holt, Rinehart and Winston, 1955).

Hersko, Marvin, Ph.D., "Incest: A Three-Way Process," *Journal of Social Therapy,* Vol. 7, No. 1, First Quarter (1961), 22-31.

"The Hidden Problem," *Time* (December 28, 1953), 29.

Hinsie, Leland E., M.D., and Shatsky, Jacob, Ph.D., *Psychiatric Dictionary* (New York: Oxford University Press, 1953).

Hirschfeld, Magnus, *Die Homosexualität des Mannes and dis Weibes* (2nd ed.) (Berlin: L. Marcus Verladsbuchjandlung, 1920).

———, *Sexual Anomalies and Perversions* (London: Encyclopedic Press, 1952).

———, *Sexual Pathology* (New York: Emerson Books, Inc., 1940).

Hite, Shere, *The Hite Report, A Nationwide Study on Female Sexuality* (New York: The Macmillan Co., 1976).

Hoch, P.H., and Zubin, J. (eds.), *Psychosexual Development in Health and Disease* (New York: Grune and Stratton, 1949).

Hoffman, Martin, "Homosexuality," *Today's Education* (November, 1970).

Holemon, R. Eugene, M.D., and Winokur, George, M.D., "Effeminate Homosexuality: A Disease of Childhood," *American Journal of Orthopsychiatry,* Vol. XXXV, No. 1 (January, 1965), 48-56.

"Homosexual Legal Rights," *Editorial Research Reports* (Washington, D.C.: Congressional Quarterly, Inc., 1974).

"Homosexuality," *New Catholic Encyclopedia,* Vol. 7 (New York: McGraw-Hill, 1967).

"Homosexuality in America," *Life,* Vol. XXXVII, No. 2 (1964), 44-58.

"Homosexual Offences," *Scots Law Times* (August 9, 1949), 84-85.

"Homosexuality, Prostitution and the Law: The Report of the Roman Catholic Advisory Committee," *The Dublin Review,* No. 471 (Summer, 1956), 57-65.

"Homosexuality and Security," *Editorial Research Reports* (Washington, D.C.: Congressional Quarterly, Inc., 1963).

Hooker, Evelyn, "The Adjustment of the Male Overt Homosexual," *Journal of Projective Techniques,* 21 (1957), 18-31.

_____, "Male Homosexuality in the Rorschach," *Journal of Projective Techniques,* Vol. 22 (1958), 33-54.

Horney, Karen, "The Flight From Womanhood: The Masculinity Complex in Women," *International Journal of Psychoanalysis,* Vol. 7 (1926), 324.

_____, "On the Genesis of the Castration Complex in Women," *International Journal of Psychoanalysis,* Vol. V (1924), 50.

_____, "The Problem of Female Masochism," *Psychoanalytic Review,* 22 (1935), 241.

Huffman, Arthur V., "Problems Precipitated by Homosexual Approaches on Youthful First Offenders," *Journal of Social Therapy,* Vol. 7, No. 4, Fourth Quarter (1961), 216-223.

_____, "Sex Deviation in a Prison Community," *Journal of Social Therapy,* Vol. 6, No. 3, Third Quarter (1960), 170-181.

Hyde, H. Montgomery, *The Love That Dared Not Speak Its Name* (Boston: Little, Brown and Co., 1970).

Jacoby, George W., *The Unsound Mind and the Law* (New York: Funk and Wagnalls Co., 1918).

Janzen, W.B., *et al.,* "Clinical and Sign Prediction: The Draw-a-Person and Female Homosexuality," *Journal of Clinical Psychology,* Vol. 31, No. 4 (October, 1975), 757-765.

Jensch, K., "Zur Genealogie der Homosexualität," *Archiv fur Psychiatrie und Nervenkrankheiten* (1941), 112.

Johnson, Adelaide, and Robinson, David B., "The Sexual Deviant (Sexual Psychopath) — Causes, Treatment and Prevention," *Journal of the American Medical Association,* 164 (August 3, 1957), 1559-1565.

Jones, E., *Life and Work of Sigmund Freud,* Vol. 2 (New York: Basic Books, Inc., 1956).

————, *The Life and Work of Sigmund Freud, The Last Phase: 1919-1939,* Vol. III (New York: Basic Books, Inc., 1957).

Journal of the American Medical Association, Vol. 185, No. 5 (August 3, 1963).

Jung, C.G., *Contributions to Analytical Psychology* (London: Routledge and Kegan Paul, Ltd., 1948).

Kahn, Eugen, and Lion, Ernest G., *American Journal of Psychiatry,* Vol. XCV (1935).

————, "Clinical Note on Self-fellator," *American Journal of Psychiatry,* 95 (July, 1938), 131-133.

Kallman, Franz J., *American Journal of Human Genetics,* Vol. IV (1952), 136-146.

————, "Comparative Twin Studies on the Genetic Aspect of Male Homosexuality," *Journal of Nervous and Mental Diseases,* 115 (1952), 283-298.

Kardiner, Abram, *Sex and Morality* (New York: The Bobbs-Merrill Co., Inc., 1954).

Karpman, Benjamin, "Sex Life in Prison," *Journal, American Institute of Criminal Law,* 38 (January-February, 1948), 475-486.

————, *The Sexual Offender and His Offense* (New York: The Julian Press, Inc., 1954).

Kates, Elizabeth M., "Sexual Problems in Women's Institutions," *Journal of Social Therapy,* Vol. 1, No. 4 (October, 1955), 187-191.

Katz, Sander, "Comparative Sexual Behavior," *Complex,* 5 (Spring, 1951), 16-25.

Kazal, H.L., *et al.,* "The Gay Bowel Syndrome: Clinico-pathologic Correlation in 260 Cases," *Annals of Clinical Laboratory Science,* Vol. 6, No. 2 (March-April, 1976), 184-192.

Kelly, Gerald, *Modern Youth and Chastity* (St. Louis: The Queen's Work Publishing Co., 1941).

Kempe, G. Th., "The Homosexual in Society," *British Journal of Delinquency,* 5 (1954), 4-20.

Kenyon, F.E., "Homosexuality in the Female," *British Journal of Psychiatry,* No. 9 (1975), 185-200.

Ketterer, Warren A., M.D., "Venereal Disease and Homosexuality," special communication in the *Journal of the American Medical Association,* Vol. 188, No. 9 (June 1, 1964), 811-812.

Kickham, Charles J.E., M.S., F.A.C.S., "The Impediment of Impotency and the Condition of Male Impotence," *The Linacre Quarterly,* Vol. 26 (February, 1959), 13-22.

Kinsey, Alfred C., "Criteria for A Hormonal Explanation of the Homosexual," *Journal of Clinical Endocrinology,* 1 (1941), 424-428.

Kinsey, Alfred C., *et al., Sexual Behavior in the Human Female* (Philadelphia and London: W.E. Saunders Co., 1953).

———, *Sexual Behavior in the Human Male* (Philadelphia and London: W.E. Saunders Co., 1948).

Kirch, A.M., (ed.), *The Homosexuals* (New York: The Citadel Press, 1954).

Klaf, Franklin S., M.D., "Evidence of Paranoid Ideation in Overt Homosexuals," *Journal of Social Therapy,* Vol. 7, No. 1, First Quarter (1961), 48-52.

———, "Female Homosexuality and Paranoid Schizophrenia: A Survey of 75 Cases and Controls," *Archives of General Psychiatry,* Vol. 4 (1961), 84.

Klaf, Franklin S., M.D., and Davis, Charles A., M.D., "Homosexuality and Paranoid Schizophrenia: A Survey of 150 Cases and Controls," *The American Journal of Psychiatry,* Vol. CXVI, No. 12 (June, 1960), 1070-1075.

Knight, R.P., "Evaluation of the Results of Psychoanalytical Therapy," *American Journal of Psychiatry,* Vol. 98 (1941), 434-436.

Kolb, L.A., and Johnson, A.M., "Etiology and Therapy of Overt Homosexuality," *Psychoanalytic Quarterly,* Vol. 24 (1955), 506-515.

Krafft-Ebing, R.v., *Psychopathia Sexualis* (New York: The Physicians and Surgeons Book Co., 1934).

———, *Psychopathia Sexualis, with Special Reference to the Antipathic Sexual Instincts: A Medico-Forensic Study* (New York: Rebman, 1906).

Kubie, Lawrence S., "The Drive to Become Both Sexes." Paper read at the American Psychoanalytical Association Meeting (1954).

Kurland, M.L., "Paedophilia Erotica," *Journal of Nervous and Mental Diseases,* Vol. 131 (1960), 394.

Laidlaw, Robert W., "A Clinical Approach to Homosexuality," *Marriage and Family Living,* Vol. XIV, No. 1 (February, 1952), 39-45.

Lang, Theodore, "Studies on the Genetic Determination of Homosexuality," *Journal of Nervous and Mental Diseases,* Vol. 92 (1940), 55-64.

Lapponi, G., "Determination of Nuclear Sex. Technical Note and Findings Obtained From a Large-Scale Survey," *Sessuologia,* Vol. IV, No. 3 (July-September, 1963), 120-123. Translated summary, *Sessuologia,* Vol. 4, No. 4 (October-December, 1963), ix.

Laycock, S.R., "Homosexuality. A Mental Hygiene Problem," *Canadian Medical Association Journal,* Vol. 63 (1950), 245.

Levin, Meyer, *Compulsion* (New York: Simon and Schuster, 1956).

Lewinsky, Hilde, "Features From a Case of Homosexuality," *Psychoanalytic Quarterly,* Vol. XXI (1952), 344-354.

Lieberman, Daniel, M.D., and Siegel, Benjamin, A., Ph.D., "A Program for 'Sexual Psychopaths' in a State Mental Hospital," *The American Journal of Psychiatry,* Vol. 113, No. 9 (March, 1957), 801-807.

Lindman, Frank T., and McIntyre, Jr. (eds.), *The Mentally Disabled and the Law* (Chicago: The University of Chicago Press, 1952).

Lindner, Robert, "Sex in Prison," *Complex,* Vol. VI (Fall, 1951), 6.

Lindzey, G., Tejessy, C., and Zamansky, H.S., "Thematic Apperception Test: An Empirical Examination of Some Indices of Homosexuality," *Journal of Abnormal Sociology and Psychology,* Vol. 57 (1958) 67-75.

Lloyd, Charles W. (ed.), *Human Reproduction and Sexual Behavior* (Philadelphia: Lea and Febiger, 1964).

Lorand, Sandor, M.D., and Balint, Michael, M.D. (eds.), *Perversions, Psychodynamics and Therapy* (New York: Random House, Inc., 1956).

Lorand, Sandor, and Schneer, Henry I., *Adolescents* (New York: Hoeber, 1961).

Low, Barbara and Gabler, R. (trans.), *The Collected Papers of Sigmund Freud,* Vol. II (London: Hogarth Press, 1920).

Lurie, L.A., "Endocrine and Disordered Sexual Behavior," *British Medical Journal,* 1 (March 9, 1957), 574.

————, "The Endocrine Factor in Homosexuality," *American Journal of Medical Science,* 208 (1944), 176-186.

MacKinnon, J., "The Homosexual Woman," *American Journal of Psychiatry,* 103 (1947), 661.

Maia, I., "A Contribution to the Study of Homosexuality in the Rorschach Test," *Arch. Dep. Assist. Psicop.* (1959-1960), Vol. 1, 25-26, 265-280.

Marcozzi, A., "Value of Homosexual Behavior in Adolescence," *Sessuologia,* Vol. IV, No. 3 (July-September, 1963), 175-177. Translated summary, *Sessuologia,* Vol. IV, No. 4 (October-December, 1963), xii.

Marcozzi, A., Pomini, P., and Caprioli, N., "Determination of Urinary 17-Ketosteroids in Females With Homosexual Tendencies," *Sessuologia,* Vol. IV, No. 3 (July-September, 1963), 178-179. Translated Summary, *Sessuologia,* Vol. IV, No. 4 (October-December, 1963), xii.

Margolese, M. Sydney, and Janiger, Oscar, "Androsterone/Etiocholandone Ratios in Male Homosexuals," *British Medical Journal* (July 28, 1973).

Marone, Silvio, "Homosexuality and Art," *International Journal of Sexology,* Vol. VII, No. 4 (May, 1954), 175-188.

Masserman, Jules H., M.D. (ed.), *Current Psychiatric Therapies,* Vol. 3 (New York: Grune and Stratton, 1963).

Masters, R.E.L., *The Homosexual Revolution* (New York: The Julian Press, Inc., 1962).

Mather, John S., and Seamon, Donald, *The Great Spy Scandal* (London: Purnell and Sons, Ltd., 1956).

McConaghy, N., "Aversive and Positive Conditioning Treatments of Homosexuality," *Behavior Research Therapy,* Vol. 13, No. 4 (October, 1975) 309-319.

McGuire, R.L., and Vallance, M., "Aversion Therapy by Electric Shock: A Simple Technique," *British Medical Journal,* 1 (1964), 151.

McNeill, John J., S.J., *The Church and the Homosexual* (Kansas City: Sheed Andrews and McMeel, Inc., 1976).

"MD tennis star's sex surgery spotlights transsexualism," *Medical World News* (September 6, 1976).

Meares, Ainslie, M.D., *A System of Medical Hypnosis* (Philadelphia and London: W.B. Saunders Co., 1961).

Medical World News (January 25, 1974).

Merloo, J.A.M., "The Concept of Psychopathy," *American Journal of Psychiatry,* Vol. 16 (1962), 645.

Mesnikoff, Alvin M., Rainer, John D., Kolb, Lawrence C., and Carr, Arthur C., "Intra-familial Determinants of Divergent Sexual Behavior in Twins," *American Journal of Psychiatry,* Vol. 119, No. 8 (February, 1963), 732.

Miller, Merle, *On Being Different: What It Means To Be A Homosexual* (New York: Random House, Inc., 1971).

Mitchell, Roger S., *Homosexual and the Law* (New York: Arco Publishing Co., Inc., 1969).

Mohr, J.W., Ph.D., Turner, R., M.D., and Ball, Richard B., M.B., "Exhibitionism and Pedophilia," *Corrective Psychiatry and Journal of Social Therapy,* Vol. 8, No. 4, Fourth Quarter (1962), 172-186.

Moll, A., *Libido Sexualis: Studies in the Psychosexual Laws of Love Verified by Clinical Sexual Case Histories* (New York: American Ethnological Press, 1933).

———, *The Sexual Life of the Child* (New York: The Macmillan Co., 1912), 314.

Money, John, "Components of Eroticism in Man I: The Hormones in Relation to Sexual Morphology and Sexual Desire," *Journal of Nervous and Mental Disease,* 132 (1961), 239-248.

————, "Components of Eroticism in Man II: The Orgasm and Genital Somesthesia," *Journal of Nervous and Mental Disease,* 132 (1961), 289-297.

Moore, Dom Thomas V., *The Nature and Treatment of Mental Disorders* (New York: Grune and Stratton, 1951).

————, "The Pathogenesis and Treatment of Homosexual Disorders," *Journal of Personality,* Vol. 14, No. 1 (September, 1945), 47-83.

Muscardin, L., "Research Into Some Morphological Features in a Group of Homosexuals," *Sessuologia,* Vol. IV, No. 4 (October-December, 1963), 124-154.

Nedoma, K., "Homosexuality in Sexological Practice," *International Journal of Sexology* (1951), 4, 219-224.

Neustadt, R., and Myerson, A., "Quantitative Sex Hormone Studies in Homosexuality, Childhood and Various Neuropsychiatric Disturbances," *American Journal of Psychiatry,* 97 (1940), 524-551.

"New Shocker," *Newsweek* (May 29, 1950), 18.

Nielson, Nils, "What Is Homosexuality?" *International Journal of Sexology,* Vol. 6, No. 3 (February, 1953), 188.

Nitsche, C.J., Robinson, J.F., and Parsons, E.T., "Homosexuality and the Rorschach," *Journal of Consulting Psychology,* Vol. 20 (1956), 196.

Norman, J., "Evidence and Clinical Significance of Homosexuality in 100 Unanalyzed Cases of Dementia Praecox," *Journal of Nervous and Mental Diseases,* Vol. 107 (1948), 484.

Odenwald, R.P., "Counseling the Homosexual," *Priest,* 9 (December, 1953), 940-944.

Oesterle, Gerard, "De Relatione Homosexualitatis ad Matrimonium," *Revista Española de Derecho Canonico,* Vol. X, No. 28 (1955).

————, "Welchen Einfluss hat die Homosexualität auf die Ehen," *Oesterreichesches Archiv fur Kirchenrecht,* Vol. XII (1961), 305-334.

Oliven, John F., M.D., *Sexual Hygiene and Pathology* (Philadelphia and Montreal: J.B. Lippincott Co., 1955).

Ovesey, Lionel, "The Homosexual Conflict," *Psychiatry,* Vol. XVII, No. 3 (August, 1954), 243-250.

————, *Homosexuality and Pseudohomosexuality* (New York: Science House, 1969).

Ovesey, Lionel, Gaylin, Willard, and Hendin, Herbert, "Psychotherapy of Male Homosexuality," *Archives of General Psychiatry,* 9 (July, 1963), 19-31.

Owensby, Newdigate M., M.D., "The Correction of Homosexuality," *The Urologic and Cutaneous Review,* Vol. XLV (August, 1941), 494-496.

Palmer, Paul, "Marriage," *New Catholic Encyclopedia: Supplement* (New York: McGraw-Hill, 1972), 279.

Pantom, J.H., "A New M.M.P.I. Scale for the Identification of Homosexuality," *Journal of Clinical Psychology,* Vol. 16 (1960), 17-21.

Pare, C.M.B., "Homosexuality and Chromosomal Sex," *Journal of Psychomatic Research,* 1 (1956), 247-251.

Pascal, G.R., *et al.,* "A Study of Genital Symbols of the Rorschach Test: Presentation of a Method and Results," *The Journal of Abnormal and Social Psychology,* Vol. 45 (1950), 286-295.

Perry, Helen Swick and Ladd, Mary (eds.), *The Interpersonal Theory of Psychiatry* (New York: Norton, 1953).

Ploscowe, M., *Sex and the Law* (New York: Prentice-Hall, Inc., 1951).

Ploss, Hermann Heinrich, Bartels, Max, and Bartels, Paul, *Woman* (London: William Heinemann, Ltd., 1935).

Poe, John S., "The Successful Treatment of a 40-Year-Old Passive Homosexual Based on an Adaptational View of Human Behavior," *The Psychoanalytic Review,* Vol. XXIX, No. 1 (January, 1952), 23-33.

Pollack, S., *et al.,* "The Dimensions of Stigma: The Social Situation of the Mentally Ill Person and the Male Homosexual," *Journal of Abnormal Psychology,* Vol. 85, No. 1 (February, 1976), 105-112.

Pope Pius XII, *The Catholic Priesthood* (Washington, D.C.: National Catholic Welfare Conference).

————, "Discourse to Delegates Attending the Fifth Congress of Psychotherapy and Clinical Psychologists (April 13, 1953)," *The Linacre Quarterly,* Vol. XX, No. 4 (November, 1953).

————, *On Holy Virginity.* An encyclical, Rome (March 25, 1954).

Pritchard, M., "Homosexuality and Genetic Sex," *Journal of Mental Science,* 108 (September, 1962), 616-623.

The Proceedings for the Institute for the Clergy on Problems in Pastoral Psychology (New York: Fordham University Press, 1956).

Psychiatric News (August, 1969; February 3, 1971; April 3, 1974).

Puxon, M., "Not as Other Men," *Solicitors' Journal,* 101 (September 28, 1957), 735.

Quinn, Rev. Joseph J., *Rotal Jurisprudence With Regard to Functional Impotence in the Male* (Washington, D.C.: Catholic University of America, 1956).

Raboch, J., and Nedoma, K., "Sex Chromatin and Sexual Behavior: A Study of 36 Men With Female Nuclear Pattern and of 134 Homosexuals," *Psychosomatic Medicine,* Vol. XX (1958), 55.

Rachman, S., Ph.D., "Sexual Disorders and Behavior Therapy," *The American Journal of Psychiatry,* Vol. CXVIII, No. 3 (September, 1961), 235-240.

Rado, Sandor, "A Critical Examination of the Concept of Bisexuality," *Psychoanalytic Medicine II* (October 4, 1940), 459-467.

Ramsey, G.V., "The Sexual Development of Boys," *The American Journal of Psychiatry,* Vol. 56 (1943), 217-234.

Rees, Tudor and Usill, Harley V., *They Stand Apart* (New York: The Macmillan Co., 1955).

Reitzell, J.M., "A Comparative Study of Hysterics, Homosexuals and Alcoholics Using Content Analysis of Rorschach Responses," *Rorschach Research Exchange,* Vol. 13 (1949), 127-141.

Ricco, D., and Petiziol, A., "Psychological Examinations in Homosexuality," *Sessuologia,* Vol. IV, No. 4 (October-December, 1963), 215-218. Translated summary, *Sessuologia,* Vol. IV, No. 4, xiii.

Rickles, N., "Exhibitionism," *Journal of Nervous and Mental Diseases,* 95 (1942), 11-17.

Rick, James E., *The Law of Catholic Marriage* (Chicago: Callaghan and Co., 1957).

Ritchey, Michael G., and Leff, Arnold M., M.D., "Venereal Disease Control Among Homosexuals: An Outreach Program," *Journal of the American Medical Association,* Vol. 232, No. 5 (May 5, 1975).

Ritty, Charles J., J.C.L., "Possible Invalidity of Marriage by Reason of Sexual Anomalies," *The Jurist,* Vol. XXIV, No. 4 (October, 1963), 394-422.

Roberts, Leigh M., and Pacht, Asher R., "Termination of Inpatient Treatment for Sex Deviates: Psychiatric, Social and Legal Factors," *The American Journal of Psychiatry,* Vol. 21, No. 9 (March, 1965), 837-880.

Robinson, B. (ed.), *Encyclopedia Sexualis: A Comprehensive Encyclopedia-Dictionary of the Sexual Sciences* (New York: Dingwall-Rock, 1936).

Rogers, C., *et al.,* "Group Psychotherapy With Homosexuals: A Review," *International Journal of Group Psychotherapy,* Vol. 26, No. 1 (January, 1976), 3-11.

"Roman Catholic Advisory Committee on Prostitution and Homosexual Offences and the Existing Law," *Dublin Review,* 230 (Summer, 1956), 60-65.

Rosenzweig, S., and Hoskins, R.G., "A Note on the Ineffectualness of Sex-hormone Medication in a Case of Pronounced Homosexuality," *Psychosomatic Medicine,* 3 (1941), 87-89.

Roth, Jack, "Nationwide Ring Preying on Prominent Deviates," *New York Times* (March 3, 1966).

Ruitenbeck, Hendrik M. (ed.), *The Problem of Homosexuality in Modern Society* (New York: E.P. Dutton and Co., Inc., 1963).

Saghir, Marcel, M.D., and Robins, Eli, M.D., *Male and Female Homosexuality: A Comprehensive Investigation* (Baltimore: Williams and Wilkins Co., 1973).

St. John-Stevas, Norman, *Life, Death and the Law* (Bloomington, Ind.: Indiana University Press, 1961).

Sakel, Manfred, *Schizophrenia* (New York: Philosophical Library, 1958).

Salzman, Leon, "The Concept of Latent Homosexuality," *American Journal of Psychoanalysis,* Vol. XVII, No. 2 (1957), 161-169.

Saul, J.L., and Beck, A.T., "Psychodynamics of Male Homosexuality," *International Journal of Psychoanalysis,* Vol. 42 (1961), 43-48.

Sawyer, G.I.M., "Homosexuality: The Endocrinological Aspects," *The Practitioner,* 72 (April, 1954), 374-377.

————, *Lancet,* 2 (December 12, 1959).

Schofield, M.G., *Society and the Homosexual* (London: Gollancz, 1952), first American edition (New York: Dutton, 1953).

Schrenck-Notzing, A.P.F. von, *Therapeutic Suggestions in Psychopathia Sexualis (Pathological Manifestations of the Sexual Sense) with Especial Reference to Contrary Sexual Instincts* (Philadelphia: Davis, 1895).

Scott, P.D., "Homosexuality, With Special Reference to Classification," *Proceedings of the Royal Society of Medicine,* 50 (1957), 655-660.

————, "Psychiatric Aspects of the Wolfenden Report," *British Journal of Delinquency,* Vol. 9 (1958), 1.

Severinghaus, E. L., and Chornyak, J., "A Study of Homosexual Adult Males," *Psychosomatic Medicine,* 7 (1945), 302-305.

"Sex: A Christian View," *New Catholic Encyclopedia,* Vol. 13 (New York: McGraw-Hill, 1967), 147.

"Sexual Offenders and Social Punishment," published for the Church of England Moral Welfare Council (1956), ed. D. S. Bailey.

Sherwin, R.V., "Sodomy: A Medicolegal Enigma," *International Journal of Sexology,* Vol. 5 (1951), 10.

———, "Some Legal Aspects of Homosexuality," *International Journal of Sexology,* Vol. 4 (1950), 22.

Silverstein, Arthur J., "Constitutional Aspects of the Homosexual's Right to a Marriage License," *Journal of Family Law,* Vol. 12, No. 4 (1973), 607-634.

Simpson, Ruth, *From The Closets To The Courts* (New York: The Viking Press, 1976).

S.I.R. and Hickerson vs. *Hamppon* (San Francisco, October, 1973); *Baker and Rau* vs. *Hamppon* (Washington, D.C., December, 1973).

Slater, Eliot, "The Sibs and Children of Homosexuals," *Journal of Nervous and Mental Diseases,* 107 (1948), 251-268.

———, "The Sibs and Children of Homosexuals," *Symposium on Nuclear Sex* (New York: Interscience Publishers, 1958).

Slater, E., and Slater, P., "A Study in the Assessment of Homosexual Traits," *British Journal of Medical Psychology,* Vol. 21 (1947), 61.

Smith, Alexander B., Ph.D., Bassin, Alexander, Ph.D., "Group Therapy With Homosexuals," *Journal of Social Therapy,* Vol. 5, No. 3, Third Quarter (1959), 225-232.

Smith, C. E., "Homosexual Federal Offender: A Study of 100 Cases," *Journal, American Institute of Criminal Law,* 44 (January-February, 1954), 582-591.

Socarides, Charles, "Meaning and Content of Paedophiliac Perversion," *Journal of the American Psychoanalytic Association,* Vol. 7 (1959), 84.

Spitzer, Robert L., M.D., "A Proposal About Homosexuality and the APA Nomenclature," *Psychiatric News* (June, 1973).

Steinach, E., and Lichtenstein, "Umstimmung der Homosexualität durch Austausch der Pubertatsdrusen," *Munchener Medizinische Wochenschrift,* Vol. 65 (1918).

Stekel, William, M.D., *The Homosexual Neurosis* (New York: The Physicians and Surgeons Book Co., 1934).

Stevenson, I., and Wolpe, J., *American Journal of Psychiatry,* Vol. 116 (1960).

Strackey, A., and J., *Collected Papers of Sigmund Freud,* Vol. III (London: Leonard and Virginia Woolf, 1925).

Tappan, Paul W., "Sentences for Sex Criminals," *Journal of Criminal Law, Criminology and Police Science,* Vol. 42 (1951), 332-336.

_____, "Treatment of the Sex Offender in Denmark," *The American Journal of Psychiatry,* Vol. CVIII, No. 4 (October, 1951), 24-49.

Teodori, V., and Morabito, F., "Endocrinological Aspects of Homosexuality," *Sessuologia,* Vol. IV, No. 3 (July-September, 1963), 156-164. Translated summary, *Sessuologia,* Vol. IV, No. 4 (October-December, 1963), xi-xii.

Thompson, Clara, "Changing Concepts of Homosexuality in Psychoanalysis," *Psychiatry,* 10 (1947), 183-189.

Thompson, G. N., "Electroshock and Other Therapeutic Considerations in Sexual Psychopathy," *Journal of Nervous and Mental Disease,* 109 (1949), 531.

Tobin, William J., Ph.D., *Homosexuality and Marriage* (Rome: The Catholic Book Agency, 1964).

Tocca, M., and Micheli, F., "The Validity of Hormonal Exploration in the Diagnosis of Homosexual Conditions," *Sessuologia,* Vol. IV, No. 3 (July-September, 1963), 165-169. Translated summary, *Sessuologia,* Vol. IV, No. 4 (October-December, 1963), xii.

Trese, Leo, "Muted Tragedy," *The Commonweal,* Vol. LI (February 17, 1950), 512ff.

Tripp, C. A., Ph.D., *The Homosexual Matrix* (New York: The New American Library, Inc., 1975).

"The Unspeakable Crime," *Time* (November 16, 1953), 36.

Vague, J., Favier, G., and Nicolino, J., "Somatic Aspects of Male and Female Homosexuality," *Sessuologia,* Vol. 4 (1963), 124-149. Translated summary, *Sessuologia,* Vol. 4, No. 4 (October-December, 1963), x-xi.

VanderVeldt, James H., O.F.M., and Odenwald, Robert P., M.D., *Psychiatry and Catholicism* (New York: McGraw-Hill, 1957).

Vann, Gerald, O.P., "Moral Dilemmas," *Blackfriars,* XXXV (January, 1954), 6-7.

Waring, Paul, and Bryce, Dean Travis, *Homosexual Freedom,* privately published, 1961.

Warren, C. A., "Women Among Men: Females in the Male Homosexual Community," *Archives of Sexual Behavior,* Vol. 5, No. 2 (March, 1976), 157-169.

Wayne, D. M., Adams, M., and Rowe, L. H., "A Study of Military Prisoners at a Disciplinary Barracks Suspected of Homosexual Activities," *Milit. Sun.,* Vol. 101 (1947), 499-534.

Weil, A., "Concerning the Anatomic Fundamentals of the Congenital Homosexual," *Arch. Frauenk-Eugen,* 10, 23-26.

_____, "The Substance of the Expression of Homosexuals About Their

Specific Constitution," *Arch. f. Entwickungsmechanik der Organismen,* 49 (1921), 538.

Weinberg, Martin S., and Bell, Alan P., *Homosexuality: An Annotated Bibliography* (New York: Harper and Row, Publishers, Inc., 1972).

Weissman, P., "Structural Considerations in Overt Male Bisexuality," *International Journal of Psychoanalysis,* 43 (1962), 159-168.

Weltge, Ralph (ed.), *The Same Sex* (Philadelphia: Pilgrim Press, 1969).

West, Donald J., M.B., *The Other Man* (New York: Whiteside, Inc., and William Morrow and Co., 1955).

————, "Parental Figures in the Genesis of Male Homosexuality," *International Journal of Sociology and Psychology,* Vol. 5 (1959), 85-97.

West, Louis J., Doidge, William T., and Williams, Robert L., "An Approach to the Problem of Homosexuality in the Military Service," *The American Journal of Psychiatry,* Vol. 115, No. 5 (November, 1958).

Westwood, Gordon, *A Minority: A Report on the Life of the Male Homosexual in Great Britain* (London: Longmans, Green and Co., Ltd., 1960).

Wheeler, W. M., "An Analysis of Rorschach Indices of Male Homosexuality," *Rorschach Research Exchange and Journal of Projected Techniques,* Vol. 13 (1949), 97-126.

Whitaker, L., Jr., "The Use of an Extended Draw-a-Person Test to Identify Homosexual and Effeminate Men," *Journal of Consulting Psychology,* Vol. 25, No. 6 (1961), 482-485.

Williams, A. H., "Problems of Homosexuality," *British Medical Journal* (August 16, 1975), 426-428.

Willink, H. U., "Legal Aspects of Artificial Insemination," *The Practitioner,* Vol. 158 (1947), 349.

Winokur, George (ed.), *Determinants of Human Sexual Behavior* (Springfield, Ill.: Charles C. Thomas, 1963).

The Wolfenden Report (Introduction by Karl Menninger, M.D.) (New York: Stein and Day, 1963).

Wolfson, William and Gross, Alfred, "A Footnote to the Etiological Study of the Homosexual Syndrome," *International Journal of Sexology,* 6 (February, 1953), 178-179.

Woodward, Mary, "Diagnosis and Treatment of Homosexual Offenders," *British Journal of Delinquency,* Vol. 9 (1958), 44-58.

Wooten, Barbara, "Sickness or Sin," *The Twentieth Century* (May, 1956).

Wortis, J., "Intersexuality and Effeminacy in a Male Homosexual," *American Journal of Orthopsychiatry*, 10 (1940), 567-569.

————, "Note on Body Build of Male Homosexual," *American Journal of Psychiatry*, 93 (1937), 1121.

Wright, C. A., Glass, S. J., and Devel, H. J., "Sex Hormone Studies in Male Homosexuality," *Endocrinology*, Vol. 26 (1940), 590-594.

Young, W. C. (ed.), *Sex and Internal Secretions,* 3rd ed. (Baltimore: Williams and Wilkins Co., 1961).

Zamansky, H. S., "A Technique for Assessing Homosexual Tendencies," *Journal Pers,* Vol. 24 (1956), 436-448.

Index

Coppen, physical constitution, 62

Cory, aim of therapy, 240; castration anxiety, 78; physical characteristics, 92

Counseling, Bier on, 259

Cunnilingus, definition, 42

Cure, 16

Curran, morality, 235ff; pastoral counseling, 252; theory of compromise, 235

Dahl-Iverson, transsexualism, 118

Darke, etiology, 66

Daughters of Bilitis, 205, 207ff

Davidman, castration anxiety, 79

Davidson, etiology, 63; recidivism, 179

Davis, Lesbianism, 126

Depressive features, 98

Deutsch, etiology, 72; Lesbianism, 127; Oedipal stage, 72

Diagnostic considerations, 112

Diagnostic and Statistical Manual of Mental Disorders (DSM II), 30

Dignity, 214ff

Dixon, chromosomal factors, 62ff

Dreams, homosexual, 159

Duel, etiology, 63

Durham Decision, 50

Edgerton, transsexualism, 119

Ellis, A., castration anxiety, 79; marriage, 149; psychotherapy, 249; sublimation, 247

Ellis, H., etiology, 60

Entrapment, 171ff; Clark on, 171; Marshall on, 171ff

Ethnic characteristics, 96ff

Etiological factors, 81

Etiology, Allen on, 60ff; Anomaly on, 81; Barr on, 63; Bieber on, 77, 86; Boss on, 89; Buckley on, 61; Coppen on, 62; Darke on, 66; Davidman on, 63; Deutsch on, 72; Dixon on, 62ff; H. Ellis on, 60; fear of genital organs, 76; Freud on, 70ff; Hacker on, 73ff; Henry on, 60; Hirschfeld on, 60; Hobbs on, 63; hormonal theory, 61; Horney on, 72; interfamily relations, 81; Janiger on, 64; Kallman on, 66ff; Keller on, 66; Krafft-Ebing on, 60; Krausz on, 74ff; Lang on, 65ff; Lorand on, 75; Maranon on, 60; Margolese on, 64; Moore on, 65; Myerson on, 63; Nedoma on, 63; Neustadt on, 63; Ovesey on, 88-89; Pare on, 63; proximate factors, 80-81; Raboch on, 63; Rado on, 87; rejection of child, 87; rejection of parent, 81; Sawyer on, 64; seduc-

344

Hypnosis, Krafft-Ebing on, 247; Meares on, 247; Schrenck-Notzing on, 247
Illness, Wooten on, 49
Immaturity, sexual, 83
Impotence, Quinn on, 151
Impotency, psychological, 151
Imprisonment, Lindner on, 241
Impulse, irresistible, 181
Incest, definition, 44
Insanity, District of Columbia, definition, 180
Intelligence services, 190ff
Interim Report, 183, 188ff
Inversion, absolute, 42; amphigenous, 42; definition, 39; sexual, 44
Invert, definition, 44
Irreversible homosexual, 23
Ishmael Complex, 73ff; Hacker on, 73
Janiger, etiology, 64
Jerome Biblical Commentary, The, 20
Johnson, seduction of child, 82
Jorgenson, Christine, 118
Kallmann, etiology, 66ff
Keller, etiology, 66
Kempff's Disease, 44
Ketterer, venereal disease, 108-109
Kierkegaard, responsibility, 50
Kinsey, classification of sex acts, 176ff; homosexuality in prisons, 242; Lesbianism, 126; physical characteristics, 91ff; rating scale, 111; transvestism, 115
Kinsey Report, The, 54; male incidence, 28
Krafft-Ebing, bisexuality, 41, 70; etiology, 60; hypnosis, 247
Krausz, etiology, 74ff
Laidlaw, etiology, 64ff; psychological types, 40
Lang, etiology, 65ff
Leff, venereal disease, 109
Le Moal, angelism, 107
Lesbian, definition, 45; derivation of, 125; marriage, 145, 152
Lesbianism, 125ff; de Beauvoir on, 126; Brody on, 126; case reports, 128ff; clinical features, 128; Davis on, 126; Deutsch on, 127; dynamics, 126; etiology, 126; Horney on, 127; incidence, 125ff; Kinsey on, 126; St. Paul on, 125
Lindner, imprisonment, 241
Lhermitte, female companions, 265

Ovesey, etiology, 88-89
Owensby, shock therapy, 247
Pacht, psychotherapy of prisoners, 243; recidivism, 178
Paranoid schizophrenia, Sakel on, 123
Paraphilia, 46; *see also* perversions, sexual
Pare, etiology, 63
Parent, absence of, 83
Parents, mistreatment of, 84
Pastoral counseling, 252ff; aim of, 258; aspects of, 253; Bier on, 253; Buckley on, 258; Curran on, 252; Felix on, 255; Tobin on, 258
Pastoral counselor, rules for, 260ff; qualities, 253, 259ff
Patient I, 68, 96, 143
Patient II, 94
Patient III, 98ff
Patient IV, 103ff
Patient V, 129ff
Patient VI, 134ff
Paul, St., Lesbianism, 125; marriage, 150
Pedophilia, 120ff; classification, 120ff; definition, 120; frequency (Table I), 121; variety (Table II), 122
Peeping Tom (voyeurism), 47
Penis envy, Freud on, 76
Personality disorders, classification, 52
Perversions, sexual, 37; definition, 46
Pervert, definition, 37
Physical appearance, 91
Physical characteristics, 91; Berg on, 92; Chart I, 93; Cory on, 95; Holemon on, 93; Kinsey on, 91ff; Winokur on, 93
Physical constitution, as a cause, 61ff; Coppen on, 62; Galbraith on, 62; Henry on, 61ff; Weil on, 61ff; Wortis on, 62
Pope Pius XII, homosexuals, 156; responsibility, 49
Prevention, 251
Procreation, 18
Procreative function, 21
Procreative love, 22
Pseudohomosexual, 41
Pseudohomosexuality, 41
Psychiatrists and homosexuals, 166ff
Psychogenic factors in etiology, 69
Psychological characteristics, 94ff
Psychosexual abnormalities, 46; *see also* perversions, sexual
Psychotherapy, A. Ellis on, 249; prisoners, 243; prognosis, 250